Paris For Dummies
4th Edition

D0969954

Métro Stops for Paris Attractions

See the Métro map on the inside front cover and the RER map on the inside back cover to find the locations listed below.

Museums

Attraction	Métro Line Number: Stop
Centre Georges Pompidou	1: St-Paul
Musée d'Art et d'Histoire du Judaïsme	11: Rambuteau
Musée Carnavalet	1: St-Paul
Musée de Cluny	10: Cluny-La Sorbonne
Musée de l'Histoire de France	1,11: Hôtel-de-Ville
Musée Jacquemart-André	9: St-Philippe-du-Roule
Musée du Louvre	1: Louvre-Rivoli
Musée des Médailles	1, 7: Palais Royal
Musée d'Orsay	12: Solférino/RER Musée d'Orsay
Musée Picasso	1: St-Paul
Musée Rodin	13: Varenne

Churches

Attraction	Métro Line Number: Stop
Notre Dame	4: Cité
Sacré Cœur	12: Abbesses
Sainte-Chapelle	4: Cité

Parks

Attraction	Métro Line Number: Stop
Jardin du Palais-Royal	1, 7: Palais-Royal
Jardin des Tuileries	1, 8, 12: Concorde/1: Tuileries
Jardin et Palais du Luxembourg	4, 10: Odéon/RER Luxembourg/RER Port Royal
Place des Vosges	1: St-Paul

Monuments and Architecture

Attraction	Métro Line Number: Stop
Arc de Triomphe	1, 2, 6: Charles de Gaulle-Étoile
Champs-Elysées	1, 8, 12: Concorde/1, 13: Champs-Elysées Clémenceau/1, 9: Franklin D. Roosevelt/1: George V/1, 2, 6: Charles de Gaulle-Étoile
Conciergerie	4: Cité
La Crypte Archéologique	4: Cité/RER St-Michel-Notre-Dame
Eiffel Tower	8: École-Militaire/6: Bir-Hakeim/RER Luxembourg
Hotel des Invalides (Napoléon's Tomb)	8: Latour-Maubourg/13: Varenne/1, 13: Champs-Elysées Clémenceau/RER Invalides
Panthéon	10: Cardinal Lemoine/RER Luxembourg
Place de la Bastille	1, 5: Bastille

Cemetery

Attraction	Métro Line Number: Stop
Père Lachaise	2, 3: Père Lachaise

Kids

Attraction	Métro Line Number: Stop
Aquaboulevard	8: Balard
Les Catacombes	4, 6: Denfert-Rochereau
Cité des Sciences et de l'Industrie	7: Porte de la Villette
Les Égouts	9: Alma-Marceau/RER Pont-de l'Alma
Jardin d'Acclimation Bois de Boulogne	1: Les Sablons
Jardin des Plantes	5, 10: Gare d'Austerlitz/7, 10: Jussieu
Parc Zoologique de Paris	8: Porte Dorée

Historic Cafés & Bars

Attraction	Métro Line Number: Stop
Brasserie	7: Pont Marie
Brasserie Lipp	4: St-Germain-des-Prés
Café les Deux Magots	4: St-Germain-des-Prés
La Closerie de Lilas	RER Port-Royal
Harry's New York Bar	3, 7, 8: Opéra

Paris
FOR
DUMMIES®
4TH EDITION

**by Cheryl A. Pientka
and Joseph Alexiou**

BICENTENNIAL
BICENTENNIAL
1807
WILEY
2007
BICENTENNIAL
BICENTENNIAL

Wiley Publishing, Inc.

Paris For Dummies,® 4th Edition

Published by
Wiley Publishing, Inc.
111 River St.
Hoboken, NJ 07030-5774
www.wiley.com

For general information on our other products and services, please contact our Customer Care Department within the U.S. at 800-762-2974, outside the U.S. at 317-572-3993, or fax 317-572-4002.

For technical support, please visit www.wiley.com/techsupport.

Wiley also publishes its books in a variety of electronic formats. Some content that appears in print may not be available in electronic books.

Library of Congress Control Number: 2007920008

ISBN: 978-0-470-08584-4

Manufactured in the United States of America

10 9 8 7 6 5 4 3 2 1

WILEY

About the Authors

Cheryl A. Pientka is a freelance writer who has contributed to *France For Dummies* and *Europe For Dummies*. A graduate of Columbia University Graduate School of Journalism and the University of Delaware, she lives in New York.

Joseph Alexiou recently graduated from Tufts University with a degree in History. A hopeless francophile, he hopes to return someday to Paris (or anywhere in Provence) in some literary capacity. For now he resides very happily in Brooklyn, New York.

Dedications

CAP: To my mother, Mary Anne Pientka, for all her help, encouragement, and advice. And to the memory of her husband and my father, Philip Pientka.

JA: To my grandmother Esther Braun Sparberg, who adores, loves, and understands so much of this world.

Authors' Acknowledgments

CAP: Once again, a big merci to two terrific Wiley people, Amy Lyons and Melinda Quintero; and to my friend, author Alice Alexiou for her endless wisdom and insight; and to Joseph. A special thank you, as well, to the coaches and support staff of A Team for Kids for helping me train for and successfully run my first NYC Marathon (when I wasn't working on this book, of course!). And to the dedicated people at A Cause for Paws for tirelessly finding homes for so many cats and dogs — and for Gypsy.

JA: Great thanks to my mother, Alice Sparberg Alexiou, my father Nick Alexiou, and my brother Alex Alexiou for their endless encouragement and love; to Cheryl for being my mentor in my first foray in the real world (en rigolant au meme temps); to LoAnn Halden, Ed Salvato, Amy Lyons, and Melinda Quintero. Thanks also to Ali Abou Hassan for being my cohort and my "French Friend"; to Stephanie Morris who opened my mind to the vast multiverse of French pastries; to Anne de Turenne for her constant affection; to my dear Sara Dalziel for loving Paris along with me and teaching me what I didn't know; to her parents Anna and Graeme for their warmth and hospitality; to Meghan "Joggles" Cain for visiting (all of Electric Ave is on this page!); to all my boys from Tufts, and a great big thank you to my friends and family from Eisner.

Publisher's Acknowledgments

We're proud of this book; please send us your comments through our Dummies online registration form located at www.dummies.com/register/.

Some of the people who helped bring this book to market include the following:

Editorial

Editors: Amy Lyons, Development Editor; Eric T. Schroeder, Production Editor

Copy Editor: Jennifer Connolly

Cartographer: Guy Ruggiero

Editorial Assistant: Melinda Quintero

Senior Photo Editor: Richard Fox

Cover Photos: Front Credit: © Jeremy Woodhouse/Masterfile. Description: Abbesses Art Nouveau subway entrance. Back Credit: © Bruce Fleming/ Masterfile. Description: Croissants on plate, close-up.

Cartoons: Rich Tennant (www.the5thwave.com)

Composition Services

Project Coordinator: Linsey Osborn

Layout and Graphics: Lissa Auciello-Brogan, Claudia Bell, Heather Ryan

Anniversary Logo Design: Richard J. Pacifico

Proofreaders: Aptara, Jessica Kramer, Susan Moritz

Indexer: Aptara

Publishing and Editorial for Consumer Dummies

Diane Graves Steele, Vice President and Publisher, Consumer Dummies

Joyce Pepple, Acquisitions Director, Consumer Dummies

Kristin A. Cocks, Product Development Director, Consumer Dummies

Michael Spring, Vice President and Publisher, Travel

Kelly Regan, Editorial Director, Travel

Publishing for Technology Dummies

Andy Cummings, Vice President and Publisher, Dummies Technology/ General User

Composition Services

Gerry Fahey, Vice President of Production Services

Debbie Stailey, Director of Composition Services

Contents at a Glance

Maps at a Glance

Table of Contents

Introduction

*I*f this is your first time in Paris, be forewarned that you just may find your heart stolen by this legendary city.

Paris has been coveted since the Romans wrested away this settlement from a tribe of peaceful fishermen called the *Parisii,* and named it *Lutetia, Parisiorum.* A fascination with the city grew over nearly 2,000 years. It's not just the culture — though you can visit a different museum every day for a year and still not hit all of them. Nor is it Paris's breathtaking beauty — from the curved Beaux-Arts apartment buildings with iron-fenced balconies protecting dripping flower boxes to the graceful bridges arching over the Seine to the eye-pleasing formal gardens balanced by natural parks to the exquisite store windows to the unexpected vistas.

Perhaps it is simply that Paris is an eternal source of discovery. Even a familiar walk will yield surprises — a passage that veers off the main road into a park; an unusual building; a cluster of houses containing some half-forgotten history from centuries past. Or maybe it's just the Parisian way of life where relaxing in a cafe and watching the world go by is a natural part of every day.

If this is your first visit or if you haven't been to Paris in a decade or more, you're in for some changes. After losing many American tourists during the days of "freedom fries" at the onset of the war in Iraq, Parisians are trying mightily to overcome (and may we add, succeeding) the stereotype they are collectively a rude bunch. Service at stores and in restaurants can actually be downright warm, especially when foreigners take the time to acknowledge storekeepers and waiters with a pleasant smile and a simple, *"bonjour"* (hello).

Most recently the **Orangerie,** the beautiful museum in the Tuileries gardens, reopened after six years of renovations — Monet's Water Lilies have never looked better! Paris's newest art museum, the **Musée du quai Branly,** is a spectacular Jean Nouvel–designed homage to the art from non-Western civilizations — and just a short walk from the Eiffel Tower to boot!

Paris is more than a city; it's an encounter. Every visitor here experiences Paris's glory in an individual and unique way, and we hope the city grabs a hold of your heart so that before your trip is even over you'll be itching to return.

Dummies Post-it® Flags

As you read this book, you'll find information that you'll want to reference as you plan or enjoy your trip — whether it be a new hotel, a must-see attraction, or a must-try walking tour. Mark these pages with the handy Post-it® Flags included in this book to help make your trip planning easier!

About This Book

Consider this a textbook of sorts that you don't have to read from front to back, with your visit to Paris your test (there are no failing grades, however)! Basically *Paris For Dummies* presents you with to-the-point information on Paris that's fun and easy to access. We explain very basic information about the city for readers who have never visited and discuss points of interest for the seasoned traveler.

Please be advised that travel information is subject to change at any time — and this is especially true of prices. Always write or call ahead for confirmation when making your travel plans. The authors, editors, and publisher cannot be held responsible for the experiences of readers while traveling. Your safety is important to us, however, so we encourage you to stay alert and be aware of your surroundings. Keep a close eye on cameras, purses, and wallets, all favorite targets of thieves and pickpockets.

Conventions Used in This Book

Paris For Dummies is a reference book, meaning you may read the chapters in any order you want. We use some standard listings for hotels, restaurants, and sights. These listings enable you to open the book to any chapter and access the information you need quickly and easily.

In this book, we include lists of hotels, restaurants, and attractions. As we describe each, we often include abbreviations for commonly accepted credit cards. Take a look at the following list for an explanation of each.

> AE: American Express
>
> DC: Diners Club
>
> DISC: Discover
>
> MC: MasterCard
>
> V: Visa

Also included is some general pricing information to help you as you decide where to unpack your bags or dine on the local cuisine. We use a system of euros and dollar signs to show a range of costs for one night in a hotel (the price refers to a double-occupancy room) in Chapter 9 or a meal at a restaurant (included in the cost of each meal is soup or salad, an entrée, dessert, and a nonalcoholic drink) in Chapter 10.

Always included are the Paris *arrondissements,* or administrative districts, in each address to give you a better idea of where each place is located. Paris is divided into 20 arrondissements, which spiral out like a snail shell from the first arrondissement in the very center of Paris (abbreviated *1er*), to the 20th on the outer edges of the city (abbreviated *20e*). The arrondissement number appears after the street address in each citation in this book. For example, "55 bd St-Michel, 5e," indicates the building numbered 55 on the boulevard St-Michel is in the 5th arrondissement. To get an idea of where each arrondissement is located, consult the "Paris at a Glance" map in Chapter 1. Street abbreviations used throughout the book include not only *bd.* (boulevard), but also *rue* (street), *av.* (avenue), *place* (square), *bis* (an odd term generally meaning an address between two buildings), *Ter* (terrace), or *quai* (quay or riverbank).

To help you orient yourself, we also give the nearest Métro (subway) stop for all destinations (for example, Métro: Pont Marie).

Although exchange rates can and do fluctuate daily, the price conversions in this book were calculated at the rate of one euro (the local currency) to $1.20 U.S. dollar. For more information about the euro, see Chapter 4.

Foolish Assumptions

As we wrote this book, we made some assumptions about you and your needs as a traveler.

- ✔ You may be an experienced traveler who hasn't had much time to explore Paris and wants expert advice when you finally do get a chance to enjoy that particular locale.

- ✔ You may be an inexperienced traveler looking for guidance when determining whether to take a trip to Paris and how to plan for it.

- ✔ You're not looking for a book that provides all the information available about Paris or that lists every hotel, restaurant, or attraction available to you. Instead, you're looking for a book that focuses on the places that give you the best or most unique experience in Paris.

If you fit any of this criteria, *Paris For Dummies* gives you the information you're looking for!

How This Book Is Organized

Paris For Dummies is divided into seven parts with two appendixes. If you read the parts in sequential order, they can guide you through all the advance-planning aspects of your trip and then get you off and running while you're in the City of Light.

Part I: Introducing Paris

Provided here is a "best-of" overview of the city, some basic history and architecture, and the variety of events Paris offers at different times of the year.

Part II: Planning Your Trip to Paris

Should I use a travel agent or go it alone? Is travel insurance a good idea? These chapters touch on everything you need to consider before planning a trip, including hints on developing a realistic budget and what options are available to travelers with special needs or interests.

Part III: Settling into Paris

Some of the city's best moderately priced hotels (with a few super-budget and some deluxe resorts thrown in for good measure), are listed here, as well as advice on how to tie up those frustrating last-minute details that can unnerve the most seasoned of travelers. You'll learn in no time what kind of accommodations to choose in Paris and why you don't have to pay full price at hotel chains.

Tips on everything from navigating your way through customs to getting to your hotel from the airport to discovering Paris neighborhood by neighborhood orient you to Paris in no time. You find out how to use the city's terrific transportation system, why you shouldn't rent a car here, and what to know when you hail a cab. You make sense of the euro, and find out where to turn if your wallet gets stolen.

Paris is known for its fine food, and Chapter 10 helps you choose some of the best restaurants for your taste and budget. Everything from moderately priced to haute cuisine restaurants are listed here, so you can discover that a fine meal is truly an art in itself. We also provide street food and light fare options for those occasions when you don't have the time, or the desire, for a full-course meal.

Part IV: Exploring Paris

How to get to Paris's top sights, how much they cost, how much time to devote to them, and handy indexes by sight, type, and neighborhood make Paris's most famous attractions (and some not so famous but just as good) easier to find. There are kid- and teen-specific sights, as well as information on orientation and other tours, a shopper's guide to Paris, three recommended itineraries, and five great daytrips if you'd like to explore outside of the city.

Part V: Living It Up After Dark: Paris Nightlife

Part V gives you all the information you need about seeing plays, opera, ballet, and live music as well as which nightclubs and bars are the most fun. We are honest about whether the spectacles for which Paris has come to be known — the cabarets — are truly worth it. Uncover what's going on and where you can get reduced-rate tickets. Nothing is more beautiful than Paris at night, when the city's monuments are lit up like a stage. Anything can happen!

Part VI: The Part of Tens

What *For Dummies* book would be complete without a Part of Tens? Included is a quick collection of such fun tidbits as what to do on a rainy day or recommendations for the best place to relax with a picnic — a quintessential Parisian pastime!

Part VII: Appendixes

In the back of this book is Appendix A, a Quick Concierge that contains lots of handy information you may need when traveling in Paris: phone numbers and addresses of emergency personnel, area hospitals, and pharmacies; lists of local newspapers and magazines; protocol for sending mail and finding taxis; and more. Check out this appendix when searching for answers to lots of little questions that may come up as you travel. You can find the Quick Concierge easily because it's printed on yellow paper.

Appendix B is a glossary of English-to-French translations of basic vocabulary and health, travel, and (of course) shopping terms.

Icons Used in This Book

The following icons are scattered throughout the margins of this guide and are meant to draw your attention to especially useful text.

Keep an eye out for the Bargain Alert icon as you seek out money-saving tips and/or great deals.

Best of the Best icon highlights the best Paris has to offer in all categories — hotels, restaurants, attractions, activities, shopping, and nightlife.

You see this icon whenever something needs your particular attention. When you need to be aware of a rip-off, an overrated sight, a dubious deal, or any other trap set for unsuspecting travelers, this icon alerts you to that fact. These hints also offer the lowdown on the quirks, etiquette, and unwritten rules of the area so you can avoid looking like a tourist and, instead, be treated more like a local.

This icon is a catchall for any special hint, tip, or bit of insider's advice that can help make your trip run more smoothly. Really, the point of a travel guide is to serve as one gigantic tip, but this icon singles out those nuggets of knowledge you may not have run across before or of which you can make immediate use.

This icon, in addition to flagging tips and resources of special interest to families, points out the most child-friendly hotels, restaurants, and attractions. If you need a baby sitter at your hotel, a welcoming relaxed atmosphere at a restaurant, or a dazzling site that delights your child, look for this icon. Information is included regarding larger, family-sized rooms at hotels and restaurants that serve meals that go easy on your little ones' tummies.

Sometimes a great hotel, restaurant, or attraction may be a bit out of the center or require a bit of effort to get to. This icon alerts you to these secret finds, and you can rest assured, no spots are included that aren't truly worth the energy. This icon also signifies any resource that's particularly useful and worth the time to seek out.

Where to Go from Here

Where else? To Paris! *Paris For Dummies* shows you just how accessible this city can be. Included is a selective list of some of the best hotel, dining, and touring options along with insider info to help you make informed decisions. Follow the advice laid out here, and you'll want to return to Paris again and again.

Part I
Introducing Paris

The 5th Wave

By Rich Tennant

"I know it's a wedding present from your niece, I just don't know why you had to wear it to the Louvre."

In this part . . .

Are you a stranger to Paris? Or has it been a long time since you last visited? Then (re)introduce yourself to the city and whet your appetite to find out more about it. In Chapter 1, you get an overview of Paris and learn about the best the city has to offer. Chapter 2 gives you a crash course in Paris's history and architecture, briefly introduces you to French cuisine, soothes any worries you may have about the language, and recommends some great books and movies to enhance your understanding of the city. In Chapter 3, the pros and cons of the seasons as well as a Paris calendar of events help you decide the perfect time for your visit.

Chapter 1

Discovering the Best of Paris

In This Chapter

▶ Discovering Paris's best sights
▶ Finding Paris's best accommodations for every price range
▶ Indulging in glorious food, the best bars, a shopping nirvana, and the best culture, parks and gardens

*Y*ou've chosen one of the world's most beautiful and celebrated cities to visit — congratulations! There is so much to do and see that perhaps you feel a bit overwhelmed. Are you wondering what you should do first, and frankly, what's a waste of time? How long should you spend at the Louvre, and if you miss the Arc de Triomphe, will you always regret it? Are you concerned that a language barrier may prevent you from doing some of the things you'd like? Just how small are the hotel rooms at budget establishments? You know you want to taste the delicious food for which the country is renowned, but who knew there were so many types?

Three words: take — it — easy. Know up front that, much as you'd like, you simply won't be able to do, see, and taste it all. Avoid "Griswold Syndrome" (think of the family in the movie *European Vacation* who rush to see all of Paris and suffer the consequences!), and enjoy what could be Paris's greatest attraction of all: a way of life in which relaxing in a cafe and watching the world go by are natural parts of the day. You'll discover that the **Louvre** Museum is as incredible as its reputation, but did you know that the **Musée du quai Branly** has opened up near the Eiffel Tower and displays some of the Louvre's former treasures? And what a great time to visit — the **Orangerie,** closed for nearly a decade, has reopened, and Monet's *Water Lilies* here are spectacular! You'll find that taking a **boat tour of the Seine** is one of the best ways to see Paris, but renting a bike for a few hours can take you to such places as the **Bois de Boulogne** and the **Bois de Vincennes,** two big, beautiful parks on each side of Paris that are a haven from the city's bustle. Whatever you do, you'll quickly discover that Paris (see map "Paris at a Glance") is more of an experience than merely a city, and each visitor experiences it in an entirely individual way.

Paris at a Glance

Paris Map Key

A Paris's Top Attractions;
More Fun Things to Do in Paris;
Paris Shopping

B Light Bites in Montmartre

C Hotels in the Heart of the Right Bank;
Restaurants on the Right Bank;
Light Bites in the Heart of the Right Bank

D Hotels in the Heart of the Left Bank;
Restaurants on the Left Bank;
Light Bites in the Heart of the Left Bank

E Père-Lachaise Cemetery

This chapter is designed as an at-a-glance reference to the absolute best — the best of the best — that Paris has to offer. Each of these experiences and places are discussed in detail later in the book; you can find them in their indicated chapter, marked with a Best of the Best icon.

The Best Accommodations

With more than 2,200 chain hotels, deluxe palacelike accommodations, hotels that cater to business travelers, budget hotels, and mom-and-pop establishments, it's difficult to narrow things down to just a few. But the hotels here are the hotels that, in our opinion, you'll want to return on your next visit (because no one can see Paris just once!). We only list hotels in the first eight arrondissements, the most central locations in Paris. See Chapter 9 for more information on the accommodations listed here.

✔ We love the **Hôtel Minerve** (5e), a welcoming, budget, kid-friendly hotel in the Latin Quarter. With wood-beamed ceilings, exposed stone walls, carved mahogany wood furnishings and decent sizes, rooms are a great value and the location is terrific! (Ask for one of the ten balconied rooms complete with a table and chairs overlooking rue des Ecoles.) Just around the corner from the Cluny Museum, this is a true Paris treasure.

✔ Located on a street full of art galleries, the pretty **Hôtel de Seine** (6e) in St-Germain-des-Près is a few blocks from the Seine and the pedestrian bridge Pont des Arts that leads to the Louvre. For just a few more euro, you can stay in this hotel where each room is distinctly decorated with French provincial furniture and flowered wallpaper or Provence-inspired jewel-toned paint and Louis XVI-era reproductions.

✔ Rooms are simply divine at the gorgeous deluxe **Pavillon de la Reine** (4e) right off place des Vosges, and this is THE place to celebrate anniversaries or honeymoons. The large standard rooms are decorated with gingham wallpaper and Louis XIII-style furniture, superior duplex rooms have modern beds located in a loft above a cozy sitting room with comfortable chairs and couches, and suites boast four-poster beds and beamed ceilings and open onto the courtyard. You'll find all the amenities here. For these prices, you can have the extravagant splendor of one of Paris's palace hotels, but Pavillon de la Reine's intimate surroundings are just as appealing.

The Best Food

It's no question that one of the greatest things about visiting Paris is eating the delicious food! No matter where you decide to dine or what kind of food you choose, you can count on having some memorable meals! The following list contains some of our favorite restaurants (the information in parentheses indicates the arrondissement in which each establishment is located). See Chapter 10 for more information on the restaurants listed here.

- **Chez Casimir (10e):** This restaurant near the Gare du Nord and far from the more touristy sides of Paris packs in loyal customers because Chef Philippe Tredgeu works magic in his kitchen, cooking with ingredients he finds at the market that morning or the night before. This is French comfort food at great prices!

- **Le Cinq (8e):** We have never been disappointed in Le Cinq (when we can afford to eat here!). This three-Michelin-starred restaurant in the Four Seasons George V is truly extraordinary, from exquisite pull-out-all-the-stops food to its award winning sommelier and fantastic wine cellar. Dining here is a sumptuous experience!

- **Chainterelle (5e):** You will feel as if you're visiting the Auvergne, the rugged, pastoral south-central region of France. Little fonts contain essential oils made from native plants; a sound system incorporates native birdsong, rain, and church bells; and the door even says "moo" when you walk in. A pretty, walled outdoor garden is a respite from Paris's bustle, and the peasant food is hearty and delicious.

The Best Sights

What's a visit to Paris without seeing the view from the Eiffel Tower? For most people, the real reason for visiting Paris is to see the quintessentially French attractions for which the city is known. Are the sights really as great as returning travelers say? Mais oui! Here are just a few of the best. See Chapter 11 for more information on the sights listed here.

- The city's most famous landmark, the **Eiffel Tower,** graces the city skyline with its lacy presence and twinkles for ten minutes each hour at night with some 30,000 bulbs installed in 2003. People have climbed it, bungee-jumped from it, and cycled down the tower's steps, but hopefully you'll be content just to enjoy its views!

- Take a **tour boat down the Seine** at night and see lights from bridges older than the United States cast reflections in the water. English-language commentary is included.

- **The Musée d'Orsay** has an unsurpassed collection of Impressionist masterpieces (and a terrific collection of Art Nouveau pieces). It's also the world's best-renovated train station! Take a moment at the top of the central staircase to envision where trains once pulled into the station under the curved roof.

- When you catch your first glimpse of the nearly 900-year-old **Cathédral de Notre-Dame,** it just may take your breath away. Flying buttresses lend a graceful air to what would otherwise be an imposing structure. Play Quasimodo and climb to the top of the bell tower (get there early — the lines grow huge from late morning through closing) or marvel at the gorgeous rose windows.

✔ The **Arc de Triomphe** was commissioned by Napoléon to honor his army and its 128 victorious battles, but the real reason people visit is for the view — one that takes in the Eiffel Tower. From the top, 49m (162 ft.) up, you can see in a straight line the Champs-Elysées, the obelisk in the place de la Concorde, the Louvre, and the Grande Arche de la Défense in St-Denis, a giant open cube built to be the modern equivalent to this arch.

✔ The **Musée Picasso** constantly rotates its exhibits that represent every phase of Picasso's prolific 75-year career. All of it is housed in a beautiful 17th-century mansion deep in the Marais, one of Paris's best and most interesting neighborhoods.

✔ The **Musée Nationale d'Auguste Rodin** is one of Paris's more relaxing museums. After taking in the sensual sculptures displayed in the beautiful former convent, stroll through the gardens here to see more of the legendary artist's masterpieces such as *The Thinker* and *The Gates of Hell.*

✔ The **Musée de Cluny** is one of the jewels of Paris museums and is home to the famous tapestry series *The Lady and the Unicorn.* It houses ancient Roman hot and cold baths, the original statues pulled off Notre-Dame in 1790 by furious revolutionaries, and so, so much more, as well as a terrific gift shop to boot.

The Best Parks and Gardens

Paris has parks for every taste and interest offering flowers, rare plants, and views of the city and puppet shows, pony rides, and museums. Here are some of its best. Chapter 11 has more information.

✔ The **Jardin des Tuileries** (1er) is Paris's most visited park, where visitors to the Louvre next door like to revive in the fresh air and rest their feet on conveniently placed wrought-iron chairs surrounding the garden's fountains. In keeping with the French style of parks, trees are planted according to an orderly design and the sandy paths are arrow straight. During the summer, a carnival features an enormous Ferris wheel (with great views of the city) and some other thrill rides, a fun house, arcade-style games, and snacks.

✔ The **Jardin du Luxembourg** in the Latin Quarter is Parisians' most beloved park. Children love it for its playground, pony rides, puppet theater, and the Fontaine de Médicis where they can sail toy boats. Make use of the tennis and *boules* courts (*boules* is a French game similar to lawn bowling or the Italian *bocce* in which players try to be the first to roll their balls closest to the small object ball called the *cochonnet*), or appreciate the art exhibited on the wrought-iron fence at the garden's northwestern entrance near boulevard St-Michel and rue de Médicis. Courses are offered here in bee keeping, and the park's orchard grows apples and pears that end up on the plates of staff at the French Senate, which is housed in the garden's Palais du Luxembourg.

✔ **Parc de la Villette** (19e) is a modern park with a series of theme gardens, including an exotic bamboo garden and one featuring steam and water jets. Scattered throughout are playgrounds and other attractions — this is a must-visit if you've spent time at the huge children's science complex, **Cité des Sciences et l'Industrie.**

✔ Rock formations and grottoes in the tranquil **Parc de Belleville** (20e) are still around from the days when the hill was a strategic point for fighting Attila the Hun. Watch the sun set over western Paris and take in the wonderful (free!) views of the city. Topped by the **Maison de l'Air,** a museum with displays devoted to the air that we breathe, you can enjoy fountains, a children's play area, and an open-air theater that holds rock concerts during the summer.

The Best Shopping

A favorable euro-to-dollar rate has seen many new stores open and others expand, though sadly, department store Samaritaine is closed for the next few years while it brings up to code its antiquated fire system. Though the city has a well-deserved reputation as a bastion of over-the-top luxury (to understand why, head for the 8th arrondissement), discount, resale, and overstock stores also abound, as well as the wonderful Monoprix (see below). Whenever we're in Paris, a visit to the following stores is a must. See Chapter 12 for more information on the stores listed here.

✔ **Monoprix,** a reasonably priced department store with branches around the city, has stylish clothing and is also great for accessories, low-priced cosmetics, lingerie, and house wares. Many locations also have large grocery stores good for gift buying. The one at 52 av. du Champs-Elysées, 8e, is chock-full of goodies and open until midnight.

✔ **Le Bon Marché** (6e) is elegant, but small enough to be manageable, and is the Left Bank's only department store. You can find the top designers here, as well as more affordable pieces, too, and the basement toy store has great gift selections. The third floor is particularly renowned for its large shoe selection and lingerie department (where dressing rooms have phones to summon your salesperson).

✔ Although it isn't cheap, Le Bon Marché's next-door grocery store, **Le Grand Epicerie** (6e) is one of the best luxury supermarkets in Paris and a great place to look for gourmet gifts such as olive oils, homemade chocolates, or wine. It makes for wonderful one-stop picnic shopping, too, offering a wide array of prepared foods and cheeses. If you're staying in an apartment or your hotel has a kitchen for guests, come here to purchase fixings for dinner.

✔ **Du Pareil au Même** is *the* store to buy clothes for every child on your list — clothes are practical, *très mignons* (very cute), and very reasonably priced.

The Best of Culture

Getting "cultured" is not a problem in Paris. There are more than 100 theaters, competing opera houses, and ballet and chamber music concerts in many churches. Even if your French is rusty or not up to par, many avant-garde productions and English-language theaters serve as alternatives to French-language plays. In this section, we list some of the best places to see theater, watch a ballet, or hear a symphony. See Chapter 15 for more information.

✔ You can see dazzling performances by the national opera and ballet troupes that perform at both the radiant **Palais Garnier** (9e) and the ultramodern **Opéra National de Bastille** (11e). The Palais Garnier conducts more ballet performances, and the Opéra Bastille puts on more opera.

✔ A good mix of modern and classic tragedies and comedies comes alive in wonderful performances in the **Salle Richelieu** of the **Comédie-Française,** 2 rue de Richelieu, 1er.

✔ For popular, contemporary plays, the **Théâtre National de Chaillot,** place du Trocadéro, 16e, is your place.

✔ Whatever your choice of the classic arts — opera, ballet, concerts, recitals — you'll find it performed at the **Châtelet, Théâtre Musical de Paris** (1er) by local and international performers of the highest caliber.

✔ For comedy in English, try **Laughing Matters,** in the historic Hôtel du Nord (10e). This company is thriving, and the lineups are always terrific, featuring award-winning comics from the United States, the United Kingdom, Ireland, and Australia.

✔ More than a dozen Parisian churches regularly schedule relatively inexpensive organ recitals and concerts. The most glorious, where the music is nearly outdone by the glorious stained glass windows, is **Sainte-Chapelle** (4e).

The Best Clubs

Each neighborhood makes a different contribution to Paris's vibrant nightlife scene. Listed here are some of the best places to dance the night away. See Chapter 16 for more information.

- **Barrio Latino** (11e) has three bars, private areas where you can see (but not be seen), a lounge complete with pool table, a second floor restaurant serving Latino food, a top-floor private club with a kitschy Che Guevara mural, and energetic Latin music that sets everyone to dancing. It's pure fun!

- **Batofar** (13e), an Irish light ship docked in the Seine, is one hot, sweaty, and ultimately fun time right on the Seine, with all types of music represented, from drum-and-bass to British pop.

- At **Red Light** (15e) — with multiple raised platforms above the floor for those who dare to dance — you can see the trendiest kids in town wearing the newest fashions available.

- **Le Wax**'s (11e) décor is very *Clockwork Orange,* with plastic bubbles on the walls, yellow plastic couches, and lots of crimson and orange. The bathrooms are very psychedelic, too, especially after your second drink.

- **Le Mix** (15e) boasts spinning provided by music gurus Ministry of Sound and David Guetta (a holy name among Parisian clubbers). Come groove with the fashionistas.

- **Le Pulp** (2e) used to be one of Paris's hippest lesbian clubs, but everyone comes here now. Reminiscent of a 19th-century French music hall, this venue is très cool, with all types of cutting-edge music.

Chapter 2

Digging Deeper into Paris

- -

In This Chapter

▶ Discovering the rich history of Paris

▶ Admiring the city's architecture

▶ Enjoying the local cuisine

▶ Getting to know the local language

▶ Previewing the city in books and movies

- -

A cultural course in a nutshell, this chapter will fill you in on the city's history, the basics of French architecture, the art of the meal, and why the French language is nothing to be afraid of. (Really, it's not!) Plus, you get your pretrip homework assignment — reading wonderful books and watching great movies!

History 101: The Main Events

The Parisii tribe settled Paris in the third century B.C. on the **Ile de la Cité** (one of two islands in the Seine around Central Paris — these days, Notre-Dame sits on Ile de la Cité). They were peaceful fishermen who traded with other tribes along the river and with travelers on the main north–south trading road that connected the Mediterranean with northern Europe. Unfortunately, the road made attacking the Parisii all too convenient for invaders. The first and most successful were the Romans led by Julius Caesar in 52 B.C. During the Romans's 500-year stay, the settlement became known as Lutetia Parisiorum (*Lutèce* in French). You can still see their public baths at the **Musée National du Moyen Age/Cluny Museum** in the **Latin Quarter.**

Years of barbarian invasions eventually weakened Rome's hold over the territory. Around A.D. 350, Attila the Hun, on his way to sack Paris, changed course at the last minute, purportedly due to the prayers of a young girl named **Geneviève.** She became the patron saint of Paris. In the 400s, Franks from the east successfully wrested control away from the Romans. In 508, Clovis, king of the Franks, chose Paris as his capital. It was abandoned as a capital 250 years later only to regain that status in 987 when Hugues Capet was proclaimed king of France. Celebrating the city's importance, two Gothic masterpieces, the cathedrals of **Notre-Dame** and **Sainte-Chapelle,** were built on the Ile de la Cité.

Across the river, on the **Left Bank,** the **Sorbonne University** was born. Under Louis XIV, who ruled for 72 years, the monarchy's power reached its height, supported by heavy taxes. Although he added monuments and splendor to the city, the Sun King moved his court to Versailles, alienating the citizenry and preparing the way for the French Revolution.

On July 14, 1789, a mob stormed the **Bastille** prison, which held many who were out of favor with French royalty. To most French citizens at the time, the Bastille was a sign of much that was wrong with the monarchy, and the attack on the Bastille came to represent the end of the monarchy. Three days later at the Hôtel de Ville, **Louis XVI** was forced to kiss the new French tricolor. On July 14, 1790, the Festival of the Federation was celebrated on the Champs de Mars, and an estimated 300,000 attended a Mass at which the king swore an oath of loyalty to the constitution. Still, radical factions grew. On August 10, 1792, revolutionary troops joined a Parisian mob storming the **Tuileries Palace,** where the king lived and took him prisoner. In 1793, he and **Queen Marie Antoinette** were beheaded in the place de la Concorde. At this time, Maximilien **Robespierre** was elected leader of the Committee of Public Safety, which conducted witch hunts for those it deemed counter-revolutionaries. This became known as the Reign of Terror. Between September 1793 and February 1794, 238 men and 31 women were tried and executed for crimes against the state. Nearly 5,500 more awaited trial in prisons until Robespierre's arrest in July 1794. He was executed the same month.

During the last stage of the French Revolution, a directory of five men was ushered into govern France. After four years, Napoléon staged a coup (1799), turning the country into a dictatorship. Five years later, (1804) at Notre-Dame, Napoléon crowned himself emperor and his wife, Joséphine, empress. He then embarked on a series of military campaigns until his defeat at Waterloo in 1815. During his reign, he gave Paris many of its most grandiose monuments, notably the **Arc de Triomphe** and the **Bourse,** but his greatest gift was starting the **Louvre.**

The **Eiffel Tower** (La Tour Eiffel), built only as a temporary structure for the 1889 World's Fair, was at one time the tallest structure in the world. Paris opened its first Métro line in 1900, and by the turn of the 20th century, had thousands of restaurants and 27,000 cafes.

In the years that followed, Paris witnessed two world wars with more than ten million military casualties, nearly one million Jews losing their lives, and four years of German occupation. Tens of thousands of soldiers died fighting the end of French colonial rule around the world.

In 1968, students took to the streets of Paris, rebelling against France's antiquated educational system among a host of other causes, including the rights of workers (this period of time is known in France as *Mai 1968*). De Gaulle's government tried to quash the strikes with police action, but only succeeded in making the situation worse. Young people hurled paving stones at police in street battles, and ten million French workers throughout the country went on strike. This nearly led to the collapse of the government, and De Gaulle called for new elections. Almost as quickly as the student and worker revolution started, it was over by June 1968 when voters elected an even stronger De Gaulle administration. DeGaulle, himself, resigned in 1969. The government flirted unsuccessfully with socialism in the 1980s and ended the decade with a great celebration of democracy: the bicentennial of the French Revolution and the centennial of the Eiffel Tower.

Former Paris Mayor **Jacques Chirac** was elected president in 1995 on his promise to jump-start the economy, but growth remained stagnant, and the president was forced to share power with Prime Minister Lionel Jospin, after the leader of the opposition called for elections in 1997. Facing rising gas prices, escalating crime, anti-Semitic vandalism, and a lack of interest in the 2002 presidential elections, Jospin lost his prime minister's seat, sending extremist Jean-Marie Le Pen into the presidential race against Chirac. French citizens took to the streets in protest, and Chirac won by a landslide. Jospin retired from politics.

One of the biggest events in 2003 was a terrible summer heat wave that left more than 15,000 mostly elderly people dead throughout the country. Many of the dead were left alone while family members went on vacation, and as a result, the whole French system of priorities was thrown into question.

In 2005, as a result of the accidental electrocution of two teenagers of African and North African descent, riots broke out in Paris resulting in the burning of thousands of cars and trucks in the Ile-de-France region. The two teenagers were attempting to hide from a police patrol when they were accidentally killed, and rioting youth cited suffering from unemployment and the supposed racism of French police, government, and general society against those of African and Arab descent, as well as Muslims in general. The anger and violence turned into a months-long series of riots that spread throughout urban areas of France. The situation was not helped when Interior Minister Nicolas Sarkozy referred to the suburban youth as *racaille,* meaning hooligans. The year 2006 saw continual clashes between the citizenry and the French government when over a million people took part in student strikes during the months of February and March. The strikes were held in opposition to proposed changes to the basic layout of workers' rights in France, specifically changes that would allow employers to fire workers under the age of twenty-six without giving an officially stated reason (previously, the process for firing an employee of any age was time-consuming and expensive). Although it was meant to encourage businesses otherwise afraid of taking on new employees to open their doors, students saw these changes as detrimental to their job security. Universities across France were shut down due to student blockades.

Building Blocks: Local Architecture

First-time visitors to Paris are struck by the graceful curves and balconies of the city's gorgeous apartment buildings, many of which were built during the reign of Napoléon III (mid-1800s). In a city bursting with architectural treasures, these are just some of the newest. In addition to the mixture of styles associated with the 19th and 20th centuries, many architectural eras are represented in Paris, among them the Ancient Roman, Romanesque, Gothic, Renaissance, classical (classicism), and rococo periods. You can see artifacts from Paris's founding in the third century B.C. by a tribe of fisherman, as well as such modern-day projects as the guts-on-the-outside Centre Georges Pompidou and I.M. Pei's glass pyramid at the Louvre.

Paris's important architectural periods are outlined here.

✔ **Ancient Roman (125 B.C.– A.D. 450):** After Julius Caesar conquered the island of Lutétia, his legions began using bricks and concrete in building and introduced the load-bearing arch, which led to the construction of stronger bridges and doorways. You can see examples of excavated Roman ruins at the **Crypte Archéologique** (see Chapter 11), about 60m (200 ft.) directly in front of the entrance of Notre-Dame. The ruins of ancient Roman baths are in the cellar at the **Cluny Museum** (also in Chapter 11), a former private residence that was built around and on top of the ruins.

✔ **Romanesque (800–1100):** This style is characterized by arches and curves, thick walls with small windows, huge piers to hold up the roof, simple geometric arrangements, and painting in decorative hues. The architects during this period built large churches; none survive intact in Paris; all were improved upon with different architectural styles or rebuilt. **St-Germain-des-Près** is a Romanesque building with a Gothic interior. **St-Julien-le-Pauvre** was originally a Romanesque church, but later Gothic additions obscure the original details.

✔ **Gothic (1100–1500):** Known for its slender vertical piers and counterbalancing buttresses and for vaulting and pointed arches that allow for taller and thinner structures, the interiors of these buildings force the eyes upward. Windows with stained glass were constructed so that most of the illiterate population could understand the stories told in each pane. Gargoyles (drain spouts), spires, flying buttresses, rose windows, and choir screens were all features of the Gothic church. The best examples are **Notre-Dame,** of course, and the **Cathédrale de Notre-Dame de Chartres** (Chapter 14 describes this cathedral in more detail).

✔ **Renaissance (1500–1630):** This architectural style is characterized by harmonious form, mathematical proportion, and a unit of measurement based on the human scale. Roofs became steeply pitched, and dormer windows were built taller, using stone. The mansions surrounding the **Place des Vosges** are all Renaissance, as is the **Hôtel Carnavalet,** home to the **Musée Carnavalet.**

✔ **Classicism (1630–1800):** In this school, the emphasis was on form, simplicity, proportion, and restraint, influenced by the architecture of ancient Greece and Rome. Exteriors in the classical style may feature Doric, Corinthian, and Ionic columns, low and simple dormer windows, mansard roofs (having two slopes on all sides with the lower slope steeper than the upper, invented by François Mansard), and simple proportions; the interiors of classical buildings went over the top. This interior style is known as **rococo,** derived from the words *rocaille* (rock) and *coquille* (shell), delicate decorative motifs that appeared along with scrolls, branches of leaves, flowers, and bamboo stems. The best example of classicism and rococo is **Versailles** (see Chapter 14). The **Louvre** is also a classical tour de force.

✔ **Nineteenth century (1800–1889):** This style began with *neoclassicism,* a return to the majesty of past civilizations, and an adoption of classical forms and styles. Examples include the **Arc de Triomphe** and the **Madeleine.** The **Second Empire** brought wide boulevards lined with six-story apartment buildings with balconies and mansard roofs with dormer windows. The **Third Republic**'s industrial age produced glass and steel structures; the most famous are the **Eiffel Tower** and **Sacré-Coeur.**

✔ **Art Nouveau (1890–1914):** This period saw the end of the 19th century and continued into the 20th with beautiful renderings of plants and flowers in wrought iron **(Abbesses Métro station entrance),** stained glass, wood, tile, and hand-painted wallpapers (for a wonderful introduction to Art Nouveau, visit the middle floor of the **Musée d'Orsay;** see Chapter 11).

✔ **Twentieth century (1900–1999):** This style may be defined by late President François Mitterand's *grands projets* (grand projects), most of which were controversial when completed. Richard Rogers' and Renzo Piano's **Centre Georges Pompidou** (see Chapter 11), with its "guts on the outside" architecture, horrified Parisians, as did I.M. Pei's glass pyramids at the Louvre, but residents have slowly come to accept them. The four looming towers shaped like open books that comprise Mitterand's last project, the Bibliothèque Nationale de France, are another story; the building, which is still suffering from the occasional technological glitch, has gotten little respect since its opening in the late 1990s. You may recall that the Parisians initially hated the Eiffel Tower, too; now, where would they be without it?

A Taste of Paris: The Local Cuisine

Parisians have such wonderful meals from which to choose — regional French, three-star haute cuisine, North African *couscouseries,* tasty crepes sold from street vendors, and more. During the last decade, the city witnessed the rise of *baby bistros,* restaurants opened by celebrity chefs and their talented young apprentices offering simpler and less-expensive meals than those served at their deluxe establishments. Also in vogue is a back-to-Grandmère's-kitchen approach featuring chefs turning out homey meals such as *blanquette de veau* (veal stew in white sauce), *cassoulet* (meat-and-vegetable casserole), and *confit de canard* (duck preserved and cooked in its own fat until it's so tender it falls off the bone). Asian influences are also in vogue; witness the success of L'Atelier de Joël Robuchon. We talk in more depth about dining in Paris in Chapter 10.

A glossary good enough to eat

Use this helpful guide when you're trying to decide what to order and how you want it cooked.

General Terms

compris (comb-*pree;* included)
déjeuner (*day*-zhu-nay; lunch)
dîner (*dee*-nay; dinner)
ménu dégustation (meh-*noo* day-goo-*stah*-sion; sampler, or tasting, menu)
petit déjeuner (pet-*tee day*-zhu-nay; breakfast)
prix fixe (pree-feeks; set price)
supplément (sup-play-*mahn;* extra charge)

Les Entrées (*layz ahn-trays; appetizers*)

charcuterie (shar-koot-*ree;* assorted cold cuts)
crudités (kroo-dee-*tay;* assorted raw vegetables)
foie gras (fwah grah; goose liver paté)
salade composée (sa-*lad* com-poh-zay; mixed salad)
salade de chèvre chaud (sa-*lad* deh-shev-rah-*sho;* salad with warm goat cheese on croutons)
salade de Niçoise (sa-*lad* nee-*shwahz;* salad with tuna, canned corn, anchovies, and potato)
salade gesiers (sa-*lad* zheh-shee-*air;* salad with sautéed chicken gizzards)
salade landaise (sa-*lad* lahn-*dehs;* salad containing duck breast, duck liver, and duck gizzards)

saumon fumé (soh-*moh foo*-may; smoked salmon)
soupe à l'oignon (soop-ah-lowh-*yon;* onion soup)
soupe à pistou (soop-ah-pees-*too;* vegetable soup with pesto)
velouté (vay-loot-*ay;* cream-based soup)
vichyssoise (vee-shee-*swahz;* cold leek and potato soup)

Boeuf (*bewf; beef*)

bavette (bah-*vet;* flank steak)
chateaubriand (cha-tow-bree-*ahn;* porterhouse)
contre-filet (*kahn*-trah-fee-lay; filet steak)
côte de boeuf (cote dah bewf; T-bone)
entrecôte (ahn-trah-*cote;* rib-eye)
faux-filet (foe-fee-*lay;* sirloin)
filet mignon (fee-*lay* mee-*nyahn;* tenderloin)
langue de boeuf (lahng dah bewf; tongue)
onglet (ahn-*glay;* hanger steak)
pavé (pah-*vay;* thick steak; *literally:* paving stone)
queue de boeuf (kyew dah bewf; oxtail)
rôti de boeuf (*roe*-tee dah bewf; roast beef)
steak haché (stake *ha*-shay; minced meat or hamburger)

steak tartare (stake tar-*tar;* a lean cut of beef minced and served raw — a high-quality dish prepared by experts, people rarely get sick from eating this)
tournedo (*tor*-nay-doe; small tender filet usually grilled or sautéed)
veau (voe; veal)

Other Meats

agneau (ah-*nyoe;* lamb)
gigot (*gee*-joe; leg — usually of lamb)
jambon (zhahm-*bon;* ham)
médaillon (meh-dah-ee-*on;* medallions — beef, veal, lamb)
merguez (mare-*gay;* spicy sausage)
porc (pork; pork)
saucisses/saucisson (soh-*sees,* soh-see-*sohn;* sausage/little sausage)

Volailles (voe-lie; fowl)

blanc de volaille (blahn dah voe-*lai;* chicken breast)
caille (kaih; quail)
canard (kah-*nahr;* duck)
dinde (dand; turkey)
magret de canard (mah-*gret* dah kah-*nahr;* duck breast)
oie (wah; goose)
pigéon (pee-jee-*ohn;* game pigeon)
pintade (pan-*tahd;* guinea fowl)
poulet (*poo*-lay; chicken)

Fruits de Mer (free duh mair; seafood)

bar (bar; bass)
coquilles St-Jacques (*koe*-kee san-*jahk;* scallops)
crevettes (kreh-*vet;* shrimp)
daurade (doe-*rahd;* sea bream)
homard (oe-*mahr;* lobster)
huîtres (wee-*tra;* oysters)
langoustine (lang-oo-*steen;* crayfish)
morue/cabillaud (moh-*roo*/ka-bee-*oh;* cod)
moules (mool; mussels)
poissons (pwah-*son;* fish)
raie (ray; skate)
rascasse (ras-*kass;* scorpion fish)

rouget (roo-*zhay;* red mullet)
saumon (soh-*moh;* salmon)
thon (than; tuna)
truite (trweet; trout)

Les Légumes (lay lay-goom; vegetables)

artichault (ar-tee-*show;* artichoke)
asperge (as-*pearzh;* asparagus)
aubergine (oe-bur-*zheen;* eggplant)
champignons/cèpes/truffes/girolles (sham-pee-*nyahn*/sep/troof/*gee*-roll; mushrooms)
choucroute (shoo-*kroot;* sauerkraut)
choux (shoo; cabbage)
choux de bruxelles (shoo dah broo-*zells;* brussels sprouts)
courgette (kore-*zhette;* zucchini)
épinard (ay-pee-*nahr;* spinach)
haricots (ahr-ee-*koe;* beans)
haricots verts (*ahr*-ee-koe-vair; string beans)
oignons (wah-*nyoh;* onions)
petits pois (*pet*-tee pwah; peas)
poireaux (pwah-*roe;* leeks)
poivron rouge (pwah-vrah-*roozh;* red pepper)
poivron vert(pwah-vrah *vair;* green pepper)
pomme de terre (pum dah *tair;* potato)
pommes frites (*pum freet;* french fries)
riz (*ree;* rice)
tomate (toe-*maht;* tomato)

Les Fruits (lay free; fruit)

abricot (*ah*-bree-koh; apricot)
ananas (a-*na*-nas; pineapple)
banane (bah-*nan;* banana)
cerise (sair-*ees;* cherry)
citron (see-*troh;* lemon)
citron vert (see-troh-*vair;* lime)
fraise (frayz; strawberry)
framboise (frahm-*bwahz;* raspberry)
myrtille (meer-*teel;* blueberry)
pamplemousse (pahm-pull-*moos;* grapefruit)
pêche (pehsh; peach)
poire (pwahr; pear)

pomme (pum; apple)
prune (proon; plum)
pruneau (proo-*noh;* prune)
raisin (rah-*zeen;* grape)
raisin sec (rah-zeen-*sek;* raisin)

Les Desserts (lay day-sair; desserts)

Charlotte (shar-*lote;* molded cream ringed with a biscuit)
clafoutis (clah-foo-*tee;* thick batter filled with fruit and fried)
crème brûlée (krem broo-*lay;* creamy custard with caramel topping)
fromage blanc (froe-*mahzh* blahn; smooth cream cheese)
gâteau (gah-*toe;* cake)
glace (glahs; ice cream)
marquise (mar-*keez;* light, mousse-like cake)
mousse au chocolat (moos oh shok-*lah;* chocolate mousse)
tarte aux (tart oh; pie)
tarte tatin (tart ta-*ta;* caramelized upside-down apple pie)
vacherin (*vahsh*-reh; cake of layered meringue, fruit, and ice cream)

Preparation Methods

à l'ail (ah lai; with garlic)
à point (ah pwahn; medium)
au four (oh fore; baked)
béarnaise (bare-*nayse;* hollandaise sauce with tarragon, vinegar, and shallots)
bechamel (beh-sha-*mel;* white sauce made with onions and nutmeg)
beurre blanc (bur blahn; white sauce made with butter, white wine, and shallots)
bien cuit (byen kwee; well done).
bleu (bluh; very rare)
bordelaise (bore-dah-*lays;* brown meat stock made with red wine, mushrooms, shallots, and beef marrow)

bouilli (bwee-*ee;* boiled)
bourguignon (bore-gee-*nyoh;* brown meat stock flavored with red wine, mushrooms, and onions)
confit (kahn-*fee;* meat — usually duck or goose — cooked in its own fat)
consommé (kahn-soe-*may;* clear broth)
coulis (koo-*lee;* any nonflour sauce, purée, or juice)
en croûte (ahn *kroot;* in a pastry crust)
cru (kroo; raw)
diable (dee-*ah*-blah; brown sauce flavored with cayenne pepper, white wine, and shallots)
en papillote (ohn pah-pee-*oat;* cooked in parchment and opened at the table — usually fish)
estouffade (ay-too-*fahd;* meat that has been marinated, fried, and braised)
farci (fahr-*see;* stuffed)
feuilleté (fwee-eh-*tay;* in puff pastry)
fumé (*foo*-may; smoked)
gratiné (*grah*-tee-nay; topped with browned bread crumbs or cheese)
grillé (*gree*-ay; grilled)
hollandaise (ahl-lan-*dehs;* white sauce with butter, egg yolks, and lemon juice)
lyonnais (lee-ohn-*nay;* with onions)
marinière (mar-ee-*nyair;* steamed in garlicky wine stock)
meunière (moo-*nyur;* fish rolled in flour and sautéed)
parmentier (pahr-men-tee-*ay;* with potato)
Provençal (pro-ven-*saw;* tomato-based sauce, with garlic, olives, and onions)
rôti (*roe*-tee roasted)
saignant (sen-*yahn;* rare)
terrine (tuh-*reen;* cooked in an earthenware dish)

Salivating over French cooking

Even with English translations, confronting a French menu can be a daunting experience. Dishes that have been familiar to French people since childhood are often unknown to outsiders. The following list is a user's guide to typical French dishes that you're likely to encounter.

- **Andouillette** (ahn-dwee-*et*): A sausage of pork organs encased in intestines. Andouillette has a strong flavor with a distinct aftertaste and is usually grilled and served with mustard and French fries. Look for the A.A.A.A.A. label — the Association Amicale des Authentiques Amateurs d'Andouillettes (Association of Real Andouillette Lovers) stamps it on the best andouillettes.

- **Blanquette de veau** (blahn-*ket* duh voe): Veal cooked in a white stew that includes eggs and cream.

- **Boeuf Bourguignon** (buhf bor-gee-*nyon*): Beef cooked with red burgundy wine, mushrooms, and onions.

- **Boudin** (boo-*dan*): A rich sausage made from pig's blood, usually combined with *créme fraîche,* onions, and eggs. More elaborate versions may feature a touch of garlic or chestnuts. The dish is often served with sautéed apples or mashed potatoes, which enhance the slightly sweet taste of the sausage.

- **Boudin blanc** (boo-*dan* blahn): A white sausage made from veal, chicken, or pork.

- **Bouillabaisse** (*bwee*-ah-bess): A fish stew from the Mediterranean that includes assorted shellfish and white fish accompanied by croutons, grated cheese, and *rouille,* a mayonnaise made with garlic.

- **Brandade** (brahn-*dahd*): Salt cod *(morue)* soaked in cold water, shredded, and cooked with garlic, olive oil, milk, and potato. It has the look and consistency of mashed potatoes but tastes like salted fish. A green salad makes a good accompaniment.

- **Carpaccio** (car-*pahsh*-shyow): Thinly sliced, cured raw beef or tuna.

- **Cassoulet** (cass-oo-*lay*): A rich stew made of white beans, dry sausage, onion, duck, prosciutto, herbs, carrots, and tomatoes. It's cooked slowly and usually served in a ceramic bowl or pot. Absolutely delicious, but heavy; don't plan any serious physical exertions after eating — digestion will be enough.

- **Cervelles** (suhr-vel): Pork or sheep brains.

- **Cheval** (sheh-vahl): Horse meat.

- **Choucroute** (shoo-*kroot*): Sauerkraut cooked with juniper berries and wine, served with an assortment of pork cuts, usually including brisket, pork shoulder, ham, frankfurters, or spicy sausage. It goes well with boiled potatoes and is served with mustard.

- ✔ **Confit de canard** (con-*fee* duh can-*ahr*): A duck leg cooked and pre-served in its own fat. The fatty skin is usually salty, but the meat underneath is tender and juicy. Mashed potatoes make a good side dish.

- ✔ **Cuisses des grenouilles** (cwees day gren-*wee*): Frogs' legs.

- ✔ **Escargots** (es-car-*go*): Snails.

- ✔ **Foie** (fwah): Liver.

- ✔ **Gesiers** (jeh-*zyay*): Gizzards; very good in salads.

- ✔ **Lapin à la moutarde** (la-*pan* ah la moo-*tard*): Rabbit cooked with mustard, créme fraîche, and sometimes white wine. The mustard perks up the rabbit meat, which has a mild flavor.

- ✔ **Lièvre** (lee-*yevr*): Hare.

- ✔ **Magret de canard** (mah-*greh* duh can-*ahr*): The sliced breast of a fattened duck, sautéed and sometimes served with a green pepper-corn sauce. The result more closely resembles red meat than poul-try. As with any meat, specify how you want it cooked.

- ✔ **Pieds de cochon** (pyay duh coh-*shon*): Pig's feet.

- ✔ **Plateau de fruits de mer** (plah-*toe* duh free duh mair): A variety of raw and cooked seafood served on ice. You usually find two kinds of oysters — flat, round *belon,* and larger, crinkly *creuse.* Both types are cultivated, not harvested. The oysters are eaten with lemon or red-wine vinegar and accompanied by thin slices of buttered rye bread. In addition to various kinds of shrimp, clams, and mussels, you also see periwinkles *(bulots)* (edible marine snails), which are eaten with mayonnaise.

- ✔ **Pot-au-feu** (*pot*-oh-fuh): A hearty dish of boiled vegetables and beef that sometimes includes the marrow bone. Scrape out the marrow, spread it on toast, and sprinkle it with salt. Sometimes the broth is served first, followed by the vegetables and beef. Mustard is the preferred condiment.

- ✔ **Ris de veau** (ree duh voe): The thymus gland of a calf (a white meat) sautéed in a butter and cream sauce. It has a delicate, pleas-ant taste but is high in cholesterol.

- ✔ **Rognons** (*ron*-yawn): Kidneys.

- ✔ **Tête de veau** (tet duh voe): Calf's head.

Words to the Wise: The Local Language

Parisians *do* speak English and are much more willing to speak English than ever before — especially to visitors who do them the courtesy of trying to speak a few phrases of French. You often find that you can't even complete a sentence in French before you're answered in English.

Don't be afraid of saying you don't understand French (*Je ne comprends pas;* juh neh cohm-*pren* pah); you will save yourself, and the person with whom you are conversing, a lot of time, and get help that much faster.

Phrases to remember are the essential *Parlez-vous anglais* (par-*lay* voo ahn-*glay;* do you speak English?); the common courtesy phrase of *Bonjour madame/monsieur* (bohn-*joor* mad-*am,* mis-*yoo*) when you enter a store or place of business; and *au revoir madame/monsieur* (oh-*vwah*) when you leave. This book, too, has an extensive glossary of words and phrases (See Appendix B for "A Glossary of French Words and Phrases") that anticipate nearly every situation.

Background Check: Books and Movies

Compiled here are lists of books and movies to help prepare you for your trip.

Books

There are so many books about the experiences of travelers who fell under the city's spell, or the doings of a particular French person, or the efforts of those who try to figure out just what it is that makes France such a peculiar culture but such a wonderful place to visit. The following list provides just a sample.

- ✔ *C'est La Vie: An American Conquers the City of Light, Begins a New Life, and Becomes — Zut Alors — Almost French* by Suzy Gershman (Viking). Frommer's (a Wiley company) *Born to Shop* author Gershman had long planned to retire in France with her husband. But when he died of an unexpected illness, she moved to Paris alone to try to work through her grief. A deliciously chatty chronicle of her first year in Paris.

- ✔ *The Flâneur* by Edmund White (Bloomsbury). Edmund White, who lived in Paris for 16 years, wanders through the streets and avenues and along the quays, taking readers into parts of Paris virtually unknown to visitors — and to many Parisians.

- ✔ *French Toast: An American in Paris Celebrates the Maddening Mysteries of the French* by Harriet Welty Rochefort (Thomas Dunne Books). Part memoir, part guide by an Iowan who picked up and moved to Paris more than 20 years ago, this book sheds light on why the French do things the way they do, and how you can, too, while you're there.

- ✔ *Paris to the Moon* by Adam Gopnik (Random House). The often humorous and tender account of the five years *New Yorker*-writer Gopnik spent in Paris with his wife and young son.

- ✔ *The Piano Shop on the Left Bank: Discovering a Forgotten Passion in a Paris Atelier* by Thad Carhart (Random House). Carhart notices an unassuming piano shop while walking his children to school one day. He eventually gains entry into a new world of the piano and its French fans as well as its art and history — and rediscovers the forgotten joys of playing the piano.

✔ *Savoir Flair* by Polly Platt (Culture Crossings Ltd.). Cultural do's and don'ts by an American who has lived in Paris since 1967. This guide is simply essential!

✔ *Sixty Million Frenchmen Can't Be Wrong* by Jean-Benoit Nadeau and Julie Barlow (Sourcebooks). Two Canadian journalists who move to France on a two-year fellowship deconstruct French ideas about land, food, privacy, and language.

✔ *A Year in the Merde* by Stephen Clarke (Bloomsbury USA). A young Englishman arrives to set up some English tearooms in Paris and writes a laugh-out-loud account of the pleasures and perils of being a Brit in France.

Movies

It's difficult to cull this down into a small list because there are so many wonderful films about France. Most of these films take place in Paris, and their shots of this beautiful city should only increase your anticipation of visiting.

✔ *Au Bout de Souffle (Breathless):* In this classic by Jean-Luc Godard, a small-time gangster kills a cop and then flees to Paris to get enough money together to leave the country with his girlfriend. Wonderful shots of Paris in the late 1950s.

✔ *Cléo de 5 à 7:* A Parisian singer, nervous about her impending doctor's appointment where she will learn test results, whiles away the time throughout Parisian neighborhoods.

✔ *Gigi:* This 1958 Lerner and Loewe musical set in Paris at the turn of the 20th century follows a young girl as she is groomed into a would-be courtesan (based on a story by the French author Colette).

✔ *Jules et Jim:* In François Truffaut's new wave classic, two best friends fall in love with the same woman in 1912 Paris. Breathtaking!

✔ *The Fabulous Destiny of Amélie Poulain:* It's hard to tell who the star is in this movie about a young woman trying to do good, actress Audrey Tautou or the city of Paris.

✔ *The Triplets of Belleville:* This animated film is about a Tour de France racer kidnapped by gangsters and the grandmother who goes in search of him with the help of a musical trio — the Triplets of Belleville. Though it doesn't take place in Paris, it's a terrific introduction to the country and fun to watch with your kids. (There isn't much talking, so not a lot of subtitles to decipher.)

✔ *Zazie Dans le Metro:* In Louis Malle's very funny 1962 film, a young girl is foisted on her unwilling transvestite uncle, and they have a series of madcap adventures in Paris.

Chapter 3

Deciding When to Go

. . . .

In This Chapter

▶ Choosing the best season to visit
▶ Checking out a calendar of events

. . . .

*H*ere we list the pros and cons of each season to help you decide when you can make the most of your visit to Paris. Also compiled is a calendar of the most memorable events in Paris; you may want to consider planning your trip to coincide with one of the festivals, sporting events, or celebrations.

Revealing the Secret of the Seasons

Residents and visitors alike find Paris ideal in spring and autumn, when weather is kind, crowds are reasonably sized, and Parisian life runs at a steady hum. Winter can be gray and bone-chillingly damp, but there are plenty of things to do inside: You can fill an entire trip with visits just to the Louvre, and don't forget the January sales. In summer, you can bask in daylight that lasts until 10 p.m. Just remember that timing your visit to Paris depends on what kind of experience you want to have.

Table 3-1 presents average temperature by month in Paris to help you plan your trip. (In Paris, temperatures are reported in Celsius.)

Table 3-1	Average Daytime Temperatures for Paris											
	Jan	Feb	Mar	Apr	May	June	July	Aug	Sept	Oct	Nov	Dec
Fahrenheit (F)	38°	39°	46°	51°	58°	64°	74°	76°	61°	53°	45°	40°
Celsius (C)	3°	4°	8°	11°	14°	18°	28°	29°	16°	12°	7°	6°

Spring fling

Spring arrives in Paris around April and brings some beautifully clear, fresh days. The parks and gardens of Paris — and those at Versailles, Fontainebleau, and Giverny — burst with colorful, fragrant blooms (see

Chapter 14). Crowds of visitors don't kick in until July summer vacation (except during the spring fashion shows in Mar), so lines are relatively short at the top sightseeing attractions, and airfares have yet to reach their summertime highs.

 But keep in mind that April in Paris is *not* as temperate as Cole Porter, who loved Paris in the springtime, would have you believe. In fact, Paris weather can be very similar to that in London: It's fickle. Pack for warm, cold, wet, dry, and every other eventuality; in other words, bring layers and don't even *think* about coming without an umbrella. Also, nearly every Monday in May is a holiday in France — stores and many museums are closed, the Métro runs on a holiday schedule, and other venues are affected.

Spectacular summer

Long and sultry days make visiting Paris in summer ideal — 6 a.m. sunrises and 10 p.m. sunsets — so you're afforded additional hours to wander and discover. You can find discounts of 30 percent to 50 percent in most stores during July, one of the two big months for shopping sales (the other is January). Hotel room rates are less expensive in July and August, considered the low season, and during August, parking is free in most of the city.

 But remember that an influx of tourists during the summer means long lines at museums and other sites. The weather also is capricious: You may have a week of rain and 55-degree temperatures, followed by days of cloudless skies and high temperatures, and much of the city is without air conditioning.

Because most Parisians take their vacations in August, the city is wonderfully tranquil in some places and devoid of life in others. Although the entire city doesn't exactly shut down in August, some shops and restaurants close for the entire month. The city's cultural calendar slows down, too, and you may have to walk an extra block or two to find an open shop or newsstand. And if you go to Paris in August with thoughts of practicing your French, think again. French may be the language you're least likely to hear in August.

Festive fall

Paris bursts into life starting the first week of September, a time typically known as *la rentrée* (the return). This season is one of the most exciting times of the year, when important art exhibitions open along with trendy new restaurants, shops, and cafes. By the middle of September, airfares drop from summertime highs. And with daytime temperatures in the 60s and 70s and nights in the 50s, the weather is pleasant.

 Keep in mind, however, that finding a hotel at the last minute in the fall can be difficult due to the number of business conventions and trade shows that take place in the city, including the October fashion shows. Be sure to book ahead.

Transportation strikes of varying intensities traditionally occur during the fall. Some go virtually unnoticed by the average traveler, but others can be giant hassles.

Winter wonders

You can find great airfare deals during the winter; airlines and tour operators often offer unbeatable prices on flights and package tours. Lines at museums and other sights are mercifully short. And, if shopping is your bag, you can save up to 50 percent during the sales in January.

But remember that although Paris winters may appear mild on paper, in reality, residents know that they are gray (sometimes the sun doesn't shine for weeks), dreary, and bone-chillingly damp. And look out for those winds that lash up and down the city's grand boulevards. Bring a warm, preferably waterproof, coat and umbrella.

Perusing a Calendar of Events: A Paris Calendar

When you arrive, check with the **Paris Convention and Visitors Bureau** (tel **08-92-68-30-00** at a charge of 0.34€ per minute, www.parisinfo.com) and buy *Pariscope, L'Officiel des Spectacles* for dates, places, and other up-to-date information. Or, if you pass by an English-language bookstore or bar, pick up a copy of the English-language *Paris Free Voice.* For a refresher course in the ways and means of Paris addresses, see the Introduction.

Below are Paris's month by month attractions.

January

A big, noisy parade on New Year's Day makes Paris more Rose Bowl than City of Light. **La Grande Parade de Montmartre** is fun and flashy with majorettes, high school bands, and elaborate floats that traverse the city streets. The parade begins at 2 p.m. (so you *can* sleep in) in the place Pigalle, 18e (the 18th *arrondissement,* or neighborhood), and ends at the place Jules-Joffrin, 18e. January 1.

The **Fête des Rois** is a holiday kids love, the celebration of the Feast of the Three Kings, and custom dictates the wearing of gold paper crowns to celebrate. The main object of celebration is a flaky, almond-paste-filled pie that conceals a ceramic charm (so watch your teeth). According to custom, whoever finds the charm becomes king or queen for the day, is entitled to wear the crown, and has free reign, as it were, in his or her choice of a consort. The pie with the charm is available at all *pâtisseries* (dessert shops). January 6.

La Mairie de Paris Vous Invite au Concert features a two-week, two-people-for-the-price-of-one special admission to a variety of jazz and classical concerts across the city. Mid-January.

An annual **Commemorative Mass for Louis XVI** attracts a full turnout of aristocrats, royalists, and even some far-right types. At the Chapelle Expiatoire, 29 rue Pasquier, 8e. Sunday closest to January 21.

Residents go all out for the **Chinese New Year Festival,** which, depending on the Chinese calendar, falls between January 21 and February 19. Celebratory events take place in Chinatown (13e). A parade features dragons, dancers, and fireworks. Plan on grabbing a bite to eat in one of the many excellent Chinese restaurants in the area.

Twice a year, in January and September, more than 40,000 buyers make their way to the **Ready-to-Wear Fashion Shows** in the Salon International de Prêt-à-Porter (Parc des Expositions, 15e; Métro: Balard or Porte de Versailles). The exposition hall at the Porte de Versailles hosts shows of the new clothing lines from some 1,200 designers. Admission for non-trade visitors is around 23€ ($28). Invitation-only fashion shows are also held at the major design houses. End of January.

February

Foire à la Feraille de Paris is one big upscale flea market. This yearly antiques and secondhand fair that takes place in the Parc Floral de Paris in the Bois de Vincennes (12e). Contact one of the branches of **The Office de Tourisme et des Congrès de Paris** for exact dates.

- The Opéra-Grands-Magasins Welcome Center, 11 rue Scribe, 9e; open Monday to Saturday 9 a.m. to 6:30 p.m. (Métro: Chausée d'Antin or Opéra; RER: Auber)

- The Welcome kiosk beneath the modern glass roofed terminal of the Gare du Nord, 18 rue Dunkerque, 10e; open 7 days a week from 8 a.m. to 6 p.m. (Métro and RER: Gare du Nord)

- The Gare de Lyon Welcome Center, 20 bd. Diderot, 12e; open Monday to Saturday 8 a.m. to 6 p.m. (Métro and RER: Gare de Lyon)

- 21 place du Tertre, 18e; open daily 10 a.m. to 7 p.m. (Métro: Abbesses)

- Carrousel du Louvre, beneath the Pyramide, 99 rue de Rivoli, 1er; open daily 10 a.m. to 7 p.m. (Métro: Palais Royal/Musée du Louvre)

- Eiffel Tower, between the north and east pillars; open daily 11 a.m. to 6:40 p.m. (Métro: Bir Hakeim; RER: Champ-de-Mars–Tour Eiffel)

Hundreds of farmers display animals and produce and win prizes for the biggest and best at **Salon de l'Agriculture,** a country fair in the heart of the city. Regional food stands offer tastes from all parts of France, and the atmosphere is friendly and quintessentially French at the Parc des

Expositions de Paris, Porte de Versailles, 15e. For more information, call the Parc des Expositions information line at ☎ **01-43-95-37-00** or the Paris Convention and Visitors Bureau. Admission is 10€ ($12) adults; 6€ ($7.20) children and students. Last week of February to first week of March.

March

Professional actors and residents of the neighborhood perform in **La Passion à Ménilmontant,** the Passion play (the events leading up to and including the Crucifixion of Christ), for a month around Easter. The play is staged at the Théâtre de Ménilmontant (20e). The event is a local tradition that's been observed since 1932. Admission is around 9€–20€ ($11–$24). Call ☎ **01-46-36-98-60** or 01-46-36-03-43 for the schedule. Mid-March to mid-April.

When the **Foire du Trône,** a tacky and fun annual carnival, comes to town, spring is just around the corner. Take a trip up on the Ferris wheel and other rides, try your hand at games, buy hokey souvenirs, and sample fairground food. The fair is located at the Pelouse de Reuilly in the Bois de Vincennes (Métro: Porte Dorée, Porte de Charenton or Liberté). Late March to end of May.

April

Follow Paris's archbishop as he performs **Le Chemin de la Croix (the Stations of the Cross)** from the square Willette in Montmartre up the steps to the basilica of Sacré-Coeur where he leads prayers to commemorate the Passion and Crucifixion of Jesus Christ. Good Friday, 12:30 p.m. March or April.

One of the most popular athletic events of the year, the **Paris Marathon** has runners sprinting past a variety of the city's most beautiful monuments. Held on a Sunday, the 42km (26.2-mile) event attracts enthusiastic crowds. Call the Paris Convention and Visitors Bureau for exact dates. Mid-April.

The huge annual fair, **Foire de Paris,** is a great place to bargain hunt and people watch, and signals the start of spring with hundreds of stands selling good-priced food and wine, and a variety of clothing and household goods. The fair takes place at the Parc des Expositions, Porte de Versailles. Late April to early May.

The **Grandes Eaux Musicales** and **les Fêtes de Nuit de Versailles** bring the sounds of classical music to life at the magnificent fountains in the gardens of the Château de Versailles every Sunday from mid-April to mid-October, and every Saturday and national holiday from June through August. Even better are the Grandes Fêtes, spectacular sound-and-light shows with fireworks that take place one Saturday in June, three Saturdays in July, one Saturday in August, and two Saturdays in September. These events are held at the Château de Versailles, Versailles. Log on to www.chateauversailles.fr for more information. (See Chapter 14 for tour companies that go to Versailles.)

May

May is a month of one holiday after the next in France. Banks, post offices, and most museums are closed for **May Day,** May 1, the French version of Labor Day, but you can watch a workers' parade that traditionally ends at the place de la Bastille. May 1.

Montmartre's **Vintage Car Rally,** is an array of antique cars that makes its way through the streets of Montmartre starting at 10 a.m. in rue Lépic and ending at the place du Tertre. Sunday closest to May 15.

The weather is usually beautiful during **Les Cinq Jours Extraordinaire** (five extraordinary days), when the shops in the rue du Bac, de Lille, de Beaune, des St-Pères, and de l'Université, and on the quai Voltaire, feature a free open house focusing on a special object chosen according to the annual theme. The whole quarter takes on a festive ambience, red carpets line the streets, and plants and flowers decorate shop fronts. Third week of May.

If you are lucky enough to procure hard-to-find tickets to the **French Open,** Paris's biggest tennis event, you'll find yourself watching the red-clay matches in the Stade Roland Garros in the Bois de Boulogne on the western edge of the city. Unsold tickets — those not reserved for corporate sponsors — go on sale two weeks before the competition starts. The stadium is at 2 av. Gordon Bennett, 16e. Call the French Federation of Tennis at the stadium for more information (☎ 01-47-43-48-00) or visit the Web site at www.frenchopen.com. Last week in May and first week in June.

June

The other Orangerie, this one in the beautiful Bagatelle gardens on the edge of the Bois de Boulogne, is the backdrop for the **Festival Chopin à Paris,** a much-loved annual series of daily piano recitals. Mid-June to mid-July (Métro: Porte Maillot, then take bus 244).

The celebration of the summer solstice has never been louder! The entire country becomes a concert venue in celebration of the first day of summer, and this musical day is called the **Fête de la Musique.** You can hear everything from classical to hip-hop for free in squares and streets around Paris. A big rock concert usually happens in the place de la République, and a fine classical concert generally takes place in the gardens of the Palais-Royal. June.

One of the most distinguished aviation events in the world is the **Paris Air Show,** which takes place in odd-numbered years at Le Bourget Airport just outside Paris. Visitors can check out the latest aeronautic technology on display. Call the Paris Convention and Visitors Bureau for more information.

Art exhibits, concerts, and a fantastic parade are staged in the Marais, the boulevard St-Michel, and in other Paris streets to celebrate **Gay Pride.** Call the Centre Gai et Lesbien for dates at ☎ **01-43-57-21-47.** Late June.

July and August

French independence day, **Bastille Day,** is July 14, but the festivities actually begin the night before on July 13, with free *bals* (dances) open to everyone at fire stations all over the city. (Some of the best *bals* are in the fire stations on the rue du Vieux-Colombier near the place St-Sulpice, 6e; the rue Sévigné, 4e; and the rue Blanche, near place Pigalle, 9e.) Although the *bals* are free, drinks cost. On July 14, be sure to get to the Champs-Elysées waaay before the 10 a.m. start of the Bastille Day military parade if you hope to see anything. Later that night a sound-and-light show with terrific fireworks can be seen at the Trocadéro. Rather than face the crowds, many people watch the fireworks from the Champs de Mars across the river, from hotel rooms with views, or even from the hill on rue Soufflot, in front of the Panthéon. July 13 and 14.

The **Paris, Quartier d'Été** (Paris, summer neighborhood) celebration has contemporary music, dance, and film as the bills of fare at outside venues around the city. The outdoor movies shown on a giant screen at Parc de la Villette (Métro: Porte de la Villette) are particularly popular. July 14 to August 15.

If you plan to be in Paris in July, bring your beach clothes! **Paris Plage,** a month-long festival, turns a bit of the Right Bank into the Riviera. From mid-July to mid-August, the city closes off 3.5km (2 miles) of its quays between the Pont Henri IV and the quai des Tuileries so that people can enjoy the same activities they would at the beach — all but swimming in the swift and dangerous Seine (a pool was added between pont Marie and pont Sully in 2004). There are three "beaches" made from sand, grass, or wooden planks; palm trees and wooden lounge chairs; snack bars and cafes; a climbing wall, trampolines, an area to play boules; and even old-time dance halls known as *guinguettes*. Concerts are organized by the electronics store Fnac, and there are dance and comedy performances as well.

The final day of the three-week long **Tour the France** is the third Sunday of July. The winner is crowned at the Champs-Elysées. If you plan to attend the celebration, be sure to arrive at the very early because the crowds are tremendous. You need a special invitation for a seat in the stands near place de la Concorde, but you can see the cyclists farther up the Champs-Elysées and, depending on the route (which changes each year), elsewhere in the city, too. Check the newspapers the day before or log on to www.letour.com.

The **Fête de l'Assomption** celebrates the journey of Mary, Jesus's mother, to Heaven after her death. Church services at Notre-Dame are the most popular and colorful on this important French holiday (many stores are closed, and transportation runs on a holiday schedule), and banners are draped over the church's towers to celebrate the day. August 15.

September

One of the largest and most prestigious antiques shows in the world, the **Biennale des Antiquaires,** opens to the public in even-numbered years in the Cour Carée du Louvre, the underground exhibition space connected to the museum. For more information, contact the Paris Convention and Visitors Bureau. Early September.

Planning your trip to Paris around September 15th? Then be sure to visit the off-limits palaces, churches, and other official buildings that throw open their doors to the public for two days during **Les Journées de Patrimoine** (the days of Patrimony). Long lines can put a damper on your sightseeing, so plan what you want to see and show up early (with a good book, just in case). Get a list and a map of all the open buildings from the Paris Convention and Visitors Bureau. Weekend closest to September 15.

The annual arts festival, **The Festival d'Automne,** is recognized through-out Europe for its innovative programming and the high quality of its artists and performers. Check the Paris Convention and Visitors Bureau for more information.

The second of two annual **Ready-to-Wear Fashion Shows** takes place in September (see the previous entry under "January").

This street party cum parade gets bigger every year, and at press time, the mid-September Paris **Techno Parade** was expecting 300,000 viewers to turn out to celebrate musical freedom with a conscience. The theme of the 2006 parade was "Turn up the sound and wipe out hunger."

October

The wine might not taste that great, but it's all about the celebration of the harvest at Montmartre's one remaining vineyard, Clos Montmartre. Watch as the wine is auctioned off at high prices to benefit local chari-ties during the **Fêtes des Vendanges à Montmartre** here. Locals dress in period costumes, and the streets come alive with music. First or second Saturday of October.

As interesting for browsing as for buying is the FIAC **(Foire Internationale d'Art Contemporain),** one of the largest contemporary art fairs in the world. With stands from more than 150 galleries, half of them foreign, the fair takes place at the Parc des Expositions, Porte de Versailles, 15e (Métro: Balard or Porte de Versailles). Admission is 14€ ($16). For more information, call ☎ **08-92-69-26-94.** Mid- to late October.

November

Many of the city's major museums celebrate the art of photography during **Mois de la Photo** (the month of the photo) with shows. Check listings in the weekly guide *Pariscope*. All month.

The French commemorate those who died fighting in both World Wars with a wreath-laying ceremony at the Arc de Triomphe, and veterans sell poppy corsages in memory of **Armistice Day.** November 11.

November in Paris can be awfully gray and chilly, but you'll warm up quickly just after midnight on the third Thursday (technically Friday) of November for the annual celebration of the public release of **Beaujolais Nouveau** — a lightweight red wine that is bottled after the fall harvest and meant for immediate consumption as it has a short shelf life. (You can find it in the States as well, right around Thanksgiving.) Wine bars and cafes are packed just for the event.

The annual **Lancement des Illuminations des Champs-Elysées** (lighting of the avenue's Christmas lights) makes for a festive evening, with jazz concerts and an international star to push the button that lights up the avenue. For more information, call the Paris Convention and Visitors Bureau. Late November.

December

Each year a different foreign city installs a life-size Christmas manger scene **(La Crèche sur le Parvis)** in the plaza in front of the Hôtel de Ville (City Hall). The crèche is open daily from 10 a.m. to 8 p.m. December 1 to January 3.

Part II
Planning Your Trip to Paris

The 5th Wave   By Rich Tennant

"And how shall I book your flight to Paris -First Class, Coach, or Medieval?"

In this part . . .

*L*ook no further than these chapters to help you plan everything for your trip — from where to stay and how much to spend to traveling successfully with children to what to do if your wallet has been stolen. Chapter 4 tells you what to expect in each expense category so you can plan a workable budget. Chapter 5 gets you to Paris, whether it be by plane, train, automobile, or hovercraft and discusses the pros and cons of package tours. Chapter 6 takes into account special interests and gives advice to families, seniors, disabled persons, and gay men and lesbians. And in Chapter 7, you get some advice about those last-minute details that can frustrate even the most frequent flyer.

Chapter 4

Managing Your Money

* *

In This Chapter

▶ Developing a workable budget
▶ Cutting costs — but not the fun
▶ Handling your money
▶ Dealing with a lost or stolen wallet

* *

A good way to budget your trip to Paris is to mentally walk through the journey, from the moment you leave to the minute you get back home, and don't forget to figure in your transportation to and from the airport. Then add in the flight cost (see Chapter 5 on how to fly to Paris for less), the price of getting from the Charles-de-Gaulle or Orly airports to your hotel, your hotel rate per day, meals, public transportation costs, admission prices to museums and the theater, and other entertainment expenses. Add another 15 percent to 20 percent to the total for good measure (you never know when you might come across a *brocante,* or flea market, selling one-of-a-kind items!).

Planning Your Budget

Cities rarely are cheap or expensive across the board; Paris tends to be pricey for dining but reasonable for accommodations, so booking a good hotel shouldn't be a problem. The following list offers guidelines for what you're likely to spend while in Paris. The rate of exchange at press time was 1€ = $1.20.

▶ **Lodging:** Before you start shelling out money for lodging, think about how much time you'll actually spend in your room. For between 70€ and 90€ ($84–$108), you can rent a clean, functionally furnished hotel room with a private bathroom and cable TV. This type of budget room is comfortable, has the basic furnishings and décor; the drawbacks are thin yet serviceable towels and thin bars of packaged soap.

If you're feeling extravagant and willing to spend 200€ ($240) or more to stay, luxury, upper-tier hotels offer more services, such as room service, air-conditioning, and toiletries.

✔ **Transportation:** The Paris Métro, the model for subways around the world since its inauguration in 1900, is one of the best transit systems around in terms of price and efficiency. Getting across town in less than a half hour is no problem, and the cost is lower when you purchase one of several available discount tickets or a *carnet* (booklet) of ten tickets. (See Chapter 8 for options and prices.)

If you thrive on labyrinthine one-way streets, a dearth of parking spaces, hellish traffic, and driving among what are statistically the worst drivers in Europe, then renting a car in Paris is for you, but we strongly discourage it! If you want to rent a car to see other parts of France or make a daytrip outside of Paris, rent on your way out of the city. (See Chapter 7 for addresses and phone numbers of car rental agencies in Paris.)

✔ **Restaurants:** The French consider dining out one of the finer joys in life, and they pay for it. You can expect to do the same. An average Parisian dining experience — a three-course dinner in a popular eatery — runs about 50€ to 70€ ($60–$84) per person.

You can find restaurants serving satisfying two-course meals for as little as 12€ ($14) and wonderful ethnic food and sandwich shops that help you save even more money. Dining reasonably in Paris isn't impossible when you know where to look. Chapter 10 helps you discover just that.

✔ **Attractions:** Entry fees to museums and other sights can add up quickly; we give you money-saving advice in Chapter 11, after which making a list of must-dos will give you a feel for how much money to set aside.

✔ **Shopping:** Paris is simply a shoppers' paradise. French shopkeepers arrange their wares in such enticing window displays that they'll have you *faites du leche-vitrines* (licking the windows) in no time. You can find some great deals during the semiannual sales in January and July, but remember that a steep 19.6 percent tax (value-added tax, abbreviated VAT or TVA) is added to most goods. If you live outside the European Union, you're usually entitled to get back part of the tax, if you meet certain requirements. See Chapter 12 for more information.

✔ **Nightlife:** Don't forgo the spectacles at the Lido or Moulin Rouge if you've always wanted to see them — just know beforehand that you'll be charged a small fortune for entry and alcoholic beverages. Plan on seeing the show without dinner, and exit with a wallet that isn't quite as light as it otherwise would be. Budget big, too, especially when you plan to visit clubs and other nightspots; nightclubs usually have covers (though the first drink is generally included) and bars are not cheap. You can save money for ballet, opera, and plays at the national theaters by buying half-price or same-day tickets. See Chapter 15 for more information.

Table 4-1 gives you approximate prices for some common expenses, listed in euro, U.S. dollars, and British pounds.

Table 4-1	What Things Cost in Paris		
Expense	*Euro*	*U.S. Dollars*	*Pounds Sterling*
Taxi from Charles-de-Gaulle Airport to the city center (depending on traffic)	45€	$54	£ 30
Taxi from Orly Airport to the city center	40€	$48	£ 27
Public transportation for an average trip on Métro within the city (from a Métro *carnet* of 10)	1.10€	$1.30	£ 0.70
Telephone card for public phones	7.50€	$8.60	£ 5.35
Glass of wine	4€	$4.80	£ 2.60
Coca-Cola (at a cafe)	3.50€	$4.20	£ 2.30
Cup of coffee	2€	$2.40	£ 1.30
Roll of ASA 100 color film, 36 exposures	10€	$12	£ 7.15
Admission to the Louvre	8.50€	$10.20	£ 6.10
Movie ticket	6€	$7.20	£ 4.30
Concert ticket (at the Opera Garnier)	5€–300€	$6–$360	£ 3.55–£ 214

Cutting Costs

One of the primary ways to save money at the outset is by booking a package tour. For many destinations, you can book airfare, hotel, ground transportation, and even some sightseeing just by making one call to a travel agent or searching the Internet, for a lot less than if you tried to put the trip together yourself. (See Chapter 5 for specific companies to call.)

We can't repeat it enough: Always ask for discount rates. Membership in AAA, frequent-flyer plans, trade unions, AARP, or other groups may qualify you for savings on car rentals, plane tickets, hotel rooms, even meals. Ask about everything; you may be pleasantly surprised.

The following list offers additional cost-cutting strategies for various expenses.

✔ **Food and drink**

- Make lunch your main meal. Many restaurants offer great deals on a fixed-price *(prix fixe)* lunch or offer a daily *formule,* or day's special of appetizer, main course, and dessert that can often be cheaper than ordering off the regular menu. After two or three courses at midday, you won't want a big dinner.

- Try the ethnic neighborhoods. You can get terrific Chinese and Vietnamese foods in the 13th arrondissement between the place d'Italie and the Porte de Choisy; and the 10e, 18e, and 20e have restaurants with North African, Turkish, Vietnamese, and Thai menus. Couscous is on the menu at many restaurants and usually is an inexpensive offering.

- Keep in mind that the *plat du jour* (daily entrée special) usually is the cheapest main dish at a budget restaurant.

- Remember that wine is cheaper than soda. Some mineral waters, likewise, are less expensive than others. Ask for tap water *(une carafe d'eau,* oon kar-*ahf* doh), which is free.

- If you're just having drinks or coffee, do it standing at the bar. You pay twice as much when you're seated at a table.

- Know the tipping rules. Most restaurants include the gratuity in the bill. Look for *service compris* on your bill, which means 15 percent has been added already. It is customary to leave extra; 5 percent if the service was good.

✔ **Lodging**

- Book your hotel room early. Rooms at the best prices fill up quickly.

- Negotiate the room price, especially in the low season. It never hurts to ask for discounts, either: Ask for a discount if you're a student or older than 60; ask for a discount when you're staying three days or more.

- Reserve a room with a kitchen. It may not seem like much of a vacation if you cook your own meals and wash your own dishes, but you can save a lot of money by not eating in restaurants three times a day. Even if you make only breakfast and pack an occasional bag lunch, you can save a little extra cash for souvenirs and gifts for your family and friends back home. Shopping the open-air markets and grocery stores offers a fun peek into the French way of life. And you won't need to fret over a hefty room-service bill.

- Try renting an apartment instead of staying in a hotel. Renting a Paris apartment can be surprisingly cheap, and apartment rental services flourish online. You save money by eating more meals in the apartment, and you experience a little of what it's like to live like a resident of Paris. (See Chapter 9 for specific rental agencies.)

✔ **Shopping and entertainment**

- For discounts on fashion, try the rue St-Placide in the 6e arrondissement. You find plenty of overstock and *dégriffe* (clothes with labels removed) items on this street near Le Bon Marché department store. Stylish inexpensive clothes also can be found at Monoprix stores located all over the city.

- If you plan to visit two or three museums a day for multiple days, buy the **Paris Museum Pass,** formerly known as the *Carte Musées et Monuments.* It's offered in three versions: two-, four-, and six-consecutive day passes costing 30€ ($36) 45€ ($54) and 60€ ($72) respectively. The pass is good at major museums and tourist sites (except the Eiffel Tower). It's a great deal if you plan to visit a lot of museums. See Chapter 11 for more information.

- Take advantage of the reduced admission fees at museums. The reduced prices usually apply after 3 p.m. (at the Louvre, it's after 6 p.m.) and all day Sunday. Remember that on the first Sunday of every month, admission to national museums is free.

- Buy half-price theater and other performance tickets. You can find same-day half-price tickets at one of the kiosks by the Madeleine or at the Gare Montparnasse. The kiosks are little huts with panels indicating whether the performance is sold out (symbolized by a little red man) or if tickets are still available (a little green man). (See Chapter 15 for more information.)

- Avoid going to clubs on weekends. Some clubs are cheaper than others, and some are cheaper during the week. Many clubs allow women in free until a certain time (usually 11 p.m.).

✔ **Transportation:**

- Fly during the week rather than on weekends. Many airlines charge less if you fly on weekdays.

- Travel during the *off season* (also called the *low season*), the period from approximately October to April.

- Pack light so that you can take the cheapest way into the city from the airport and won't have to worry about lugging around heavy bags. You can save around 35€ ($42) by taking a train or bus instead of a cab from Roissy–Charles-de-Gaulle Airport and about 26€ ($31) from Orly.

- While in Paris, use the bus or Métro or walk.

- Buy a *carnet* of ten Métro tickets at a time. A single ticket costs 1.40€ ($1.70), but one ticket from an 11€ ($13) carnet costs 1.10€ ($1.30). Better yet, if you know you're going to be in Paris from two to five consecutive days, buy a *Paris Visite pass,* which is good for unlimited subway and bus travel. A one-day Paris Visite card costs €8.35 ($9.60), two-day 14€ ($16), three-day 18€ ($21), and five-day 27€ ($31).

Handling Money

The euro, the single European currency for much of the European Union, became the official currency of France and 11 other participating countries on January 1, 1999, but it didn't go into general circulation until January 1, 2002. The old currency, the French franc, disappeared into history on March 1, 2002. Exchange rates of participating countries are locked into a common currency fluctuated against the dollar.

Converting to euro

In converting prices to U.S. dollars, we used a conversion rate of 1€ = $1.20. For up-to-the minute exchange rates between the euro and the dollar, check the currency converter Web site at www.xe.com/ucc.

At this writing, £1 equals approximately 1.80€. These were the rates of exchange used to calculate the values in Table 4-1.

You can withdraw euro at any ATM in Paris, and ATMs are everywhere and open 24 hours. Find them outside nearly every bank, in major department stores, airports, and train stations. MasterCard and/or Cirrus cards can be used at any ATM that displays the MasterCard and/or Cirrus marks. Visa and/or PLUS can also be used at ATMs displaying Visa and PLUS signs.

Keep in mind you won't be able to check your balance or transfer funds, so keep track of your withdrawals while you travel.

Remember that every time you withdraw cash from an ATM, your bank hits you with a fee, sometimes as much as $5. Check how much your bank charges before leaving home. On top of this fee, the bank from which you withdraw cash may also include its own fee. Thus, taking out larger amounts of money every two to three days makes more sense than more frequent withdrawals of smaller denominations. Likewise, remember that your bank places a limit on the amount of money you can take out per day, usually between 300€ and 500€ ($360–$600).

If you need to withdraw more than your bank's limit, visit any Parisian bank where a teller can swipe your ATM card for the amount you need, as long as the amount doesn't surpass the Parisian bank's own limit.

Approach the bank's information desk first to explain in English what you need done.

Pulling out your plastic: Using credit cards

Master Card and Visa are accepted at nearly any establishment that takes credit cards in Paris. But American Express and Diner's Club aren't widely accepted at small restaurants, shops, or budget hotels in Paris or the rest of the country.

Remember that you pay interest on cash advances on your credit card from the moment you receive the cash. And, many credit-card companies now tack on additional fees for foreign currency transactions — sometimes up to 4 percent, on top of the 1 percent service charge that MasterCard and Visa charges. If you don't know how much your credit card charges for currency conversion, contact a company representative.

Going the way of the dinosaur: The extinction of traveler's checks

These days, there's no need to waste valuable time standing in long lines at the American Express office or in search of *bureaux de change* to cash traveler's checks. Simply use your ATM card to withdraw the money you need. Relatively few banks in Paris exchange currency or cash traveler's checks, preferring to send visitors to bureaux de change in touristy areas that charge a hefty fee.

If you want the safety of the traveler's check without the hassle, check out American Express's Traveler's Cheque Card. It's a reuseable, reloadable card that is not linked to your bank account. You can even add more funds when you're out of the country by calling American Express collect at ☎ 801-945-9450. To learn more, consult the Web site at www. americanexpress.com.

You can cash traveler's checks at **American Express,** 11 rue Scribe, 9e, ☎ 01-47-77-70-00 (Métro: Auber or Opéra); **Travelex,** 194 rue de Rivoli, 1er, ☎ 01-42-60-37-61 (Métro: Tuileries); or **Global Change,** 99 rue de Rivoli, Galerie du Carrousel du Louvre, 1er, ☎ 01-40-20-09-42.

Dealing with a Lost or Stolen Wallet

Every credit card company has an emergency international number that you can call if your wallet or purse is stolen. In the unlikely event that this happens, be sure to block charges against your credit card account immediately. Your credit card company may be able to wire you a cash advance off your credit card immediately, and in many places, can deliver an emergency credit card in a day or two. Call ☎ 0-800-90-11-79 if you've lost or had your **Visa** card stolen. **American Express** card and traveler's check holders in France can call collect ☎ 336-393-1111 for money and lost card emergencies. For **MasterCard,** call ☎ 0800-90-13-87.

If your traveler's checks are lost or stolen, you need to be able to report exactly which checks are gone in order to get them replaced. The check issuer can tell you where to pick up the new checks.

Here's what to do if your pocket has been picked: First, make a police report as soon as possible. There are three or four police stations *(commissariats)* in each arrondissement (the train stations also have small police stations). Go to the station closest to where the crime took place. If you were robbed in the subway, however, you can go to any police station. You will receive a *Récépissé de Déclaration de Perte ou de Vol* (receipt for declaration of loss or theft). If you have lost your passport, identification documents, and/or valuables, you are given separate receipts — one for your papers *(pièces d'identité)* and one for your valuables. The police receipts are sometimes necessary in applying for the replacement of airline tickets, **INTERAIL** passes (Europass and Eurail), passports, and traveler's checks or for supporting insurance claims.

The report must be made in person and most police stations have English-speaking personnel. Call the U.S. Embassy (☎ **01-43-12-22-22,** or 01-43-12-45-01 for assistance in interpreting if you have difficulty being understood).

Though it's unlikely the police will recover your lost or stolen items, contact the police and file a police report anyway — you may need it for credit card or insurance purposes later.

Finally, you can visit the lost and found office, run by the French police, to verify whether your belongings were returned: **Centre des Objets trouvés de la Prefecture de Police de Paris,** 36 rue des Morillons, 75015, ☎ **08-21-00-25-25 (0.10€/15¢ per minute);** Métro: Convention; open Monday, Wednesday, and Friday 8:30 a.m. to 5 p.m. and Tuesday and Thursday 8 a.m. to 8 p.m.

Chapter 5

Getting to Paris

● ●

In This Chapter

▶ Discovering which airlines fly to Paris
▶ Finding the best fare
▶ Arriving by train or ferry
▶ Choosing a package tour

● ●

*T*he Internet has drastically changed travel planning with its online travel agents, airline, lodging, and car rental Web sites — and plenty of information about your destination. But you still need to decide what kind of travel best suits you. In this chapter, you'll be an expert in no time and well able to get yourself to Paris simply and easily.

Flying to Paris

Though Paris has two major airports: Charles de Gaulle and Orly, most non-European visitors will probably land at the larger, busier and more modern Charles de Gaulle. Known as CDG, and sometimes called Roissy–Charles de Gaulle, it's located 23km (14½ miles) northeast of downtown Paris. Orly Airport is located 14km (8½ miles) south of the city. Web sites and phone numbers for the major airlines serving Paris are in the list that follows. These sites offer schedules, flight bookings, and package tours. Most have Web pages where you can sign up for e-mail alerts that list weekend deals and other late-breaking bargains.

Airlines that fly there from the United States and Canada:

- ✔ **Air Canada** (☎ **888-247-2262;** www.aircanada.ca) flies direct to Paris from Montréal and Toronto.

- ✔ **Air France** (☎ **800-237-2747;** www.airfrance.com) flies direct from Atlanta, Boston, Chicago, Cincinnati, Houston, Los Angeles, Miami, Newark, New York, Philadelphia, and Washington, D.C.

- ✔ **Air Tahiti Nui** (☎ **877-824-4846;** www.airtahitinui-usa.com) flies from Los Angeles.

- ✔ **American Airlines** (☎ **800-433-7300;** www.aa.com) flies direct from Boston, Chicago, Dallas, New York, and Miami.

✔ **British Airways** (☎ 800-247-9297; www.ba.com) flies to Paris with a layover in London from Atlanta, Baltimore, Boston, Chicago, Detroit, Houston, Los Angeles, Miami, Orlando, Philadelphia, Phoenix, Newark, New York, San Francisco, Tampa, and Washington, D.C.

✔ **Continental Airlines** (☎ 800-523-3273; www.continental.com) flies direct to Paris from Houston and Newark.

✔ **Delta Air Lines** (☎ 800-221-1212; www.delta.com) flies direct from Atlanta, Cincinnati, and New York and shares flights with Air France from Boston, Chicago, Cincinnati, Detroit, Dulles, Houston, Los Angeles, Philadelphia, and San Francisco.

✔ **Iceland Air** (☎ 800-223-5500; www.icelandair.com) flies to Paris with a layover in Reykjavic from Baltimore, Boston, Minneapolis, Orlando, New York, and San Francisco.

✔ **Northwest/KLM** (☎ 800-225-2525; www.nwa.com) flies direct to Paris from Detroit; KLM flies from other cities including Los Angeles, Memphis, Minneapolis and Seattle with a layover in Amsterdam.

✔ **United Airlines** (☎ 800-864-8331; www.united.com) flies direct from Chicago, Los Angeles, San Francisco, and Washington, D.C.

✔ **US Airways** (☎ 800-428-4322; www.usairways.com) flies from Charlotte and Philadelphia.

Airlines that fly there from the United Kingdom:

✔ **Air France** (☎ 0870-142-4-343; www.airfrance.co/uk) flies from London and Manchester.

✔ **British Airways** (☎ 0870-850-9-850; www.ba.com) flies direct to Paris from London and with a layover in London from Edinburgh, Glasgow, and Manchester.

✔ **British Midland** (☎ 0870-6070-222; www.flybmi.com) flies from Aberdeen, Belfast, Dublin, Leeds, London, and Manchester.

✔ **easyJet** (☎ 0871-244-2366; www.easyjet.com) flies from Aberdeen, Belfast, Bristol, Inverness, Glasgow, Edinburgh, New Castle, Liverpool, East Midlands, London, Stansted, and Luton.

Airlines that fly there from Australia and New Zealand:

✔ **Qantas** (☎ 13-13-13 anywhere in Australia; www.qantas.com.au) flies from Sydney.

✔ **Singapore Airlines** (check the Web site for phone booking from your particular city; www.singaporeairlines.com) flies from Sydney and Auckland.

Getting the best deal on your airfare

Though every airline offers virtually the same product, prices can vary by hundreds of dollars. Competition among the major U.S. airlines is unlike that of any other industry.

Business travelers who need the flexibility to buy their tickets at the last minute and change their itineraries at a moment's notice — and who want to get home before the weekend — pay the premium rate, known as the *full fare*. If you're lucky enough to fly to Paris this way, more power to you. We know it did not come cheap! But if you can book your ticket far in advance, stay over Saturday night, and are willing to travel mid-week (Tues–Thurs), you can qualify for the least expensive price — usually a fraction of the full fare. On most flights, even the shortest hops within the United States, the full fare is close to $1,000 or more, but a 7- or 14-day advance purchase ticket may cost less than half of that amount. Obviously, planning ahead pays.

The airlines also periodically hold sales, in which they lower the prices on their most popular routes. These fares have advance purchase requirements and date-of-travel restrictions and may be nonrefundable, but you can't beat the prices. As you plan your vacation, keep your eyes open for these sales, which tend to take place in seasons of low travel volume — November 1st to December 1st and January to April. You almost never see a sale around the peak summer vacation months of July and August, or around Thanksgiving or Christmas, when many people fly, regardless of the fare they have to pay.

Consolidators, also known as *bucket shops,* negotiate bulk quantities of airline tickets and sell them at a discount. They are great sources for international tickets, although they usually can't beat the Internet on fares within North America. Start by looking in Sunday newspaper travel sections; their ads are usually formatted to look like classified ads. U.S. travelers should focus on the *New York Times, Los Angeles Times,* and *Miami Herald.*

Bucket-shop tickets are usually nonrefundable or rigged with stiff cancellation penalties, often as high as 50 percent to 75 percent of the ticket price, and some put you on charter airlines with questionable safety records.

Several reliable consolidators are worldwide and available on the Net. **STA Travel** (☎ 800-781-4040; www.statravel.com), the world's leader in student travel, offers good fares for travelers no matter your age. **ELTExpress** (☎ 201-541-3826 for air travel originating in the U.S. and Canada; www.flights.com) started in Europe and has excellent fares worldwide, but particularly to that continent. **LowestFare.com** (☎ 800-FLY-CHEAP; www.1800flycheap.com) is owned by priceline.com. **Air Tickets Direct** (☎ 888-858-8884; www.airticketsdirect.com) is based in Montreal and leverages the currently weak Canadian dollar for low fares.

Booking your ticket online

The big three online travel agencies, **Expedia** (www.expedia.com), **Travelocity** (www.travelocity.com), and **Orbitz** (www.orbitz.com) sell most of the air tickets bought on the Internet. (Canadian travelers should try www.expedia.ca and www.travelocity.ca; U.K. residents can go for expedia.co.uk and opodo.co.uk.) Each has different business deals with the airlines and may offer different fares on the same flights, so shopping around is wise. Expedia and Travelocity will also send you an **e-mail notification** when a cheap fare becomes available to your favorite destination.

Of the smaller travel agency Web sites, **SideStep** (www.sidestep.com) receives good reviews from users. It's a browser add-on that purports to "search 140 sites at once," but in reality only beats competitors' fares as often as other sites do.

Great **last-minute deals** are available through free weekly e-mail services provided directly by the airlines. Most of these deals are announced on Tuesday or Wednesday and must be purchased online. Most are only valid for travel that weekend, but some (such as Southwest's) can be booked weeks or months in advance. Sign up for weekly e-mail alerts at airline Web sites or check megasites that compile comprehensive lists of last-minute specials, such as **Smarter Living's Smarter Travel** (www.smartertravel.com). For last-minute trips, **www.site59.com** in the U.S. and **www.lastminute.com** in Europe often have better deals than the major-label sites.

If you're willing to give up some control over your flight details, use Priceline's (www.priceline.com) *opaque* fare service. We say opaque because it offers rock-bottom prices in exchange for travel on a mystery airline at a mysterious time of day, often with a mysterious change of planes en route. The mystery airlines are all major, well-known carriers, but your chances of getting a 6 a.m. or 11 p.m. flight are pretty high. Priceline also has nonopaque service; you can pick exact flights, times, and airlines from a list of offers/

Great last-minute deals are also available directly from the airlines themselves through a free e-mail service called *E-savers*. Each week, the airline sends you a list of discounted flights, usually leaving the upcoming Friday or Saturday and returning the following Monday or Tuesday. Airline sites also offer schedules, flight booking, and information on late-breaking bargains.

Arriving by Other Means

If you're arriving in Paris by **train** from northern Germany, Belgium, or London, you disembark in the **Gare du Nord.** Trains from Normandy come into the **Gare St-Lazare,** in Northwest Paris by Galeries Lafayette and Opéra Garnier. Trains from western France (Brittany, Chartres,

Versailles, Bordeaux) head to the **Gare de Montparnasse** in the 14e; those from the southwest (the Loire Valley, Pyrénées, Spain) arrive at the **Gare d'Austerlitz** near the Jardin des Plantes, 13e. Those from the south and southeast (the Riviera, Lyon, Italy, Geneva) pull in at the **Gare de Lyon.** Trains coming from Alsace and eastern France, Luxembourg, southern Germany, and Zurich arrive at the **Gare de l'Est.** All train stations connect to Métro stations with the same name. All Paris train stations are located within the first 15 arrondissements, and are easily accessible.

Buses connect Paris to most major European cities. European Railways operates **Europabus** and **Eurolines.** The companies don't have American offices, so you must make bus transportation arrangements after arriving in Europe. In Great Britain, contact Eurolines (☎ **08-705-808080** [7.90p/mn]). In Paris, contact Eurolines (at their Latin Quarter agency at 55 rue St. Jacques, 5e; ☎ **43-54-11-99**). International buses pull into the **Gare Routière Internationale** (International Bus Terminal) in the suburb of Bagnolet, just across the *périphérique* (ring road) from the Galliéni Métro station. To go into Paris proper, take Line 3 and change buses according to your final destination.

If you are arriving in Paris from the UK, about a dozen companies run **hydrofoil, ferry,** and **hovercraft** across the English Channel, or *La Manche* ("the sleeve," pronounced la mahnsh), as the French say. Services operate daily and most carry cars. Hovercraft and hydrofoils make the trip across the Channel in about 40 minutes; the shortest ferry route between Dover and Calais is about 1½ hours. The major routes are between Dover and Calais and Folkestone and Boulogne (about 12 trips a day). Depending on weather conditions, prices and timetables can vary. This is not the best way to get to Paris from the UK; the entire trip from London to Dover by train, then from Dover to Calais by ferry, and Calais to Paris by train takes about 10½ hours. You can check schedules and reserve space on ferries on **Ferrybooker.com** (www.ferrybooker. com). Special fares at press time included Dover to Calais for 60€ per car with up to five passengers.

It's important to make reservations because ferries are crowded.

The **Channel Tunnel** (Chunnel) opened in 1994, and the popularity of its Eurostar train service has had the happy effect of driving down prices on all cross-channel transport. This remarkable engineering feat means that if you hop aboard Le Shuttle in Britain, you can be eating a meal in France two to four hours later. You can purchase tickets in advance or at the tollbooth. Eurostar tickets start at $70 one way off season if you book seven days in advance. Prices rise in April and in June. Eurostar transports *passengers only* (no vehicles) between London or Ashford in Kent and Paris, Brussels, Lille, and beyond. For more information on Eurostar, including online booking, go to www.eurostar.com. For special packages information in the U.S., visit RailEurope (www.raileurope. com) or the TravelPro Network (www.travelpro.net).

A separate company known as **Eurotunnel** (☎ **08-05-35-35-35** in the U.K.; www.eurotunnel.com) can transport passengers with their cars between Folkestone in the United Kingdom and Calais in France. Car prices start at £ 49 ($88) for a round-trip daytrip and rise to £180 ($324) for a round-trip journey longer than five days. One-way prices start at £49 (88).

Joining an Escorted Tour

An *escorted tour* spells out nearly everything in advance: your flights, your hotels, your meals, your sightseeing itineraries, and your costs. It's the least independent way to travel, but some travelers find escorted tours liberating — no hassles with public transportation, no deciphering maps, and the comfort of knowing what you're getting. Others fervently despise escorted group tours, because they feel as if they're being herded from one sight to the next, missing the element of surprise and individuality that independent travel affords.

On escorted tours, the tour company takes care of all the details, and tells you what to expect at each leg of your journey. You know your costs up front, and you don't get many surprises. Escorted tours can take you to the maximum number of sights in the minimum amount of time with the least amount of hassle.

If you decide to go with an escorted tour, we *strongly* recommend purchasing travel insurance, especially if the tour operator asks to you pay up front. But don't buy insurance from the tour operator! If the tour operator doesn't fulfill its obligation to provide you with the vacation you paid for, there's no reason to think that they'll fulfill their insurance obligations either. Get travel insurance through an independent agency. (I tell you more about the ins and outs of travel insurance in Chapter 7.)

When choosing an escorted tour, along with finding out whether you have to put down a deposit and when final payment is due, ask a few simple questions before you buy.

- ✔ **What is the cancellation policy?** Can they cancel the trip if they don't get enough people? How late can you cancel if you are unable to go? Do you get a refund if you cancel? If they cancel?

- ✔ **How jam-packed is the schedule?** Does the tour schedule try to fit 25 hours into a 24-hour day, or does it give you ample time to relax by the pool or shop? If getting up at 7 a.m. every day and not returning to your hotel until 6 or 7 p.m. at night sounds like a grind, certain escorted tours may not be for you.

- ✔ **How large is the group?** The smaller the group, the less time you spend waiting for people to get on and off the bus. Tour operators may be evasive about this, because they may not know the exact size of the group until everybody has made reservations, but they should be able to give you a rough estimate.

✔ **Is there a minimum group size?** Some tours have a minimum group size, and may cancel the tour if they don't book enough people. If a quota exists, find out what it is and how close they are to reaching it. Again, tour operators may be evasive in their answers, but the information may help you select a tour that's sure to happen.

✔ **What exactly is included?** Don't assume anything. You may have to pay to get yourself to and from the airport. A box lunch may be included in an excursion but drinks may be extra. Beer may be included but not wine. Find out how much flexibility you have: Can you opt out of certain activities, or does the bus leave once a day, with no exceptions? Are all your meals planned in advance? Can you choose your entree at dinner, or does everybody get the same chicken cutlet?

Depending on your recreational passions, I recommend one of the following tour companies.

✔ **The French Experience, (☎ 201-216-0024;** www.frenchexperience. com), offers several fly/drive programs through different regions of France (the quoted price includes airfare and a rental car). You can specify the type and price level of hotels you want. The agency arranges the car rental in advance, and the rest is up to you.

✔ **American Express Vacations (☎ 800-335-3342;** www.american expressvacations.com), is perhaps the most instantly recognizable tour operator in the world. Its offerings in Paris and the rest of Europe are probably more comprehensive than those of any other company and include package tours and independent stays.

Choosing a Package Tour

For lots of destinations, package tours can be a smart way to go. In many cases, a package tour that includes airfare, hotel, and transportation to and from the airport costs less than the hotel alone on a tour you book yourself. That's because packages are sold in bulk to tour operators who then resell them to the public. It's kind of like buying your vacation at a buy-in-bulk store — except the tour operator is the one who buys the 1,000-count box of garbage bags and resells them ten at a time.

Package tours can vary as much as those garbage bags, too. Some offer a better class of hotels than others; others provide the same hotels for lower prices. Some book flights on scheduled airlines; others sell charters. In some packages, your choice of accommodations and travel days may be limited. Some let you choose between escorted vacations and independent vacations; others allow you to add on just a few excursions or escorted day trips (also at discounted prices) without booking an entirely escorted tour.

To find package tours, check out the travel section of your local Sunday newspaper or the ads in the back of national travel magazines such as *Travel + Leisure, National Geographic Traveler,* and *Condé Nast Traveler.* **Air France Holidays (☎ 800-2-FRANCE;** www.airfranceholidays. com) has France-specific package tours; their six-night Presenting Paris special starts at $1,259 and includes air and hotel fare, breakfast, and a Seine River cruise. **Liberty Travel** (call ☎ **888-271-1584** to find the store nearest you; www.libertytravel.com) is one of the biggest packagers in the Northeast, and usually boasts a full-page ad in Sunday papers.

Another good source of package deals is the airlines themselves. Most major airlines offer air/land packages, including **American Airlines Vacations (☎ 800-321-2121;** www.aavacations.com), **Delta Vacations (☎ 800-654-6559;** www.deltavacations.com), **Continental Airlines Vacations (☎ 800-301-3800;** www.covacations.com), and **United Vacations (☎ 888-854-3899;** www.unitedvacations.com). Several big **online travel agencies** — Expedia, Travelocity, Orbitz, Site59, and Lastminute.com — also do a brisk business in packages. If you're unsure about the pedigree of a smaller packager, check with the Better Business Bureau in the city where the company is based, or go online at www.bbb.org. If a packager won't tell you where it's based, don't fly with them.

Chapter 6

Catering to Special Travel Needs or Interests

●●

In This Chapter

▶ Traveling with the brood
▶ Getting discounts for seniors
▶ Locating wheelchair-accessible attractions and accommodations
▶ Identifying resources for gay and lesbian travelers

●●

*N*ot everyone finds traveling a piece of cake (actually does anyone anymore in these days of "take off your shoes and deposit your water in the garbage bin"?). If you're bringing your family to Paris, if you have a disability and are wondering how to pilot yourself down cobblestone streets and winding Métro corridors, if you're a senior citizen, or if you want to see the gay side of Paris, this is the chapter for you.

Taking the Family Along

The City of Light is full of attractions worthy of your children's attention, and they only benefit from the experience! Parks and playgrounds are plentiful, as are kid-specific sights and museums, interesting boat rides, and bike tours. And you're less than an hour away from Disneyland Paris. Paris is just as safe as, if not safer than, most big American cities. Though taking your children thousands of miles away may seem at times like an insurmountable challenge, it can be immensely rewarding, giving you new ways of seeing the world through smaller pairs of eyes.

You can find good family-oriented vacation advice on the Internet from sites like the **Family Travel Forum** (www.familytravelforum.com), a comprehensive site that offers customized trip planning; **Family Travel Network** (www.familytravelnetwork.com), an award-winning site that offers travel features, deals, and tips; **Traveling Internationally with Your Kids** (www.travelwithyourkids.com), which was started by parents whose daughters were born abroad and is a clearinghouse for information on traveling (and living abroad) with your children from those who have been there; and **Family Travel Files** (www.thefamilytravel files.com), which offers an online magazine and a directory of off-the-beaten-path tours and tour operators for families.

If you plan your trip well in advance, your kids may get a kick out of learning the language from one of the many French-language instructional videotapes on the market.

Such books as Ludwig Bemelmans's *Madeline* series, Albert Lamorisse's *The Red Balloon,* and Kay Thompson's *Eloise in Paris* are great for kids under eight years of age. Look for them at your local library or bookstore. Older teens may appreciate Ernest Hemingway's *A Moveable Feast* (Scribner paperback reissue), Victor Hugo's *Les Misérables,* Mark Twain's *Innocents Abroad,* and Rose Tremain's *The Way I Found Her* (Washington Square Press paperback reprint).

Children younger than 18 are admitted free to France's national museums (although not necessarily to Paris's city museums), and some attractions offer a lower rate for families of four or more. When purchasing tickets, ask if there is a family rate (*carte famille nombreus,* pronounced kart fam-*ee* nohm-*brooz*).

If your children are younger than 12 and you're traveling by rail through France, check out the **Carte Enfant Plus,** a children's rail pass. It's available at any SNCF (French National Railroads) station or, for non-Americans, online at www.sncf-voyages.com (if you scroll all the way to the bottom of the home page, you will see a tiny British flag; click on this for English). Unfortunately, SNCF does not sell directly to North Americans, who have to purchase these cards at a French train station. The pass offers a 50 percent discount for the child and up to four adult travel companions on non-TGV (Train Grand Vitesse, France's high-speed train) mainline trains in off-peak periods, and 25 percent off on TGV trains (except overnight trains) and mainline trains during peak travel times. The pass costs 68€ ($82), and you can reserve it online right before you leave, and pick it up at any Paris train station within the time limit (usually two days). Similarly, a discount travel card is available for those ages 12 to 25 called **Carte 12–25.** For 49€ ($59), a cardholder is entitled to 50 percent discounts on all non-TGV rail services (except overnight services) and couchette berths on non-TGV mainline services at all times. A guaranteed 25 percent reduction is available on all TGV rail services (except overnight services) and couchette berths on non-TGV mainline services at all times where no seats are available at the 50 percent reduction rate. A passport photo must be presented when applying for these cards. *Note:* To find out where to buy or pick up these passes within the train station, go to the Acceuil (Welcome) information kiosk and have an English-speaking representative direct you.

If you're traveling with a baby, you can arrange ahead of time for such necessities as a crib and bottle warmer at your hotel, and, if you're driving, a car seat (small children are prohibited from riding in the front seat). Find out whether your hotel stocks baby food; if not, take some with you for your first day, but then plan to buy some. Plenty of choices are available, from Nestlé to Naturalia.

Transportation in Paris isn't as stroller-friendly as in the United States. Be prepared to lift your child out of the stroller when boarding buses, climbing up and down stairs, and/or walking long distances in some Métro subway stations. The upside of all of this is that once you get to your destination, you and your child can stroll and play in some of the world's prettiest parks and gardens.

And when you need some kid-free time, consider one of the following agencies that employ English-speaking baby sitters: **Allo Maman Dépannage,** 38 rue Greuze, 16e (☎ **01-47-55-15-75**), or **Kid Services** (☎ **08-20-00-02-30;** .10€/15¢ per min.). Specify when calling that you need a sitter who speaks English. Also, try the **American Church**'s basement bulletin board where English-speaking (often American) students post notices offering baby-sitting services. The church is located at 65 quai d'Orsay, 7e (☎ **01-45-62-05-00;** Métro: Invalides).

The books *Family Travel* (Lanier Publishing International) and *How to Take Great Trips with Your Kids* (The Harvard Common Press) are full of good, general advice that can apply to travel anywhere. Another reliable tome with a worldwide focus is *Adventuring with Children* (Foghorn Press).

You can also check out *Family Travel Times,* published six times a year by **Travel with Your Children,** 40 Fifth Ave., Seventh floor, New York, NY 10011 (☎ **212-477-5524;** www.familytraveltimes.com). It includes a weekly call-in service for subscribers. Subscriptions are $39 for one year, $49 for two years. A free publication list and a sample issue are available on request.

 Finally, a word of advice: Although French people love kids and welcome them just about anywhere, they expect them to be well mannered. Proper behavior is expected everywhere, but especially in restaurants and museums. French children are taught at an early age to behave appropriately in these settings, and French adults expect the same from your kids.

Making Age Work for You: Tips for Seniors

 Mention that you're a senior citizen when you first make your travel reservations; you may be entitled to some discounts before you even get to Paris. When you arrive in Paris, don't be shy about asking for senior discounts, and always carry a form of identification that shows your date of birth.

 People over the age of 60 qualify for reduced admission to theaters, museums, and other attractions and for other travel bargains like the **Carte Senior,** which entitles holders to 50-percent discounts on TGV rail services (except overnight services) and couchette berths on non-TGV mainline services, subject to seating availabilities. There is 25 percent off all TGV rail services (except overnight services) and couchette berths on non-TGV mainline services at all times, where no seats are available at the 50-percent reduction. The Carte Senior also triggers some discounts on admission to museums and historic sites. It's valid for one year, costs 53€ ($64), and you can buy it at any SNCF (train) station. You have to present a passport photo when applying for these cards. *Note:* To find out where to buy these passes within the train station, go to the Acceuil (Welcome) information kiosk, where an English-speaking representative will direct you.

Membership in certain organizations can qualify you for some discounts. Be sure to bring whatever membership card the organization issues. If you're older than 50, consider joining **AARP,** 601 E St. NW, Washington, DC 20049 (☎ **888-687-2277;** www.aarp.org), for discounts on hotels, airfares, and car rentals. As a member, you're eligible for a wide range of special benefits, including *Modern Maturity* magazine and a monthly newsletter.

Hundreds of travel agencies specialize in senior travel, and although many of the vacations are of the tour-bus variety, which may cramp the style of an independent senior, one bonus is that free trips are often thrown in for organizers of groups of 20 or more. Obtain travel information from **SAGA International Holidays,** 222 Berkeley St., Boston, MA 02116 (☎ **800-343-0273;** in the U.K. contact 0800-096-0074; www.saga holidays.com). This is a British-owned company offering inclusive tours and cruises for those age 50 and older.

Recommended publications offering travel resources and discounts for seniors include the quarterly magazine *Travel 50 & Beyond* (www.travel50andbeyond.com); *101 Tips for Mature Travelers,* available from Grand Circle Travel (☎ **800-959-0405;** www.gct.com); and *Unbelievably Good Deals and Great Adventures That You Absolutely Can't Get Unless You're Over 50* (McGraw-Hill), by Joan Rattner Heilman.

Accessing Paris: Advice for Travelers with Disabilities

Unfortunately, the features that make Paris so beautiful — uneven cobblestone streets, quaint buildings with high doorsills from the Middle Ages, and twisting lanes too narrow and traffic-clogged to simultaneously admit pedestrians and autos — also make using a walker or a wheelchair a nightmare. According to French law, newer hotels with three stars or more are required to have at least one wheelchair-accessible guest room. Most of the city's older, budget hotels, which are exempt from the law, occupy buildings with winding staircases, or elevators smaller than phone booths, and generally aren't good choices for travelers with disabilities.

Few Métro stations have elevators, most feature long tunnels, and some have wheelchair-unfriendly moving sidewalks and staircases. Escalators often lead to flights of stairs, and many times when you climb a flight of stairs, you're faced with another set of stairs leading down. However, line 14 of the Métro is wheelchair accessible, and so are the stations at Nanterre-Université, Vincennes, Noisiel, Saint-Maur-Créteil, Torcy, Auber, Cité-Universitaire, Saint-Germain-en-Laye, Charles-de-Gaulle–Étoile, Nanterre-Ville, and several others.

Currently, wheelchair lifts aren't standard equipment on city buses, and the buses don't kneel closer to the curb to make that first step any lower. Bus 91, which links the Bastille with Montparnasse, is wheelchair accessible, and so are new buses on order. Some high-speed and inter-city trains are equipped for wheelchair access, and a special space is available in first class (at the price of a second-class ticket) for wheel-chairs, although you must reserve well in advance.

Don't let these inconveniences change your mind about visiting Paris. Before your trip to Paris, go to the **Paris Convention and Visitor's Bureau website,** which provides an overview of facilities for people with disabilities in the French transportation system and at monuments and museums in Paris and the provinces (http://en.parisinfo.com/ guide_paris/rub5978.html&id_article=14572). This list contains everything from tour guides to accessible parks to organizations for per-sons with disabilities to specialized transport.

L'Association des Paralysés de France (The Association of the Paralyzed of France), 17 bd. Auguste-Blanqui (☎ **01-40-78-69-00;** Web site in French: www.apf.asso.fr), publishes (in French only, unfortu-nately) *Le Guide Vacances (The Vacation Guide),* 5.30€ ($6.35), which lists accessible hotels as well as cultural and sporting activities taking place all over France.

 Click on www.ratp.info/informer/reseau_ferre.php and scroll down for a list of Métro and RER stops that offer elevator access to the platforms, either with the assistance of an attendant *(avec agent)* or free service *(service libre).*

If you speak French, contact the **Groupement pour l'Insertion des Personnes Handicapées Physiques** (Help for the Physically Handi-capped), Paris Office, 10 rue de Georges de Porto Riche (☎ **01-43-95-66-36**), and **Les Compagnons du Voyage** of the **RATP** (Paris public trans-portation; ☎ **01-53-11-11-12;** Web site in French: www.ratp.fr) for help in planning itineraries using public transportation.

A good English-language resource is the UK organization, RADAR. They last updated their guidebook for people with disabilities, *Access in Paris,* in 2001 and at press time a new update was imminent. For more informa-tion, go to www.accessinparis.org/index.php.

Check out *A World of Options* (www.miusa.org/publications/books/worldofoptions), a 658-page book of resources for travelers with disabilities that covers everything from biking trips to scuba outfitters to living abroad as a student for $18. You can order it from **Mobility International USA,** P.O. Box 10767, Eugene, OR 97440 (☎ **541-343-1284** voice and TTY). Another place to try is **Access-Able Travel Source** (www.access-able.com), a comprehensive database of travel agents who specialize in travel for people with disabilities and a clearinghouse for information about accessible destinations around the world.

Many travel agencies offer customized tours and itineraries for travelers with disabilities. **Flying Wheels Travel** (☎ **507-451-5005;** www.flyingwheelstravel.com) offers escorted tours and cruises that emphasize sports and private tours in minivans with lifts. **Access-Able Travel Source** (☎ **303-232-2979;** www.access-able.com) offers extensive access information and advice for traveling around the world with disabilities. **Accessible Journeys** (☎ **800-846-4537** or 610-521-0339; www.disabilitytravel.com) addresses the needs of wheelchair travelers and their families and friends.

Organizations that offer assistance to travelers with disabilities include **MossRehab** (www.mossresourcenet.org), which provides a library of accessible-travel resources online; **SATH (Society for Accessible Travel and Hospitality;** ☎ **212-447-7284;** www.sath.org; annual membership fees are $45 adults, $30 seniors and students), an educational nonprofit membership organization whose mission is to raise awareness of the needs of all travelers with disabilities, remove physical and attitudinal barriers to free access, and expand travel opportunities in the United States and abroad. SATH offers a wealth of travel resources for all types of disabilities and informed recommendations on destinations, access guides, travel agents, tour operators, vehicle rentals, and companion services, and includes *Open World Magazine* (subscription: $13 per year, $21 outside the United States); and the **American Foundation for the Blind (AFB;** ☎ **800-232-5463;** www.afb.org), a referral resource for the blind or visually impaired that includes information on traveling with guide dogs.

For more information specifically targeted to travelers with disabilities, check out the quarterly magazine **Emerging Horizons** ($17 per year, $22 outside the United States; www.emerginghorizons.com); **Twin Peaks Press** (☎ **800-637-2256**), offers books for travelers with special needs.

Following the Rainbow: Resources for Gay and Lesbian Travelers

France is one of the world's most tolerant countries toward gays and lesbians. It has no laws that discriminate against them. Technically, sexual relations are legal for consenting partners ages 16 and older. Everyone from hotel clerks to servers treats same-sex couples with polite indifference. This casual attitude led many to settle here: Oscar Wilde and James Baldwin lived in Paris, as did Gertrude Stein and Alice B. Toklas.

 Paris's gay center is the Marais, which stretches from the Hôtel de Ville to the place de la Bastille. The biggest concentration of gay bookstores, cafes, bars, and clothing boutiques is here, and so is the best source of information on Parisian gay and lesbian life — the **Centre Gai et Lesbien,** 3 rue Keller, 11e (☎ **01-43-57-21-47;** www.cglparis.org; Métro: Bastille), is open Monday to Saturday from 4pm until 8pm. The center is a source of information, and members of its staff coordinate the activities and meetings of gay people around the world. Another helpful source is **La Maison des Femmes,** 163 rue Charenton, 12e (☎ **01-43-43-41-13;** maisondesfemmes.free.fr; Métro: Reuilly-Diderot), which has a cafe and a feminist library for lesbians and bisexual women. Meetings about everything from sexism to working rights and informal dinners and get-togethers all take place here. Call Monday, Wednesday, or Friday from 3 to 8 p.m. for more information.

Gay magazines that focus mainly on cultural events include *Illico* (free in gay bars) and *Tetu,* available at almost all newspaper stands. This magazine is similar to the U.S. publications *Out* and *The Advocate,* and each issue has a separate pull-out section with cultural and nightlife events in Paris and every major city in France. *Lesbia* is available for women. You can find these and others at Paris's largest and best-stocked gay bookstore, **Les Mots à la Bouche,** 6 rue Ste-Croix-la-Bretonnerie, 4e (☎ **01-42-78-88-30;** www.motsbouche.com; Métro: Hôtel-de-Ville). Open 11 a.m. to 11 p.m. Monday through Saturday and 1 to 9 p.m. Sunday, the store carries French- and English-language publications.

For advice on HIV issues, call **F.A.C.T.S.** (☎ **01-44-93-16-32**) from 6 to 10 p.m. Monday, Wednesday, and Friday. The acronym stands for Free Aids Counseling Treatment and Support, and the English-speaking staff provides counseling, information, and doctor referrals.

The **International Gay and Lesbian Travel Association (IGLTA; ☎ 800-448-8550** or 954-776-2626; www.iglta.org) has been around since 1983 and is the trade association for the gay and lesbian travel industry. It offers an online directory of gay- and lesbian-friendly travel businesses.

Many agencies offer tours and travel itineraries specifically for gay and lesbian travelers. **Now, Voyager** (☎ **800-255-6951;** www.nowvoyager.com) is a well-known San Francisco–based gay-owned and -operated travel service. Canada's **GayTraveler** (www.gaytraveler.ca) is a Web site dedicated to travel for the gay, lesbian, bisexual, and transgendered communities. The site has discussion boards and a free monthly newsletter in addition to lists of all-gay cruises, tours, packages, and other holiday events.

The following travel guides are available at most bookstores; *Frommer's Gay & Lesbian Europe* (Wiley), an excellent travel resource (www. frommers.com); *Out and About* (www.outandabout.com), which offers such guidebooks as *Three Days in Paris* packed with solid information on the global gay and lesbian scene; *Spartacus International Gay Guide* (Bruno Gmünder Verlag; www.spartacusworld.com/gayguide) and *Odysseus* (Odysseus Enterprises; www.odyusa.com/html/trvlguide. html), both good, annual English-language guidebooks focused on gay men; and the *Damron* guides (www.damron.com), with separate annual books for gay men and lesbians.

Chapter 7

Taking Care of the Remaining Details

- -

In This Chapter

▶ Obtaining a passport

▶ Discovering why you *don't* need to rent a car in Paris

▶ Understanding travel and medical insurance

▶ Guarding your health while traveling

▶ Keeping in touch via e-mail and cellphone

▶ Navigating airline security

- -

*T*his chapter advises and helps you organize those innumerable loose ends and last-minute tasks so that planning your trip to Paris doesn't last longer than the trip itself!

Getting a Passport

A valid passport is the only legal form of identification accepted around the world. You can't cross an international border without it. Getting a passport is easy, but the process takes some time. For an up-to-date country-by-country listing of passport requirements around the world, go to the "Foreign Entry Requirement" Web page of the U.S. Department of State at http://travel.state.gov.

Applying for a U.S. passport

If you're applying for a first-time passport, follow these steps.

1. Complete a **passport application** in person at a U.S. passport office; a federal, state, or probate court; or a major post office. To find your regional passport office, either check the **U.S. Department of State** Web site, http://travel.state.gov/passport/passport_1738.html, or call the **National Passport Information Center** (☎ 877-487-2778) for automated information.

2. Present a **certified birth certificate** as proof of citizenship. (Bringing along your driver's license, state or military ID, or social security card is also a good idea.)

3. Submit **two identical passport-sized photos,** measuring 2-x-2 inches in size. You often find businesses that take these photos near a passport office. *Note:* You can't use a strip from a photo-vending machine because the pictures aren't identical.

4. Pay a **fee.** For people 17 and over, a passport is valid for ten years and costs $97. For those 16 and under, a passport is valid for five years and costs $82.

 Allow plenty of time before your trip to apply for a passport; processing normally takes three weeks but can take longer during busy periods (especially spring).

If you have a passport in your current name that was issued within the past 15 years (and you were over age 16 when it was issued), you can renew the passport by mail for $67.

Applying for other passports

The following list offers more information for citizens of Australia, Canada, New Zealand, and the United Kingdom.

✔ **Australians** can visit a local post office or passport office, call the **Australia Passport Information Service** (☎ **131-232** toll-free from Australia), or log on to www.passports.gov.au for details on how and where to apply. The fee for Australian passports rose on July 1, 2006 from AU$172 to AU$193 for adults, and from AU$86 to AU$96 for children and seniors.

✔ **Canadians** can pick up applications at passport offices throughout Canada, post offices, or from the central **Passport Office, Department of Foreign Affairs and International Trade,** Ottawa, ON K1A 0G3 (☎ **800-567-6868**; www.ppt.gc.ca). Applications must be accompanied by two identical passport-sized photographs and proof of Canadian citizenship. Processing takes five to ten days if you apply in person, or about three weeks by mail The cost is CAN$87 for adults; CAN$37 for children.

✔ **New Zealanders** can pick up a passport application at any New Zealand Passports Office or download it from their Web site. For information, contact the **Passports Office** or check out their Web site. Contact the **Passports Office** at ☎ **0800-225-050** in New Zealand or log on to www.passports.govt.nz. The cost for an adult passport is NZ$150; NZ$ 80 for a child's passport.

✔ **United Kingdom** residents can pick up applications for a standard ten-year passport (five-year passport for children under 16) at passport offices, major post offices, or a travel agency. For information, contact the **United Kingdom Passport Service** (☎ 0870-521-0410; www.passport.gov.uk/index.asp). An adult passport is £51; a child's passport costs £34.

Always keep a photocopy of the inside page of your passport with your picture packed separately from your wallet or purse. In the event your passport is lost or stolen, the photocopy can help speed up the replacement process. When traveling in a group, never let one person carry all the passports. If the passports are stolen, obtaining new ones can be much more difficult, because at least one person in a group needs to be able to prove his or her identity to identify the others.

If you're a U.S. citizen and either lose or have your passport stolen in Paris, go to the Consulate of the American Embassy at 2 rue St. Florentin, 1er (☎ 01-43-12-22-22; Métro: Concorde; http://paris.usembassy. gov/consul/acs/passports/lost.htm). Canadians in the same circumstances need to visit the Consulate of the Canadian Embassy, 35 av. Montaigne, 8e (☎ 01-44-43-29-00; Métro: Franklin-D-Roosevelt or Alma Marceau). Australians must go to the Ambassade d'Australie at 4 rue Jean Rey, 15e (☎ 01-40-59-33-00; Métro: Bir-Hakeim). New Zealanders need to visit the New Zealand Embassy, 7 Ter rue Léonard de Vinci, 16e (☎ 01-45-01-43-43; Métro: Victor-Hugo).

Why Not to Rent a Car in Paris

Extreme sports aficionados, driving in Paris is for you. In the 1998 movie, *Ronin,* starring Robert De Niro, a former U.S. intelligence agent tries to track down a mysterious package wanted by both the Irish and the Russians. Naturally, there's a car chase, and this one is edge-of-the-seat: The bad guys in a BMW are fleeing from the good guys in a Mercedes through the center of Paris. The BMW speeds through traffic the wrong way with the Mercedes in hot pursuit, and after nearly ten nail-biting minutes, one of the cars flips over (I won't tell you which one) in a flaming crash. To the uninitiated, simply driving a car in Paris makes you feel like you're in this Paris chase. Why? Parisian drivers are ruthlessly aggressive. Traffic is dense. Roundabouts pop up everywhere, and cars seem to hurtle at you from the left — no better example than the circle called Étoile that surrounds the Arc de Triomphe, where cars enter and exit from *12 different locations* at high speeds. Parking is difficult, both in terms of finding a space and the size of the spaces available. Most hotels, except luxury ones, don't have garages. And if you drive to Paris from somewhere else and get on the limited-access roadway called the *périphérique* that circles the city, you'll find that its exits aren't numbered. Because the Paris Métro is one of the world's best urban transportation systems, having a car in Paris seems highly unnecessary. Even the daytrips described in Chapter 14 are easily accessible by public transportation.

If you must drive in Paris, make sure that you have a copilot helping you navigate the streets. Children, by law, are required to sit in the back, and backseat passengers must wear seat belts. And remember that the majority of rentals available in France (and, indeed, most of Europe) have manual (stick-shift) transmissions. In fact, if you request an automatic transmission, you'll probably end up paying more for the car, if a car is even available.

When you rent a car, try doing so for three days or more because the cost usually works out to be less per day than renting for one day, and unlimited mileage is thrown in. Reserve before you leave home (make sure to print out your reservation!), and keep in mind that government taxes are calculated at an eye-popping 20.6 percent of the total contract, collision damage insurance tacks on 15€ to 20€ ($18–$24) per day, gas is very expensive, and a surcharge of about 15€ ($18) is assessed if you pick up the car at the airport.

Car rental agencies in Paris include

- ✔ **Avis,** gare d'Austerlitz, arrivals gate, 13e (☎ **01-45-84-22-10;** www.avis.com). A compact car, such as a Renault Megane, that seats four runs about 64€ ($77) per day unlimited mileage before tax.

- ✔ **Europcar,** 60 bd Diderot, 12e (☎ **08-25-35-23-52;** .15€/20¢ per minute; www.europcar.fr). A compact four-door with air conditioning, such as the Volkswagen Golf, costs 87€ ($104) per day with unlimited miles before tax.

- ✔ **Hertz France,** gare de l'Est, 10e (☎ **01-42-05-50-43;** www.hertz.com). A compact car such as an Opal Corsa costs about 92€ ($110) per day with limited mileage but with all taxes.

- ✔ **National,** Charles de Gaulle Airport, Terminal One, (☎ **01-48-62-65-81;** www.nationalcar.com). A compact five-door car that seats four, such as a Citröen C4 1.6, costs 121€ ($145) per day limited mileage before tax.

The major highways *(autoroutes)* to Paris are the **A1** from the north (the United Kingdom and Belgium); the **A13** from Normandy and other points in northwest France; the **A109** from Spain and the southwest; the **A7** from the Alps, the Riviera, and Italy; and the **A4** from eastern France. At the beginning and end of long weekends, school breaks, and August summer vacations, these roads become parking lots.

Playing It Safe with Travel and Medical Insurance

Three kinds of travel insurance are available: trip-cancellation insurance, medical insurance, and lost luggage insurance. The cost of travel insurance varies widely, depending on the cost and length of your trip, your age and health, and the type of trip you're taking, but expect to pay between 5 percent and 8 percent of the vacation itself.

✔ **Trip-cancellation insurance** helps you get your money back if you have to back out of a trip, if you have to go home early, or if your travel supplier goes bankrupt. Allowed reasons for cancellation can range from sickness to natural disasters to the Department of State declaring your destination unsafe for travel. (Insurers usually won't cover vague fears, though, as many travelers who tried to cancel their trips in Oct 2001 because they were wary of flying discovered.)

Protect yourself by paying for the insurance with a credit card — by law, consumers can get their money back on goods and services not received if they report the loss within 60 days after the charge is listed on their credit card statement.

Note: Many tour operators, particularly those offering trips to remote or high-risk areas, include insurance in the cost of the trip or can arrange insurance policies through a partnering provider, a convenient and often cost-effective way for the traveler to obtain insurance. Make sure the tour company is a reputable one, however: Some experts suggest you avoid buying insurance from the tour or cruise company you're traveling with, saying it's better to buy from a third-party insurer than to put all your money in one place.

✔ Most health plans (including Medicare and Medicaid) do not provide **medical insurance** coverage for travel overseas, and the ones that do often require you to pay for services up front and reimburse you only after you return home. Even if your plan does cover overseas treatment, most out-of-country hospitals make you pay your bills up front and send you a refund only after you return home and file the necessary paperwork with your insurance company. As a safety net, you may want to buy travel medical insurance, particularly if you're traveling to a remote or high-risk area where emergency evacuation is a possible scenario. If you require additional medical insurance, try **MEDEX Assistance** (☎ 410-453-6300; www.medexassist.com) or **Travel Assistance International** (☎ 800-821-2828; www.travelassistance.com).

✔ **Lost luggage insurance** is not necessary for most travelers. On international flights (including U.S. portions of international trips), baggage coverage is limited to approximately $9.07 per pound, up to approximately $635 per checked bag. If you plan to check items more valuable than the standard liability, see if your valuables are covered by your homeowner's policy, get baggage insurance as part of your comprehensive travel-insurance package, or buy Travel Guard International's "BagTrak" product (☎ 800-454-7107; www.travelguard.com). Don't buy insurance at the airport, as it's usually overpriced. Be sure to take any valuables or irreplaceable items with you in your carry-on luggage, as many valuables (including books, money, and electronics) aren't covered by airline policies.

If your luggage is lost, immediately file a lost-luggage claim at the airport, detailing the luggage contents. For most airlines, you must report delayed, damaged, or lost baggage within 4 hours of arrival. The airlines are required to deliver luggage, once found, directly to your house or destination free of charge.

For more information on travel insurance, contact one of the following recommended insurers: **Access America** (☎ 800-729-6021; www.access america.com); **Travel Insured International** (☎ 800-243-3174; www.travelinsured.com); **Travelex Insurance Services** (☎ 800-228-9792; www.travelex-insurance.com); and **InsuranceToGo.com** (☎ 877-598-8646; www.insurancetogo.com).

Staying Healthy when You Travel

We know you're not going to get sick on this vacation, so feel free to skip over this section! Of course, the last time we checked, those nasty flu bugs weren't listening to us any more than they probably listen to you, so just in case you're bitten . . . .

The French government pays 70 percent of the cost of doctor visits, and its national health insurance covers 99 percent of France's population. Visitors needing medical care in France find that same-day appointments are easily made, and patient fees are relatively inexpensive. Patients almost always have to pay up front, unless they're citizens of European Union countries with reciprocal medical arrangements. U.S. health insurance companies usually reimburse you for most of the cost of treating illnesses in foreign countries; make sure to keep all your receipts.

If you do get sick, ask the concierge at your hotel to recommend a local doctor — even his or her own doctor, if necessary. You can also call SOS Medecins (☎ 01-47-07-77-77), a 24-hour service. Ask for an English-speaking doctor. The **Centre Médicale Europe,** 44 rue d'Amsterdam, 9e (☎ 01-42-81-93-33), is another good and efficient option. It has a host of specialists, and foreigners pay about 30€ ($36) for a consultation. If you're in urgent need of a dentist, try **SOS Urgences Stomatologiques et Dentaires,** 87 bd. Port-Royal (☎ 01-43-36-36-00).

Talk to your doctor before leaving on a trip if you have a serious and/or chronic illness. For conditions such as epilepsy, diabetes, or heart problems, wear a **MedicAlert identification tag** (☎ 888-633-4298; www.medic alert.org), which immediately alerts doctors to your condition and gives them access to your records through MedicAlert's 24-hour hotline. Contact the **International Association for Medical Assistance to Travelers (IAMAT;** ☎ 716-754-4883 or, in Canada, 416-652-0137; www.iamat. org) for tips on travel and health concerns in the countries you're visiting, and lists of local, English-speaking doctors. The United States **Centers for Disease Control and Prevention** (☎ 800-CDC-INFO; www.cdc.gov) provides up-to-date information on health hazards by region or country and offers tips on food safety.

Staying Connected by Cellphone or E-mail

The three letters that define much of the world's **wireless capabilities** are GSM (Global System for Mobiles), a big, seamless network that makes for easy cross-border cellphone use throughout Europe and dozens of other countries worldwide. In the United States, T-Mobile, AT&T Wireless, and Cingular use this quasi-universal system; in Canada, Microcell and some Rogers customers are GSM, and all Europeans and most Australians use GSM.

If your cellphone is on a GSM system, and you have a world-capable multiband phone (for example, a "triband" phone — check your phone specifications or call your service provider), such as many Sony Ericsson, Motorola, or Samsung models, you can make and receive calls across civilized areas on much of the globe, from Andorra to Uganda. Just call your wireless operator and activate *international roaming* on your account. Unfortunately, per-minute charges can be high — usually $1 to $1.50 in Western Europe and up to $5 in such places as Russia and Indonesia.

That's why it's important to buy an *unlocked* world phone from the get-go. Many cellphone operators sell *locked* phones that restrict you from using any other removable computer memory phone chip card (called a **SIM card**) other than the ones they supply. Having an unlocked phone allows you to install a cheap, prepaid SIM card (found at a local retailer) in your destination country. (Show your phone to the salesperson; not all phones work on all networks.) You get a local phone number — and much, much lower calling rates. Getting an already locked phone unlocked can be a complicated process, but it can be done; just call your cellular operator and say you're going abroad for several months and want to use the phone with a local provider.

For many, **renting** a phone is a good idea. (Even owners of cellphones with international calling capabilities have to rent new phones if they're traveling to non-GSM regions, such as Japan or Korea.) Although you can rent a phone from any number of overseas sites, including kiosks at airports and at car rental agencies, we suggest renting the phone before you leave home. One good place is *www.roadpost.com*. You can rent a phone from them that starts at $49 for basic service (plus $1.79/minute; the most popular option is the 100-minute plan for $139; additional minutes are $1.39) for up to 30 days. The phone comes with your own number, voice mail, call forwarding, adaptors and accessories for your travel destinations, and free 24/7 technical support. When you return home, just ship the phone back to Road Post in the prepaid envelope they provide. You can give loved ones and business associates your new number, make sure the phone works, and take the phone wherever you go — especially helpful for overseas trips through several countries, where local phone-rental agencies often bill in local currency and may not let you take the phone to another country.

In France, phone rental isn't cheap. You usually pay $40 to $50 per week, plus airtime fees of at least a dollar a minute. One option is www. mobirent.fr, a French company that specializes in phone rental and will deliver to your lodging. The phone and its accessories are accompanied by one of three pricing plans: first class, business class, or economy. Economy rates are 52€ ($62) for 90 minutes of calling in France, 162€ ($194) for 90 minutes of calls to North America, and 243€ ($292) for 90 minutes of calls to the rest of the world. With rates like this, it may be more prudent to just buy a cellphone in France. For under $100, you get a phone and accessories, and some free minutes — don't forget that unlike mobile phone services in the States, receiving calls and text messages in France is free, and you can still call most places in Europe or America at somewhat reasonable rates. Cellphone stores abound in Paris: the biggest are **SFR** (there's a branch at 87 rue de Sèvres, 6e; Métro: Vaneau), **France Télécom** (a central location is 46 bis rue de Louvre, 1e; Métro: Les Halles), and **Bouygues Télécom** (33 rue de Rivoli, 4e; Métro: Hôtel de Ville). The first two companies provide better quality service and less blackout periods, while Bouygues Télécom is generally cheaper. You can also ask about rental policies at these stores, however at the time of this writing these companies are ceasing to offer this service.

Accessing the Internet Away from Home

Travelers have any number of ways to check their e-mail and access the Internet on the road. Of course, using your own laptop — or even a PDA (personal digital assistant) or electronic organizer with a modem — gives you the most flexibility. But even if you don't have a computer, you can still access your e-mail and even your office computer from cybercafes.

It's hard nowadays to find a city that *doesn't* have a few cybercafes. Although there's no definitive directory for cybercafes — they are independent businesses, after all — two places to start looking are at www. cybercaptive.com and www.cybercafe.com.

Aside from formal cybercafes, most **youth hostels** nowadays have at least one computer you can use to get on the Internet. And most **public libraries** across the world offer Internet access free or for a small charge. You can always find a cybercafe near a college; in France the Latin Quarter abounds with them around rue des Écoles and boulevard St-Michel. Try **Cybercafé de Paris,** 15 rue Halles, 1e (☎ 01-42-21-11-11; Métro: Les Halles), or Luxembourg Micro, 81 bd St-Michel, 5e (☎ 01-46-33-27-98; Métro: St-Michel). Avoid **hotel business centers** unless you're willing to pay exorbitant rates.

Most major airports now have **Internet kiosks** scattered throughout their gates. These kiosks, which you also see in shopping malls, hotel lobbies, and tourist information offices around the world, give you basic Web access for a per-minute fee that's usually higher than cybercafe prices. The kiosks' clunkiness and high price mean they should be avoided whenever possible.

To retrieve your e-mail, ask your **Internet Service Provider (ISP)** if it has a Web-based interface tied to your existing e-mail account. If your ISP doesn't have such an interface, you can use the free **mail2web** service (www.mail2web.com) to view and reply to your home e-mail. For more flexibility, you may want to open a free, Web-based e-mail account with **Yahoo! Mail** (http://mail.yahoo.com). (Microsoft's Hotmail is another popular option, but Hotmail has severe spam problems.) Your home ISP may be able to forward your e-mail to the Web-based account automatically.

If you need to access files on your office computer, look into a service called **GoToMyPC** (www.gotomypc.com). The service provides a Web-based interface for you to access and manipulate a distant PC from anywhere — even a cybercafe — provided your target PC is on and has an always-on connection to the Internet (such as with Road Runner cable). The service offers top-quality security, but if you're worried about hackers, use your own laptop rather than a cybercafe computer to access the GoToMyPC system.

If you're bringing your own computer, the buzzword in computer access to familiarize yourself with is **Wi-Fi** (wireless fidelity) — more and more hotels, cafes, and retailers are signing on as wireless hotspots from where you can get high-speed connection without cable wires, networking hardware, or a phone line. You can get Wi-Fi connection one of several ways. Many laptops sold in the last year have built-in Wi-Fi capability (an 802.11b wireless Ethernet connection). Mac owners have their own networking technology, Apple AirPort.

You sign up for wireless access service much as you do cellphone service, through a plan offered by one of several commercial companies that make wireless service available in airports, hotel lobbies, and coffee shops, primarily in the United States (followed by the United Kingdom and Japan). **T-Mobile Hotspot** (www.t-mobile.com/hotspot) serves up wireless connections at more than 1,000 Starbucks coffee shops nationwide and at the Starbucks locations in Paris. **Boingo** (www.boingo.com) and **Wayport** (www.wayport.com) have networks in airports and high-class hotel lobbies. **iPass** (www.ipass.com) providers also give you access to a few hundred wireless hotel lobby setups. Best of all, you don't need to be staying at the Four Seasons to use the hotel's network; just set yourself up on a nice couch in the lobby. The companies' pricing policies can be complicated, with a variety of monthly, per-connection, and per-minute plans, but in general you pay around $30 a month for limited access — and as more and more companies jump on the wireless bandwagon, prices are likely to get more competitive.

If Wi-Fi is not available at your destination, most business-class hotels throughout the world offer dataports for laptop modems, and a few thousand hotels in the United States and Europe now offer free high-speed Internet access using an Ethernet network cable. You can bring your own cables, but most hotels rent them for around $10. **Call your hotel in advance** to see what your options are.

Keeping Up with Airline Security Measures

Today security procedures at airports around the world mean longer waits in lines and getting to the airport earlier, especially for an international flight. Generally, you'll be fine if you arrive at the airport **one and a half hours** before a domestic flight and **three hours** before an international flight.

Bring a **current, government-issued photo ID** such as a driver's license or passport (of course you will need your passport if you are traveling to France). Keep your ID at the ready to show at check-in, the security checkpoint, and sometimes even the gate. (Children under 18 do not need government-issued photo IDs for domestic flights, but they do for international flights to most countries.)

Speed up security by not wearing metal objects such as big belt buckles and make sure to pack all liquids (this includes makeup, toothpaste, and so on) in your check-in baggage. If you have metallic body parts, a note from your doctor can prevent a long chat with the security screeners. Keep in mind that only ticketed passengers are allowed past security, except for folks escorting passengers or children with disabilities.

Travelers in the U.S. are allowed one carry-on bag, plus a "personal item" such as a purse, briefcase, or laptop bag. The Transportation Security Administration (TSA) has stabilized **what you can carry on** and **what you can't.** The general rule for carry-on luggage is that sharp things are out as are all liquids, including water bottles, gels, lotions, and any similar items (makeup, lipstick, and toothpaste, etc . . .). Be sure to pack any of these items in your checked baggage or they will be confiscated. Baby formula, breast milk, and prescriptions are some of the exceptions to the rule (the name on prescription must match the name of the passenger). To be safe, visit the TSA Web site at **www.tsa.gov** for a current list of restricted items.

Part III
Settling into Paris

The 5th Wave   By Rich Tennant

"Welcome to the Hotel de Notre-Dame. If there's anything else I can do for you, please don't hesitate to ring."

In this part . . .

*T*his section helps you go from point A to point B without wasting time and money. Better yet, it suggests great places to stay and tells you all you want to know about eating French-style and then directs you to some memorable eateries. Chapter 8 guides you from the airport to your hotel, describes the most popular neighborhoods, and tells you where to go for information after you're in Paris. Read Chapter 9 for reviews of the best accommodations in Paris — for all budgets. Chapter 10 proves that Paris is indeed a feast with an overview of the local dining scene, advice on how to trim the fat from your food budget, and recommendations for some of the best restaurants, brasseries, cafes, wine bars, tea salons, and sandwich places in the city. A handy index cross-references all the dining establishments by neighborhood, price, and type.

Chapter 8

Arriving and Getting Oriented

In This Chapter

▶ Passing through passport control and Customs
▶ Securing transportation to your hotel
▶ Discovering Paris by neighborhood
▶ Getting information on Paris in Paris
▶ Navigating the city

*T*he Paris experience begins for most on the plane, where announcements are made in English and French. For others it begins at the airport — with bi- and trilingual signs directing you to passport control and baggage claim. The smell of cigarettes. Free luggage carts! Horrendous lines at passport control (see the first section for an explanation). Little dogs peek out of bags or prance at the end of leashes. People dress more formally than at home. It all may seem a little astonishing. But, the important thing is you've arrived! Now you can move on to the first item of the day — getting from the airport to your hotel.

Navigating Your Way through Passport Control and Customs

Most visitors to Paris land at Charles de Gaulle Airport, currently under renovation. It's known as CDG and sometimes called Roissy-Charles de Gaulle. Nearly all direct flights from North America land at Charles de Gaulle. Bilevel Terminal 1 (Aérogare 1) is the older and smaller of the two terminals and is used by foreign airlines. Narrow escalators and moving sidewalks connect its podlike cement terminals. The bright and spacious Terminal 2 (Aérogare 2) is divided into halls A through F and is used by Air France, domestic and intra-European airlines, and some foreign airlines, including Air Canada.

A free shuttle bus *(navette)* connects Terminal 1 and 2. Signs in French and English in both terminals direct you to Customs, baggage claim, and transportation to the city. Staff at information desks also are on hand to answer questions.

Two lines are set up for passport control, one for European Union nationals and the other for everyone else. These lines can move quite quickly or horrendously slowly; it usually depends on the clerk checking your passport.

When passing through Customs, keep in mind that restrictions are different for citizens of the European Union than they are for citizens of non-EU countries. As a non-EU national, you can bring in 200 cigarettes or 100 cigarillos or 50 cigars or 250 grams of smoking tobacco duty-free. You can also bring in two liters of wine and one liter of alcohol of more than 80 proof. In addition, you can bring in 50 grams of perfume, a quarter-liter of toilet water, 500 grams of coffee, and 100 grams of tea. Travelers age 15 and older can also bring in 171€ ($205) in other goods; for those age 14 and younger, the limit is 86€ ($103). (See Chapter 12 for what you're allowed to bring home.) Because you probably aren't going to need to make a claim, you should be waved through by an officer pretty quickly. Customs officers do, however, pull random travelers over to check luggage. Whenever that happens to you, don't be offended; be polite and as helpful as you can, and if you don't speak French, let them know by saying, "Je ne parle pas français" (zhe ne *parl* pah frahn-*say*).

Regardless of the terminal, you need euro to get from the airport into Paris. You can find ATMs in the arrival areas of the airports along with *bureaux de change,* where you can exchange dollars for euro, but you're better off buying and bringing 200€ ($240) from your bank at home. Airport ATMs are notorious for being broken when you need them most, and the airport bureaux de change are just as notorious for their bad rates of exchange.

Making Your Way to Your Hotel

You can travel to and from the airports by several different means, and the amount of text here notwithstanding, they're all easy!

If you fly into Charles de Gaulle

Charles de Gaulle Airport (CDG) is located 23km (14½ miles) northeast of downtown Paris. Transportation into the city is plentiful.

Taking a taxi

Probably the easiest, but certainly not the cheapest, mode of transportation to your hotel from the airport is by **taxi.** A cab into town from Charles de Gaulle takes 40 to 50 minutes, depending on traffic, and costs about 50€ ($60) from 7 a.m. to 8 p.m. and about 15 percent more at other times. Taxi drivers are required to turn the meter on and charge the price indicated plus 0.90€ ($1.10) for each piece of luggage stowed in the trunk. If your French is poor or nonexistent, write down the name and full address of your hotel. The five-digit postal code is the most important morsel of information, because it tells the driver to the arrondissement where to take you. Check the meter before you pay — rip-offs of arriving tourists are not uncommon. Whenever you strongly think that you may have been overcharged, demand a receipt (*un réçu*, *ray*-soo), which drivers are obligated to provide, and contact the **Paris Préfecture of Police** (☎ **01-53-71-53-71**).

The taxi stands at Charles de Gaulle (***Note:*** Due to the construction at CDG, the location of these stands are subject to change) are located at

 ✔ **CDG Terminal 1:** Exit 20, arrivals level

 ✔ **CDG Terminals 2A and 2C:** 2A Exit 6, 2C Exit 6

 ✔ **CDG Terminals 2B and 2D:** 2B Exit 8, 2D Exit 8

 ✔ **CDG Terminal 2F:** Exit 0.10, arrivals level

 ✔ **CDG Terminal 3:** Arrivals level

Taking a shuttle

If you don't want to schlep your bags through Paris's streets and Métro stations, taking an airport shuttle is definitely the way to go. Although more expensive than airport buses and trains, shuttles are much cheaper and roomier than taxis. And you can reserve a seat in advance and pay by credit card. **World Shuttle,** 13 rue Voltaire, 94400 Vitry-sur-Seine (☎ **01-46-80-14-67;** www.world-shuttles.com) costs 26€ ($31) for one person, 17€ ($21) per person for two or more from Charles de Gaulle and Orly. Before 5:30 a.m., it's 70€ ($84) for two to four people.

PariShuttle, (☎ **01-53-39-18-18;** www.parishuttle.com) offers a similar service. You're picked up in a minivan at Orly or Charles de Gaulle and taken to your hotel for 25€ ($30) for one person, 19€ ($23) per person for groups of two to four people, and 16€ ($19) per person for five to eight people. The cost for children ages three to ten is 10€ ($12).

Riding the rails

A good option when you're not overloaded with baggage and want to keep your expenses down is to take the suburban commuter train to the Métro. **RER** (Réseau Express Régional) **Line B** stops near Terminals 1 and 2. Easy, cheap, and convenient, you can ride both to and from the airport from 5 a.m. to midnight Monday through Friday and 7 a.m. to 9 p.m. weekends.

Free shuttle buses connect terminals CDG 1 and CDG 2 to the RER train station. You can pick up the free shuttle bus at

 ✔ **CDG Terminal 1:** Follow RER signs to exit on arrivals level

 ✔ **CDG Terminal 2A:** Exit A8

Paris Neighborhoods

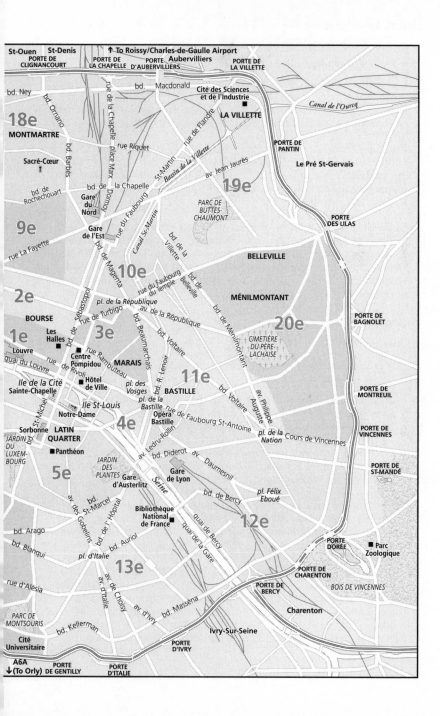

St-Ouen   St-Denis   ↑ To Roissy/Charles-de-Gaulle Airport
PORTE DE   PORTE DE   PORTE   Aubervilliers   PORTE DE
CLIGNANCOURT   LA CHAPELLE   D'AUBERVILLIERS   LA VILLETTE

bd. Ney   bd. Macdonald   Cité des Sciences
                                  et de l'Industrie   Canal de l'Ourcq
18e   LA VILLETTE
MONTMARTRE   PORTE DE
                                                           PANTIN
Sacré-Cœur   av. Jean Jaurès   Le Pré St-Gervais

Gare   PARC DE
du   BUTTES-
9e   Nord   CHAUMONT   PORTE
                                                           DES LILAS
Gare
de l'Est   BELLEVILLE
rue La Fayette
                        10e
2e   rue du Faubourg   MÉNILMONTANT
                                  du Temple
BOURSE   pl. de la République
                rue de Turbigo   av. de la République   PORTE DE
1e   Les   BAGNOLET
         Halles   **3e**   **20e**
Louvre   CIMETIÈRE
quai du Louvre   Centre   DU PÈRE-
         rue   Pompidou   MARAIS   LACHAISE
Ile de la Cité   Hôtel   pl. des   PORTE DE
Sainte-Chapelle de Ville Vosges   MONTREUIL
         Ile St-Louis   **11e** BASTILLE
Notre-Dame   pl. de la
Sorbonne LATIN   Bastille rue de Faubourg St-Antoine PORTE DE
JARDIN   QUARTER Opéra   VINCENNES
DU   Bastille   pl. de la
LUXEM-   ■Panthéon   Nation Cours de Vincennes
BOURG   PORTE DE
5e   JARDIN   ST-MANDÉ
         DES
         PLANTES Gare
                  d'Austerlitz
                  Gare
                  de Lyon   PORTE DE
bd. Arago   pl. Félix   DORÉE   ■Parc
bd. Blanqui   Bibliothèque   Eboué   Zoologique
              National   **12e**
         pl. d'Italie de France   PORTE
                                            DORÉE
         13e   PORTE DE   BOIS DE VINCENNES
rue d'Alésia   CHARENTON
                        PORTE DE
PARC DE   BERCY   Charenton
MONTSOURIS
Cité   Ivry-Sur-Seine
Universitaire
A6A   PORTE   PORTE   PORTE
↓(To Orly) DE GENTILLY   D'ITALIE D'IVRY

✔ **CDG Terminal 2B:** Exit B6

✔ **CDG Terminal 2C:** Exit C8

✔ **CDG Terminal 2D:** Exit D6

✔ **CDG Terminal 2F:** Exit 2.06

You can also take a walkway to the RER station — ask an airport employee or look for the round RER logo. (RER is pronounced air-uh-air in French.)

Buy the **RER** ticket, which costs 12€ ($14) for adults, 5.55€ ($6.40) for children, at the RER ticket counter and hang onto it in case of ticket inspection. (You can be fined if you can't produce your ticket for an inspector.) In any case, you need your ticket later to get off the RER system and onto the Métro.

Depending where your hotel is located, you exit either on the Right or the Left Bank. From the airport station, trains depart about every 15 minutes for the half-hour trip into town and stop on the **Right Bank** at Gare du Nord and Châtelet–Les Halles, and on the **Left Bank** at St-Michel, Luxembourg, Port-Royal, and Denfert-Rochereau, before heading south out of the city.

Boarding the bus

A bus is better than the RER if

✔ You're heading into Paris during off-peak driving hours, and you're not in a hurry.

✔ Your hotel is located near one of the drop-off points. *Note:* The bus is most convenient for the hotels I recommend in the 2e and 8e arrondissements. If you're staying outside these arrondissements, you can take a taxi from the shuttle drop-off point or board the closest subway if you aren't loaded down with luggage. If a bus isn't convenient, check out the door-to-door airport shuttle services in the earlier "Taking a shuttle" section.

If your hotel is located on the **Right Bank,** in the **8e, 16e,** or **17e** arrondissements, take **Air France coach Line 2,** which stops at rue Gouvion Saint-Cyr at Porte Maillot before ending up at 1 av. Carnot at place Charles de Gaulle–Étoile, the name for the huge traffic roundabout at the Arc de Triomphe. The bus costs 10€ ($12) one-way and runs every 15 minutes from 5:45 a.m. to 11:30 p.m. You do not have to be a passenger on an Air France flight to use the service, and tickets are available in a small office next to the bus. The trip from the airport into the city and vice versa takes about 40 minutes in light traffic, such as on weekend mornings. During weekday morning rush hour, however, the same trip can take twice as long, if not longer. Pick up the coach from

- ✔ **CDG Terminal 1:** Exit 34, arrivals level

- ✔ **CDG Terminals 2A: Exit 5; Terminal2C:** Exit 6

- ✔ **CDG Terminals 2B and 2D:** Exit 6

- ✔ **CDG Terminal 2F:** Exit 0.07, arrivals level (*Note:* Due to construction at CDG, bus terminals could change.)

If your hotel is located on the **Right Bank** near the **Bastille** (11e or 12e) or on the **Left Bank** in **Montparnasse** (14e), take the **Air France Line 4** coach, which stops at boulevard Diderot in front of the Gare de Lyon before ending up on rue du Commandant Mouchotte near the back of the Gare de Montparnasse. The bus costs 11.50€ ($14) one-way and runs every 30 minutes from 7 a.m. to 9:30 p.m. both to and from the airport. It takes about 50 minutes to get from the airport into the city in light traffic. Catch this coach from

- ✔ **CDG Terminal 1:** Exit 34, arrivals level

- ✔ **CDG Terminals 2A and 2C:** Exit 2 from Terminal 2C

- ✔ **CDG Terminals 2B and 2D:** Exit 2 from Terminal B

- ✔ **CDG Terminal 2F:** Exit 0.07, arrivals level

Take the **Roissybus** if your hotel is on the **Right Bank** near the **Opéra** (2e or 9e). It costs 8.30€ ($9.55) and leaves every 15 minutes from the airport between 6 a.m. and 11 p.m. (from 5:45 a.m. to 11:46 p.m. back to the airport). The drop-off point is on rue Scribe, a block from the **Opéra Garnier** near American Express. You can get to your destination in 45 to 50 minutes in regular traffic. Buy your tickets in the small office next to where the bus is parked. Pick up this coach from

- ✔ **CDG Terminal 1:** Exit 30, level 5, Arrivals

- ✔ **CDG Terminals 2A and 2C:** Exit 9 from Terminal 2A

- ✔ **CDG Terminal 2B:** Exit 12

- ✔ **CDG Terminal 2D:** Exit 11

- ✔ **CDG Terminal 2F:** Exit 0.08, arrivals level

If you fly into Orly

Orly Airport, 14km (8½ miles) south of the city, has two terminals — **Ouest** (West) and **Sud** (South) — and English speakers find the terminals easy to navigate. French domestic flights land at Orly Ouest, and intra-European and intercontinental flights land at Orly Sud. Shuttle buses connect these terminals, and other shuttles connect them to Charles de Gaulle every 30 minutes or so. A tourist information desk is conveniently located on the arrivals level of both terminals.

Like Charles de Gaulle Airport, two lines are set up for passport control; one for European Union nationals, one for visitors carrying passports from all other countries, and you should be waved through Customs. (See the previous section, "Navigating Your Way through Passport Control and Customs" for information about what you can bring into France.)

Taking a taxi

A cab from Orly into Paris costs about 35€ ($42), depending on traffic, and takes anywhere from 25 minutes to an hour. The taxi stand at Orly Sud is just outside Exit L; at Orly Ouest it's at Exit I. The same advice as when taking a taxi from Charles de Gaulle holds true here: Write down the full name and address of your hotel for the driver. And remember that cabs charge 0.90€ ($1.08) for each piece of luggage put in the trunk.

Busing is best — sometimes

Take the **Air France coach Line 1** if your hotel is located on the **Left Bank** near Les Invalides (7e). Buses leave Orly Sud at Exit K, and Orly Ouest at Exit D, arrivals level, every 12 to 15 minutes. The trip takes 30 minutes and costs 7.50€ ($9). You can request that the bus stop at Montparnasse-Duroc (14e).

The cheapest trip into town is on the **Jetbus.** You take this bus from Orly to Métro station Villejuif–Louis Aragon in south Paris (13e). It costs 5.15€ ($6) for the 15-minute journey. Beginning at 6:34 a.m., the bus leaves every 15 minutes from Orly Sud, Exit H and Platform 2, and from Orly Quest at Exit C on the arrivals level. The bus departs Paris for Orly from 6:15 a.m. to 10:15 p.m. An **Orly bus** also operates from 6 a.m. to 11:30 p.m. from Exit J, arrivals level, at Orly Ouest, and from Exit H, Platform 4, at Orly Sud to the Left Bank's Denfert-Rochereau station. It costs 5.80€ ($6.70) for the 25-minute journey. It departs Paris for Orly from 5:35 a.m. to 11 p.m.

Taking the train

If you're staying on the Left Bank, take the **RER C line** by catching a free shuttle bus from Exit G, Platform 1, at Orly Sud and Exit G, on the arrivals level, at Orly Ouest to the **Rungis** station, where RER C trains leave every 15 minutes for **Gare d'Austerlitz** (13e). A one-way fare is 5.65€ ($6.80). The trip into the city takes 30 minutes, making various stops along the Seine on the **Left Bank.** If you're staying on the **Right Bank,** you can take the **Orlyval/RER B line** to **Antony** Métro station. You connect at the **Antony** RER station where you board the RER B train to Paris. Hold on to the ticket because you will need it to get into the Métro/RER system. A trip to the Châtelet station on the Right Bank takes about 30 minutes and costs 9.05€ ($11). Once in Paris, the train stops at **Denfert-Rochereau, Port-Royal, Luxembourg,** and **St-Michel** on the Left Bank, and then crosses to the Right Bank for stops at **Châtelet** and **Gare du Nord.**

Figuring Out the Neighborhoods

You arrive at your hotel, check in, and maybe unpack a little. But taking a nap prolongs your jet lag. So, go out and act like a Parisian by having a cup of coffee at a cafe before getting ready to explore.

The Seine River divides Paris into two halves: the **Right Bank** *(Rive Droite)* on the north side of the river and the **Left Bank** *(Rive Gauche)* on the south side of the river. The larger Right Bank is where you find the city's business sector, stately monuments, and high-fashion industry. The Left Bank has the publishing houses, universities, and a reputation as bohemian because students, philosophers, and creative types have been congregating here for centuries. Two of the city's tallest monuments are on the Left Bank — the **Tour Montparnasse** (that lonely tall black building hovering on the edge of the city) and the **Eiffel Tower.**

The city is divided into 20 numbered *arrondissements* (municipal districts). The layout of these districts follows a distinct pattern. The first (abbreviated 1er for *premiere*) arrondissement is the dead center of Paris, comprising an area around Notre-Dame and the Louvre. From there, the rest of the districts spiral outward, clockwise, in ascending order. The lower the arrondissement number, the more central the location. To get a better idea, consult the "Paris Neighborhoods" map.

Arrondissement numbers are key to locating an address in Paris. And this book lists addresses the way they appear in Paris, with the arrondissement number following the specific street address (for instance, 29 rue de Rivoli, 4e, is in the fourth arrondissement). Arrondissement numbers are noted on street signs and are indicated by the last two digits of the postal code. For instance, an address with a postal code of 75007 is located in the seventh arrondissement. Once you know in which arrondissement an address is located, finding that spot is much easier. Numbers on buildings running parallel to the Seine usually follow the course of the river east to west. On north-south streets, numbering begins at the river.

Neighborhoods in the following sections are listed first by arrondissement, and then by neighborhood name. Only the better-known arrondissements — meaning the ones that you're most likely to stay in or visit — are mentioned here.

On the Right Bank

The following are the neighborhoods you're likely to visit on the Right Bank.

1er: Musée du Louvre/Palais-Royal/ Les Halles/Île de la Cité

Ile de la Cité is connected to the nearby posh residential island of **Ile de Saint-Louis.** Traditionally, people consider the Right Bank to be more upscale, with Paris's main boulevards, such as **Champs-Elysées,** and museums such as the **Louvre.** One of the world's greatest art museums (some say *the* greatest), the **Louvre,** still lures all visitors to Paris to the 1er arrondissement. You can see the contrast between many of the city's elegant addresses along the rue de Rivoli and arched arcades under which all kinds of touristy junk is sold. Walk through the **Jardin des Tuileries,** the most formal garden of Paris, and take in the classic beauty, opulence, and wealth of the **place Vendôme,** which is home to the Ritz Hotel. Browse the arcaded shops and view the striped columns and seasonal art on display in the garden of the **Palais Royal,** once the home to Cardinal Richelieu. The slightly seedy **Forum des Halles,** an above- and below-ground shopping and entertainment center, is also here.

This arrondissement tends to be crowded, and hotel prices are higher during Paris's high tourist season (in early fall) because the area is so convenient. Aristocratic town houses, courtyards, and antiques shops, flower markets, the **Palais de Justice,** and **Notre-Dame Cathedral** and **Sainte-Chapelle** (the chapel built in 1243 for St. Louis, famous for its gorgeous stained glass windows) are also part of the 1er on Ile de la Cité, an island in the Seine. This is one of Paris's prettiest and most crowded neighborhoods, as is its sister island, Ile St-Louis (see "4e: Ile St-Louis/Centre Pompidou" below).

2e: La Bourse

Often overlooked by tourists, the 2e houses the **Bourse** (stock exchange), and some of the pretty 19th-century covered shopping passageways. The district, lying between the Grands Boulevards and the rue Etienne Marcel, is also home to the **Sentier** area, where the garment trade is located, and wholesale fashion outlets abound. Sex shops and prostitutes line parts of the rue St-Denis.

3e: Le Marais

Le Marais (translated as "the swamp") is one of Paris's hippest neighborhoods, and one of the city's most popular attractions, the **Musée Picasso** and one of the more interesting museums, **Musée Carnavalet,** are located here. Paris's old Jewish neighborhood is located around the rue des Rosiers, and the rue Vieille-du-Temple is home to numerous gay bars and boutiques.

4e: Ile St-Louis/Centre Pompidou

Aristocratic town houses, courtyards, and antiques shops, the **Brasserie Ile-St-Louis** (a historic brasserie with literary associations), **Berthillon** (reputed to be Paris's best ice cream), the **Centre Georges Pompidou museum,** and the **place des Vosges** make up the 4e arrondissement, which is partly on the Ile St-Louis and partly in the Marais district. The area around the Centre Pompidou is one of Paris's more eclectic; you see everyone from pierced and Goth-style art students to chic Parisians sipping coffee at Café Beaubourg to tourists buying football shirts from one of the many souvenir stores.

8e: Champs-Elysées/Madeleine

The 8e is the heart of the Right Bank, and its showcase is the **Champs-Elysées.** The Champs stretches from the **Arc de Triomphe** to the city's oldest monument, the Egyptian obelisk on **place de la Concorde.** The fashion houses, the most elegant hotels, expensive restaurants and shops, and the most fashionably attired Parisians are here.

9e: Opéra Garnier/Pigalle

Everything, from the **Quartier de l'Opéra** (the neighborhood around the Opéra Garnier) to the strip joints of **Pigalle,** falls within the 9e, which was radically altered by Baron Haussmann's 19th-century redevelopment projects; his Grands Boulevards radiate through the district. You'll probably pay a visit to the 9e to shop at its famous department stores **Au Printemps** and **Galeries Lafayette.** Try to visit the **Opéra Garnier** (Paris Opera House), which recently reopened after an expensive restoration, worth a visit for its gorgeously restored ceiling by Marc Chagall.

10e: Gare du Nord/Gare de l'Est

In the movie *Amélie,* the young heroine likes to skip stones on the Canal St-Martin in the newly hip neighborhood of the same name with a burgeoning night scene, located here. Though most of this arrondissement is dreary (**Gare du Nord** and **Gare de l'Est** are two of the city's four main train stations), the canal's **quai de Valmy** and **quai de Jemmapes** are scenic, tree-lined promenades. The classic movie *Hotel du Nord* was also filmed here.

11e: Opéra Bastille

The 11e has few landmarks or famous museums, but the area has become a mecca for hordes of young Parisians looking for casual, inexpensive nightlife. Always crowded on weekends and in summer, the overflow retires to the steps of the **Opéra Bastille,** where inline skaters and skateboarders skate and teens flirt.

16e: Trocadéro/Bois de Boulogne

This area of Paris is where the moneyed live. Highlights include the **Bois de Boulogne** (the huge wooded park on Paris's western edge), the **Jardin du Trocadéro** (known for its famous fountains bordering the Eiffel Tower), the **Musée de Balzac,** the **Musée Guimet** (famous for its Asian collections), and the **Cimetière de Passy,** resting place of Manet, Talleyrand, Giraudoux, and Debussy. One of the largest arrondissements, the 16e is known today for its exclusivity, its BCBG residents (*bon chic bon genre,* or yuppie), its upscale rents, and some rather posh (and, according to its critics, rather smug) residential boulevards. The arrondissement includes what some visitors consider the best place in Paris from which to view the Eiffel Tower, the **place du Trocadéro.**

18e: Montmartre

The **Moulin Rouge,** the **Basilica of Sacré-Coeur** (the white domed structure on a hill overlooking Paris), and the **place du Tertre** (the square filled with restaurants behind it) are only some of the attractions in this outer arrondissement. Take a walk through the winding old streets here, and you feel transported into another era. The **Bateau-Lavoir,** Picasso's first studio in Paris, is also here. The city's most famous flea market, **Marché aux Puces de la Porte de St-Ouen,** is nearby in the 20e.

On the Left Bank

The following are neighborhoods you're likely to visit on the Left Bank.

5e: Latin Quarter

Bookstores, schools, churches, nightclubs, student dives, Roman ruins, publishing houses, and expensive boutiques characterize this district, which is called *Latin* because students and professors at the Sorbonne, located here, once spoke Latin exclusively. Stroll along **quai de Montebello,** inspecting the inventories of the *bouquinistes* (booksellers), and wander the shops in the old streets of rue de la Huchette and rue de la Harpe (but don't eat here; you can find much better places). The 5e also stretches down to the **Panthéon** and to the steep cobblestone rue Mouffetard behind it, where you can visit one of the city's best produce markets, eat at a variety of ethnic restaurants, or raise a glass in très cool Café Contrescarpe.

6e: St-Germain and the Luxembourg Gardens

The art school that turned away Rodin, the **École des Beaux-Arts,** is here, and so are some of the chicest designers around. But the secret of the district lies in discovering its narrow streets and hidden squares. Everywhere you turn here, you encounter famous historical and literary associations. For instance, the restaurant **Brasserie Lipp** is where Hemingway lovingly recalls eating potato salad in *A Moveable Feast,* and the **Café les Deux Magots** is depicted in the movie adaptation of Hemingway's *The Sun Also Rises.* The 6e takes in the **rue de Fleurus** where Gertrude Stein lived with Alice B. Toklas, and down the street is the wonderful **Luxembourg Gardens,** probably local residents' most loved park. (Try to find the Statue of Liberty in the garden.)

7e: Near the Eiffel Tower and Musée d'Orsay

The city's most famous symbol, the **Eiffel Tower,** dominates the 7e, and part of the **St-Germain** neighborhood is here, too. The **Hôtel des Invalides,** which contains **Napoléon's Tomb** and the **Musée de l'Armée,** is also in the 7e, in addition to the **Musée Rodin** and the **Musée d'Orsay,** the world's premier showcase of 19th-century French art and culture. The Left Bank's only department store, **Le Bon Marché,** is also located here, and so is a warren of streets along which beautiful shoes, clothing, and objects for the home are sold.

13e: Butte-aux-Cailles and Chinatown

Although high-rises dominate much of 13e, a nightlife scene has emerged on the dance barges along the **quai Tolbiac** (where the new **Bibliothèque François Mitterand** sits) and in the cozy network of winding streets that make up the **Butte-aux-Cailles** (literally hill of pebbles) neighborhood. The 13e has also become a lively hub for Paris's Asian community with Vietnamese and Chinese restaurants along **avenue d'Ivry** and **avenue de Choisy** next to stores selling all kinds of items from France's former colonies in Southeast Asia. The Chinese New Year Parade takes place here in late January or February.

14e: Montparnasse

Montparnasse is the former stomping ground of the *lost generation* — writers Gertrude Stein, Ernest Hemingway, Edna St. Vincent Millay, Ford Madox Ford, and other American expatriates gathered here in the 1920s. After World War II, it ceased to be the center of intellectual life in Paris, but the memories linger. Some of the world's most famous literary cafes, including **La Rotonde, Le Select, Le Dôme,** and **La Coupole,** are in the northern end of this large arrondissement, near the Rodin statue of Balzac at the junction of boulevard Montparnasse and boulevard Raspail. Some of those same literary giants (most notably Jean-Paul Sartre and Simone de Beauvoir) are buried nearby, in the Cimitière du Montparnasse. At its southern end, the arrondissement contains pleasant residential neighborhoods filled with well-designed apartment buildings, many built between 1910 and 1940.

Finding Information after You Arrive

The **Office de Tourisme et des Congrès de Paris** (www.parisinfo.com) has branches throughout the city at the following locations *Note:* These centers are closed on May 1.

- ✔ **The Opéra-Grands-Magasins Welcome Center,** 11 rue Scribe, 9e; open Monday to Saturday 9 a.m. to 6:30 p.m. (Métro: Chausée d'Antin or Opéra; RER: Auber)

- ✔ **The welcome kiosk beneath the modern glass roofed terminal of the Gare du Nord,** 18 rue Dunkerque, 10e; open seven days a week from 8 a.m. to 6 p.m. (Métro and RER: Gare du Nord)

- ✔ **The Gare de Lyon Welcome Center,** 20 bd. Diderot, 12e; open Monday to Saturday 8 a.m. to 6 p.m. (Métro and RER: Gare de Lyon)

- ✔ **21 place du Tertre,** 18e; open daily 10 a.m. to 7 p.m. (Métro: Abbesses)

- ✔ **On median strip facing 72 bd Rochechouart,** Montmartre, 18e; open daily 10 a.m. to 6 p.m. (Métro: Anvers)

✔ **Carrousel du Louvre, beneath the Pyramide,** 99 rue de Rivoli, 1er; open daily 10 a.m. to 7 p.m. (Métro: Palais Royal/Musée du Louvre)

✔ **Eiffel Tower between the North and East pillars;** open daily 11 a.m. to 6 p.m. May through September (Métro: Bir Hakeim, RER: Champ-de-Mars/Tour Eiffel)

Getting Around Paris

Probably your best introduction to Paris, and to the way the city is laid out, is from the north tower at Notre-Dame. You can see the magnificent cathedral from many parts of the city, and a visit helps you get oriented. From the cathedral, you see that the river Seine is actually Paris's most important "street."

By Métro

The best way to get around Paris is to walk, but for longer distances the Métro, or subway, rules. The **Métropolitain** is fast, safe, and easy to navigate. Open from 5:45 a.m. to 12:45 a.m., it's an efficient and cheap way to get around. The only times you may want to avoid it are the hours between 7 to 10 a.m. and 6 to 8 p.m. — in other words, rush hour. Operated by the RATP (Régie Autonome des Transports Parisiens), the Métro has a total of 16 lines and more than 360 stations, making it likely that one is near your destination. The Métro is connected to the suburban commuter train, the **Réseau Express Régional** (RER), which connects downtown Paris with its airports and suburbs.

You can recognize a Métro station either by an elegant Art Nouveau gateway reading *Métropolitain* or by a big yellow *M* sign. Unless otherwise marked, all Métro stations have a ticket booth, where you purchase a single ticket (1.40€/$1.70) or a group of ten tickets called a *carnet* (kar-*nay*; 11€/$13) from an attendant or, in most stations, from a machine that accepts only bills and coins (no credit cards). Every Métro stop has maps of the system; you can get portable maps by asking at a ticket booth for *une carte* (oon kart). Near the exits, you can find a *plan du quartier,* a very detailed pictorial map of the streets and buildings surrounding the station, with all exits marked. A good idea is to consult the *plan du quartier* before you exit the system, especially at very large stations. You may want to use a different exit to reach the other side of a busy street or wind up closer to your destination.

Navigating the Métro is easy, and you'll be a pro in no time. Here's what you do.

1. **Use the Métro map on the inside front cover of this book to figure out which station is closest to you.**

   For example, if you want to go to the Louvre and are in your hotel in the Latin Quarter, say the Familia, check the listing in this book for your hotel. The book tells you that your nearest Métro station, or your starting point, is Jussieu. Look at the Métro map on the Cheat Sheet at the front of this book for the line that the Jussieu station is on. (Each end of the lines on the Métro map is marked with the number of the line.) The Jussieu station is on Line 7.

2. Look for your destination station.

In the example, you look for the Louvre. You see that the Louvre has two stops: the Palais Royal-Musée du Louvre station on Line 7 and the Louvre Rivoli station on Line 14. Choose the Palais-Royal Musée du Louvre station, and you won't have to change trains.

3. Enter the Métro system through a turnstile with two ticket slots.

With the magnetic strip facing down, insert your ticket into the nearer slot. Your ticket pops out of the second slot. Remove it, and either walk through a set of rubberized doors that briskly open on each side or push through a turnstile.

Keep your ticket with you until you exit the station. At any point while in you're the Métro, an inspector may ask to see your ticket again. If you fail to produce it, you're subject to a steep fine. When you ride the RER, you must keep your ticket because you have to insert it in a turnstile when you exit the station.

4. Make sure you're going in the right direction.

When you're past the entrance, look at your subway map and trace the line past your destination to its end. The station's name at the end of the line is the name of the subway train on which you'll be traveling; in the case of Line 7 the train is La Corneuve. To get back to your hotel from the Louvre, you take the train going in the opposite direction, marked Villejuif Louis Aragon and exit at the Jussieu station.

5. Enter the train and exit at the station you want.

Blue signs reading *Sortie* mark all exits.

See? Pretty easy! Suppose, however, that the Métro line nearest to you doesn't directly go to your destination. For example, you want to go to the Arc de Triomphe from Jussieu, and the stop is Charles de Gaulle–Étoile. Find the Charles de Gaulle–Étoile stop on the Métro map. You see that you can reach Charles de Gaulle–Étoile on Line 6 or Line 1. But you're on Line 7. You have to change trains. Changing trains is called a *correspondance,* or transfer.

To make a **transfer** *(correspondance),* follow these steps.

1. Figure out which transfer station you need.

On your map, blank white circles indicate where a number of lines intersect. These circles are *transfer stations,* where you can change subway trains.

To figure out where you need to change from the 7 train to Line 1 or Line 6 (to get from Jussieu to the Arc de Triomphe), use the map to see where Line 7 intersects with Line 1 and with Line 6. Line 7 and Line 6 intersect at Stalingrad, opposite from where you want to go. But Line 7 and Line 1 intersect at Concorde, very close to Charles de Gaulle–Étoile. This is the train you want to take. To make sure you go in the right direction on Line 1, look on your map for the name of the station at the very end past Charles de Gaulle–Étoile. It's called Grande Arche de la Défense, and this is the name of the train you want to ride.

2. **Look for a bright orange *Correspondance* sign above the platform at the transfer station.**

   Beneath it is a white sign that has the number of the line you can transfer to in a circle (in the example, Line 1).

3. **Follow the direction the sign indicates for the line you want.**

   You eventually come to two stairwells leading to the platforms. Navy blue signs mark this area, indicating the train's direction and listing all the stops the train makes. Make sure you choose the stairwell leading to the train going in the direction you want — in the example, you want the train to Grande Arche de la Défense, so that you can exit at Charles de Gaulle–Étoile.

The distances between platforms at the *correspondance* (transfer) stations can be very long. You may climb stairs, walk a short distance, only to descend stairs to walk some more. Châtelet is particularly long. Some lines are connected by moving sidewalks that seem to do nothing but make a very long walk a little less long. For those with limited mobility, take the bus or a cab.

The Métro connects with the suburban commuter train, the RER, in several stations in the city. The RER operates on a zone fare system, but Métro tickets are valid on it in the city. You probably won't go past the first two zones, unless you visit Disneyland on the A4 or Versailles on the C5. When you ride the RER, keep your ticket because you need to insert it into a turnstile to leave the station.

The doors on most Métro cars don't open automatically. You must lift a door handle or press a button to get on and off.

Anyone who has ever been crushed on a Paris subway at rush hour can attest that commuters don't easily give up their places. If you step out of the train to let someone off, you may just be giving others on the platform the chance to squeeze in before you. Be polite, but stand your ground.

After the subway shuts down around 1 a.m., the RATP operates **Noctambuses** that run on the hour from 1:30 a.m. to 5:30 a.m. from Châtelet-Hôtel de Ville, but they don't cover every arrondissement. Check the maps at the entrance to Métro stations to determine if a

Noctambus services your destination. The bus has a distinctive yellow-and-black owl symbol, and tickets cost 2.70€ ($3.10).

A ten-ticket *carnet* good for the Métro and on buses is a good deal for 11€ ($13) because a single ticket costs 1.40€ ($1.70). You can purchase a *carnet* at all Métro stations as well as *tabacs* (cafes and kiosks that sell tobacco products). The heavily publicized **Paris Visite** card, which starts at 8.35€ ($10) a day offers free or reduced entry to some minor attractions and free souvenirs from others in addition to unlimited travel on Métro and buses, but make sure the attractions that interest you are included on the list (ask for it at the ticket window first) or visit the Paris Visite Web site before you leave home (www.ratp.fr/Paris Visite/Eng/index.htm).

How long do you plan to be in Paris? If you plan to use public transportation frequently, consider buying the **Carte Orange.** The weekly or monthly pass is inexpensive — 16€ ($17) for zones 1 and 2 and 21€ ($25) for zones 1 to 3 for a week's unlimited travel (*coupon hebdomadaire,* koo-poh eb-*doh*-muh-dare) or 46€ ($53) for a month's pass (*coupon mensuel* koo-*poh men*-soo-ell) covering the first 20 arrondissements. The only catch is that you must supply a passport-sized photo of yourself. Bring one from home or visit a photo booth at one of the many Monoprix stores, major Métro stations, department stores, or train stations, where you can get four black-and-white pictures for less than 5€ ($6). The weekly Carte Orange is on sale Monday through Wednesday morning and is valid through Sunday, but the monthly card is only sold the first two days of the month.

The **Mobilis** pass is good for unlimited travel on subway and bus lines (except to and from the airports) for one day. The cost is 5.30€ ($6). If you will be hopping on and off subways for more than one day, you may want to try one of the other passes. **Paris Visite** is good for unlimited travel for one, two, three, or five days. Though it has discounts for some museums and monuments, check the brochure to make sure you want to see the listed sites. Otherwise, the Paris Visite card turns out to be more expensive than a Carte Orange or a one-day Mobilis pass. A one-day Paris Visite card costs 8.35€ ($9.60), two-day 14€ ($16), three-day 19€ ($21), and five-day 27€ ($31). **Paris l'Open Tour** is good for one or two days of unlimited travel around Paris on special open-air buses. You can get on and off whenever you like. It's a bit pricey at 25€ ($29) for one day and 28€ ($32) for two days, but it's a good way to get to know Paris.

For more information on the city's public transportation, call the RATP's English information line (0.35€/80¢ per min.; ☎ 08-92-68-41-14; www.ratp.fr).

By bus

The bus system is convenient and can be an inexpensive way to sightsee without wearing out your feet. Most Parisian buses run from 6:30 a.m. to 8:30 p.m.; a few run until 12:30 a.m. Each bus shelter has a route map, which you want to check carefully. Because of the number of one-way streets, the bus is likely to make different stops depending on its direction. Main stops are written on the side of the buses with the endpoint shown on the front above the driver. Furthermore, the back of every bus shelter has posted large bus maps and smaller maps inside the shelter showing the specific bus route. Métro tickets are valid for bus travel, and although you can buy single tickets from the conductor, you can't buy ticket packages *(carnets)* on the bus.

Board at the front of the bus. If you have a single-trip ticket, insert it into the slot in the small machine right behind the driver. The machine punches your ticket and pops it back out. If you have a pass, show it to the driver. To get off at the next stop, press one of the red buttons on the safety poles; the *arrêt demandé* (stop requested) sign above the driver lights up.

The downside of taking the bus is that it often gets mired in heavy Parisian traffic, so I don't recommend it if you're in a hurry. And, like the Métro, avoid the bus during rush hours when it seems *le monde* (the world) is sharing the bus with you.

Bus routes great for sightseeing include

- ✔ **Bus 69:** Eiffel Tower, Invalides, Louvre, Hôtel de Ville, place des Vosges, Bastille, Père-Lachaise Cemetery

- ✔ **Bus 80:** Department stores on boulevard Haussmann, Champs-Elysées, avenue Montaigne *haute couture* shopping, Eiffel Tower

- ✔ **Bus 96:** St-Germain-des-Prés, Musée de Cluny, Hôtel de Ville, place des Vosges

By taxi

You have three ways to get a taxi in Paris, and I rank them in order of how successful they are.

- ✔ The best way to find a cab is by **phoning Alpha Taxis (☎ 01-45-85-85-85)** or **Taxis G7 (☎ 01-47-39-47-39)**. Keep in mind, however, that phoning ahead is more expensive because the meter starts running as soon as the driver commences the journey to get you.

- ✔ You can also **wait at a taxi stand** *(station de taxis);* a blue Taxi sign denotes the stands. Depending on the time of day, however, you may wait in a long line of people, or a very limited number of cabs stop.

- ✔ Finally, you can **hail a cab,** as long as you're not within 60m (200 ft.) of a taxi stand. Look for a taxi with its white light illuminated, which means the cab is available. An orange light means the cab is occupied or on the way to a pickup. You may get a cab driver who refuses to take you to your destination; by law, a driver can do this only during his or her last half-hour at work. Be prepared, as well, for the selective vision of drivers, especially when you hail a cab. Don't be surprised to see a free taxi or two pass you by.

Keeping the picks out of your pockets

Over the past few years, petty crime has been making a comeback in Paris, a city that is otherwise relatively safe. Anywhere where you find a high concentration of tourists, you also find pickpockets — including in the Métro, hovering around the lines outside the Eiffel Tower and Notre-Dame, and in the church and its bell tower. Keep an eye out for little bands of scruffy children, who often surround you, distract you, and make off with your belongings.

Your best bet is to use common sense. Be aware of the people around you at all times. Get a money belt. Women wear purses diagonally across the body with the flap facing the body. Make sure zipper purses are closed at all times. (In fact, zippered purses aren't recommended.) See Chapter 4 for what to do if you get pickpocketed.

For one to three people, the fare in Paris proper is around 2€ to 3€ ($2.30–$3.45); the rate per kilometer is 0.60€ ($.70) from 7 a.m. to 7 p.m. (otherwise known as Rate A); otherwise, it's 1€ to 2€ ($1.15–$2.30) (Rate B). You pay a 0.70€ (85¢) supplement for taxi stands at train stations and at the Air France shuttle-bus terminals, as well as 0.90€ ($1.05) for each piece of luggage weighing more than 5kg. If the driver agrees to do so, it's 1.50€ ($1.70) for transporting a fourth person. Common practice is to tip your driver 10 percent to 15 percent on longer journeys when the fare exceeds 15€ ($17); otherwise round up the charge and give the driver the change.

By car

Streets are narrow, parking is next to impossible, and nerve, skill, ruthlessness, and a knowledgeable copilot are required if you insist on driving in Paris. I *strongly* recommend that you don't. (If you must drive in Paris, do it in August when residents are away on vacation, and traffic is lighter.)

A few tips: Get an excellent street map and ride with another person; traffic moves so lightning-fast you don't have time to think at intersections. For the most part, you must pay to park in Paris. Depending on the neighborhood, expect to pay 1.80€ ($2.10) to 2.30€ ($2.65) an hour for a maximum of two hours. Place coins in the nearest meter, which issues you a ticket to place on your dashboard. You can also buy parking cards at the nearest *tabac* (tobacco shop) for meters that accept only parking cards. Parking is free on Sundays, holidays, and for the entire month of August.

Drivers and all passengers must wear seat belts. Children under 12 must ride in the back seat. Drivers are supposed to yield to the car on the right, except where signs indicate otherwise, as at traffic circles.

 Watch for the *gendarmes* (police officers), who lack patience and who consistently contradict the traffic lights. Horn blowing is frowned upon except in emergencies. Flash your headlights instead.

By bicycle

The banks of the Seine are closed to cars and open to pedestrians and cyclists March to November each Sunday from 10 a.m. to 5 p.m. It may not make much of a dent in the air quality, but bicycling is a fun and healthy way to spend a Sunday afternoon.

City planners have been trying to encourage more cycling by setting aside 100km (62 miles) of bicycle lanes throughout Paris. The main routes run north–south from the Bassin de La Villette along the Canal St-Martin through the Left Bank and east–west from Château de Vincennes to the Bois de Boulogne and its miles of bike lanes. The RATP (which runs the city's buses and subways) in partnership with the mayor's office rents bikes through its *Roue Libre* program (www.rouelibre.fr). To rent a bike, you need to put down a 200€ ($240) deposit per bike by traveler's check, credit card or with cash and show a passport or driver's license. Costs are 9€ ($11) per weekday, 32€ ($38) for eight days. A Roue Libre location is at 1 passage Mondétour, in front of 120 de la rue Rambuteau, 1er (☎ **08-10-44-15-34**; Métro: Les Halles; open daily 9 a.m.–7 p.m.). Roue Libre also gives 25€ ($30) three-hour guided tours of Paris in English (see Chapter 11.)

For more information and a bike map, pick up the *Plan Vert* from the tourist office. (For bike tours of the city, see Chapter 11.)

Paris à pied (On foot)

Paris is one of the prettiest cities in the world for strolling, and getting around on foot is probably the best way to really appreciate the city's character. The best walking neighborhoods are **St-Germain-des-Prés** on the Left Bank and the **Marais** on the Right Bank, both of which are filled with romantic little courtyards, wonderful boutiques, and congenial cafes and watering holes. The **quays of the Seine,** as well as its bridges, are also lovely, especially at sunset when the sun fills the sky with a pink glow that's reflected on the water. And try not to miss the pretty **Canal St-Martin** with its arched bridges and locks in the 10e, featured in the movies *Amélie* and *Hôtel du Nord* or the tiny streets off the Montmartre *butte* (hill).

Take special care when crossing streets, even when you have the right of way. The number-one rule of the road in France is that whoever is coming from the right side has the right of way. Drivers often make right turns without looking, even when faced with pedestrians at crosswalks. And don't ever attempt to cross a traffic circle if you're not on a cross-walk. The larger roundabouts, such as the one at the Arc de Triomphe, have pedestrian tunnels.

Chapter 9

Checking in at Paris's Best Hotels

*P*art of the fun of traveling to Paris is waking up in a new place with unlimited opportunities for exploring! If this is your first trip to Paris, your expectations about what a hotel room should look like may be based on what you have seen in your own country. For those visiting from North America, one important thing to know is that rooms in Paris tend to be smaller than they are in hotels in North America, even in expensive places (unless you opt for a modern chain hotel, which can lack charm). Parisian doubles are almost never big enough to hold two queen-sized beds, and the space around the bed usually isn't big enough for more than a desk and perhaps a chest of drawers. The story is the same in London, Rome, and most other continental capitals where buildings date back two, three, four, or more centuries, when everything was smaller.

Parisian hotels also vary widely in their plumbing arrangements. Some units come equipped with only a sink; others may also have a toilet and either a shower or tub. Private bathrooms with tubs often have hand-held shower devices, and some shower stalls don't have curtains — so pay attention that water isn't flooding the floor. The trend is toward renovating small hotels by installing a small shower, toilet, and sink in each room, but don't count on having *all* these amenities in your room unless you're in a pricier hotel.

Acoustics tend to be unpredictable in old Parisian hotels. Your quarreling neighbors may compete with street noise for the prize of most annoying, so bring earplugs for the neighbors, or ask for a room in the rear of the hotel to avoid the street noise. Another point to remember: Most budget hotels in Paris don't have air-conditioning, but fortunately, their solid stone walls tend to keep out the summer heat.

Getting to Know Your Options

More than 2,200 hotels are located in Paris — chain hotels, deluxe palacelike accommodations, hotels that cater to business travelers, budget hotels, and mom-and-pop establishments.

The French government grades hotels with a star system, ranging from one star for a simple motel or inn to four stars for a deluxe hotel. Moderately priced hotels usually get two or three stars. This system is based on a complex formula of room sizes, facilities, plumbing, elevators, dining options, renovations, and so on.

To find the hotel that's right for you, you need to weigh five variables: price, location, room size, amenities, and — the least tangible, but perhaps most desired of them all — a charming Parisian ambience. If the first variable, price, poses no problem, then you can have it all: great location, huge room, super perks, and sumptuous surroundings. Most travelers, however, need to make some compromises.

Before committing to a hotel, keep in mind that Paris offers additional options for lodging — renting an apartment, for example. Nothing beats living in Paris as a Parisian. In your own **apartment,** you can cook with fresh and unusual ingredients from the local green markets, taste fine wines that would be too expensive in a restaurant, and entertain new friends. Although the daily rate can be higher than a budget hotel, the room will be larger, you can save money on meals, and in the end, you may end up paying the same rate you would for room and board at a hotel — or less.

The most practical way to rent an apartment is through an agency. Most agencies require a seven-day minimum stay and offer discounts for longer stays. We've found that apartments vary quite a bit in size, location, and amenities. At the bottom end — for about 100€ ($120) per day — you'll find yourself in either a small, centrally located studio, or a larger studio in a neighborhood a bit far from the center of Paris. Studio apartments usually feature a convertible couch; an armchair or two; a bathroom with a tub or shower; and a tiny kitchenette with a refrigerator, stove, coffeemaker, and maybe a microwave. Dishes, cutlery, pots and pans, telephone, TV, iron, vacuum cleaner, linen, and sometimes a washing machine are also provided. Pay a bit more — around 150€ ($180) per day — and you get a more centrally located one-bedroom apartment. As with anything else, higher prices pay for larger, more luxurious spaces.

You can find many rental agencies online and comparison shop among them. Companies offering attractive apartments at reasonable prices are **Apartment Living in Paris** (www.apartment-living.com) and **Lodgis Solutions** (www.lodgis.com), which also rents apartments in New York, the French Riviera, and Marrakech. **Paris Vacation Rentals** (www.rentals-paris.com) is an agency that deals in short-term rental of upscale apartments at very good prices. More expensive is **New York Habitats** (www.newyorkhabitat.com), a New York real estate brokerage that rents Paris flats as a sideline. **Bonjour Paris** (www.bonjourparis.com) has reviews and information about apartment rental agencies.

Keep in mind that this is a short-term apartment rental. You have to sign a contract and put down a security deposit, which may not be refunded if you damage the apartment in any way.

If the agency offers optional gift baskets or transportation to and from the airport, refuse them. The gift basket usually contains items you can buy more cheaply at the grocery store, and the transportation is usually twice as much as a cab.

If you bring the kids with you to Paris, your best option may be the *aparthotel,* a hybrid between an apartment and a hotel where you can have the autonomy of an apartment with some of the amenities of a hotel. You book an aparthotel just like you do any other hotel, through its Web site or phone number. And, like hotels, they have 24-hour reception desks, satellite TV, housekeeping services, kitchenettes, and laundry. For a family of four, a one-bedroom apartment is a good-value alternative to two double rooms in a cheap hotel. And if you use your kitchenette to prepare even half of your own meals in Paris, you can reap huge savings on your dining bill.

Finding the Best Room at the Best Rate

The *rack rate* is the maximum rate a hotel charges for a room. It's the rate you get if you walk in off the street and ask for a room for the night. But you often don't have to pay it! This section gives tips on finding the best rooms in Paris at the best rate.

Finding the best rate

At chain hotels (especially the American ones) and other luxury hotels, you can often get a good deal simply by asking for a discounted rate. Your odds of getting a reduced rate improve drastically if you're staying for more than a few nights.

Keep in mind that bartering for a cheaper room isn't the norm at Paris's budget hotels. Small and privately owned; these establishments post their rates in the reception area and may not be willing to negotiate. To be fair, they may not be able to afford to let rooms go for less.

Room rates change with the seasons as occupancy rates rise and fall. In Paris, summer is low season. Yes, you're reading that correctly: Room rates tend to be lower in July and August, which is typically when the French flee the big cities for the beaches and the mountains. November and December are also low season, but early fall is high season, with October, in particular, heavy with conventioneers, making it difficult to find a room. If a hotel is close to full, it's less likely to extend discount rates; if it's close to empty, it may be willing to negotiate.

Prices for the hotels recommended here are designated with dollar signs; Table 9-1 explains how this works. In a nutshell, the more dollar signs you see, the more expensive the hotel. The number of dollar signs corresponds to the hotel's rack rates (full rate), from the cheapest double room in low season to the most expensive in high season. The most noticeable difference between budget hotels and the most expensive hotels is better amenities and services, followed by a more luxurious décor. None of the recommended hotels listed in this chapter is a dump; the places are decent and reputable. Naturally, the luxury level in a 1,000€ ($1,200) room is substantially higher than in a 100€ one ($120).

Table 9-1: Key to Hotel Prices

Dollar Sign(s)	Price Range	What to Expect
$	Less than 75€ ($90)	These accommodations are relatively simple and inexpensive. Rooms are likely to be small, and televisions are not necessarily provided. Parking is not provided but is rather catch-as-you-can on the street.
$$	76€–150€ ($91–$180)	A bit classier, these midrange accommodations offer more room, more extras (such as irons, hair dryers, a trouser press, and even Wi-Fi access), and a more convenient location than the preceding category.
$$$	151€–300€ ($181–$360)	Higher-class still, these accommodations begin to look plush. Think chocolates on your pillow, a classy restaurant, room service, and maybe a view of the Eiffel Tower or another landmark.
$$$$	Above 300€ ($360)	These top-rated accommodations come with luxury amenities such as on-premise spas, deluxe toiletries, stereo and DVD players, multistarred gourmet restaurants with room service, views, robes — frankly nearly every luxury you can imagine but you pay through the nose for 'em.

Room prices are subject to change without notice, so the rates quoted in this book may be different than the actual rate you receive when you make your reservation. Be sure to mention membership in AAA, AARP, frequent-flyer programs, and any other corporate rewards programs you belong to when making your reservation at a chain hotel. You never know when it may be worth a few dollars off your room rate. Family-run establishments rarely have arrangements with large organizations.

Keep this advice in mind when you're trying to save money on a room.

- A **travel agent** may be able to negotiate a better price at top hotels than you can get yourself. (The hotel gives the agent a discount for steering business its way.)

- Always ask if the hotel offers any **weekend specials,** which typically require you to stay two nights (either Fri–Sat or Sat–Sun). In Paris, you can find this kind of deal from September through March at almost all price levels.

- A *forfait* (*fohr*-feh) is a discount that requires you to stay a certain number of nights — perhaps a minimum of three or five. Sometimes something else is thrown in (like a bottle of champagne) to sweeten the deal. If you're going to be in Paris for more than three days, always ask if there's a *forfait,* and then pick the hotel with the best deal.

- Don't forget about **package deals** (see Chapter 5) that include airfare, hotel, and transportation to and from the airport.

- Look on the **Internet** for deals (see below).

Surfing the Web for hotel deals

Although the major travel booking sites (such as Travelocity, Orbitz, Expedia, and Cheap Tickets; see Chapter 5 for details) offer hotel booking, using a site devoted primarily to lodging can be best because you may find properties that aren't listed on more general online travel agencies. **The Paris Convention and Visitors Bureau** (www.parisinfo.com) gives detailed information on hotels and other lodging they sanction and provides links to accommodation reservation centers (but the Web site doesn't tell you about special rates). Some lodging sites specialize in a particular type of accommodation, such as bed-and-breakfast accommodations, which you won't find on the more mainstream booking services. Others offer weekend deals on major chain properties that cater to business travelers and have more empty rooms on weekends. And finally, some individual hotels will offer an "Internet bonus" for a reservation made on their personal Web site. Therefore, checking out some of the online lodging sites, many of which offer discounts, is in your best interest.

Hotel Discounts (www.hoteldiscounts.com), offers bargain room rates at hotels in more than two dozen U.S. and international cities. The service prebooks blocks of rooms in advance, so sometimes it has rooms —

at discount rates — at hotels that otherwise are considered sold out. **TravelWeb** (www.travelweb.com) lists more than 16,000 hotels worldwide, focusing on chains such as Hyatt and Hilton, and you can book almost 90 percent of these online. **France Hotels Online** (www.france-hotel-online.com) offers detailed listings of independent hotels, apartments, and bed-and-breakfasts according to budget and neighborhood. **All Hotels on the Web** (www.all-hotels.com) lists tens of thousands of lodgings throughout the world. (The hotels on this site pay a fee to be listed.) **Places to Stay** (www.placestostay.com) lists inns, B&Bs, resorts, hotels, and properties you may not find anywhere else. **Hostelworld** (www.hostelworld.com) lists youth hostels and cheap hotel deals in Paris and major cities around the world and offers ratings written by former clients of the various accommodations. Budget travelers can find excellent deals here.

Arriving Without a Reservation

If you arrive in Paris without a reservation, you have two choices. You can pick up a phone and start dialing (after you purchase a phone card for public phones at the nearest *tabac,* a cafe or kiosk that sells tobacco products). Or you can walk into one of the branches of the **Paris Convention and Visitors Bureau** and let the multilingual staff make you a reservation. The main switchboard for any branch is ☎ **08-92-68-30-00** (.34€/mn). Only the staff at three of the office's six branches offer reservations services, so call before you go. (*Note:* These centers are closed on May 1.).

- ✔ The **Opéra-Grands-Magasins** welcome center, 11 rue Scribe, 9e; open Monday through Saturday 9 a.m. to 6:30 p.m. The main entryway is on the corner of the building; it also shares space with an American Express office and has an American Express sign on the door. (Métro: Chausée d'Antin La Fayette or Opéra; RER: Auber)

- ✔ The welcome kiosk beneath the modern glass roofed terminal of the **Gare du Nord,** 18 rue Dunkerque, 10e; open seven days a week from 8 a.m. to 6 p.m. (Métro and RER: Gare du Nord)

- ✔ The welcome kiosk at the **Gare de Lyon,** 20 bd. Diderot, 12e; open Monday through Saturday 8 a.m. to 6 p.m. (Métro and RER: Gare de Lyon)

Hotels with unsold rooms offer them through the Paris Convention and Visitors Bureau at rock-bottom prices, so you may get a three-star hotel at a two-star price. The staff will make a reservation for you on the same day that you want a room, free of charge, but it must be on a credit card or check card (which will act as a credit card while in a foreign country).

Note that during the summer season, you'll have to wait in a long line, and you aren't guaranteed a room.

Paris's Best Hotels

There are more than 2,200 hotels in Paris ranging from small alcove singles in historic buildings to the historic and palatial that anticipate a traveler's every need. But only around 50 are described here. The reason? You don't need an overwhelming, encyclopedic list of all the hotels, just ones that are right for you, and an equally right backup in case your first choice is booked solid. In compiling this list, the first step was considering the typical traveler's wish list. And for most of you, the main priority is location. Thus, the first criterion, though ruthless, was simple.

If a hotel isn't located in the first eight arrondissements, it isn't recommended in this book.

The second concern was price. The most expensive category listed here, $$$$, contains hotels that cost more than 300€ ($360) a night, which is expensive by nearly anyone's standards. Only a few hotels described here fall into the $$$$ category because most travelers are on a budget. (For a complete rundown on the $ system, see Table 9-1.) Three-quarters of the hotels in this chapter rent doubles for less than 150€ ($180) night but nevertheless give you comfort, some nice amenities, and that *frisson* of Parisian character for which the city's hotels are known. And none of the hotels listed here is a dive.

Finally, a variety of neighborhoods between the first and eighth arrondissements is represented here with a nice range of styles from conservative to trendy. The aim? We want to make sure that everyone is accounted for, regardless of budget, taste, or style of travel.

In this chapter, two maps pinpoint the locations of the hotels: "Hotels in the Heart of the Right Bank" and "Hotels in the Heart of the Left Bank." Reviews are arranged alphabetically for easy reference. Hotels that are especially good for families are designated with the kid-friendly icon. Listed immediately beneath the name of the hotel is the neighborhood in which it's located and the number of dollar signs corresponding to the hotel's rack rates, from the cheapest double room in low season to the most expensive in high season. At chapter's end are indexes of accommodations by price and neighborhood for easy reference.

Almost all hotels service breakfast in some form. Note that a normal *petit déjeuner* (breakfast), also referred to as *continental,* will usually include coffee or tea, juice, a croissant, *pain au chocolat* (a croissant with a thin thread of chocolate filling) or similar pastry, and toast with various *confitures* (jams). If a hotel also offers *un petit déjeuner Américain* (American breakfast), it means they offer a buffet with eggs and meats — this breakfast will probably be more filling than the tiny little French breakfasts!

Hotels in the Heart of the Right Bank (1–4, 8–12, & 16–18)

Castex Hôtel **23**
Citadines Les Halles Aparthotel **16**
Citadines Louvre Aparthotel **9**
Citadines Paris Opéra-Grands
   Boulevards Aparthotel **6**
Four Seasons George V **4**
Hôtel Agora **15**

Hôtel Alison **2**
Hôtel de L'Elysée **2**
Hôtel de la Place des Vosges **22**
Hôtel des Deux-Iles **18**
Hôtel du Jeu de Paume **19**
Hôtel du Vieux Saule **13**
Hôtel Jeanne d'Arc **20**

Castex Hôtel
$$ Le Marais (4e)

Less than five minutes from one of Paris's most famous brasseries, Bofinger, the Castex is a popular budget classic, near *everything* in the eastern part of the Marais. Each large room has a writing table or a desk and chair; some have views overlooking the courtyard. The renovations of the exterior have resulted in a pleasant entry to a wonderful, family-owned space. Staff is friendly and accommodating. Rooms don't have televisions, but you can watch TV or read the papers in the TV salon. Reserve at least a month in advance. The Café de la Poste is located just a few doors away at 13 rue Castex, to gently ease just-arrived travelers into the Paris lifestyle.

See map p. 104. 5 rue Castex. ☎ *01-42-72-31-52. Fax: 01-42-72-57-91.* www.castex hotel.com. *Métro: Bastille or Sully-Morland. Rates: 85€–115€ ($102–$138) single; 100€–140€ ($120–$168) double; 190€–220€ ($228–$264) triple/quad. Breakfast 10€ ($12). AE, DC, MC, V.*

Citadines Les Halles Aparthotel
$$–$$$ Louvre (1er)

Staying here is like living in your own high-rise apartment in Paris. Studios and one-bedrooms have fully equipped kitchenettes, and services include a 24-hour reception desk, satellite TV, air-conditioning, housekeeping, baby-equipment rental, and laundry facilities. The Les Halles neighborhood is a bit shady at night, so if you're a single traveler, this hotel may not be the best bet.

See map p. 104. 4 rue des Innocents (91m/299 ft. from the Forum des Halles). ☎ *01-40-39-26-50.* www.citadines.com. *Métro: Les Halles. Rates: 135€–255€ ($185–$306). AE, MC, V.*

Citadines Louvre Aparthotel
$$$ Louvre (1er)

This seven-story aparthotel is in a terrific location in an upscale and pretty neighborhood just opposite the Comédie-Française and next to the Jardin du Palais-Royal. It has several studios (each with a double fold-out sofa) and apartments equipped for travelers with disabilities. Studios and one-bedrooms (a separate bedroom with two single beds and pull-out double sofa) have fully equipped kitchenettes, and services include a 24-hour reception desk, satellite TV, air-conditioning, housekeeping, baby-equipment rental, and laundry facilities. Book well in advance.

See map p. 104. 8 rue de Richelieu (1 block north of the Louvre). ☎ *01-55-35-28-00.* www.citadines.com. *Métro: Palais-Royal or Pyramides. Rates: 180€–305€ ($216–$366). AE, MC, V.*

Citadines Paris Opéra-Grands Boulevards Aparthotel
$$$–$$$$ Opéra (2e)

Around the corner from the Opéra Comique and the Comédie-Française and near the Grands Boulevards, this five-story aparthotel is the most central in the Citadines chain. It's located in a peaceful passage, and rooms come with fully equipped kitchenettes; available services include a 24-hour reception desk, satellite TV, Internet, air-conditioning, baby-equipment rental, dry cleaning, laundry facilities, housekeeping, bar, billiards table, and fitness center. A one-bedroom apartment here (two single beds in the bedroom, a double pull-out couch) can be a good alternative to renting two rooms in a cheap hotel because cooking in the kitchenette saves on your dining costs.

See map p. 104. 18 rue Favart. ☎ *01-40-15-14-00.* www.citadines.fr. *Métro: Richelieu-Drouot. Rates: 120€–138€ ($144–$166) per night 1–6 days, 157€–177€ ($188–$212) 7–29 days for a 2-person studio; 251€–281€ ($301–$337) 1–6 days, 220€–247€ ($264–$296) per night 7–29 days for a 3-person duplex (1 bedroom) apt.; 271€–300€ ($325–$360) per night 1–6 days, 240€–285€ ($288–$342) 7–29 days 4-person (1 bedroom) apt. AE, MC, V.*

Familia Hôtel
$–$$ Latin Quarter (5e)

In this hotel owned by the Gaucherons, flowers spill out of window boxes; the stone walls in some of the bedrooms have been painstakingly restored or have had provincial-inspired wallpaper added. In other rooms, artists from l'École des Beaux-Arts (Paris's best art school) have painted sepia-toned murals of Parisian scenes. The cozy lobby exudes the atmosphere of a tiny castle with rich tapestries, a winding staircase, and frescoed walls. Some rooms have balconies (numbers 22, 23, 52, 53, 61, 62, 65) with captivating views of the Latin Quarter. From the fifth and sixth floors, you can see Notre-Dame. Bathrooms are small but modern and tiled. All rooms have cable TV and hair dryers. The staff provides kid-friendly services (such as bottle heating) and larger rooms for the weary traveler who requests ahead. Take note that most rooms in the hotel are on the small side, and the least expensive doubles in the corners are tiny. No air-conditioning is provided — remember that it can get hot in Paris heat waves! Located on rue des Ecoles, which is full of interesting people-watching, movie theaters featuring classic cinema of France and America, great cafes, and such attractions as the Jardin des Plantes and the Arenes de Lutece are down the street.

See map p. 108. 11 rue des Écoles. ☎ *01-43-54-55-27. Fax: 01-43-29-61-77.* www.hotel-paris-familia.com. *Métro: Cardinal Lemoine or Jussieu. Parking: 20€ ($24). Rates: 74€–85€ ($89–$102) single; 95€–115€ ($114–$138) double; 136€ ($163) triple; 152€ ($182) quad; 105€ ($126) single or double with balcony. Breakfast 6€ ($7.20). AE, DC, MC, V.*

Hotels in the Heart of the Left Bank (5–7 & 13–14)

Familia Hôtel **17**	Hôtel de Fleurie **8**
Grand Hôtel de Suez **10**	Hôtel de l'Abbaye Saint-Germain **6**
Grand Hôtel des Balcons **9**	Hôtel de Seine **7**
Grand Hôtel Lévêque **3**	Hôtel du Champ de Mars **2**
Hôtel Amélie **1**	Hôtel du Lys **11**
Hôtel Claude-Bernard **14**	Hôtel Esmeralda **12**

Hôtel Henri IV **18**
Hôtel le Tourville **2**
Hôtel Lindbergh **4**
Hôtel Marignan **13**
Hôtel Minerve **16**
Hôtel Prince **1**

Hôtel St-Jacques **15**
Hôtel Saints-Pères **5**

Four Seasons George V
$$$$ **Champs-Elysées (8e)**

This is one of Paris's truly legendary palace hotels. When the Four Seasons bought the slightly decaying George V in the late 1990s, they restored fixtures such as the Murano chandeliers and Louis XIV tapestries, yet added modern touches, too. The molding on the ceilings and tall mirrors demonstrate the classic French attention to detail — also look out for reproduction Greek statues and murals of beautiful Arabic script. From the elegant light-wood-and-marble lobby opening onto an outside marble courtyard decorated with bright blue awnings and umbrellas, to the cascading displays of fresh flowers, to the friendly welcome of the team of concierges, you'll wake up happy to be staying here. The 245 rooms, separated from the public corridors by their own hallways for more peace and quiet, start at 42 sq. m (450 sq. ft.), are decorated with Louis XVI–style furniture, have marble bathrooms, stereo systems, and VCRs, and have Wi-Fi Internet access. The Honeymoon Suite has three terraces, and other suites offer a stone's-throw view of the Eiffel Tower — some from their bathtubs. Amenities include the signature Four Season mattresses (930 coils instead of the industry-standard 800), a spa (with its own elevator) offering 24-hour massages and a huge pool, an American bar, and a multistarred gourmet restaurant, Le Cinq (reviewed in Chapter 10). Check online for package deals that include daily breakfast at Le Cinq.

See map p. 104. 31 av. George V, 1½ blocks from the Champs-Elysées. ☎ *01-49-52-70-00. Fax: 01-49-52-70-10. Métro: George V. Rates: 710€–910€ ($852–$1,092) double; 1,290€–9,500€ ($1,548–$11,400) suite. Continental breakfast at Le Cinq 33€ ($40); American breakfast 45€ ($54), or a Japanese breakfast at 47€ ($56). You can also have breakfast in the hotel gallery itself, the "petit déjeuner parisien" at 35€ ($42) and "déjeuner Americain" at 37€ ($44), which is a continental breakfast plus cereal. AE, DC, MC, V.*

Grand Hôtel des Balcons
$$–$$$ **St-Germain-des-Prés (6e)**

Steps from Théâtre de l'Odéon is this gracious and comfortable hotel with balconied rooms, modern light oak furnishings, bright fabrics, 19th-century stained-glass windows, and Art Nouveau lobby furnishings (look for the voluptuous statue of Venus in the breakfast room). Although most rooms and their wrought-iron balconies are small, clever use of space allows for large closets and full-length mirrors. Bathrooms are also small but well designed and come equipped with a clothesline. The higher-priced doubles, triples, and quads are big and luxurious; some have double-sink bathrooms. All rooms have satellite television and Internet access. If you're celebrating your birthday while in Paris, treat yourself to a stay here; the sumptuous and filling breakfast buffet (which includes sausage and eggs) is free for the birthday boy or girl. The Jardin du Luxembourg is a five-minute walk south.

See map p. 108. 3 rue Casimir Delavigne. ☎ *01-46-34-78-50. Fax: 01-46-34-06-27.* www.hotelgrandsbalcons.com. *Métro: Odéon. RER: Luxembourg. Rates:*

85€–125€ ($102–$150) single; 110€–160€ ($132–$192) double; 200€ ($240) triple. Buffet breakfast 10€ ($12), free on your birthday. AE, DC, MC, V.

Grand Hôtel de Suez
$–$$ Latin Quarter (5e)

Guests return for this hotel's 49 good-sized rooms at great prices at this hotel in a great Latin Quarter location. Beds are firm, storage space is ample, and the modern bathrooms have hair dryers. Décor is typical modern hotel: a comfortable mirrored lobby furnished with couches and art nouveau lamps, rooms with striped or flowered bedspreads, and curtains with color-coordinated artwork and blonde furniture. Each room has satellite TV with 30 channels and Wi-Fi is available throughout the whole building. But you may want to keep the windows to the street-side balconies shut — the Boulevard St-Michel is as noisy as a carnival way past midnight on weekends. The hotel is near Musée de Cluny, Jardin du Luxembourg, and the Panthéon. The Seine and Notre-Dame are a ten-minute walk away. There is a high-speed Internet access terminal in the salon.

See map p. 108. 31 bd. St-Michel. ☎ 01-53-10-34-00. Fax: 01-40-51-79-44. www.hotel desuez.fr. *Métro: St-Michel. Rates: 70€–125€ ($84–$150) single; 75€–130€ ($90–$156) double; 110€–155€ ($132–$186) triple. Breakfast 5€ ($6). AE, DC, MC, V.*

Grand Hôtel Lévêque
$ Eiffel Tower (7e)

This 1930s-era hotel has two amenities that many Parisian hotels do not: air-conditioning and an elevator! It's just three blocks from the Eiffel Tower on a colorful pedestrian street with the bustling rue Cler market, bakeries, restaurants, a terrific crêpe stand, wine shops, florists. The lobby has a comfortable lounge area with plush circular sofas, a soda- and ice-dispenser, and a daily newspaper. Rooms are snug, with just enough space to be comfortable, and have new, if not inspired, decorations. The bathrooms are small but in excellent condition, and each room has a satellite TV, hair dryer, Internet access, and ceiling fan. Staff members are very friendly and helpful, and if you ask, they may be able to give you a higher-priced room on the fifth floor with a balcony and partial view of the Eiffel Tower. This hotel fills up fast, so book well in advance. Street-side rooms (which have good views) cost a little more than interior rooms; as always, check online for deals.

See map p. 108. 29 rue Cler (where rue Cler meets rue de Grenelle). ☎ 01-47-05-49-15. Fax: 01-45-50-49-36. www.hotel-leveque.com. *Métro: École-Militaire or Latour-Maubourg. Rates: 57€ ($68) single room without bathroom; 87€–93€ ($104–$112) double bed with bathroom; 87€–110€ ($104–$132) twin beds with bathroom; 125€ ($150) triple (the third bed is "for children only") with bathroom. Breakfast 8€ ($9.60). AE, MC, V.*

Hôtel Agora
$–$$ Louvre (1er)

Don't worry about the ugly entryway here; it's a disguise for a very good find. This two-star hotel on a busy pedestrian street near Les Halles has a traditional French air once you mount a curved staircase (after the initial climb, an elevator leads from reception to upper floors) to its eclectic reception area. Rooms have antique furniture, marble mantelpieces, floral prints, and old-fashioned wallpapers. The windows are double-glazed, thankfully, which helps muffle the outside noise. The bathrooms are decently sized; some have bathtubs and even bidets, an often confusing French charm, which is rarely offered at hotels with such reasonable prices. Fifth-floor rooms have balconies with views of the impressive St-Eustache Church.

See map p. 104. 7 rue de la Cossonnerie. ☎ *01-42-33-46-02. Fax: 01-42-33-80-99.* www.parisby.com/agora. *Métro: Châtelet. Rates: 110€–116€ ($132–$139) single; 133€–136€ ($160–$163) double; 146€ ($175) triple. Breakfast 10€ ($12). AE, MC, V.*

Hôtel Alison
$$ Madeleine (8e)

Located between the Madeleine and the Elysée Palace and near the Champs-Elysées and rue Faubourg St-Honoré, this hotel has a retro 1970s ambience that somehow manages to be perfectly in tune with the classy neighborhood. The large, well-appointed rooms are furnished in modern style, with black furniture and light walls, and have plenty of storage space, a safe, minibar, trouser press, satellite TV, Internet access, and double-glazed windows. Hair dryers and Roger & Gallet toiletries grace gleaming, tiled bathrooms with wall-mounted showers. You can relax on low, orange-leather couches in the plush lobby or enjoy a drink in the vaulted brick lounge. Breakfast is served under a vaulted stone ceiling that is a signature of historical Parisian buildings.

See map p. 104. 21 rue de Surène. ☎ *01-42-65-54-00. Fax: 01-42-65-08-17.* www.hotel-alison.com. *Métro: Madeleine or Concorde. Rates: 79€–142€ ($95–$170) single; 112€–142€ ($134–$170) double; 129€–142€ ($155–$170) twin beds; 160€ ($192) triple; 204€–284€ ($245–$341) for two adjoining rooms. Breakfast 8€ ($9.60). AE, DC, MC, V.*

Hôtel Amélie
$ Eiffel Tower (7e)

This is a modest 16-room hotel bedecked with blooming flowers overflowing pots at each window. The renovated rooms are small with tiny closets, but the white-tiled bathrooms offer hair dryers and good-quality toiletries. Nothing is exceptional about the appearance of the rooms, but they are clean and well kept and often have small writing desks. The location is excellent for seeing such seventh arrondissement sights as the Eiffel Tower and Napoléon's Tomb, yet the atmosphere is peaceful, almost serene. Stroll down nearby rue Cler for some great fruit and veggie markets or for an expert crêpe made by a lovely Greek *vendeur* who has been there for years. There is no elevator. The owners often have special seasonal promotions; in summer 2006 rooms were offered at up to 20€ ($24) off of low-season rates!

See map p. 108. 5 rue Amélie. ☎ *01-45-51-74-75. Fax: 01-45-56-93-55.* www.hotel amelie.fr. *Métro: Latour-Maubourg. Rates: 70€–90€ ($86–$94) single; 80€–100€ ($96–$120) double with shower; 95€–110€ ($114–$132) double with tub; 90€–120€ ($108–$144) twin beds. Breakfast: 7€ ($8.40) free. Check Web site for special offers July–Aug. AE, DC, MC, V.*

Hôtel Claude-Bernard
$$–$$$ Latin Quarter (5e)

This highly recommended hotel keeps very high standards and wins much repeat business. The red exterior is chic without pretension; inside features a lobby bar (but it's not manned by a regular bartender; you have to ask at reception if you want to be served), a lounge area with comfortable chairs and a two-person elevator. The decently sized rooms have warm and tasteful wallpaper, sleek bathrooms, minibars, Wi-Fi, satellite TV, decorative balconies with flowers, and often a well-preserved piece of antique furniture. Some particularly attractive suites come with couches and armchairs. A sauna is available for guests to use, and all rooms are air-conditioned. Nearby are the Panthéon, the Sorbonne, and the fantastic Cluny Museum. Check the Web site for promotions and "last-minute" deals.

See map p. 108. 43 rue des Écoles. ☎ *01-43-26-32-52. Fax: 01-43-26-80-56.* www.paris-hotel-booking.com. *Métro: Maubert-Mutualité. Rates: 96€–149€ ($115–$175) single; 114€–174€ ($137–$209) double; 150€–218€ ($180–$262) triple; 189€–284€ ($227–$341) quad. Continental breakfast 7.90€ ($9.50). AE, DC, MC, V.*

Hôtel de Fleurie
$$$–$$$$ St-Germain-des-Prés (6e)

Just off place Odéon on a pretty side street, the Fleurie has all the comforts, including air-conditioning, marble bathrooms with heated towel racks, quality toiletries, Oriental carpets, high-speed Internet connections, and satellite TV. The jewel-toned rooms are small but comfortable, and all are furnished in a modern or classic style with such touches as fresh flowers, pretty gingham curtains, and wood-paneled accents. Book at least six weeks in advance for one of the *chambres familiales* — two connecting rooms with two large beds in each room. A continental breakfast is served in the cozy vaulted stone cellar dining room; the selection of different home-style jams is sure to please. The Marolleau family has owned this superb hotel since 1988 and earned many repeat visitors not only for the rooms but for the friendly staff, and a superb location near the church of St-Germain-des-Prés, the historic Café de Flore, Café les Deux Magots, and Brasserie Lipp. It's a few blocks from the Seine and the Jardin du Luxembourg. As with all hotels, check the Web site for specials deals or last-minute offers under "promotions."

See map p. 108. 32–34 rue de Grégoire-de-Tours. ☎ *01-53-73-70-00. Fax: 01-53-73-70-20.* www.fleurie-hotel-paris.com. *Métro: Odéon. Rates: 135€–150€*

single ($162–$180); 170€–190€ ($204–$228) double with queen-size bed; 270€ ($324) deluxe rooms (large room with 2 twin beds or 1 king-size bed); 300€–340€ ($360–$408) family suite. Breakfast 12€ ($14). AE, DC, MC, V.

Hôtel de l'Abbaye Saint-Germain
$$$–$$$$ St-Germain-des-Prés (6e)

This former convent is a popular stop for travelers on a budget who have a taste for chic surroundings. You enter through a courtyard and check in at the reception desk, which is in the convent's original vault. Some of the 42 rooms and two- and four-bedroom suites have their original exposed oak ceiling beams, 19th-century-style furnishings and damask upholstery; all are air-conditioned, with hair dryers, and satellite TV. The rooms are a good size by Paris standards, and the suites are absolutely spacious. The style of décor is modern with funky bedspreads and framed drawings and prints of famous Andy Warhol creations. Some first-floor rooms open onto a vine-covered terrace; late Italian actor Marcello Mastroianni preferred room no. 3. Rooftop suites have terraces. In summer you can eat breakfast — included in the price of your room — in the flower-filled courtyard; in winter, you can lounge in front of the lobby fireplace. The hotel provides a money-changing service.

See map p. 108. 10 rue Cassette, 4 short blocks from the northwest corner of the Jardin du Luxembourg. ☎ 01-45-44-38-11. Fax: 01-45-48-07-86. www.hotel-abbaye.com. *Métro: St-Sulpice. Rates: 205€–305€ ($246–$366) double room; 380€ ($456) suite; 420€ ($504) duplex suite. Rates include breakfast. AE, MC, V.*

Hôtel de la Place des Vosges
$$–$$$ Le Marais (4e)

The entrance to the place des Vosges is only steps away from this hotel which used to be the stables of King Henri IV. Now the exposed stone walls and beamed ceilings complement a plush, antiques-filled lobby. The small rooms have beamed ceilings, satin-cotton blend bed sheets with anti-allergen spreads and tiled bathrooms. All rooms have satellite TVs (suspended by a chain from the ceiling), Wi-Fi, safes, desks, and hair dryers, but there is a lack of storage space. The larger top-floor room (no. 10) has a pretty view over the Right Bank and a Jacuzzi, but the elevator stops a floor down, which is a consideration if you have a lot of luggage.

See map p. 104. 12 rue de Birague. ☎ 01-42-72-60-46. Fax: 01-42-72-02-64. www.hotelplacedesvosges.com. *Métro: Bastille. Rates: 107€–140€ ($128–$168) single, double, or twin beds with shower or tub; 207€–300€ ($248–$360) top-floor room with shower, tub, or Jacuzzi. Breakfast 7€ ($8.40). MC, V.*

Hôtel de L'Elysée
$$$ Champs-Elysées (8e)

Wallpaper of stamped 18th-century etchings, built-in closets, half-headboards and stucco ceilings are just some of the touches added to this hotel during a recent renovation. The wonderful, but small mansard suite no. 60 features wood beams overhead and skylights set into the low, sloping ceilings that provide peek-a-boo vistas of Parisian rooftops, including a perfectly framed view of the Eiffel Tower. All fifth- and sixth-floor rooms enjoy at least rooftop views, the former from small balconies (nos. 50–53 offer glimpses of the Eiffel Tower).

See map p. 104. 12 rue des Saussaies (off rue Faubourg St-Honoré at place Beauvau, 2 blocks north of Champs-Elysées). ☎ **01-42-65-29-25.** *Fax: 01-42-65-64-28.* www.france-hotel-guide.com/h75008efsh.htm. *Métro: Champs-Elysées-Clemenceau or Miromesnil. Rates: 145€–230€ ($174–$276) double. Breakfast 12€ ($14). AE, DC, MC, V.*

Hôtel des Deux-Îles
$$–$$$ Ile St-Louis (4e)

This appealing jewel box of a hotel is superbly located on the Ile St-Louis (practically in Notre-Dame's backyard). The owners are interior decorators, and it shows; the 17 rooms have exposed oak ceiling beams and provincial upholstery, and the lobby is a warm and cozy gem with fresh flowers and bamboo furniture. Off the lobby is a garden that some of the rooms overlook and a basement breakfast room with a fireplace. Although amenities include bathrooms, hair dryers, cable TV, Wi-Fi and air-conditioning, rooms run from tiny to small, so if you have a large amount of luggage, you may want to look elsewhere. Paris's best ice cream shop, Berthillon (closed in Aug), is just around the corner, and you can find Berthillon ice cream in nearby brasseries, too. So much is nearby — the Memorial de la Déportation, which commemorates the French Jews sent to Auschwitz; Sainte-Chapelle; the Conciergerie; and the bird and flower markets on Ile de la Cité, to name only a few — you may not know where to begin. *Hint:* Start early in the morning with Notre-Dame.

See map p. 104. 59 rue St-Louis-en-l'Ile. ☎ **01-43-26-13-35.** *Fax: 01-43-29-60-25.* www.hotel-ile-saintlouis.com. *Métro: Pont Marie. Rates: 150€ ($180) single with shower; 170€ ($204) double or twin beds. Breakfast 11€ ($13). AE, V.*

Hôtel de Seine
$$–$$$ St-Germain-des-Près (6e)

More like a private mansion than a hotel, the Hôtel de Seine is centrally located on a street full of art galleries in St-Germain-des-Près, between boulevard St-Germain and rue Jacob. It's a few blocks from the Seine and the pedestrian bridge Pont des Arts that leads to the Louvre. Each room is distinctly decorated with either French provincial furniture and flowered wallpaper or Provence-inspired jewel-toned paint and Louis XVI reproductions. Rooms have satellite TV, marble bathrooms, hair dryers. Check the Web site for specials and promotions.

See map p. 108. 52 rue de Seine. ☎ **01-46-34-22-80.** *Fax: 01-46-34-04-74.* www.paris-hotel-seine-river.com. *Métro: St-Germain-des-Près, Mabillon. Rates: 140€– 150€ ($168–$180) single; 160€–170€ ($192–$204) double; 170€–180€ ($204–$216) twin; 205€–215€ ($246–$258) triple. Breakfast 10€ ($12); breakfast served in room 11€ ($13). V.*

Hôtel du Champ de Mars
$–$$ Eiffel Tower (7e)

This 25-room hotel is like a country house tucked away on a colorful street near the Eiffel Tower, and it's a bargain that's hard to beat. The proprietors, the Gourdals, have decorated the rooms with flowered drapes, fabric-covered headboards, throw pillows, and cushioned high-backed seats. Along with the countryside feel are modern urban amenities: satellite TV and bathrooms with hair dryers, large towels, and good lighting; those with tubs have wall-mounted showers. A cozy breakfast room is located in the remodeled basement. Reserve at least four months in advance. In the summer, the two best rooms are on the ground floor and open onto the leafy courtyard; they stay cool despite the lack of air-conditioning. A grocery store is two doors down for travelers needing provisions at 27 rue Cler, and the rue Cler outdoor market (open Tuesday-Sunday mornings) is right around the corner.

See map p. 108. 7 rue du Champ de Mars. ☎ *01-45-51-52-30. Fax: 01-45-51-64-36.* www.hotel-du-champ-de-mars.com. *Métro: École-Militaire. RER: Pont de l'Alma. Rates: 78€–84€ ($94–$101) single with shower; 84€ ($101) double with tub; 88€ ($106) twin beds with tub; 105€ ($126) triple. Breakfast 7€ ($8.40). AE, MC, V.*

Hôtel du Jeu de Paume
$$$$ Ile Saint-Louis (4e)

The impressive, airy, three-story, ancient wood skeleton inside this former *jeu de paume* (a precursor to tennis) court incorporates public lounges, an indoor breakfast terrace, a hanging corridor, and a glass elevator. Most accommodations are on the snug to medium size, but the simplicity of the stylishly modern décor under hewn beams keeps rooms from feeling cramped. The three standard duplexes with spiral stairs are roomier (and don't cost any more than a double), but if you are staying five days or longer and want true bliss, check into the 900€ ($1,080) apartment, a duplex with two bedrooms and living room below and bedroom above, two baths, and a private terrace overlooking the small stone garden rimmed with flowers where guests — the suite can accommodate five people — can breakfast in nice weather. A 600€ ($720) two-bedroom apt is also available for stays of five days or longer.

54 rue Saint-Louis-en-L'Ile. ☎ *01-43-26-14-18. Fax: 01-40-46-02-76.* www.jeude paumehotel.com. *Métro: Pont-Marie. Rates: 205€–545€ ($246–$402) double; 350€–545€ ($420–$654) suite. Breakfast 18€ ($22). AE, DC, MC, V.*

Hôtel du Lys
$$ St-Germain-des-Prés (6e)

Hôtel du Lys is the perfect place for a romantic tryst on a budget. Housed in a 17th-century mansion with original tall casement windows, the homey, intimate rooms are decorated in floral wallpaper with exposed-beam high ceilings. Rooms feature double glazing to keep out the noise, and rooms 19 and 22 have balconies. People with disabilities need to heed the lack of an elevator, and the staircase, although historic, is narrow. The Lys is just a few blocks from the Seine and Notre-Dame in an area that gets quite crowded in summer; fortunately, a room here is a haven — and breakfast is included.

See map p. 108. 23 rue Serpente. ☎ *01-43-26-97-57. Fax: 01-44-07-34-90. Métro: St-Michel or Odéon. Rates: 95€ ($114) single; 115€ ($138) double; 130€ ($156) triple. Rates include breakfast. MC, V.*

Hôtel du Vieux Saule
$–$$ Le Marais/Bastille (3e)

This hotel in the Marais near place de la République offers not only air-conditioning but a free sauna, too. Ironic, perhaps, considering the giant display of cacti and other desert plants in the lobby — a welcome unique feel compared to other Parisian hotels. The cheerful, but small, rooms have tiled bathrooms, hair dryers, safes, double-glazed windows, luggage racks, Wi-Fi, satellite TV, trouser presses, and even small irons and ironing boards. The rooms on the fifth floor tend to be bigger. Breakfast is a buffet served in the original 16th-century cozy vaulted cellar accessed by a winding staircase (no elevator). Check online for promotions.

See map p. 104. 6 rue de Picardie. ☎ *01-42-72-01-14. Fax: 01-40-27-88-21.* www.hotel vieuxsaule.com. *Métro: République. Parking: 12€ ($14) for 12 hours. Rates: 91€ ($109) single with shower; 121€–136€ ($145–$163) double with shower or tub; 136€–151€ ($163–$187) deluxe double; 166€ ($199) triple. Buffet breakfast 10€ ($12). AE, DC, MC, V.*

Hôtel Esmeralda
$–$$ Latin Quarter (5e)

It's off-beat and ramshackle with creaky wood floors and cramped hallways (and even dusty in some places), but its superior location just steps away from the Seine and Notre-Dame and its prices — a budget traveler's dream — make this a favorite of many travelers, and you may have to book as far in advance as three months. However, if you prefer hotels with such amenities as satellite TV, free toiletries, or space, then the Esmeralda is probably not for you. There are an old, winding wooden staircase (no elevator) and outstanding views of Notre-Dame and the Seine from the hotel's front rooms (make sure to specify these rooms when you reserve). East rooms overlook St-Julien-le-Pauvre and square Viviani. Shabby-chic velvet coverings and antique furniture create homey warmth that almost makes up for the disappointingly dark rear rooms. The front rooms with a view have modern bathrooms with tubs, and some are exceptionally large for the location and relative size of this hotel, making them perfect for travelers with children.

See map p. 108. 4 rue St-Julien-le-Pauvre. ☎ *01-43-54-19-20. Fax: 01-40-51-00-68. Métro: St-Michel. Rates: 35€ ($42) single with sink; 65€ ($78) double; 85€ ($102) double with view of Notre-Dame; 95€ ($114) double with bathroom; 110€ ($132) triple; 120€ ($144) quad. Breakfast 6€ ($7.20). Shower 2€ ($2.40) per person. No credit cards.*

Hôtel Henri IV
$ Louvre (1er)

This place is old. It doesn't have an elevator; only five rooms have showers or tubs, only two have toilets, and none have phones. The stairs are
creaky, and no matter how old you may be, this place will make you feel
young in comparison. But this super-budget hotel is one of Europe's most
famous and nearly always is full. It occupies a dramatic location on place
Dauphine — the northernmost tip of Ile de la Cité, across the river from St-
Germain and the Louvre and a few steps from Pont-Neuf. The 17th-century
building houses cozy rooms that are past their prime, though many find
them romantically evocative (others think they're just run down). Each
room has a sink, but guests share the spotless toilets and showers on each
of the five floors. One of the communal bathrooms has an enormous tub,
and a few rooms have beautiful views of place Dauphine. All in all, staying
here is an adventure. Book far in advance.

See map p. 108. 25 place Dauphine. ☎ *01-43-54-44-53. Métro: Pont Neuf. Rates: 27€–*
35€ ($32–$42) single with sink; 47€ ($56) single with shower; 35€ ($42) double with
sink; 47€ ($65) double with shower but no toilet; 58€ ($70) double with toilet and tub
or shower; 70€ ($84) triple. Rates include breakfast. MC, V.

Hôtel Jeanne d'Arc
$–$$ Le Marais (4e)

Reserve well in advance for this great budget hotel on a pretty little street
just off the place St-Catherine. The outside facade has classically beautiful Parisian lanterns to light the way in. Full of eccentric furniture and
countryside touches, the managers insist that it is unique among Parisian
hotels. Soft tangerine colored wallpaper decorates the halls of the ground
floor, except for the fresh white dining area with billowing white curtains
and the blue sitting area directly down the hall from the entrance.
Reception is through a door on the right where I was delighted to see hanging on the wall the hotel's signature mosaic mirror tribute to French pride.
Rooms are small to decent-sized with large windows, card-key access, and
large bathrooms, but storage space is a bit cramped. Other room features
include direct-dial telephones, cable TV, and bedside tables. If a view is
important, make sure you request one because some rooms don't have
one. The hotel is in the center of the Marais, and it can be a little noisy,
but you're near the Musée Picasso, place des Vosges, and the Bastille, and
the fabulous Au Bistro de la Place cafe is in the square next door.

See map p. 104. 3 rue de Jarente. ☎ *01-48-87-62-11. Fax: 01-48-87-37-31.* www.hotel
jeannedarc.com. *Métro: St-Paul or Bastille. Rates: 58–72€ ($70–$86) single; 82€–97€*
($98–$116) double; 116€ ($139) triple; 146€ ($175) quad. Breakfast 6€ ($7.20). MC, V.

Hôtel le Faubourg Paris, Sofitel Demeure
$$$$ Champs-Elysées (8e)

If you want a luxurious but cozy place to stay near the Jardins des
Tuileries, the Louvre, and Place Vendôme shopping, Le Faubourg is the

spot. Opened in 1999, Le Faubourg is comprised of two buildings — one 18th-century, the other 19th-century and formerly the offices of *Marie Claire* magazine (reflected in the décor: a mix of contemporary and classic styles, with feng shui touches). The 174 rooms are decently sized, and all are comfortable and quiet, with stone bathtubs and terrycloth bathrobes for added comfort. In fact, the short-stay, one-person Classic rooms are small without being the least bit claustrophobic. If you want a specific feature — a balcony, a view, high ceilings — be sure to ask when booking your room. All rooms include Sofitel's cloud-like "MyBed" and thoughtful touches such as bottles of Evian, Lenôtre chocolates, a card of recommended jogging routes in the nearby gardens, and Roger & Gallet toiletries (suites and the apartment kick it up a notch with Hermès toiletries), satellite television with pay movies and video games, air-conditioning, CD players, Wi-Fi, minibars, and hair dryers. The hotel is frequented primarily by business travelers, including fashionistas in town for the biannual shows, but such celebrity guests as David Bowie and Plácido Domingo seem to appreciate Le Faubourg's low-key, high-quality accommodations and the relaxed, personalized service. Complimentary coffee is served in the library (yes, there is a library) every morning, and Bar30 has live music Monday through Saturday from 7 p.m. till 1:30 a.m. There is a very small fitness center available. Be sure to ask about packages and special rates in July and August, when business is a bit slower. Baby-sitting is available.

See map p. 104. 15 rue Boissy d'Anglas. ☎ *800/SOFITEL or 01-44-94-14-00. Fax:* ☎ *01-44-95-14-28.* www.sofitel.com. *Métro: Concorde. Parking: 25€ ($30). Rates: 435€–535€ ($522–$642) single; 495€–600€ ($594–$720) double; 575€–1,213€ ($690–$1,456) suite; 2,000€–2,500€ ($2,400–$3,000) apartment. Breakfast 23€ ($28), American breakfast 27€ ($32). AE, MC, V.*

Hôtel le Tourville
$$–$$$ Eiffel Tower (7e)

This splendid restored mansion, located just steps behind Les Invalides, can be addictive. It boasts a four-star rating: you receive almost all the amenities of a pricier hotel — Roger & Gallet toiletries, hair dryers, air-conditioning, chic décor with antiques — for rates miraculously below four-star prices. Rooms are decorated in soft yellows, pink, or sand, with crisp white damask upholsteries, antique bureaus and lamps, fabulously mismatched old mirrors, and marble bathrooms. Rooms also have satellite TV, hair dryers, and 24-hour room service. You may want to ask for one of the four magnificent rooms with walk-out vine-draped terraces or a junior suite with whirlpool bath. The staff is wonderfully helpful and polite. A grocery store a few doors down is open until 10 p.m., and a *tabac* is right next door.

See map p. 108. 16 av. de Tourville. ☎ *01-47-05-62-62. Fax: 01-47-05-43-90. Métro: École-Militaire. Rates: 170€ ($204) standard double; 220€ ($264) superior double; 250€ ($300) double with private terrace; 310€–330€ ($372–$396) junior suite. Breakfast 12€ ($14). AE, DC.*

Hôtel Lindbergh
$$ St-Germain-des-Prés (7e)

Aviation-themed photos add a tasteful touch to the décor at this pretty hotel named for the American aviator. The standard rooms are simple and delightful, with colorful bedspreads and matching bathrooms. The deluxe rooms have floor-length draperies, fabric headboards, and color-coordinated cushioned seats. The garnet-toned lobby is inviting; you can chat there with the friendly owners who like to talk about their collections of photos that include Charles Lindbergh in his plane, Lindbergh standing with Louis Blériot (the first man to fly across the English Channel), and Lindbergh with Antoine de Saint-Exupéry, the pilot author of *Le Petit Prince*. The hotel is right at the edge of the St-Germain-des-Prés shopping district, and Le Bon Marché department store, with its terrific L'Épicerie supermarket, is only a few short blocks away. The Musée Rodin is within walking distance. Those with energy can hoof the long blocks over to the Eiffel Tower; otherwise catch bus 69 from nearby rue du Bac to the Champ du Mars.

See map p. 108. 5 rue Chomel. ☎ *01-45-48-35-53. Fax: 01-45-49-31-48.* www.hotel lindbergh.com. *Métro: Sévres-Babylone. Rates: 116€–136€ ($139–163) smaller double with shower; 136€–160€ ($163–$192) double (or twin beds) with shower and tub; 156€–180€ ($187–$216) triple; 166€–190€ ($199–$228) quad. Breakfast 8€ ($9.60). AE, MC, V.*

Hôtel Louvre Forum
$ Louvre (1er)

For a truly central, reasonably priced hotel just steps from the Louvre, this comfortable modern hotel is difficult to beat. The brightly colored rooms have tiled bathrooms (with hair dryers) and simple furniture that includes writing tables, lamps, and chairs. Each room has a small armoire with hanging space and shelves; however, the rooms on the lower floors are a bit cramped. The lobby features a mural of the neighborhood, which is only a short walk from the elegant Palais Royal and the Louvre.

See map p. 104. 25 rue du Bouloi. ☎ *01-42-36-54-19. Fax: 01-42-36-66-31.* www.paris-hotel-louvre-forum.com. *Métro: Louvre-Rivoli. Rates: 81€ ($97) single with shower; 91€ ($109) double with shower; 101€ ($121) double with full bathroom. Continental breakfast 9€ ($11). AE, DC, MC, V.*

Hôtel Louvre Richelieu
$–$$ Louvre (1er)

This is a very basic hotel with good-sized rooms and a great location — halfway between the Louvre and the Opéra, but without that touristy hustle-and-bustle. Enter through a corridor with restored stone walls; the pleasant reception area and lobby are on the second floor where the staff is helpful and receptive. The two-bed double rooms are dark, but spacious with high ceilings. Each room has a writing table, a small closet, and a suitcase rack. The lack of an elevator here means that you may want to book elsewhere if you're loaded down with luggage. Reserve at least two weeks in advance for summer. A bakery is right next door.

See map p. 104. 51 rue de Richelieu. ☎ *01-42-97-46-20. Fax: 01-47-03-94-13.* www.louvre-richelieu.com. *Métro: Palais-Royal–Musée du Louvre, Pyramides. Rates: 65€ ($78) single with toilet; 90€ ($108) single with bathroom; 78€ ($94) double with toilet; 90€ ($108) double with bathroom; 94€ ($113) twin with bathroom; 117€ ($140) triple with bathroom; 136€ ($163) quad with bathroom. Breakfast 6€ ($7.20). MC, V.*

Hôtel Marignan
$–$$ Latin Quarter (5e)

It's plain and unassuming on the outside, but owners Paul and Linda Keniger have invested much time and energy in their hotel and have many repeat customers. Opened in the 1930's, Paul is proud to state that he is the third generation of his family to care for this very warm establishment. They welcome families, don't mind if you bring your own food into the dining room, and they even make the kitchen available during the low season. You also have a washer/dryer and iron at your disposal. Signs in English recommend neighborhoods to visit and tours to take, and you can always ask one of the Kenigers for recommendations. The hotel is very close to the Sorbonne — it's around the corner from the Panthéon, near the outdoor green market on rue Mouffetard — and its good rates attract students. One of the best organized Web sites for a hotel we've seen, check it out for individual floor plans of each room, as well as the ever-present promotions. Rooms fill up quickly in July and August, so if you plan to travel then, book well in advance.

See map p. 108. 13 rue du Sommerard. ☎ *01-43-54-63-81. Fax: 01-43-25-16-69.* www.hotel-marignan.com. *Métro: Maubert-Mutualité or St-Michel. Rates: 45€–150€ ($54–$208). Rates include continental breakfast. MC, V.*

Hôtel Meurice
$$$$ Louvre (1er)

This palatial hotel is positively regal, from its mosaic and marble floors to its towering ceilings with chandeliers, gold-leaf walls, hand-painted friezes, and 18th-century furnished grand lobby. You'll think you're staying at Versailles, and, indeed, royalty stays here (the hotel's slogan is "The Hotel of Kings"). Each floor corresponds to a particular period of décor. Rooms are spacious, soundproof, air-conditioned, and have ornate molded ceilings. They lack nothing in the way of luxuries, from fresh flowers and antique furnishings to walk-in closets, satellite television, and wireless Internet. On-site restaurants include the marble-trimmed Meurice, for a true French gastronomic experience, and the lighter-fare Winter Garden with its splendid Art Nouveau glass roof and live piano music. Amenities include an on-site health club and spa with Jacuzzi, Turkish baths, and massage; a laundry and dry cleaners; office and translation services; and round-the-clock maid service. The hotel faces the Jardin des Tuileries and is around the corner from the couture houses of rue Faubourg St-Honoré and the elegant place Vendôme. The Louvre is just a few minutes' walk away on rue de Rivoli. Rooms in the upper price categories have Tuileries views.

See map p. 104. 228 rue Rivoli. ☎ *01-44-58-10-10. Fax: 01-44-58-10-15.* www.meurice hotel.com. *Métro: Tuileries, but if you're going to stay here, you want to arrive by limo or taxi, at the very least. Rates: 510€–2,600€ ($612–$3,120). Continental breakfast 35€ ($42), American breakfast 45€ ($54). AE, DC, MC, V.*

Hôtel Minerve
$–$$ Latin Quarter (5e)

Owners of the Familia Hotel (reviewed earlier in this chapter), Eric and Sylvie Gaucheron, also own Hotel Minerve next door. More upscale than the Familia, rooms are larger and have wood-beamed ceilings, exposed stone walls, carved mahogany wood furnishings, and expensive wallpapers (the quality decorations, some of which have been more recently renovated are amusingly described as *"materiaux nobles"* or "noble materials"). Pretty hand-painted sepia frescos can be found in several of the rooms, as well as provincial fabrics. All have modern bathrooms with hair dryers, satellite TV, Internet access via Wi-Fi, and air-conditioning throughout the hotel. Ten rooms have large balconies with tables and chairs overlooking the street. The Minerve is as welcoming to kids as the Familia. If you're craving an American breakfast, head just a few blocks down to the delicious fare at Breakfast in America at 73 rue des Écoles. The Minerve offers airport transportation using Parishuttle (www.parishuttle.com), a van-transportation service.

See map p. 108. 13 rue des Écoles. ☎ *01-43-26-26-04. Fax: 01-44-07-01-96.* www.hotel-paris-minerve.com. *Métro: Cardinal Lemoine or Jussieu. Parking: 20€ ($24). Rates: 86€–132€ ($103–$158) single; 100€–132€ ($120–$158) double; 102€–132€ ($122–$158) twin; 152€ ($182) triple; 152€ ($182) large double with balcony or patio. Breakfast 8€ ($9.60). AE, MC, V.*

Hôtel Montpensier
$–$$ Louvre (1er)

Supposedly the former residence of Mademoiselle de Montpensier, cousin of Louis XIV, this hotel's high ceilings and windows, the stained-glass ceiling in its lounge, and its grand staircase all work together to create a sense of faded grandeur. Many rooms on the first two floors, which date from the 17th century, are either drab or have a faded elegance (depending on your point of view — some of the bright colored paneling makes the more recently renovated rooms seem elegant and classically French, but consistency is key), while rooms on the fifth floor (an elevator is available) have attractive slanted ceilings and good views over the rooftops. They are smaller than the first- and second-floor rooms, but all the sizes here are quite impressive given the rates. Most rooms are comfortably outfitted with easy chairs, ample closet space, and modern bathrooms with hair dryers. Reserve at least a month in advance for July. The prices are terrific for this location, just two blocks from the Jardin du Palais Royal and right down the street from the Louvre and the Jardin des Tuileries. In

August 2006, there were many promotions for a few euro off the price of rooms, online reservation only.

See map p. 104. 12 rue Richelieu. ☎ *01-42-96-28-50. Fax: 01-42-86-02-70.* www.hotel-paris-montpensier.com. *Métro: Palais-Royal–Musée du Louvre. Rates: 61€–149€ ($73–$179). Ask about special promotions when booking or check the Web site. Breakfast 7€–8€ ($8.40–9.60). AE, MC, V.*

Hôtel Prince
$–$$ Eiffel Tower (7e)

Just a ten-minute walk from the Eiffel Tower, the Prince is a good value for the location. Rooms are modern, soundproof, and have exposed stone walls, matching curtains and bedspreads, and big bathrooms with fluffy towels. Although they vary in size, all rooms are pleasant, comfortable, and well kept, with double-glazed windows, suitcase racks, TV, minifridges, and ample closets, and even hair dryers and safes. If you're too worn out from sightseeing to stagger out the door to the two downstairs cafes (not a part of the hotel), the hotel can arrange for a local restaurant to deliver a meal. A ground-floor room is available with facilities for travelers with disabilities.

See map p. 108. 66 av. Bosquet. ☎ *01-47-05-40-90. Fax: 01-47-53-06-62.* www.hotel-paris-prince.com. *Métro: École-Militaire. Rates: 79€ ($79) single with shower; 99€–117€ ($119–$140) double; 101€–119€ ($121–$143) twin; 125€ ($150) triple (comes with tub). Buffet breakfast 10€ ($12). AE, MC, V.*

Hôtel Saint-Merry
$$$–$$$$ Le Marais (4e)

The prices have not changed in several years at this Gothic hotel to the delight of regular visitors (don't worry the service has remained as good as ever!), so you're bound to spend a few less euro here than you would in a different hotel of the same caliber. Located on a pedestrian-only street in the Marais, the hotel was formerly the 17th-century presbytery of the Church of Saint-Merry next door (and was once a brothel as well), and it retains a medieval atmosphere. Beds have wood screens for headboards, except for room no. 9, in which the bed has flying buttresses on either side (easy to trip over in the dark, but original, nonetheless!) that make you feel as if you're sleeping in Notre-Dame. The rooms are dark with beamed ceilings, stone walls, wrought-iron chandeliers, sconces, and candelabras. Fabrics are sumptuous; rugs are Oriental; and bathrooms are pleasantly modern, fully tiled, and equipped with hair dryers. Staff is very helpful and friendly. Higher prices are for larger rooms with views. In keeping with its medieval churchlike feeling, the phone in the lobby is in a confessional, and you won't find an elevator in the building. TVs are in suites only. The hotel location is a few short blocks from the Seine and Hôtel de Ville. The Louvre is about a 15-minute walk down nearby rue de Rivoli.

See map p. 104. 78 rue de la Verrerie. ☎ *01-42-78-14-15. Fax: 01-40-29-06-82.* www.hotel marais.com *(for booking only). Métro: Hôtel-de-Ville or Châtelet. Rates: 160€–230€*

($192–$276) double; 160€–230€ ($192–$276) room with twin beds; 205€–275€ ($246–$330) triple; 335€–407€ ($402–$488) suites. In-room breakfast 11€ ($13). AE, V.

Hôtel Saints-Pères
$$–$$$ St-Germain-des-Prés (6e)

The poet Edna St. Vincent Millay loved the garden filled with camellias, and travelers have made this romantic hotel one of the Left Bank's most popular. Designed in the 17th century by Louis XIV's architect, the hotel is furnished with antiques, old paintings, tapestries, and gilt mirrors, but its 39 rooms have modern amenities such as air-conditioning, satellite TVs, and minibars. The most requested room is the *chambre à la fresque* (shawmbr ah lah *fresk*), which has a 17th-century painted ceiling. Breakfast and cocktails are served in the garden when the weather is good. The hotel is a stone's throw from celebrated Brasserie Lipp, Café de Flore, and the Deux Magots. Definitely check this Web site — during the summer of 2006, they offered discounts between 12 percent and 16 percent off of regular room prices.

See map p. 108. 65 rue des St-Pères. ☎ *01-45-44-50-00. Fax: 01-45-44-90-83.* www. esprit-de-france.com *(booking only). Métro: St-Germain-des-Prés or Sèvres-Babylone. Rates: 160€–185€ ($192–$222) double; 190€–195€ ($228–$234) twin; 280€ ($336) duplex with twin beds; 295€ ($354) suite; 345€ ($414) for la chambre à la fresque. Rates include breakfast. AE, MC, V.*

Hôtel St-Jacques
$$ Latin Quarter (5e)

This building was designed by Baron Haussmann (architect of modern Paris and its grand boulevards) and has been beautifully preserved. Several of its 35 rooms have restored 19th-century ceiling murals, and most of the high ceilings have elaborate plasterwork, giving the décor an old-Paris feel that is accentuated with traditional furniture and fabric-covered walls. The owners have added their own touches in the hallways, with stenciling on the walls and *trompe l'oeil* painting (a clever technique in which architectural elements are added to a room by painting them in to appear real) around the doors and walls and ceiling murals in the breakfast room and lounge. Modern comforts include generally spacious rooms, an elevator, immaculate tiled bathrooms with hair dryers and toiletries, double-glazed windows, ample closet space, fax and computer outlets, safes, and satellite TV. Although they aren't accessible by elevator (which stops a floor down), the rooms on the top floor are less expensive and have great views (be sure to ask for them specifically). The hotel is in a good location near the Sorbonne, Panthéon, and the Musée de Cluny, and a short walk from boulevard St-Germain, boulevard St-Michel, and rue Mouffetard.

See map p. 108. 35 rue des Écoles (at rue des Carmes). ☎ *01-44-07-45-45. Fax: 01-43-25-65-50.* www.hotel-saintjacques.com. *Métro: Maubert-Mutualité. Rates: 55€ ($66) single without shower or toilet, 84€ ($101) single with bathroom; 95€–124€ ($114–$149) double; 152€ ($182) triple. Breakfast 8.50€ ($10). AE, DC, MC, V.*

Hôtel Tiquetonne
$ Opéra (2e)

If a view is more important than space, ask the owner, Madame Sirvain, to give you one of the top rooms at this no-frills budget hotel. Rooms at the top boast views of the Eiffel Tower or Sacré-Coeur. Renovations happen continuously here: most of the rooms have new bathrooms and newer wallpaper, however the age of this hotel is made apparent by the shabbier chambers which have yet to be updated. Room 7, for example, has the hilarious oddity of a bathroom sink and a bidet in the middle of the room, as well as an optional bathroom with a shower (if you ask, the room can be 6€ ($7.20) cheaper if they close off the shower access). Nevertheless, the rooms are spotless, with firm beds and adequate storage space. Each has the basics: a bed with a wall-mounted wooden headboard, table, and comfortable chairs. Walls tend to be thin. The Tiquetonne is located just off the busy pedestrian street, rue Montorgueil (Montorgueil is the name of the small neighborhood that surrounds this street area). This up-and-coming hip micro-village has fresh grocery stores, funky restaurants, body-piercing establishments, and artsy jewelry shops. It is a stone's throw from the red-light district of rue St-Denis and a five-minute walk to the Marais and the Georges Pompidou center. Still, it manages to be a haven from the outside world of central Paris. Ask for rooms facing the quieter rue Tiquetonne. *Note:* The hotel is closed in August.

See map p. 104. 6 rue Tiquetonne. ☎ *01-42-36-94-58. Fax: 01-42-36-02-94. Métro: Etienne Marcel or Réaumur-Sébastopol. Rates: 30€ ($36) single with toilet, 40€ ($48) single with shower; 50€ ($58) double with shower or tub. Shower 6€ ($7.20) per person. Breakfast, ordered directly to the room, is 6€ ($7.20). V*

Hôtel Vivienne
$–$$ Opéra (2e)

Hôtel Vivienne is well located between the Louvre and the Opéra and offers comfortable rooms at a good price. The rooms, which are simply decorated and very clean, are updated every year and come with satellite television and Internet jacks. They have the traditional molding found in classic Parisian apartments; and have soundproofing — something lacking in most Parisian apartments. The bathrooms vary in size from adequate to huge, and all have hair dryers and wall-mounted showers in the tubs. Some of the rooms have adjoining doors, perfect for families; others have small terraces. A few have views of the Eiffel Tower. The staff is extremely warm and welcoming. Before venturing from the neighborhood, explore the Galeries Vivienne and Colbert, gorgeous historic covered passageways with pretty shops, intimate restaurants, and art galleries. There's an entrance at 6 rue Vivienne down the street.

See map p. 104. 40 rue Vivienne. ☎ *01-42-33-13-26. Fax: 01-40-41-98-19. E-mail:* paris@ hotel-vivienne.com. *Métro: Bourse, Richelieu-Drouot, Grands Boulevards. Rates: 56€ ($67) single with shower, shared toilet; 71€ ($85) double with shower, shared toilet; 83€–110€ ($100–$132) double with toilet and shower; 86€–110€ ($103–$132) twin with toilet and a tub. Breakfast 7€ ($8.40), and 9€ ($11) in room. MC, V.*

Lord Byron Hôtel Residence
$$–$$$ Champs-Elysées (8e)

Located just off the Champs-Elysées on a narrow street lined with town houses, the Lord Byron is one of the best values in the neighborhood, which is calm and not subject to the bustle of France's widest avenue. Exuding a sense of luxury and peacefulness, draperies filter the sun in the Lord Byron's lobby, the reception desk is under an arch, and a pleasant little garden makes you feel miles away from the busy Champs-Elysées. Rooms are furnished with antique reproductions, Provençal and classic French fabrics, and framed landscapes. They also feature minibars, satellite TVs, hair dryers, and full bathrooms. Near the Arc de Triomphe, this is a good hotel to stay in during the Tour de France or the Bastille Day military parade; you're close enough to walk to the action early yet are on a side street so that crowds won't interfere.

See map p. 104. 5 rue de Chateaubrand. ☎ *01-43-59-89-98. Fax: 42-89-46-04. Métro: George V, walk down rue Washington for 1 block, turn left. Rates: 132€–162€ ($158–$194) single with bathroom; 162€–180€ ($194–$216) double or twin; 255€ ($306) apartment/suite. An extra bed is 28€ ($34). Breakfast 12€ ($14). AE, MC, V.*

Pavillon de la Reine
$$$$ Le Marais (3e)

Enter through wrought-iron gates and pass through the pretty flowered courtyard and on into a cozy wood-beamed and flagstone-floored lobby where in winter, a fire burns in the marble fireplace in the antique-filled lounge. You can be assured of a welcome as warm as the fire at this hotel right off the Place des Vosges, The large standard rooms are decorated with such country touches as gingham wallpaper and Louis XIII–style furniture, the superior duplex rooms have modern beds (some decorated in purple velvet and taffeta) located in a loft above a cozy sitting room with comfortable chairs and couches, and the beamed-ceiling open onto the courtyard. Rooms overlook the courtyard or a flowered patio and have all the amenities: air-conditioning, cable TV, Internet, room service, minibar, and laundry service. Breakfast is served in the vaulted cellar, amidst tapestries; pastries are made at the *boulangerie* next door. You will definitely be treated like a queen (or king) here.

See map p. 104. 28 place des Vosges. ☎ *01-40-29-19-19. Fax: 01-40-29-19-20.* www. pavillon-de-la-reine.com. *Métro: St-Paul. Rates: 350€–430€ ($420–$516) double; 550€–800€ ($660–$960) suites. Continental breakfast 20€–22€ ($24–$26), buffet breakfast 25€–28€ ($30–$34). AE, DC, MC, V.*

Pierre & Vacances Haussmann–Champs-Elysées
$$$$ Champs-Elysées (8e)

Originally part of the Citadines chain of apartment-like hotels, this location was bought by Pierre & Vacances and offers almost identical services. Located near Galeries Lafayette and Au Printemps and in walking distance of the Champs-Elysées, the Madeleine Church, and parc Monceau, this seven-story hotel is quite luxurious. Studios and apartments are spacious and beautiful — featuring rare wood furnishings and granite bathrooms. Services and amenities include satellite TV, Internet access, baby-equipment rental, dry cleaning, laundry facilities, housekeeping every day, bar, and fitness center.

See map p. 104. 129–131 bd. Haussmann. ☎ *01-56-88-61-00.* www.pierreet vacances-city.com. *Métro: Miromesnil. Rates: 215€ ($258) per night 1–6 days, 194€ ($232) 7–29 days for a 2-person studio; 327€–368€ ($392–442) per night 1–6 days, 294€–331€ ($353–$397) 7–29 days for a 4-person apt. AE, MC, V.*

Index of Accommodations by Neighborhood

Louvre (1er)

Citadines Les Halles Aparthotel $$–$$$
Citadines Louvre Aparthotel $$$
Hôtel Agora $–$$
Hôtel Henri IV $
Hôtel Louvre Forum $
Hôtel Louvre Richelieu $–$$
Hôtel Meurice $$$$
Hôtel Montpensier $–$$

Opéra (2e)

Citadines Paris Opéra-Grands Boulevards Aparthotel $$$–$$$$
Hôtel Tiquetonne $
Hôtel Vivienne $–$$

Le Marais (3e, 4e)

Castex Hôtel $$
Hôtel de la Place des Vosges $$–$$$
Hôtel des Deux-Iles $$–$$$
Hôtel du Vieux Saule $–$$
Hôtel Jeanne d'Arc $–$$
Hôtel Jeu du Paume $$$$
Hôtel Saint-Merry $$$–$$$$
Pavillon de la Reine $$$$

Latin Quarter (5e)

Familia Hôtel $–$$
Grand Hôtel de Suez $–$$
Hôtel Claude-Bernard $$–$$$

Hôtel Esmeralda $–$$
Hôtel Marignan $–$$
Hotel Minerve $–$$
Hôtel St-Jacques $$

St-Germain-des-Prés (6e)

Grand Hôtel des Balcons $$–$$$
Hôtel de Fleurie $$$–$$$$
Hôtel de l'Abbaye Saint-Germain $$$–$$$$
Hôtel de Seine $$–$$$
Hôtel du Lys $$
Hôtel Lindbergh $$
Hôtel Saints-Pères $$–$$$

Eiffel Tower (7e)

Grand Hôtel Lévêque $
Hôtel Amélie $
Hôtel du Champ de Mars $–$$
Hôtel le Tourville $$–$$$
Hôtel Prince $–$$

Champs-Elysées–Madeleine (8e)

Four Seasons George V $$$$
Hôtel Alison $$
Hôtel de l'Elysée $$$
Hôtel le Faubourg Paris, Sofitel Demeure $$$$
Lord Byron Hôtel Residence $$–$$$
Pierre & Vacances Haussmann–Champs-Elysées $$$$

Index of Accommodations by Price

$

Familia Hôtel (5e)
Grand Hôtel de Suez (5e)
Grand Hôtel Lévêque (7e)
Hôtel Agora (1er)
Hôtel Amélie (7e)
Hôtel du Champ de Mars (7e)
Hôtel du Vieux Saule (3e)
Hôtel Esmeralda (5e)
Hôtel Henri IV (1er)
Hôtel Jeanne d'Arc (4e)
Hôtel Louvre Forum (1er)
Hôtel Louvre Richelieu (1er)
Hôtel Marignan (5e)
Hôtel Minerve (5e)
Hôtel Montpensier (1er)
Hôtel Prince (7e)
Hôtel Tiquetonne (2e)
Hôtel Vivienne (2e)

$$

Castex Hôtel (4e)
Citadines Les Halles Aparthotel (1er)
Citadines Louvre Aparthotel (1er)
Familia Hôtel (5e)
Grand Hôtel des Balcons (6e)
Grand Hôtel de Suez (5e)
Hôtel Agora (1er)
Hôtel Alison (8e)
Hôtel Claude-Bernard (5e)
Hôtel de la Place des Vosges (4e)
Hôtel des Deux-Iles (4e)
Hôtel de Seine (6e)
Hôtel du Champ de Mars (7e)
Hôtel du Lys (6e)
Hôtel du Vieux Saule (3e)
Hôtel Esmeralda (5e)
Hôtel Jeanne d'Arc (4e)
Hôtel le Tourville (7e)
Hôtel Lindbergh (7e)
Hôtel Louvre Richelieu (1er)

Hôtel Marignan (5e)
Hotel Minerve (5e)
Hôtel Montpensier (1er)
Hôtel Prince (7e)
Hôtel Saints-Pères (6e)
Hôtel St-Jacques (5e)
Hôtel Vivienne (2e)
Lord Byron Hôtel Residence (8e)

$$$

Citadines Les Halles Aparthotel (1er)
Citadines Paris Opéra-Grands
Boulevards Aparthotel (2e)
Grand Hôtel des Balcons (6e)
Hôtel Claude-Bernard (5e)
Hôtel de Fleurie (6e)
Hôtel de l'Abbaye Saint-Germain (6e)
Hôtel de la Place des Vosges (4e)
Hôtel de l'Elysée (8e)
Hôtel des Deux-Iles (4e)
Hôtel de Seine (6e)
Hôtel le Tourville (7e)
Hôtel Saint-Merry (4e)
Hôtel Saints-Pères (6e)
Lord Byron Hôtel Residence (8e)

$$$$

Citadines Paris Opéra-Grands
Boulevards Aparthotel (2e)
Four Seasons Georges V (8e)
Hôtel de Fleurie (6e)
Hôtel de l'Abbaye Saint-Germain (6e)
Hôtel Jeu du Paume $$$$ (4e)
Hôtel le Faubourg Paris, Sofitel
Demeure (8e)
Hôtel Meurice (1er)
Hôtel Saint-Merry (4e)
Pavillon de la Reine (3e)
Pierre & Vacances
Haussmann–Champs-Elysées (8e)

Chapter 10

Dining and Snacking in Paris

. . . .

In This Chapter

▶ Getting the inside scoop on Paris's dining scene
▶ Eating well without breaking the bank
▶ Grabbing something on the go
▶ Discovering the best bakeries, cafes, wine bars, and tea salons
▶ Finding a restaurant by location, cuisine, and price

. . . .

*T*his chapter is designed to make you feel comfortable about dining in Parisian restaurants, so that your experiences are pleasant and memorable, as well as delicious because, let's face it, unless you grew up in France, it can be quite intimidating to translate a menu and figure out what to eat. If you want to experience a true French meal that stretches blissfully over several courses, you can do just that at the establishments listed in this chapter. Each has all the ingredients of an excellent dining spot — fantastic cooking, reasonable prices, and great atmosphere — and creates the kind of experience that lingers on in your memory after the last dish is cleared away. Then, when you just can't sit down to another multiple-course meal, you can choose from street food and sandwiches to tea salons to cafes.

For detailed culinary information, see Chapter 2, where we give a little history of French cuisine, a useful glossary of French culinary terms, and a user's guide to typical French dishes.

Getting the Dish on the Local Scene

In France, as anywhere, you should never underestimate the importance of good manners. Your meal will be much smoother if you remember essential but basic phrases such as *"Bonjour, monsieur"* (hello, sir) and *"Merci, madame"* (thank you, madam). Keep in mind, too, that French table manners require that all food, even fruit, be eaten with a knife and fork.

Contrary to what you may have seen in the movies, *never, ever* refer to the waiter as *"garçon,"* (boy) and don't snap your fingers at him or her. Instead, say, *"Monsieur, s'il vous plaît!"* or *"Madame/Mademoiselle, s'il vous plaît!"* (Sir/Madam/Miss, if you please!).

Most French restaurants are small enough that you may feel as if all eyes are upon you. To feel more comfortable, follow the advice set out in this section, and you can dine in Paris like a local.

Making reservations for dinner

The vast majority of French restaurants are very small establishments with limited seating, and tables are scrupulously saved for folks who book. Always try to make at least a same-day reservation, even for a modest neighborhood bistro. If you are concerned about your language skills, you can always visit the establishment before service starts to make a same-day or next-day reservation. Or, ask the concierge in your hotel, or the hotel's desk clerk to make a reservation for you. Some top restaurants require several weeks' notice. Remember to call if you're going to be more than 20 minutes late. Showing up late is considered bad form.

If you're staying at a hotel with a staff concierge, phone or fax ahead and ask the concierge to make a reservation if you'd like to eat at a sought-after restaurant. Make the call as early as possible, specifying your preferred date with a back-up date or two. Don't forget to tip the concierge (slip 10€/$12 into an envelope and discreetly present it when checking out).

Dressing to dine

Only the most expensive restaurants enforce dress codes (suit and tie), and in theory, you can dress up or down as you like. Parisians, however, are a pretty stylish lot (how do Frenchwomen get their scarves to *do* that?), even when dressing informally in jeans. Relaxed dressing doesn't mean sloppy jeans and sneakers — *especially* sneakers. The look to aim for is casual Fridays at work. You can't go wrong if you dress in neutrals — think black, beige, cream, navy, and chocolate. If you wear jeans, pair them with a nice jacket, sweater, or shirt and good shoes and nice accessories. Go a notch dressier than what you'd wear at home.

Knowing the difference between a cafe and a bistro

Eateries go by various names in France, and in theory at least, these labels give you some clue to how much a meal costs. From most expensive to least expensive, the lineup generally goes like this: restaurant, bistro, brasserie, cafe. The key word is *generally.* Never rely on the name of an establishment as the sole price indicator; some of the city's most expensive places call themselves cafes. Furthermore, the awnings above quintessential cafes often claim the labels of restaurant, cafe, brasserie, or some other combination. The only way to be sure of the price is to read the menu, which by law is posted outside.

The following is a list of the different types of establishments and what you should expect.

- ✔ **Restaurants** are where you go to savor French cuisine in all its glory. At their best, classic dishes are excellent, and new dishes are inventive. Dining is usually more formal than in bistros or brasseries, and service is slower. You may also have more than one server. Generally, restaurants serve lunch between noon and 2:30 p.m. and dinner between 7 and 10 p.m. You must be seated for lunch no later than 2 p.m., if you want a full meal.

Between 3 and 7 p.m., you may find it nearly impossible to have a sit-down meal in a Paris restaurant or bistro. During this swing shift, your best bet is to head to a cafe, tearoom, or wine bar. Dining at 7 p.m. is considered very early for dinner in Paris; most Parisians wouldn't think about sitting down before 8 p.m. But starting too late — 10 p.m. is getting dangerous — can also leave you without many options.

Restaurant critics are divided about the *ménu dégustation* (sampler, or tasting, menu; meh-*noo* day-goo-*stah*-see-oh), featured in many of the city's top restaurants. Made up of small portions of the chef's signature dishes, it offers tremendous value because you have the opportunity to try more dishes. But some say there are too many portions for a customer to get a sense of the chef's artistry, and the mixture of so many flavors just confuses, instead of enriches, the palate.

- ✔ The typical **bistro** used to be a mom-and-pop operation with a menu confined to such Parisian standbys as *boeuf bourguignon* (braised beef in red wine sauce), and *tarte Tatin* (caramelized upside-down apple pie). Today, many bistros have expanded upon the old classics but retain the tradition of offering hearty, relatively low-priced dishes in a convivial, intimate atmosphere. Think crush of elbows and the sounds of corks popping, glasses clinking, multitudes of conversations, and people having a good time. Bistros are where Parisians come to dine most often.

- ✔ Literally, the word **brasserie** means "brewery" and refers to the Alsatian menu specialties that include staples such as beer, Riesling wine, and *choucroute* (a sauerkraut-based dish, usually topped by cuts of ham). Most brasseries are large, cheerful, brightly lit places that open early and close late (some are open 24 hours a day), and have an immense selection of dishes on the menu, although many no longer specialize in Alsatian fare. At brasseries, you can usually get a meal at any time of day, even in hours when restaurants and bistros are closed, and the food is relatively inexpensive.

Sadly, brasseries began to fall to corporate acquisition in the 1970s, and today most are part of one all-encompassing chain. Although this fact shouldn't stop you from visiting some of Paris's legendary eateries, look out for places that list mundane and repetitive food on their menus — they're more numerous than you think. Your best bet is to get a look at the menus of brasseries that interest you and compare costs, as well as listings. If *poulet rôti* (rotisserie chicken), *steak frites* (steak and fries), and omelets seem to be highlights, you may want to try eating somewhere else.

✔ **Cafes** are typically open from about 8 a.m. to 1 a.m. They serve drinks and food all day from a short menu that often includes salads, sandwiches, steak, mussels, and French fries. Prime locations or famous literary cafes carry higher price tags. Most cafes offer reasonably priced omelets, *croques* (see below) sandwiches, soups, or salads. Omelets come plain with just a sprinkling of herbs or filled with cheese, ham, or other hearty additions. Onion soup *(soupe à l'oignon)* is a traditional Parisian dish, and you may see *soupe de poisson* (fish soup) on the menu. Another cafe favorite is the *croque monsieur,* a grilled ham sandwich covered with melted cheese (which often comes open-faced), or a *croque madame,* the same dish topped with an egg. Or try a *salade Niçoise,* a huge bowl filled with lettuce, boiled potatoes, tuna, hard-boiled eggs, capers, tomatoes, olives, and anchovies or a *salade de chèvre chaude,* fresh greens topped with warm goat cheese on croutons. These dishes make a light, pleasant meal for 6€ to 12€ ($7.20–$14).

Parisians use cafes the way the British use pubs — as extensions of their living rooms. They're places where you meet friends before heading to the movies or a party, read your newspaper, write in your journal, or just hang out and people watch. Regardless of whether you order a cup of coffee or the most expensive cognac in the house, no one will ask you to leave. Coffee, of course, is the chief drink. It comes black in a small cup, often with a thin wrapped square of dark chocolate, unless you order a *café crème* or *café au lait* (coffee with steamed milk, which Parisians usually have at breakfast). *Thé* (tay; tea) is also fairly popular but generally isn't high quality (check on the menu for mentions of a specific brand — "Thé Mariages Frères" for example, will be very good. *Chocolat chaud* (shock-o-*lah*-shoh; hot chocolate), on the other hand, is absolutely superb and made from real ground chocolate. The result is a thick, rich, yet not too sweet taste of heaven.

✔ **Tearooms,** or *salons de thé,* usually open midmorning and close by early evening. Some serve light lunches, but most are at their best in the afternoon for desserts with coffee or tea.

✔ **Wine bars** operate from midmorning to late evening when you can order wine by the glass and munch on snacks such as *tartines* (open-face sandwiches), olives, and cheese. Some offer simple lunch menus, but like cafes and tearooms, they're generally better for light bites.

Understanding the order of a meal

A proper meal consists of three, or sometimes four, courses, so portions are usually moderate. Be aware of the traditional way French restaurants serve food.

To tip or not to tip

In France, waiting tables is an esteemed profession with benefits and retirement security, and waiters are treated with respect. When it comes to tipping them, you may have heard not to leave anything since a gratuity is already included in the bill. It's true that an 18 percent service charge, which appears on the bill as *service compris,* is added. But waiters never get the full 18 percent. Thus, it's customary to leave a few euro, or about 5 percent of the bill after a meal, unless the service was truly terrible.

✔ An *apéritif* is a light drink that precedes the meal. The French don't like to start a meal by numbing the palate with strong liquor. They usually stick to such offerings as a *kir,* a mixture of white wine and *crème de cassis* (black currant liqueur), which is light and the most common premeal drink.

✔ You're always served bread with your meal, but you must request butter.

✔ Water isn't placed on the table automatically — you must ask for it. To get regular tap water (which is perfectly fine to drink), as opposed to the pricey equivalent in a bottle, simply ask for *une carafe d'eau* (oon kar-*aff* doh).

✔ Cheese comes after the main course and is usually accompanied by a red wine.

✔ Dessert comes after the cheese course, but dessert and cheese can be served at the same time at your request.

✔ Diners traditionally don't drink coffee during the meal. Black coffee is served after dessert in a demitasse cup with sugar cubes on the side. If you want milk with your coffee, you must ask for a *café au lait* (ka-*fay* oh lay) or *café crème* (ka-*fay* krem).

✔ After the meal is finished, it is possible to order a *digestif,* or a small glass of liquor or fortified wine, thought to aid the digestion. Some classic *digestifs* are cognac, Calvados (an apple brandy from Normandy), sherry, and port.

✔ If you have food left on your plate, don't ask for a doggie bag. Restaurants are not accustomed to handling these types of requests.

The *menu du jour* at many establishments includes red or white wine. The standard measure is *un quart* (a quarter-liter carafe), sometimes served in *un pot* or *un pichet* (a pitcher). If wine isn't included, you can order *vin ordinaire* (house wine) or a Beaujolais (a light, fruity red wine), a Côtes du Rhône (a dry red wine), or a Chardonnay (a light white wine), which are very reasonably priced. And you can always opt for soda, juice, or water instead (*l'eau plat* is still water; *l'eau gazeuse* is carbonated water).

Cocktails are available but discouraged because they're thought to numb the palate.

Trimming the Fat from Your Budget

If you're watching your pocketbook when it comes to dining out, following a few of these simple tips can go a long way toward making the bill as appealing as the food.

- ✔ **Order prix-fixe (set-price) meals.** These set-price meals are up to 30 percent cheaper than ordering the same dishes a la carte. What's the trade-off? Your options are more limited than if you order from the main menu. Review the prix-fixe option carefully to determine what you're getting at that price. Does the meal come with wine, and if so, how much — a glass or a half-bottle? Is dessert or coffee included?

- ✔ **Make lunch your main meal.** Many restaurants offer great deals on a fixed-price lunch. You probably won't be hungry for a full meal at dinnertime after two or three courses at lunch.

- ✔ **Try the crêperies.** Crêperies (many are off the boulevard du Montparnasse around the square Délambre) offer a great value. Try savory meat- or vegetable-filled crêpes, called *galettes,* with a bowl of cider for your main meal and honey, jam, *chantilly* (whipped cream), chocolate, or fruit-filled crêpes for dessert. Surroundings are usually Brittany-inspired with red-checked tablecloths, wooden beams, maritime souvenirs, and pictures of Bretagnons in native dress.

- ✔ **Try chain restaurants or sandwich shops.** Batifol, Léon de Bruxelles, and l'Écluse offer some good-value, though not inspired, meals. Pomme de Pain, Cosi, and Lina's have fresh and tasty sandwiches.

- ✔ **Pay attention to the menu's details.** On most menus, the cheaper dishes are made of cheaper cuts of meat or the organs of animals, such as brains, tripe, and the like.

- ✔ **Don't eat breakfast at your hotel.** Doing so adds, at the very least, $5 more per person to your hotel bill. Grab a croissant or a *pain au chocolat* (chocolate-filled pastry) from a *boulangerie* (bakery).

- ✔ **Know the tipping rules.** Service is usually included at restaurants but it's customary to leave about 5 percent for your server.

Paris's Best Restaurants

Restaurants are listed alphabetically for easy reference, followed by the price range, neighborhood, and type of cuisine for each. Price ranges reflect the cost of a three-course meal for one person ordered a la carte, featuring an appetizer, main dish, dessert, and coffee — alcohol is not included.

The number of dollar signs used to describe each restaurant gives you a general idea of how much a meal costs at dinner, but don't make price your only criteria for choosing a restaurant. Most establishments offer fixed-price menus (also called *formules* or *prix fixe*) that can bring the cost down one whole price category. Likewise, if you're dying to try a place that's above your budget, visit it at lunch when meals are cheaper. See Table 10-1 for a key to the restaurant prices.

Table 10-1	Key to Restaurant Prices
Dollar Sign(s)	*Price Range*
$	Less than 20€ ($24)
$$	21€–50€ ($25–$70)
$$$	51€–100€ ($61–$120)
$$$$	Over 101€ ($121)

The restaurants listed here range from moderately priced establishments to homey neighborhood favorites to chic "in" spots. Also included are some bargain eateries and a few of the city's most sumptuous restaurants where haute cuisine is an art form.

See the "Restaurants on the Right Bank" and "Restaurants on the Left Bank" maps for locations of restaurants in this section.

A La Petite Chaise
$$ St-Germain-des-Prés (7e) CLASSIC FRENCH

If shopping Le Bon Marché department store makes you ravenous for classic French fare, come to this nearby restaurant, which is a favorite of the "ladies who lunch" crowd. Founded in 1680, this small gem is alleged to be the oldest restaurant in Paris. The restaurant is definitely older than the rest of the building it resides in. The entryway, adorned with a smoky antique mirror from the early 18th century, leads to a softly illuminated, cozy dining room reminiscent of an old country inn, which it once was. Start with *saumon mariné à l'aneth avec crème de moutard* (smoked salmon marinated in dill with cream of mustard on the side) or the poached eggs made with carrots and a cream sauce of goat cheese. Main courses may include a *filet de cabillaud avec l'estragon* (cod fillet cooked in tarragon) or leg of lamb cooked in its own juices. The house special dessert is *gateau au chocolat* — a rich chocolate cake topped with English cream.

See map p. 138. 36 rue de Grenelle. ☎ *01-42-22-13-35. Métro: Sèvres-Babylone. (Exit the station on bd. Raspail and walk 1 block north to rue de la Chaise. Follow the street*

Restaurants on the Right Bank

Au Bascou **19**	Chez Casimir **6**
Au Pied de Cochon **10**	Chez Marie **3**
Au Poulbot Gourmet **2**	Chez Michel **5**
Auberge de Jarente **19**	Georges **15**
Bofinger **21**	Jo Goldenberg **18**
Brasserie Ile St-Louis **17**	L'Ambroisie **20**
Caveau du Palais **13**	La Poule au Pot **18**
Chardenoux **22**	La Tour de Montlhéry Chez Denise **11**

Le Cinq **8**
L'Ébauchoir **23**
Le Kokolion **4**
Michel Rostang **1**
Restaurant du Palais-Royal **9**
16 Haussmann **7**
Zimmer **16**

Restaurants on the Left Bank

A La Petite Chaise **4**	Jacques Cagna **4**
Au Bon Accueil **2**	La Bastide Odéon **6**
Brasserie Balzar **11**	L'Atelier de Joël Robuchon **1**
Breakfast in America **12**	La Cigale **5**
ChantAirelle **13**	Le Grenier de Notre-Dame **10**

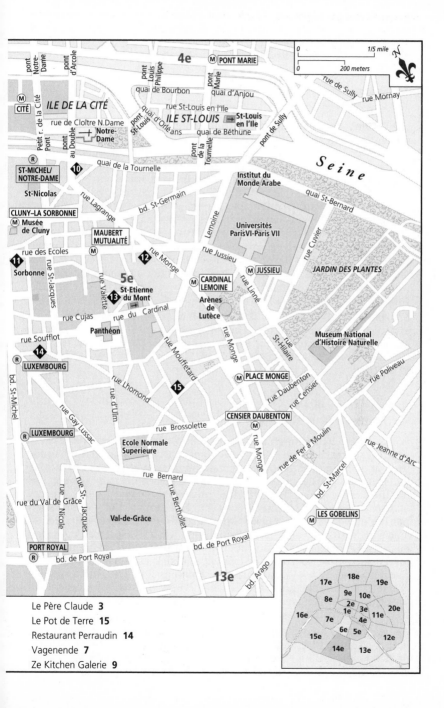

Le Père Claude **3**
Le Pot de Terre **15**
Restaurant Perraudin **14**
Vagenende **7**
Ze Kitchen Galerie **9**

to the end, where it intersects rue de Grenelle.) Prix-fixe lunch menu comes with a glass of wine and a café: 19€, 25€, or 29€ ($23, $30, or $35); dinner prix fixe (main course with appetizer or dessert) 29€ ($28) for two courses, or 31€ ($33) for three courses. AE, MC, V. Open: Daily noon–2 p.m. and 7–10:45 p.m.

Au Bascou
$$ Le Marais (3e)   BASQUE/SOUTHWEST

Specializing in dishes from the Basque country, the corner of southwestern France along the Spanish border, Au Bascou offers excellent meals and fills up fast. Start with *piperade basquaise,* a delicious concoction of sautéed peppers and onions served on salad leaves and topped with ham; then try some superb seasonal seafood, like baby squid sautéed in Espelette pepper (a staple in the flavor of Basque cuisine), or you can try the *axoa de veau cuisiné à l'Espelette* (tender chopped veal cooked in red and green peppers, with onion, garlic, herbs, and Espelette pepper). Finish up with a plate of sheep or goat cheese served with a cherry jam (a southwestern specialty), unique Basque cakes, or at least some fantastic homemade ice cream (pear flavored ice cream topped with pear liqueur is an unforgettable experience). A bottle of Irrouleguy, a smooth red Basque wine, makes a nice accompaniment to meals, and the service is friendly without being condescending.

See map p. 136. 38 rue Réaumur. ☎ 01-42-72-69-25. Métro: Arts et Métiers. (Exit the station at rue de Turbigo and cross over it to rue Réamur. Head east 1 block; the restaurant is on the corner of rue Réamur and rue Volta.) Main courses: 16€–22€ ($19–$28); three-course menu 28€ ($34). AE, V. Open: Mon–Fri noon–2 p.m. and 8–10:30 p.m.

Auberge de Jarente
$$ Le Marais (4e)   BASQUE

When you've had enough of cream sauces, come here for the taste of southwest France. Since 1964, cooks here have been using olive oil, tomatoes, and all kinds of peppers to create mouth-watering fare; Christophe Inderbitzin and his young family may have changed the management, but not the Basque genius. The 30€ ($36) prix-fixe menu may include starters of *timbale de calamars et chorizo* (calamari and chorizo cooked in a molded pan) or an escargot in a thick soup of sea salt and puréed vegetables — snails so fresh you can crunch on the sand. Or try *l'escalope de saumon au piment d'espelette* (salmon cutlet spiced with Basque hot pepper), and for a main course, such Basque-influenced dishes as sliced duck breast in a barely-sweet honey lemon sauce and potatoes. Top it off with a massive crème brûlée and sheep's cheese with jam. Order this menu because a half-bottle of wine is included — this is rare! The rustic décor includes a cave-like, cozy downstairs, and service is downright familial.

See map p. 136. 7 rue de Jarente (between rue de Sevigné and rue de Turenne, just west of place des Vosges). ☎ 01-42-77-49-35. Métro: Bastille or St-Paul. (Take rue de Turenne and follow it 1 block to rue de Jarente.) Prix fixe: 30€ ($36). AE, V. Open: Tues–Sat noon–2:30 p.m. and 7:30–11 p.m.

Au Bon Accueil
$$ Eiffel Tower (7e)   MODERN BISTRO

Almost as much ingenuity goes into the menu at vibrant and fun-filled Au Bon Accueil as it did into designing the Eiffel Tower, of which you have a spectacular view from one of the outside tables. The ingredient-based menu here is simply amazing. It changes daily according to what owner Jacques Lacipière finds in the markets. If you're ordering from the prix-fixe menu, you may start with cold cucumber soup followed by *steack de thon poélé et son caviar d'aubergine aux olives* (seared tuna steak with eggplant, caviar, and olives). Main dishes are divine and can include *rognon de veau au vin* (veal kidney in a red wine sauce) or whole lobster from Brittany roasted in herbs and tomatoes. Fantastic desserts include fig tart and crème brûlée made with walnuts. The dining room only seats 25, so reserve in advance.

See map p. 138. 14 rue de Monttessuy. ☎ *01-47-05-46-11. Métro: Alma Marceau. (Exit the station, cross the Pont l'Alma and the quai Branly, and turn onto av. Rapp; follow av. Rapp 2 blocks to rue de Monttessuy and turn right.) Reservations strongly recommended. Main courses: 15€–52€ ($18–$62); three-course prix fixe 27€ ($32). MC, V. Open: Mon–Fri noon–2:30 p.m. and 7:30–10:30 p.m.*

Au Pied de Cochon
$$ Les Halles (1er)   CLASSIC FRENCH

The welcoming gardenia-bedecked restaurant on a side street in Les Halles opened in 1946 and has played a vibrant part of the history of this old market neighborhood. With marble, murals, elaborate sconces, chandeliers, and plenty of tourists, the restaurant provides great fun at manageable prices. The waitstaff is exceptionally friendly and open. You can have a goat cheese and tomato millefeuille (a thin-layered pastry dough) or onion soup to start. Follow with grilled salmon with two kinds of rice or an *entrecôte maître d'hôtel* (rib steak in a rich red wine sauce) or their specialty and namesake, *pied de cochon* (pigs' feet). Or, if you're daring — and hungry — have the *plateau rouge:* half a Canadian lobster, crayfish, shrimp, crabs, and other red fish served on a towering pile of shaved ice. Finish with mouth-watering *profiteroles* (cream puffs).

See map p. 136. 6 rue Coquillière (between rue du Jour and rue Jean-Jacques Rousseau on the northwest side of the garden of the Forum des Halles shopping center). ☎ *01-40-13-77-00. Métro: Châtelet–Les Halles. Main courses: 14€–30€ ($17–$36). AE, DC, V. Open: Daily 24 hours.*

Au Poulbot Gourmet
$–$$ Montmartre (18e)   CLASSIC FRENCH

Photos of old Montmartre and original drawings by illustrator Francisque Poulbot adorn the walls, and chic burgundy leather banquettes are usually filled with a local crowd savoring moderately priced classic cuisine. Chef Jean-Paul Langevin brings tremendous finesse to the preparation and presentation of dishes such as *noisette d'agneau* (lamb slices) served with delicate splashes of mashed potatoes and spinach, and *poulet de Bresse aux morilles* (an especially tender breed of chicken roasted with morels). As an appetizer, try the *mosaique de chevre frais et ratatouille sur paillason de radis* (fresh goat cheese and a stew of eggplant, tomatoes, zucchini, peppers, and onions, seasoned with herbs and garlic and served with radishes). Desserts are made on the premises and the selection changes often however, you can count on a *moelleux aux chocolat* (chocolate cake with a wonderfully liquid center) served with an orange purée, or a light custard cream. The *coulis de fruits rouges* (red fruit purée) is also very refreshing during summertime.

See map p. 136. 5–7 rue de la Bastille. ☎ *01-46-06-86-00. Métro: Lamarck-Caulincourt. (Follow rue Lamarck from Sacré-Coeur; the restaurant is about a third of the way down the hill.) Three-course lunch (Mon–Fri) 18€ ($21); three-course dinner 35€ ($40). MC, V. Open: Mon–Sat noon–1:30 p.m. and 7:30–10 p.m.; lunch served Sun between Oct–May noon–1:30 p.m.*

Bofinger
$$ Bastille (4e)   ALSATIAN/BRASSERIE

Though Bofinger is owned by the Flo brasserie chain, which means you'll see similar menus in the chain's other restaurants, including Julien and Brasserie Flo, this is still one of Paris's best-loved restaurants. Dark wood, gleaming brass, bright lights, curved and painted glass ceiling, and waiters with long white aprons delivering good food all make dining here a wonderful experience. The downstairs dining room is ornately decorated with Art Nouveau flourishes and a glass-domed ceiling. Upstairs is cozier with wood paneling and separate rooms for smokers. The 24€ ($29) lunch menu may feature Brittany oysters to start, Langoustine royale (king crayfish) roasted with olive oil and herbs and accompanied by mashed potatoes garnished with *fleur de sel* (salt flower), and *floating island* (soft custard with mounds of beaten egg whites or whipped cream floating on its surface) for dessert. The restaurant is renowned for its oysters and foie gras. Best of all: The prices are actually quite moderate for Paris. Children under 12 can get the prix fixe for 14€ ($17). The more intimate Le Petit Bofinger is directly across the street; prices and fare are similar.

See map p. 136. 5–7 rue de la Bastille. ☎ *01-42-72-87-82. Métro: Bastille. (Exit the station at bd. Beaumarchais and turn left at rue de la Bastille.) Main courses: 14€–39€ ($17–$47); lunch and dinner prix fixe only on weekdays 24€ ($25) and 31€ ($37), respectively (there is also a faim de nuit menu ["night hunger"] which is the same price as the first menu, which allows a starter and entree after 11 p.m.). AE, MC, V. Open: Daily until 1 a.m.*

Brasserie Balzar
$$ Latin Quarter (5e)   ALSATIAN/BRASSERIE

Brasserie Balzar is always full of rich yuppies, even during off hours. The brasserie was the center of a controversy a few years ago when a group of regulars, including Adam Gopnik of the *New Yorker,* fought but ultimately failed to keep the Flo chain from buying it (see Mr. Gopnik's account in

Paris to the Moon, [Random House]). Nothing obvious has changed, however. People still stop into this brasserie that opened in 1898 for coffee and pastries between lunch and dinner and drop in for drinks in the evening. With authentic twinkle-eyed French waiters and the ever-interesting rue des Écoles, anyone who dines here could be a resident of the Latin Quarter. Regulars go for such hearty French classics as *poulet rôti avec frites* (roast chicken with French fries) or *choucroute garni* (sauerkraut garnished with cuts of meat, usually ham) but you can also get a good veal liver *(foie de veau),* steak au poivre (steak with crushed peppercorns), and a few fresh fish dishes. Portions are copious, French fries are crunchy and have just enough salt.

See map p. 138. 49 rue des Écoles (on the corner of rue de la Sorbonne and rue des Écoles, 1 block south of the Musée de Cluny). ☎ *01-43-54-13-67.* www.brasserie balzar.com. *Métro: Cluny-Sorbonne. Main courses: 15€–30€ ($18–$28). AE, MC, V. Open: Daily noon–midnight. Closed Aug.*

Brasserie Ile St-Louis
$$ Ile St-Louis (4e)   ALSATIAN/BRASSERIE

Brasserie Ile St-Louis is loud and bustling. The food is quintessentially Alsatian — including *choucroute* (heaps of tender, biting sauerkraut and meaty slices of ham); the hearty cassoulet, laden with rich beans and tender pieces of lamb and pork; and ham shank atop a bed of lentils. Although the food is not all that it used to be, the location is worth the trip: directly off the footbridge from Ile de la Cité to Ile St-Louis with an unparalleled view of the eastern tip of Ile de la Cité (including the back of Notre-Dame).

See map p. 136. 55 quai de Bourbon. ☎ *01-43-54-02-59. Métro: Pont Marie. Main courses: 15€–30€ ($18–$36) lunch and dinner. V. Open: Thurs–Tues noon–12 a.m.*

Breakfast in America
$ Ile de la Cité (5e)   AMERICAN

When the charm of spending 15€ ($18) on a Continental breakfast wears off, or when your longing for a hamburger becomes so powerful that McDonald's is actually tempting, get thee to Breakfast in America. Connecticut-born filmmaker Craig Carlson opened this diner in 2003 after years of craving American-style big breakfasts. The food here is even better than what you get in the roadside spots back home. American travelers and expats in need of a fix are often outnumbered by Parisians who've discovered the joys of a rib-sticking breakfast; they pack the place for fluffy pancakes, crispy bacon, omelets, and a 2€ ($2.40) "bottomless mug o' joe." Breakfast is served all day every day except Sundays, but the menu also includes burgers, nachos, chicken wings, and sandwiches. Sunday brunch is, of course, particularly busy, and Friday night is *Student Night* featuring an all night "happy hour" prices of 4€ ($4.80) mixed drinks from the full bar, which is a steal. Service is efficient and friendly and in English; you may even be seated by Craig himself. There is another location in the Marais at 4 rue Malher, Métro: Saint-Paul. *Note:* Tip is *not* included in the final tab here.

See map p. 138. 17 rue des Ecoles, 5e. ☎ 01-43-54-50-28. www.breakfast-in-america.com; *Métro: Cardinal Lemoine or Jussieu. Main courses: 6.50€–11€ ($7–$10). MC, V. Open: Daily 8:30 a.m.–11 p.m.; Mon–Sat lunch and dinner menu noon–closing; Sun brunch menu all day, lunch/dinner 4pm–closing.*

Caveau du Palais
$$ Ile de la Cité (4e)   CLASSIC FRENCH

The artist André Renoux painted the interior *(Interior Restaurant Caveau du Palais)* of this cozy wood-beamed restaurant (a well-kept Parisian secret) which is a lunch favorite of lawyers from the nearby Palais de Justice and locals (who once included Yves Montand and Simone Signoret). It's located in the heart of the serene, tree-lined place Dauphine, a secluded cobblestoned park nestled off Pont Neuf near the tip of Isle de la Cité. Try the house's special *côte de boeuf,* a kilo of grilled giant ribs prepared for two. The *confit de canard et pommes Sarladaise,* duck served with crispy potato bits sautéed in goose liver drippings, is another must. Finish it off with a classic crème brûlée or a few *boules* of ice cream. The owners display the work of up-and-coming artists.

See map p. 136. 19 place Dauphine. ☎ 01-43-26-04-28. Métro: Pont Neuf. Main courses: 19€–28€ ($23–$34). AE, DC, MC, V. Open: Mon–Sat noon–2:15 p.m. and 7:30–11 p.m.

ChantAirelle
$$ Latin Quarter (5e)   AUVERGNE

The door normally "moos" for arriving and departing customers — this summer during mid-July the cow was mostly likely on vacation, like everyone else. Don't be surprised by any other wildlife noises, such as birds, crickets, babbling brooks, or even the (albeit slow) movements of the restaurant's enormous and affectionate black cat. There's a high-walled backyard garden that children will love, and parents can appreciate an atmosphere that literally reeks of the Auvergne, the rugged south-central region of France. (The area by the cash register sells products from the region including tiny bottles of essential oils made from native plants and wines.) An old church door and a tiny fountain are incorporated into the décor, and a sound system plays bird songs, rainstorms, and church bells. The delicious peasant food is presented in good-sized portions, and appetizers may include a *torte aux poireaux gratinée* (leek torte with leeks topped with breadcrumbs) or *oeuf pochés à la fourme d'Abert* (poached eggs with regional cheese). Main courses include a tender *magret de canard au miel de Montagne et à la fleur de thym* (duck filet cooked in mountain honey and thyme blossom) or a *truffade* (a casserole of thinly sliced potatoes cooked in cream, with smoked ham in the center). Although most dishes use ham or pork, vegetarians (though not vegans) enjoy the delicious *croustade forestière "Julia":* assorted mushrooms and eggs poached with Fourme d'Ambert cheese. The best Auvergne wine is the Chateaugay, a fine fruity red. The restaurant is a block from the Panthéon.

See map p. 138. 17 rue Laplace. ☎ 01-46-33-18-59. Métro: Maubert-Mutualité. (Take the street behind the Panthéon, rue Valette, and turn right onto rue Laplace.) Main courses: 16€–21€ ($15–$24); three-course prix fixe: lunch, 21€ ($25) with glass of wine included; dinner 32€ ($38). MC, V. Open: Mon–Fri noon–2 p.m.; Mon–Sat 7–10:30 p.m.

Chardenoux
$$ Bastille (11e)   CLASSIC BISTRO

This restaurant's turn-of-the-20th-century décor is the very essence of old Paris (it has been appointed a Monument Historique), though the management has changed and is experimenting with classic French food. Service is friendly and English-speaking. A variety of French regional dishes are served in a dining room filled with swirling stucco decorations and brightened by etched windows with lacy curtains. The menu changes often, but will always be enticing — appetizers may include *fois gras au pain d'épices* (duck liver pâté with spiced bread), or *pôelée de chapignons aux herbes* (fresh regional mushrooms pan-fried in olive oil in basil and sage). Main courses may include *sautée d'agneau aux petits légumes* (lamb sautéed with chopped broccoli, carrots, and peas) or *cabillaud roti avec courgette aux rosmarin* (saltwater cod roasted with zucchini in rosemary sprigs). Desserts are classically Gallic. Try the layered pastry topped with powdered sugar and raspberries or a crème brûlée infused with jasmine.

See map p. 136. 1 rue Jules-Valles. ☎ 01-43-71-49-52. Métro: Charonne. (Exit the station on rue Charonne and walk 1 block to rue Jules-Valles. Turn left and walk to the end of the street. The restaurant is on the corner of rue Jules-Valles and rue Chanzy.) Main courses: 19€–22€ ($23–$26). AE, MC, V. Open: daily noon–2:30 p.m.; 7–10:30 p.m.

Chez Casimir
$$ Gare du Nord (10e)   CLASSIC FRENCH

Book well in advance for this restaurant far from the more touristy sides of Paris, which packs in loyal customers. It's on the same street as another restaurant well worth the trip, Chez Michel (reviewed later in this list). Chef Philippe Tredgeu works magic in his kitchen, cooking with ingredients he finds at the market that morning or the night before. Start with the refreshing *riz au lait façon de grand'maman* (rice pudding like your grandmother makes it), which is creamy and textured like velvety comfort-food, and then have *cuisse de lapin aux jus avec pommes de terres sautées aux sorrells* (leg of rabbit cooked in its own juices with potatoes sautéd in sorrel leaf), or be almost-too-adventurous and try the *tete de veau*, a French comfort-food classic — meat from the head and neck region of a young calf. For dessert, indulge in *clafoutis aux prunes rouges* (baked pancake with red plums). The wine list is highly affordable with prices starting at 7.50€ ($9) for half a bottle.

See map p. 136. 6 rue Belzunce. ☎ 01-48-78-28-80. Métro: Gare du Nord. (Exit the station on rue de Dunkerque and look for rue de Compiegne. Follow rue de Compiegne across bd. Magenta, turn left on Magenta and walk a few steps to the corner. This is rue Belzunce. Make a right here, and walk a block to the top of the street. The restaurant is on your right.) Main courses: 12€–15€ ($14–$18). MC, V. Open: Mon–Fri noon–2 p.m. and 7–11:30 p.m.; Sat 7–11:30 p.m.

Chez Marie
$$ Montmartre   (18e)   CLASSIC FRENCH

At the base of the steps heading to the place de Tertre, you can find some of the cheapest eats in this neighborhood, which isn't exactly known for bargain dining. Food is hearty, the owners are charming and friendly, and they welcome children in their humbly decorated, cozy dining room with wood benches, red-and-white picnic tablecloths, and a collage of Toulouse-Lautrec period posters and Lautrec-style paintings of cats dining. Stick to such basics as onion soup, cassoulet, or *cuisse de canard avec pommes de terre* (leg of duck with potatoes) and you're guaranteed to leave full and content and still have money in your wallet.

See map p. 136. 27 rue Gabrielle. ☎ 01-42-62-06-26. Métro: Abbesses. Three-course menus (including apéritif) 15€ ($18), 18€ ($22), 11€ ($13) for kids. AE, DC, MC, V. Open: Daily noon–3:30 p.m. and 6 p.m.–1:30 a.m. Closed Jan.

Chez Michel
$$ Gare du Nord (10e)   BRETON

Crowds of Parisians come here for excellent, unusual food at very fair prices. Look for succulent scallops, hand picked by scuba divers, served with truffles in the winter. The menu may include *crème d'homard Bréton* (cream of lobster soup topped with shaved Parmesan cheese) or beef cheeks served atop a *ficelle* (small thin baguette) with fresh young vegetables, or it may venture South to Nîmes with such local specialties as a *brandade de morue legerment gratinée au parmesan* or a salt-cod casserole, baked lightly with parmesan cheese. A nougat ice cream with spiced honey and thin almond cookies makes a satisfying dessert (ask if they have *kouign amann,* a Breton pastry made of layers of brioche dough, butter, and caramelized sugar). You can choose to sit in the more casual cellar at wooden tables and eat all the shellfish, pâtés, and salads you can fit into your stomach — which we guarantee will be stretched by the end of the night! Choose from more than 100 different wines at retail cost, a truly dizzying experience.

See map p. 136. 10 rue Belzunce. ☎ 01-44-53-06-20. Métro: Gare du Nord. (Exit the station on rue de Dunkerque and look for rue de Compiegne. Follow rue de Compiegne across bd. Magenta, turn left on Magenta and walk a few steps to the corner. This is rue Belzunce. Make a right onto Belzunce, walk a block to the top of the street. Make another right, passing restaurant Chez Casimir, and walk to the corner of rue Belzunce and rue St-Vincent de Paul. Chez Michel is here.) Three-course prix fixe 30€ ($36). MC, V. Open: Tues–Fri noon–2 p.m.; Mon–Fri 7 p.m.–midnight. Closed last week of July and first three weeks of Aug.

Georges
$$–$$$ Les Halles (4e)   MODERN BISTRO

Perched atop the museum, library, and modern piece of industrial architecture, le Centre Georges Pompidou, Georges boasts a 360-degree view of
Paris from its windows and outside terrace. Owned by the famed Costes
brothers, who have ten ultrahip restaurants across the city and the Hotel
Costes, this place is modern and chic. The waitresses must all be models —
rail thin, six-feet tall, and radiant. The décor is made of up of white plastic
tables and chairs and large abstract sculptures, and even the bathrooms
are funky. The menu changes every month, but modern French food is
fused with Asian-inspired creations. You might find a starter of avocado-
stuffed king crab, or a salmon carpaccio. Move on to turbot grilled in béarnaise sauce, "mandarina crispy duck," or the mysterious *tigre qui pleure*
(crying tiger — you'll just have to ask). Desserts usually combine in-season
fruits in French-inspired tarts and cakes. Dress chic, in black, or something
as funky as this place is.

See map p. 136. 27 rue Gabrielle. ☎ *01-44-78-47-99. Métro: Rambuteau. Reservations
required. Main courses 22€–150€ ($24–$180). AE, MC, V. Open: Daily noon–11 p.m.*

Jacques Cagna
$$$ St-Germain-des-Prés (6e)   HAUTE CUISINE

This Michelin-starred restaurant has been overshadowed by more recent
openings by celebrity chefs, but it should not be overlooked. It's housed on
the second floor of a 16th-century townhouse with wood beams and Flemish
paintings, where Chef Jacques Cagna creates delectable dishes served by a
solicitous but not overbearing staff that makes dining here a first-class expe-
rience. Starters may include *carpaccio de coquilles Saint-Jacques d'Erquy,
chips de racines de persil et pommes de terre roseval*t (sea scallop carpaccio
served with parsley-root chips and potatoes "rosevalt"), while main courses
can include a delicious *noix de veau en croûte de sel avec romarin,
champignons des bois et épinards* (veal sweetbreads in salted pastry flavored
with rosemary and served with wood mushrooms and spinach) or *le canard
croisé de Vendée, rôti aux épices, sauce à la crème de cassis* (cross-bred
Vendée duck roasted with spices, served with a currant cream sauce).
Desserts include *mangue émincée sur son sable, sorbet aux fruits de la pas-
sion* (sliced mango on shortbread served with a passion fruit sorbet) or *le
chocolat "Guanaja" moelleux à la pistache, glace à la confiture de lait* (a soft
"Guanana" chocolate cake with a creamed pistachio filling, served with a
caramelized milk jam). This is a truly special dining experience.

See map p. 138. 14 rue des Grands Augustins. ☎ *01-43-26-49-39. Métro: St-Michel,
Odéon. Reservations required. Main courses: 32€–95€ ($38–$114); prix-fixe lunch:
45€ ($54); Le Menu Jacques Cagna (chef's choice tasting menu): 100€ ($98). MC, V,
DC. Open: Tues–Fri noon–2 p.m.; Tues–Fri 7–10:30 p.m. Closed Aug.*

Jo Goldenberg
$-$$ Le Marais (4e)   CENTRAL EUROPEAN

Jo Goldenberg is a nearly 100-year-old institution that is the closest thing to a New York deli you'll find in Paris. Plump sausages dangle from the ceiling and baklava beckons from a glass case in the front. The atmosphere in the restaurant is convivial amid long red banquettes surrounded by photographs of famous patrons, including former French President François Mitterand, and original paintings of up-and-coming artists. Eastern-European/Ashkenzi Jewish specialties abound, such as chicken paprika, goulash, bagels, and Wienerschnitzel, along with typical deli offerings such as pastrami and corned beef — allegedly invented right here by Goldenberg senior in the 1920s. After almost suffering shutdown in early 2006, the restaurant is still here and welcoming all sorts of clientele. The food, while filling, can be bland, so keep that in mind when making your decision to dine here. Musicians begin playing around 9 p.m. most evenings.

See map p. 136. 7 rue des Rosiers. ☎ *01-48-87-20-16. Métro: St-Paul. (Exit the station and cross over rue de Rivoli to rue Pavée. Follow rue Pavée to rue des Rosiers, about 240m/800 ft. Turn left onto rue des Rosiers and walk about 105m/350 ft.) Main courses: 13€–20€ ($16–$24). AE, DC, MC, V. Open: Daily 11 a.m.–midnight.*

L'Ambroisie
$$$$ Le Marais (4e)   HAUTE CUISINE

This gorgeous, three Michelin-starred, spare-no-expense restaurant located in a 17th-century townhouse is one of the best in France. It counts among its diners former U.S. President Bill Clinton, who ate here as a guest of Jacques Chirac. Chef Bernard Pacaud creates exquisite food with an emphasis on perfection. Served in two mirrored and frescoed high-ceilinged dining rooms and a cozy back room (in summer there is an outdoor terrace), the seasonal specialties may include an anise-flavored cold fennel soup with crawfish, or young preserved pigeon stuffed with savory leaves. For dessert, try Pacaud's *tarte fine,* which has won awards: It's a chocolate pie served with bitter chocolate and mocha ice cream. If you don't like chocolate, opt for another cold soup — this time made from local white peaches and sided with pain de genes, a spectacular almond pound cake. If you can afford it, this restaurant just begs to be the setting for marriage proposals, anniversaries, and other special and romantic events.

See map p. 136. 9 place des Vosges. ☎ *01-42-78-51-45. Métro: St-Paul. (Exit the station on rue St-Antoine and head east to rue de Biragh, which leads into the place des Vosges. Turn left at the place des Vosges and follow the arcade around the corner to the restaurant.) Reserve at least four weeks ahead. Jacket and tie advised. Main courses: 86€–190€ ($103–$235). AE, MC, V. Open: Tues–Sat noon–1:30 p.m. and 8–9:30 p.m. Closed two weeks in Feb and three weeks in Aug.*

La Bastide Odéon
$$ St-Germain-des-Prés (6e)   PROVENÇAL

Delicious Provençal cooking has been served here since 1994 in a lovely cream-colored dining room accented with weathered wood and Provençal fabrics in shades of red. The menu changes regularly, but the dynamic creations may include starters of Paimpol coco beans prepared in poached eggs and a finely chopped Bilboa cod cooked in olive oil, or a warm grilled eggplant layered pastry with tomato and ricotta cheese. Main dishes may include roast quail in its own juices, served with a mushroom and Reggiano parmesan risotto, or a grilled, thick tuna steak served wok-fried fennel leaves and a spicy sauce of grilled pistachios. For dessert, try a *millefeuille* (multilayered pastry) with bourbon vanilla ice cream, or roasted figs in a confit of *"fruit rouges"* or strawberries, raspberries, and red currant; all accompanied by an almond *financier* and ice cream. There's a nice, slightly pricey selection of wine. The restaurant is located on a narrow stretch of sidewalk next to the Théâtre de l'Odéon and a short walk from the Jardins du Luxembourg's place Edmond Rostand/boulevard St-Michel entrance.

See map p. 138. 7 rue Corneille. ☎ *01-43-26-03-65. Métro: Odéon. (Exit the station and take rue de l'Odéon south to place de l'Odéon, where the Théâtre de l'Odéon is located. To the left of the theater is rue Corneille; take this about 45m/150 ft. to the restaurant.) Main courses: 10€–18€ ($12–$22). Lunch menu at 26€ ($31). AE, MC, V. Open: Tues–Sat 12:15–2 p.m. and 7:30–10:30 p.m. Closed first three weeks in Aug and Dec 25–Jan 1.*

La Cigale
$$ Invalides (7e)   CLASSIC BISTRO

Located on rue Récamier, a stone-paved garden square, La Cigale allows for elegant outdoor dining during the warm weather. Serving its delicious soufflés (among other specialties) to a sophisticated clientele, the food is simply some of the best you can get in Paris for these prices. The delicate soufflés are beaten high and brim with Camembert or tarragon cream. Try the Henri IV with regional cheese and a sauce *volaille* (chicken gravy), one made of goat cheese and fresh artichoke, or perhaps Camembert and morels, a seasonal luxury. If you're not in the mood for a soufflé, other tempting entrées include steak au poivre (steak with coarsely ground peppercorns) or *filet de dorade* (filet of sea bream). For dessert try — you got it! — a soufflé made with, among other things, pistachios or melt-in-your-mouth chocolate (with a chocolate fondue!) or Grand Marnier or almonds with rhubarb marmalade.

See map p. 138. 4 rue Récamier. ☎ *01-45-48-86-58. Métro: Sèvres-Babylone. (Exit the station at rue de Sèvres and cross over bd. Raspail to the Hôtel Lutétia. Rue Récamier is the street just behind the hotel. The restaurant is about 24m/80 ft. down.) Reservations recommended. Main dishes: 17€–20€ ($20–$24). MC, DC, V. Open: Mon–Sat noon–2 p.m. and 7:30–11 p.m.*

L'Atelier de Joël Robuchon
$$–$$$ Eiffel Tower (7e)   Modern Bistro

This place is still a bonne addresse among the dining chic. Joel Robuchon, arguably the most famous chef in France when he retired in the 1990s, came out of retirement in 2004 to open this chic red-and-black lacquered, sushi bar–type restaurant that serves simple French and Asian fusion food in which the ingredients are the real stars. Seating is at a 40-person sushi bar that wraps around the open kitchen. The idea is to give diners a "behind the line" experience, so you may see Robuchon giving orders, sous-chefs saucing main dishes, or a pig being roasted on a spit. The menu continually changes. Instead of starters, Robuchon offers 22 small tasting plates that diners are encouraged to share. Main dishes can include sushi (served with delicious sourdough bread) or steak tartare in a creamy morel sauce and hand-cut fries. Robuchon has a no-reservations policy, so get here early.

See map p. 138. In the Hôtel Pont-Royal, 5–7 rue de Montalembert. ☎ *01-42-22-56-56. Métro: Rue du Bac. Reservations not accepted. Main courses: 17€–65€ ($20–$78); prix fixe 80€ ($96). AE, DC, MC, V. Open: Daily 11 a.m.–2 a.m.*

Le Pot de Terre
$ Latin Quarter (5er)   CLASSIC FRENCH

Parisians fill up this restaurant on rue du Pot de Fer faster than any other. Those in the know relish its quality fresh food and its down-to-the-floor prices. The interior is made up of stone walls, an exposed wooden ceiling and support beams. The classic market fare served by charming waitstaff includes such starters as a fantastic onion soup, fowl-liver salad with raspberry vinaigrette, tender escargot. Main courses could be sautéed pork with plums, duck confit with French fries (they have two forms of fries: strips, and round, each spiced with different herbs for an especially homey taste), or a classic entrecote with peppercorns or Roquefort cheese. You couldn't say that the food is terribly unique for a French restaurant, but it is very well prepared and, at 15€ ($40) for a three-course menu, is definitely worth a visit.

See map p. 138. 22 rue du Pot de Fer. ☎ *01-43-31-15-51. Métro: Place Monge. (Exit the station and walk up the place to Rue Ortolan. Cross rue Mouffetard and continue on rue du Pot de Terre, just before rue Tournefort.) Main courses: 9.50€–12€ ($23–$30); 15€ ($40) prix fixe. MC, V. Open: Tues–Fri noon–2:30 p.m. and 7–11 p.m.; Sat–Sun noon–11:30 p.m.*

La Poule au Pot
$$ Les Halles (1er)   CLASSIC BISTRO

When Les Halles still was Paris's marketplace, its workers came to La Poule au Pot to share this signature dish, an old French recipe of chicken stewed with broth and vegetables, which has been served here since 1935 (in 2006 they celebrated their 71st birthday with a special reduced menu) with much success — if the *livre d'or* (a gold book filled with the names of visiting celebrities) means anything. After the market's demise, visits from such celebrities as Maurice Chevalier, Miou Miou, the Rolling Stones, and Prince kept this Parisian bistro on the map. The atmosphere created by the long zinc bar, *pots* of wine, red leather banquettes, wood paneling, and waiters in long aprons transports you to another era. How can the menu serve anything other than traditional French fare? Begin with *foie gras maison cuit au torchon* (house goose liver pâté cooked with a torch) or *oeufs cocotte à la crème* (eggs baked with cream), then try the *rognons de veau à la graine de moutarde* (veal kidneys cooked with mustard grains), or the succulent house *poule au pot* (33€/$40) with a tureen of the broth on the side. Finish with a velvety crème brûlée.

See map p. 138. 9 rue Vauvilliers. ☎ *01-42-36-32-96. Métro: Louvre-Rivoli. (Exit the station on rue de Rivoli and cross the street to rue du Louvre. Walk 2 blocks to rue St-Honoré and make a right. Proceed 2 blocks to rue Vauvilliers. The restaurant is near the end of the street, close to the gardens of the Forum des Halles.) Main courses: 23€–33€ ($23–$30); 33€ ($40) prix fixe. MC, V. Open: Mon–Sat 7 p.m.–5 a.m.*

Fast French food zones

When you're short on time or money, the following streets have many restaurants with fast service at low prices.

✔ **Avenue d'Ivry** and **Avenue de Choisy, 13e:** Far off the tourist track, the Vietnamese, Chinese, and Thai restaurants along these wide avenues cater to the local Southeast Asian population. Prices are low and quality is high, and you can eat like the locals.

✔ **Boulevard de Belleville, 11e:** This street features many *couscouseries* (couscous restaurants) that are reasonably priced and satisfactory, if not outstanding. Middle Eastern snacks, pastries, and a glass of mint tea make an exotic and inexpensive meal.

✔ **Boulevard du Montparnasse, 14e:** The block between rue Vavin and boulevard Raspail has four cafes with literary associations (early-20th-century writers such as Hemingway, Fitzgerald, Joyce, and St-Vincent Millay spent a lot of time at La Coupole, Le Dôme, Le Select, and La Rotonde) as well as high and moderately priced seafood restaurants, crêperies, sandwich shops, and ethnic eateries.

✔ **Métro Belleville, 11e:** The streets radiating out from this station are the northern headquarters for Asian cuisine. You can usually slurp down noodle soup at any hour of the day and well into the night.

✔ **Rue des Rosiers, in the Marais, 3e:** People have been known to trudge across town for the huge pita-bread sandwiches sold on this street. Stuffed with falafel (deep-fried chickpea balls), eggplant, and salad, and then topped with your choice of sauce, this must be the best 5€ ($6) meal in town.

✔ **Rue du Montparnasse, 14e:** The street between boulevard Edgar Quinet and boulevard du Montparnasse is a crêperie row of inexpensive Breton eateries. Whether the *crêpes* are sugared up with syrups and jam or stuffed with vegetables and meat (these are often called *galettes*), they make a tasty light meal for less than 11€ ($13).

✔ **Rue Sainte-Anne, 2e:** Sushi usually is expensive in Paris, but because this street lies within the same neighborhood as many Japanese businesses, you find the freshest fish and most authentic Japanese dishes at moderate prices.

La Tour de Montlhéry Chez Denise
$$–$$$ Les Halles (1er)   CLASSIC FRENCH

This is a meat lover's paradise as evidenced by the hams and sausages dangling from the wood beams of this true Parisian restaurant that features a zinc bar with barrels of wine and a homey dining room. The less expensive items on the menu tend to be dishes like tripe Calvados, stuffed with potatoes, and stuffed cabbage and kidneys, though the proprietors do pay a nod to fish lovers with a tasty seafood terrine and haddock in a *beurre blanc* (white butter) sauce. Other typical dishes are grilled lamb chops, *steak-frites* (beef filet and French fries) and, for those who want to try truly authentic, reputably delicious French fare, *cervelles d'agneau* (sautéed lamb's brain). *Bon courage!*

See map p. 136. 5 rue des Prouvaires. ☎ 01-42-36-21-82. Métro: Louvre-Rivoli. (Exit the station on rue de Rivoli and head east to rue du Roule. Follow rue du Roule to rue St-Honoré, where Roule becomes rue des Prouvaires. The restaurant is near the corner of Prouvaires and St-Honoré.) Reservations required. Main courses: 22€–35€ ($26–$42). V. Open: Mon–Fri 24 hours. Closed mid-July to mid-Aug.

L'Ébauchoir
$$ Bastille (12e)   CLASSIC BISTRO

A mural here pays homage to the working-class roots of the neighborhood, and the space is just large enough to render dining in this local bistro a bit noisy. Friendly but rushed waiters show diners seated at the first-come, first-served tables the day's offerings written on a tall chalkboard. Once you sample lunch or dinner, you'll find the superb food more than makes up for the decibel level. Diners may be offered appetizers of gazpacho and tuna tartare, and entrees such as a homemade terrine of goat cheese and sardines (a house specialty), or a deliciously spicy cod in Spanish-style sofrito. The head waiter insists on their wine list made of *"vins d'auteurs"* inexpensive wines made from small vineyards. For dessert, the specialty is a rice-cake *"façon grandmère"* (made like Grandma would) with chocolate ice cream, or rose-flavored macaroons served with litchi ice cream.

See map p. 136. 45 rue de Citeaux. ☎ 01-43-42-49-31. Métro: Faidherbe-Chaligny. (Exit the station on rue du Faubourg St-Antoine. Walk 1 block to rue de Citeaux and turn left. The restaurant is next to a small alley called the Impasse Druinot.) Reservations not accepted. Main courses: three-course lunch menu 14€ ($16); dinner is a la carte only; Sat afternoons you can order from the dinner menu at a 25€ ($30) for a three-course meal. MC, V. Open: Mon–Sat noon–2:30 p.m.; Tues–Sat 8–10:30 p.m.

Le Cinq
$$$$ Champs-Elysées (8e)   HAUTE CUISINE

We've been raving about this place since 2000 and still find it a heavenly experience. Chef Phillippe Legendre has earned three Michelin stars, where every element is in place, from the stately yet serene dining room with its high ceilings and overstuffed chairs to the Limoges porcelain and Riedel stemware created for the restaurant to the perfect waitstaff. The sumptuous and inventive cuisine may start with *coquilles St Jacques et palourdes à la tartare et au caviar Osciètre* (scallop and clam tartare served with Osetra caviar (from the Caspian Sea), and continue with *côtelette de veau de lait poêlé aux capres Pantelleria (pan-sautéed milk-fed veal chop with Pantelleria capers)*. The wine list here is magnificent; make sure to consult the sommelier, Enrico Bernardo, who, in 2002, won the prestigious Ruinart Trophy declaring him Best Sommelier in Europe.

See map p. 136. 31 av. George V (in the Four Seasons George V Hotel). ☎ *01-49-52-71-54. Métro: George V. Reservations required. Light tasting menu: 120€ ($144); gourmet tasting menu (without beverage) 210€ ($252); main courses: 50€–200€ ($52–$242). AE, MC, V. Open: Daily noon–2:30 p.m. and 6:30–10:30 p.m.*

Le Grenier de Notre-Dame
$–$$ Latin Quarter (5e)   VEGETARIAN

This cozy two-level restaurant near Notre-Dame blooms with live plants hanging from the ceiling and decorating the spiral staircase. The food is good, filling, and nearly all vegetarian (but not vegan as eggs, cheese, and some fish are used here). Especially recommended is the miso soup with tofu and seaweed and the vegetable paté served with warm toast, *les lasagnes végétarienne* (with eggplant, onions, tomatoes, cheese, tofu, and mushrooms), and the enormous portions of lentil moussaka made with lentils, white cheese, egg, tomatoes, and eggplant. Le Grenier has a well-deserved reputation for desserts, such as the hot apple tart with caramel and vanilla ice cream and a homemade chocolate cake with orange sauce. The wine list includes a variety of organic offerings.

See map p. 138. 18 rue de la Bûcherie. ☎ *01-43-29-98-29. RER: St-Michel/Notre-Dame. (Exit onto quai de Montebello; turn right onto rue d'Arcole, then left onto rue de la Bûcherie.) Three courses at lunch: 16€ ($15), dinner 18€ ($17); main courses: 13€–15€ ($14–$16). MC, V. Open: Mon–Sat noon–2:30 p.m. and 7:30–11 p.m.; Sun noon–3 p.m.*

Le Kokolion
$–$$ Montmartre (18e) CLASSIC FRENCH

Tucked away on the quiet rue d'Orsel in Montmartre is this hidden gem. A red facade and colored lights illuminate the entrance of this small and adorable little French "resto." Atmosphere is key here: Funky glass spheres hang from the ceiling and provide some dim lighting, posters of old movies and recent plays in the quarter are also displayed, along with the occasional kitschy photograph. Open only for dinner, service can be slow once it gets crowded. The food quality is even higher than the prices you pay. A 24€ ($29) dinner menu can start out with an *os à moelle gratiné avec sel du cuve ronde et toast* (a beef bone-marrow casserole made with reservoir salt), dinner could be a half a rooster roasted in tarragon gravy served with homemade potato purée. And if you opt for a la carte, you can treat yourself to foie gras in armagnac with Espelette hot pepper, and then *abrandade de morue nîmoise,* a specialty of smoked cod pounded with olive oil, garlic, cream, and saffron and parmesan. Their wine list is great and inexpensive: Ask the Kevin Spacey look-alike waiter for recommendations (he may be the only one present). The desserts will unfortunately leave something to be desired (at these low prices you can't have everything!) so think about that before you decide on a prix-fixe menu that includes dessert. The Kokolion starts late, and ends late, as it serves as an after-theater dinner for the nearby Théâtre de l'Atelier. You can start dining as late as midnight, but be warned that by 10 p.m., though patrons' excitement is high, reaction time is decidedly lower for the waiters.

See map p. 136. 62 rue d'Orsel. ☎ *01-42-58-24-41. Métro: Abbesses or Anvers. Reservations suggested. Dinner menu is 24€ ($29), main courses 12€–18€ ($14–$22). MC, V. Open Tues–Sat 8 p.m.–12:30 a.m.*

Le Père Claude
$$ Eiffel Tower (5e)   CLASSIC BISTRO

Le Père Claude is known for its enormous portions of red meat dishes. Starters include warm sausage with pistachios and apples, *terrine de gibier et foie gras de canard* (game terrine with duck liver) and yes, *cuisses de grenouilles,* frogs' legs. The *panaché de viandes* is an assortment of perfectly roasted meats served with a comforting heap of mashed potatoes. Make sure you specify how you want the beef cooked, or it will be served the way the French like it — *bleue,* which means very, very rare (refer to Chapter 2 for more about how meat is cooked). Seafood lovers won't be disappointed in the mussel soup with saffron or the *assiette de pecheur aux pates fraiches* (fisherman's plate with fresh terrine). President Jacques Chirac and Don King have been spotted (separately) chowing down here, but it's usually home to families and, to a lesser extent, tourists with big appetites. After dinner, you can stroll up the avenue de La Motte-Picquet and take in a view of the spectacular illuminated Eiffel Tower.

See map p. 138. 51 av. de La Motte-Picquet. ☎ *01-47-34-03-05. Métro: La-Motte-Picquet–Grenelle. (Exit the station on av. de La Motte-Picquet and head northeast about 1/4-mile, toward the Champ de Mars.) Main courses: 15€–28€ ($18–$34). AE, MC, V. Open: Daily 11:30am–2:30 p.m. and 7 p.m.–midnight.*

Michel Rostang
$$$$ Ternes (17e)   CLASSIC FRENCH

Sampling a *menu de dégustation,* a tasting menu made up of five to nine different courses, each with its own wine selected to taste (courses are usually small), is a wonderful way to experience a celebrated chef's specialties, and Michel Rostang's flagship restaurant is an ideal place to have such an experience. Four different rooms offer four different themes (one features Art Nouveau, another mimics the interior of the famous Orient Express), and the décor is pleasing and beautiful: Everything matches, from the couture tablecloths to the cutlery and flatware. The dishes are meticulously prepared for artistic presentation, and their tastes and textures are unique and outstanding — at 175€ ($210) a person. Ordering a la carte can be equally rewarding, however. Desserts change daily and are baked on the spot, and the creaminess of the ice cream as well as inventive flavors are sure to please. After a meal like this you will understand the lengths to which the French have gone to perfect the art of preparing, serving, and yes, eating food. This place is expensive, certainly, but you will pay for impeccable service, presentation, and quality food. Down the street one can find M. Rostang's "baby bistro," le Bistro d'à Côté, which is also delicious and more normally priced. One should dress nicely for this place; a jacket and tie for men is highly recommended.

See map p. 136. 20 rue Rennequin. ☎ 01-47-63-40-77. Métro: Ternes. Reservations necessary. Lunch menu: 70€ ($84); dinner menu de dégustation: 175€ or 230€ ($210 or $276); main courses: 83€–88€ ($100–$106). AE, MC, V. Open: Tues–Fri 12:30–2:30 p.m.; Mon–Sat 7:30–10 p.m.

Restaurant du Palais-Royal
$$–$$$ Louvre (1er)   CLASSIC FRENCH

The elegant arcade that encircles the gardens inside the Palais-Royal also surrounds this restaurant, making it one of the most romantic locations in Paris. Service is lacking during midday, as it is favorite lunch spot for professionals working in the area; better to eat dinner here and avoid overworked waiters and waitresses. Sit at the terrace on warm, sun-filled days and begin your meal with starters such as escargot with chives or duck liver terrine with red onion. Main dishes vary with the season but may include lamb roasted with rosemary and a side of creamy polenta or a tartare of red tuna during the summer. They have a special risotto section on their menu and promise smooth and buttery results. Try the good house red wine, served Lyonnaise-style in thick-bottomed bottles. The desserts are delicious; the pistachio and chocolate *mille-feuille* (puff pastry) are divine. Whenever dining outside just isn't an option, enjoy the recently renovated dining room that shines in tones of gold, silver, and warm red.

See map p. 136. 43 rue Valois or 110 gallerie Valois (on the northeast side of the Palais-Royal arcade). ☎ 01-40-20-00-27. Métro: Palais-Royal-Musée du Louvre. Main courses: 24€–46€ ($29–$55). AE, DC, MC, V. Open: Mon–Fri noon–2:30 p.m. and 7–10 p.m. Closed late Dec–late Jan.

Restaurant Perraudin
$$ Latin Quarter (5e)   CLASSIC BISTRO

The delicious home cooking and low prices draw a big clientele made up of students and professors from the nearby. At this historic bistro, with its red-checked tablecloths and lace lampshades, jolly atmosphere, and staff that welcomes kids, you can get a bargain three-course lunch that may start with *pot au feu de compote oignons* (a hearty stew of boiled vegetables with a compote of onions), or filet of kippers, followed by the house specialty, *chateaubriand* (porterhouse steak) served in a variety of ways, including with foie gras, or try the calf kidneys cooked with a homemade mustard. Classic dishes such as duck confit and *gigot d'agneau* (leg of lamb) with *gratin Dauphinois* (cheese-topped potatoes) are on the a la carte menu. For dessert, the *tarte Tatin* (caramelized upside-down apple pie) is heavenly. Arrive early for a table because reservations aren't accepted here.

See map p. 138. 157 rue St-Jacques (on the west side of the Panthéon, take rue Soufflot to rue St-Jacques and turn left). ☎ *01-46-33-15-75. RER: Luxembourg. Reservations not accepted. Main courses around 14€–23€ ($17–$29); three-course lunch menu 18€ ($22); three-course dinner menu 28€ ($34). No credit cards. Open: Mon–Sat noon–2 p.m. and 8–11.p.m.*

16 Haussmann
$$ Opéra (9e)   CLASSIC FRENCH

Located in the Hotel Ambassador just five minutes from Opéra Garnier, Galeries Lafayette, and Printemps, the Phillipe Starck furniture and bold color scheme — royal blue, bright yellow, and mahogany — reflects the bold and delicious concoctions that are the hallmarks of Chef Michel Hache. Starters may include *oeufs coques à la crème d'épices et caramel de xérés* (soft-boiled eggs in sherry cream sauce with caramel and spices) or *raviolis de langoustines à la crème mousseuse de basilic* (scampi ravioli in a heavily-beaten basil mousse-crème sauce), while choices for main courses could be a wild-mushroom risotto with truffle oil and a slice of parmesan, or a Bordeaux pan-filet, with butter and Sichuan pepper. The two-course menu may not satisfy a large appetite, so plan on sampling such luscious desserts as a crunchy praline "givara" milk biscuit with peanuts and apricot sorbet, or a velvety Caribbean chocolate cake made with bitter cocoa. A good selection of wines is available by the glass, and the plant and teak-furnished outdoor terrace, open in summer, is the perfect place to relax after a day of shopping the nearby department stores.

See map p. 136. In the Hôtel Ambassador, 16 bd. Haussmann. ☎ *01-48-00-06-38. Métro: Chausée d'Antin or Richelieu-Drouot. Two-course menu: 26€ ($31); three-course menus: 32€ ($38) and 37€ ($44). AE, DC, MC, V. Open: Mon–Fri noon–2:30 p.m. and 7–10:30 p.m.*

Vagenende
$–$$ St-Germain-des-Prés (6e)   ALSATIAN/BRASSERIE

This is one of the few remaining independent brasseries in Paris. Founded in 1904 as a *bouillon* (a workers' canteen or soup kitchen), the restaurant evolved into a brasserie that is now classified as a Monument Historique. The Art Nouveau décor is authentic — mirrors, frescoes, and swirling floral patterns abound within walls of dark wood. Lace curtains, globe lights, and spacious booths enhance the classic atmosphere. The menu is extensive and classic; start with escargot, liver pâté cooked in Armagnac, or a freshwater-fish soup served with *rouille,* a slightly spicy garlic mayonnaise sauce. Next, dive into a chateaubriand steak with dauphinois potatoes, perhaps brave a mustard-grilled Andouillette (sausage), or even taste a Gatinais-roast rabbit with a tomato confit and polenta. A "minestrone" of seasonal fruit marinated in wine from the Pays d'Oc region of France makes a refreshing dessert. If it's not too busy, maybe your waiter will crank up the old mechanical piano for a little taste of times past.

See map p. 138. 142 bd. St-Germain. ☎ *01-43-26-68-18. Métro: Odéon. Main courses: 11€–34€ ($13–$41); prix fixe (two courses, drinks not included served noon–6 p.m.): 19€ ($23); dinner prix fixe (three courses, drinks not included): 23€ ($28). AE, MC, V. Open: Daily noon–1 a.m.*

Ze Kitchen Galerie
$$ St-Germain-des-Prés (6e)   MODERN BISTRO

William Ledeuil became a popular chef at the trendy Les Bouquinistes and in 2002 opened this hip and sophisticated place nearby. It is indeed an art gallery and kitchen: As their only decoration, the walls of the spacious and spare dining room feature art work that changes every three months. The innovative, Asian-inspired menu, created from a tiny windowed kitchen at the far side of the room, changes every five weeks. The menu is broken down into four parts: soup, raw (usually fish), pasta, and grilled *(à la plancha)*. Starters may include a cold artichoke soup with lemongrass or raw tuna sashimi style. Mains may be marinated tuna served with a tomato-ginger marmalade and a supplement of green potatoes with turmeric or grilled piglet flavored with tamarind, violet mustard, and a Thai sauce. Since portions are on the small side, you'll more than likely have room for dessert, which may include flavored cappuccinos: strawberry, pistachio, even lemongrass and wasabi, or try a chocolate crème brûlée with roasted cherries and chocolate ice cream. Reservations are recommended because this restaurant fills up fast.

See map p. 138. 4 rue des Grands Augustins. ☎ *01-44-32-00-32. Métro: St-Michel. Reservations recommended. Main courses: 19€–34€ ($23–$41). AE, DC, MC, V. Open: Mon–Fri noon–2:30 p.m.; Mon–Sat 7–11 p.m.*

Zimmer
$$ Louvre (1er)   BRASSERIE

Founded by the Alsatian Zimmer family after the Franco-Prussian war of 1870, this beautiful, centrally-located brasserie was restored in 2000 by the Costes brothers, who also own the hotel by the same name and ten other restaurants in Paris. Diners relax in plush surroundings of blue and rose velvet beneath a gorgeous gold molded ceiling and doorways framed by rose velvet draperies. Separated by a door from the Théâtre du Châtelet, it has counted among its patrons actors such as Sarah Bernhardt and such artists as Toulouse-Lautrec and Picasso. One of its three basements, now sealed, was used by the Résistance during World War II as a meeting place, an arsenal, and a hiding place for Jews. The food here is simple and delicious. You may start with a dish from the south of France like thin slices of beef marinated in olive oil and basil and sprinkled with Parmesan cheese or a *brick provençale,* which is goat cheese, basil, and zucchini fried in batter. Main courses include traditional *choucroute* (sauerkraut made with seafood or Frankfurt, Montbéliard, and Nuremberg sausages, cured bacon, and short ribs) or a sirloin steak grilled in a shallot fondue. Desserts change daily, but may include a cake with melted banana filling, or litchis in ginger ice cream.

Keep it Fresh: Eating Veggie

Being a vegetarian can be challenging for those who also like dining out. Paris is no exception: Everyone's primary food group seems to be ham. Luckily for those "veggies" among us, there are several places that one can eat fantastic French food without involving any butchers. Below is a list of places to get vegetarian grub during your time in Paris.

✔ **Au Grain de Folies** (24 rue de la Vieuville, 18e; ☎ 01-42-58-15-57; Métro: Abbesses) is a tiny restaurant that feels like you're eating in someone's kitchen. Soups, veggie tarts, and homemade desserts leave nothing to be desired.

✔ **Les 5 Saveurs d'Anada** (rue Cardinal Lemoine, 5e; ☎ 01-43-29-58-54; Métro: Cardinal Lemoine) is a totally organic restaurant (in French it's *bio*): No smoking allowed anywhere and even the wine is organic!

✔ **Le Grenier de Notre-Dame** (see above).

✔ **Piccolo Teatro** (9 rue des Ecouffes, 4e; ☎ 01-42-72-17-79; Métro: St-Paul) offers a wide range of entrees, inspired by French, Italian, and Indonesian cuisine. Their gratins are especially filling.

✔ **Le Potager du Marais** (22 rue Rambuteau, 4e; ☎ 01-42-74-24-66; Métro: Rambuteau) is highly recommended among the vegetable-eating community. The space is tiny, but the food is extremely fresh (try the mushroom tart).

✔ Take out from **Chez H'anna** (54 rue des Rosiers, 4e; ☎ 01-42-74-74-99; Métro: St-Paul) may include a massive falafel with a big cucumber and tomato salad on the side, or you can stay here and watch the family chop vegetables for their daily fare. Try especially their eggplant dishes.

✔ **Le Boutegrill Chez Hamadi** (12 rue Boutebrie, 5e; ☎ 01-43-54-03-30; Métro: St-Michel) is a Tunisian restaurant that also prepares excellent couscous meals, one of which is only stewed vegetables. Sip along with your meal a glass of *Mascara*, a well regarded Algerian wine.

See map p. 136. 1 place du Châtelet. ☎ 01-42-36-74-03. Métro: Châtelet. Main courses: 16€–19€ ($19–$23); two-course menu: 19€ ($23). AE, DC, MC, V. Open: Daily 7 a.m.–midnight.

Dining and Snacking on the Go

Face it: Who can sit down to multiple-course meals every day — even if they are cooked by legendary chefs? Fortunately, many alternatives to a full meal are available. Choose from street carts, sandwich places, and tea salons. And of course, there's that Parisian institution, the cafe. Listed here are some of Paris's best cafes and their more sophisticated sisters, the wine bars where you, too, can join in the great French art of people watching!

See the "Light Meals in the Heart of the Right Bank" and "Light Meals in the Heart of the Left Bank" maps for locations of establishments in this section.

Partaking of Paris street food

Some street vendors sell Belgian waffles, called *gaufres,* served warm with powdered sugar or chocolate sauce, but the Parisian street food you see the most is the *crêpe* — a thin wheat pancake stuffed with a filling that's either salty or sweet. When served with savory fillings, such as cheese or mushrooms, a street vendor may either call it a crêpe salé (salted or savory), or a *galette.* A true *galette,* a specialty from Normandy, is made with buckwheat and is only cooked on one side, unlike a traditional crêpe cooked on both sides. However it is cooked, both are delicious and constitute a meal. Sweet crêpe fillings include plain powdered sugar, chocolate-hazelnut spread, ice cream, or jam (called *compote*). Talk about a sugar rush!

You can find stalls or carts selling crêpes near most of the major attractions, in the parks and bigger gardens, and along the rue de Rivoli between the Marais and the place de la Concorde. When you buy a crêpe from a street vendor, you won't have much of a choice of sweet fillings; for a more extensive menu visit a crêperie.

 Make a meal of crêpes at one of the many good establishments on rue du Montparnasse, where you can settle down in a peaceful atmosphere with a bowl of cider (a Breton specialty), a galette for a main course, and a crêpe for dessert — usually under 12€ ($14) a person (Métro: Edgar Quinet or Montparnasse-Bienvenüe).

The other typical Parisian street food, *panini,* is also sold just about anywhere. Named for the Italian-style bread with which they're made, panini can be almost any filling stuck between two slices of bread, then flattened and grilled between two hot plates. The most common fillings are mozzarella, basil, and sun-dried tomatoes (a pizza sandwich, if you will). Panini are cheap, tasty, and easy to eat on the run.

Snacking on sandwiches

Even sandwiches are delicious in France. Sandwich (and more) shops Lina's, Cosi, and Le Pain Quotidien, open until the early evening, make their own breads. Following is a list of sandwich shops you may want to try:

- ✓ **Cosi,** 54 rue de Seine, 6e (☎ **01-46-33-35-36;** Métro: St-Germain-des-Prés; see map p. 162), serves its sandwiches on delicious home-made flatbread, and fillings are plentiful and delicious. You can even build your own salads if you want — this place is a bit of New York–style service in the heart of Paris.

- ✓ **Le Pain Quotidien,** 18 place du Marché-St-Honoré, 1er (☎ **01-42-96-31-70;** Métro: Tuileries; see map p. 160), is part of a Belgian

Light Meals in the Heart of the Right Bank

A Priori Thé **18**	Café de L'Industrie **29**	La Tartine **35**
Angelina **12**	Café Marly **23**	Ladurée **10**
Au Bistro de La Place **32**	Clown Bar **26**	Lafayette Gourmet **6**
Au Négociant **3**	Fauchon **8**	Le Bistrot du Peintre **30**
Au Progrès **1**	Fouquet's **11**	L'Eté en Pente Douce **2**
Au Rendez-Vous des Amis **36**	Hédiard **9**	L'Étoile Manquante **33**
BE (Boulangepicier) **7**	La Butte Glacée **25**	Le Griffonnier **5**
Berthillon **39**	La Chaise au Plafond **34**	Le Pain Quotidien **13**
Café Beaubourg **37**	La Cloche des Halles **19**	Lina's **17**

Light Meals in the Heart of the Left Bank

Amorino **14**	Café Mabillon **12**
Berthillon **20**	Cosi **16**
Bonneau **3**	La Contrescarpe **26**
Boulangerie Kaysers	La Coupole **18**
(Organic &Traditional) **25**	La Fourmi Ailée **22**
Café de Flore **9**	La Grande Épicerie **6**
Café de la Place **7**	Le Bac à Glaces **4**
Café les Deux Magots **10**	L'Écluse **18**

pont Notre-Dame
pont d'Arcole
4e

PONT MARIE

pont Louis Philippe
pont Marie

quai de Bourbon
quai d'Anjou

20

rue St-Louis en l'Ile

ILE DE LA CITÉ
CITÉ
rue de la Cité
rue de Cloître N.Dame
quai d'Orléans
St-Louis d'Orléans

ILE ST-LOUIS
St-Louis en l'Ile

Petit r. de la Cité
Pont
pont au Double
Notre-Dame
quai de Béthune

pont de Sully

rue Mornay

Seine

ST-MICHEL/NOTRE-DAME
21
quai de la Tournelle
pont de la Tournelle

St-Nicolas
22

rue Lagrange
bd. St-Germain

Institut du Monde Arabe

quai St-Bernard

23
CLUNY–LA SORBONNE
Musée de Cluny

24
25
MAUBERT MUTUALITÉ

Lemoine

Universités ParisVI-Paris VII

rue Cuvier

rue des Ecoles

rue Monge
rue Jussieu

Sorbonne
rue St-Jacques

5e
St-Etienne du Mont

JUSSIEU
CARDINAL LEMOINE

rue Linné

JARDIN DES PLANTES

rue Valette
Arènes de Lutèce

rue Cujas
rue du Cardinal

rue Buffon

Panthéon

rue Soufflot

rue Mouffetard

rue Monge

rue St-Hilaire

Museum National d'Histoire Naturelle

LUXEMBOURG

27
PLACE MONGE

rue Daubenton
rue Censier

rue Poliveau

rue Lhomond
rue Gay Lussac
rue d'Ulm

28
rue Brossolette

CENSIER DAUBENTON

rue Monge

rue du Fer à Moulin

rue Jeanne d'Arc

Ecole Normale Superieure

LUXEMBOURG

bd. St-Michel

rue Bernard

rue St-Jacques
rue Nicole

rue Berthollet

rue du Val de Grâce

Val-de-Grâce

bd. St-Marcel

LES GOBELINS

PORT ROYAL
bd. de Port Royal

bd. de Port Royal

bd. Arago

13e

0   1/5 mile
0   200 meters

Le Comptoir du Relais
  Saint-Germain **13**
Le Sancerre **1**
M.P Gourmandises **23**
Marché Biologique **5**
Mariage Frères **19**
Moulin de la Vierge **2**
Octave **28**

Poujauran **1**
Rue Cler **3**
Rue de Buci **15**
Salon de Thé de la
  Mosquée de Paris **27**
The Tea Caddy **21**

17e 18e 19e
8e 9e 10e
16e 2e 3e 11e 20e
1e 4e
7e 6e 5e 12e
15e
14e 13e

chain serving mouth-watering tartines (open-faced sandwiches) made with combinations such as country ham and Gruyère cheese, a goat-cheese-and-honey duo; or a combination of tuna, hummus and fresh vegetables. There are five locations all around Paris; one is in the Marais at 18 rue des Archives, 4e (☎ 01-44-54-03-07) and another is in the Latin Quarter, not far from the Panthéon at 138 rue Mouffetard, 5e (☎ 01-55-43-91-99).

✔ **Lina's,** 22 rue St-Pères, 6e (☎ 01-40-20-42-78; Métro: St-Germain-des-Près; see map p. 160), packs an assortment of fillings onto whole-meal breads and rolls, American deli–style. Other locations are at 15 rue du Louvre, 1er (☎ 01-40-41-15-00), and 1 bd. de Courcelles, 8e (☎ 01-40-08-01-00), not far from the designer boutiques.

✔ **Pomme de Pain,** 76 rue de Rivoli, 4e (☎ 01-42-78-57-29; Métro: Hôtel de Ville; see map p. 160), boasts a fast-food–style counter where staff slice baguettes in half and layer on the toppings of your choice. The menu specials (a sandwich, potato or dessert, and one drink) are usually a fair deal. Branches are located all across the city, including one at 2 bd. Haussmann, 9e (☎ 01-48-24-20-60) and another at 1–7 rue Pierre Lescot, Basement level 3, Forum des Halles, 1er (☎ 01-40-39-94-63).

✔ **Sam's Bagels (formerly The Bagel Place),** 51 pass Choiseul, 2e (☎ 01-42-86-07-36; Métro: Pyramides; see map p. 160), offers New York–style bagels and a blackboard full of bagel sandwich specials. You will pay several euro more than you would for a bagel back home, however.

Assembling a picnic, Parisian style

Grab a crusty baguette or two, some dried sausage, a wedge of cheese, and a few pieces of fruit and head to the nearest park or to a garden that strikes your fancy. Picnicking in Paris can be as fun and as unforgettable as a meal in a three-star restaurant at just a fraction of the cost. In this section, discover where to stock up on provisions. (*Note:* You can also assemble picnic fixings cheaply at Parisian supermarkets all across the city.)

The traiteurs (gourmet food shops)

Look for the word *traiteur,* which designates a food shop that sells ready-made meat, pasta, and salad dishes. The two most famous, **Fauchon** and **Hédiard,** have main stores at place de la Madeleine, 8e (Métro: Madeleine), and branches all across Paris. Every neighborhood has several good *traiteurs,* so be on the lookout, and don't hesitate to ask your hotel staff for recommendations.

✔ **Fauchon,** 30 place de la Madeleine, 8e (☎ 01-70-39-38-00; Métro: Madeleine; see map p. 160), was founded in 1886. It is *the* high-end food shop with everything from foie gras and Norwegian smoked salmon to caviar to fancy breads and cheeses. Their epicerie and cave together will entirely stock your picnic basket. Open Monday to Saturday 9 a.m. to 8 p.m.

✔ **Hédiard,** 21 place de la Madeleine, 8e (☎ 01-43-12-88-88; Métro: Madeleine; see map p. 160), is a gourmet food shop that sells upscale products, wine, and readymade food to go. Open Monday to Saturday from 9 a.m. to 10 p.m.

✔ **La Grande Épicerie, Le** Bon Marché, 38 rue de Sèvres, 7e (☎ 01-44-39-81-00; Métro: Sèvres-Babylone; see map p. 162), may be the best grocery store on the Left Bank. It has large *traiteur* and wine departments and sells everything from cleaning supplies to gourmet chocolate to fresh fish. Picnics just aren't complete without fresh salad expertly measured and mixed from this wonderland. Open Monday to Saturday from 8:30 a.m. to 9 p.m.

✔ **Lafayette Gourmet,** 48 bd. Haussmann, 9e (☎ 01-42-82-34-56, or 01-42-81-25-61; Métro: Havre-Caumartin; see map p. 160), is another wonderful grocery store that has everything you need for a picnic. It's located smack in the middle of the Galeries Lafayette complex (in the men's store). Open Monday to Saturday from 9:30 a.m. to 7:30 p.m.; open Thursday until 9 p.m.

The street markets

Every neighborhood in Paris has its street market, and it's probably the best place to find the freshest produce, cheeses of excellent quality, and other picnic supplies. Even when you don't buy anything, visiting one or two is worth the authentic reflection of Parisian society you encounter. Markets are generally open from Tuesday through Saturday, from around 7 a.m. to 1 p.m., and of course, the pickings are better the earlier you go. The ones open on Sunday are indicated. Some of the more well known include

✔ **Marché Bastille,** 11e (Métro: Bastille; see map p. 160): This huge market sells everything from game, cheese, and vegetables to fish and condiments. Open Thursday from 7 a.m. to 2:30 p.m. and Sunday 7 a.m. to 3 p.m.

✔ **Marché Biologique,** boulevard Raspail between rue du Cherche-Midi and rue de Rennes, 6e (Métro: Rennes; see map p. 162): This all-organic market features greengrocers, winemakers, butchers, and bakers. Open Sunday 9 a.m. to 2 p.m. An "inorganic" market takes place here Tuesday and Friday from 7 a.m. to 2:30 p.m.

✔ **Rue Cler,** 7e (Métro: Ecole-Militaire; see map p. 162): See how diplomats shop for their dinner in this chic market. Open Tuesday through Saturday mornings between 8:30 a.m. and 1 p.m. and again from 5 to 7 p.m. Sundays open only in the morning up to noon.

✔ **Rue de Buci,** 6e (Métro: Odéon; see map p. 162): This lively market is close to all the Latin Quarter action. Open Tuesday to Sunday mornings between 8 a.m. and noon.

✔ **Rue Montorgueil,** 1er (Métro: Les Halles/Châtelet; see map p. 160): Have breakfast at one of the many sidewalk cafes before choosing your produce. Open Tuesday through Saturday from 8 a.m. to 1 p.m. and 4 p.m. to 7 p.m.

✔ **Place Monge,** 5e (Métro: Monge; see map p. 162): One of the oldest markets in Paris on one of the city's more interesting streets. Sing along with accordion players on Sunday mornings. Open Wednesday and Friday between 7:30 a.m. and 2:30 p.m., 7 a.m. to 3 p.m. on Sundays.

✔ **Rue Poncelet,** 17e (Métro: Ternes; see map p. 160): The Poncelet market is especially renowned for its fresh fruit stalls. Open Tuesday through Saturday mornings between 8:30 a.m. and noon and again from 2:30 until 6 p.m.

The best bakeries

You want a fresh baguette for your picnic, and you can find bakeries *(boulangeries)* on nearly every corner in residential neighborhoods. Keep in mind that quality of the breads varies considerably.

Long lines of locals on weekend mornings or evenings before dinner give away the best bakeries. You can get a sandwich or a quiche to go, but be warned that bakeries here offer what seem to be very plain sandwiches — often just a slice of bread or cheese on a baguette with no condiment or other accoutrement. If you want a sandwich with more filling, look for the name of an ingredient plus *"crudités,"* which means that it comes with raw vegetables, usually lettuce, cucumbers, or even tomatoes, and mayonnaise). For a chicken sandwich with raw veggies, for example, ask for *poulet crudités* (poo-*lay* crew-dee-tay). Below are some of Paris's best bakeries.

✔ **BE (Boulangepicier),** 73 bd. de Courcelles, 8e; ☎ **01-46-22-20-20.** Open Monday to Saturday from 7 a.m. to 8 p.m. Métro: Courcelles or Ternes; see map p. 160.

✔ **Bonneau,** 75 rue d'Auteuil, 16e; ☎ **01-46-51-12-25.** Open Tuesday through Sunday from 6:30 a.m. to 8:30 p.m. Métro: Michel–Ange–Auteuil; see map p. 162.

✔ **Boulangerie Kayser** (organic), 14 rue Monge, 5e; ☎ **01-44-07-17-81.** Open Tuesday through Sunday 8 a.m. to 8 p.m. Métro: Maubert Mutualité; see map p. 162.

✔ **Boulangerie Kayser** (traditional), 8 rue Monge, 5e; ☎ **01-44-07-01-42.** Open Wednesday through Monday from 6:30 a.m. to 8:30 p.m. Métro: Maubert Mutualité; see map p. 162.

✔ **Caumont,** 33 rue Coquillière, 1e; ☎ **01-45-08-57-60.** Open Monday through Friday from 7 a.m. to 8 p.m.

- ✔ **Le Grenier à Pain,** 38 rue des Abbesses, 18e; ☎ **01-46-06-41-81.**
  Open Friday through Tuesday, from 7:30 a.m. to 8 p.m. Métro:
  Abbesses.

- ✔ **Moulin de la Vierge,** 166 av. de Suffren, 15e; ☎ **01-47-83-45-55.**
  Open Friday to Wednesday from 7 a.m. to 8 p.m. Métro: Sèvres-
  Lecourbe; see map p. 162.

- ✔ **Poilâne,** 8 rue du Cherche-midi, 6e; ☎ **01-45-48-42-59.** Open Monday
  to Saturday from 7:15 a.m. to 8:15 p.m. Métro: St-Sulpice or Sèvres
  Babylone; see map p. 160.

- ✔ **Poujauran,** 20 rue Jean Nicot, 7e; ☎ **01-43-17-35-20.** Open Tuesday
  to Saturday from 8 a.m. to 8:30 p.m. Métro: La Tour Maubourg; see
  map p. 162.

There are so many different types of bread available in these bakeries,
that a complete list would probably be impossible to compile accurately.
However, the most staple bread for sampling is the *baguette,* which is
long, crispy, and delicious. If you're feeling a little adventurous, spend
a euro and change, instead of the requisite 85 centimes, on a *baguette
de campagne, à l'ancienne,* or *de tradition.* These names mean that the
baguette dough, which is prepared by hand, is left overnight to let
the yeast develop. The result is a much more flavorful and chewier interior with an off-white, more rustic look than the simple white-interior
baguettes. The extra 20 to 40 centimes will go a long way. Look for
boulangeries that say ARTISINAL, which means that they prepare all of
their goods on the spot: These places sell pastries and bread with a
mouthwatering taste that cannot be described in any language!

Watching the world go by at a cafe

There are just too many good cafes in Paris — after all, the French have
been perfecting these institutions for centuries — and to list them all
here would be *am-poh-seebl,* as they say in French. Instead, we've compiled some of our favorites — places where you'll be comfortable reading the paper, writing postcards, watching people, and soaking up the
city's atmosphere while relaxing with a cup of coffee, a glass of wine or
beer, or a sandwich, salad, or traditional French specialty like *pot-au-feu*
(beef boiled with vegetables). Cafes are generally open from about 8 a.m.
until 1 a.m., and most take MasterCard and Visa.

Au Bistro de La Place

This square on the place du Marché Sainte-Catherine is a pedestrian zone
on the site of an 18th-century market, and this is the prettiest of all the
bistros on the outdoor terrace here. The food is also the best; you may
find fresh vegetable soup served hot or cold or an artichoke pâté with
salad, topped off with butter-browned salmon served with a saffron sauce.
Even if you don't come here for a meal, visit after the lunch hour (noon–
2:30 p.m.) to enjoy a leisurely drink or pastry on the terrace.

See map p. 160. 2 place du Marché Sainte-Catherine (between rue de Turenne and rue de Sevigné), 4e. ☎ *01-42-78-21-32*. Métro: St-Paul. Closed Fri.

Au Progrès

Situated on a pleasant corner near the footsteps of Sacre Coeur, le Progrés is quirky and simple. The benches and closely arranged tables put funky and bohemian locals next to tourists; all to be served by a youthful staff who yell jokes back and forth over the midday din. A croque *jeune homme* (their tongue-in-cheek name for a croque monsieur) is only 7.50€ ($9), or you can just sip wine while watching the denizens of Montmartre pass you by. During the winter, order their *vin chaud* (hot wine, with spices), it will warm you right up!

See map p. 160. 7 rue des Trois Frères, 18e. ☎ *01-42-64-07-37*. Métro: Abbesses or Anvers.

Au Rendez-Vous des Amis

You will find at the "meeting place of friends" a pleasant throwback to the Marais cafe of a previous era. They avoid the ultramodern décor of the modern metropolis in favor of beautiful wood-lined counters and well-worn chairs, with simple sketches, old photos, and stained-glass panes on the walls. A hot goat cheese salad with some red wine is mouth-watering, and the people-watching on the chic and beautiful rue Saint-Croix de la Bretonnerie is never boring.

See map p. 160. 10 rue Sainte-Croix de la Bretonnerie, 4e. ☎ *01-42-72-05-99*. Métro: Hôtel de Ville.

Café Beaubourg

This is the hip cafe overlooking the Centre Pompidou; the backs of its white terrace chairs (nearly always full with a good mix of tourists and locals) resemble the lips in the Stravinsky Fountain just around the corner. The best time to sit here is around opening time — have their breakfast special (fresh-baked croissants or *pain chocolat,* juice, and coffee or tea, for 8€/$10) and watch, with the classy regulars, last-night's partiers walk home. The dark bilevel interior has large circular columns that soar to an illuminated ceiling. The walls are filled with books, and a small wooden bridge spans the upper part of the cafe and leads to quieter, artistically designed tables. Even the bathrooms are attractions in themselves; they have the serenity of Zen gardens. Simple food may include a smooth gazpacho, salmon club sandwich, or goat cheese salad. You'll become a main attraction yourself as passersby cast curious glances at the people chic enough to eat here.

See map p. 160. 43 rue St-Merri, 4e. ☎ *01-48-87-63-96*. Métro: Rambuteau or Hôtel-de-Ville.

Café de Flore

In the heart of St-Germain-des-Prés, this cafe is still going strong, even though the famous writers have moved on and you now pay high prices.

Sartre is said to have written *Les Chemins de la Liberté (The Roads to Freedom)* at his table here, and he and Simone de Beauvoir saw people by appointment here. Other regulars included André Malraux and Guillaume Apollinaire. Paris's leading intellectual bookstore, La Hune, is right next door.

See map p. 162. 172 bd. St-Germain, 6e. ☎ *01-45-48-55-26. Métro: St-Germain-des-Prés.*

Café de la Place

If you're headed out of Paris via the Gare Montparnasse and you have a bit of extra time, skip the train station food stalls and come to this old-fashioned cafe overlooking small, tree-lined place Edgar Quinet, just around the corner and down the street. It's a calm and popular spot for young neighborhood residents. Browse the menu of inexpensive bistro specialties, or opt for a simple sandwich and a glass of wine. If you're lucky, there will be a *brocante* (flea market) or art fair in the square across the street.

See map p. 162. 23 rue d'Odessa, 14e. ☎ *01-42-18-01-55. Métro: Edgar-Quinet.*

Café de L'Industrie

This cafe is young, friendly, casual, and extremely popular; so much so that at night the crowd constantly overflows to the sidewalks next door and even across the street. To capitalize on its popularity, Café de l'Industrie bought its next door neighbor and the former Moroccan restaurant across the street. Mod meets retro meets country in the spacious rooms that also have a vaguely colonial flavor. Hip Bastille denizens drift in and out all day. Bartenders like to mix "specialties," and if you ask for one with a winning smile, you may get a reduced price. An 18€ ($22) brunch is served on weekends.

See map p. 160. 15–17 rue St-Sabin (the corner of rue Sedaine and rue St-Sabin), 11e. ☎ *01-47-00-13-53. Métro: Breguet-Sabin or Bastille.*

Café les Deux Magots

Like its neighbor, Café de Flore, Café les Deux Magots was a hangout for Sartre and Simone de Beauvoir. The intellectuals met here in the 1950s, and Sartre wrote at his table every morning. Hemingway also haunted this place, at least, when he had the money. With prices that start at 4€ ($5) for coffee, the cafe is an expensive place for literary-intellectual pilgrims, but a great spot to watch the nightly promenade on the boulevard St-Germain.

See map p. 162. 6 place St-Germain-des-Prés, 6e. ☎ *01-45-48-55-25. Métro: St-Germain-des-Prés.*

Café Mabillon

If you only have one night in Paris, make the most of it and welcome the dawn at Café Mabillon, which stays open all night. During the day, pleasant lounge music draws the young and hip as well as older BCBG locals, who dine in fantastic outfits that you'd be afraid to spill food on. If you're hungry, try the ravioli with foie gras; it's to die for. Or just have a cafe or glass of wine and relax on the outdoor terrace or in the ultramodern interior. At night the music changes to techno and electro, and the bordello-red banquettes fill with a wide assortment of night owls. As dawn approaches, the sound drops to a level just loud enough to keep you from dozing off in your seat.

See map p. 162. 164 bd. St-Germain, 6e. ☎ 01-43-26-62-93. Métro: Mabillon.

Café Marly

Sinking into one of the plush red chairs here amid high ceilings, warmly painted pastel walls, and luxurious sofa chairs with a drink or cup of tea is the best antidote to Louvre fatigue! This stunning cafe has a gorgeous view of the glass pyramid that is the museum's main entrance. You almost forget food is served here, but that would be a mistake — it's very good, if not abundant. It is certainly a bit on the expensive side, but that is normal considering your location. Enjoy the exquisite lighting on the pyramid and surrounding 18th-century facades from the outdoor balcony. After 8 p.m., seating is for dinner only.

See map p. 160. 93 rue de Rivoli, cour Napoléon du Louvre, 1er. ☎ 01-49-26-06-60. Métro: Palais-Royal–Musée du Louvre.

Fouquet's

This 20th-century Parisian institution is the place with the red umbrellas on the Champs-Elysées, not far from the Arc de Triomphe. The restaurant has undergone a renovation that restored the red plush and wood splendor of the days when it hosted such guests as James Joyce, Charlie Chaplin, Marlene Dietrich, Winston Churchill, Franklin D. Roosevelt, François Truffaut, Claude Chabrol, and Jean-Luc Godard. Opened in 1899, it is now registered as a historic monument.

See map p. 160. 99 av. des Champs-Elysées, 8e. ☎ 01-47-23-50-00. Métro: George V.

La Chaise au Plafond

This friendly, stylish place tucked away on a pedestrian-only side street in the heart of the Marais is always packed. Maybe that's because it's the perfect spot to refuel after visiting the Musée Picasso. It serves enormous salads, imaginative sandwiches, and thick tartes to a local crowd sprinkled with tourists in the know. The menu and kitchen here is the same as another well known cafe just around the corner, les Philosophes, but la Chaise au Plafond has more personality and more twinkly-eyed waiters.

See map p. 160. 10 rue Trésor, 4e. ☎ 01-42-76-03-22. Métro: Hôtel-de-Ville.

La Contrescarpe

Patrons have been gravitating to this cafe just across the pretty place de la Contrescarpe after the demise of neighborhood cafe La Chope. The view looks out on four lilac trees and a fountain. This is a good place to take a break after marketing on rue Mouffetard or visiting the nearby Panthéon. The 14€ ($17) menu is a good deal.

See map p. 162. 57 rue Lacépède, 5e. ☎ *01-43-36-82-88. Métro: Cardinal Lemoine.*

La Coupole

You won't know which is more interesting, the scene on the street, or the parade that passes through the revolving doors of this infamous cafe which has been packing them in since Henry Miller came here for his morning porridge. The cavernous interior is always jammed and bristling with energy. Japanese business people, French yuppies, models, tourists, and neighborhood regulars keep the frenzied waiters running until 2 a.m. The food is good, too, though prices are high, and dancing happens down-stairs on the weekends.

See map p. 162. 102 bd. Montparnasse, 14e. ☎ *01-43-20-14-20. Métro: Vavin.*

Le Comptoir du Relais Saint-Germain

The spunky waitstaff at this tiny cafe serves restaurant class meals and quick pick-me-ups: You can get cheese or charcuterie with a traditionally-made baguette while you sip some house red wine, but also try their chicken cream soup with spices — mmm. With plenty of outdoor seating, Le Comptoir is perfectly situated in the carrefour de l'Odéon, and you can watch curious Left Bank habitués and students walk by, or even watch the people in the other cafes across the street.

See map p. 162. 9 carrefour de l'Odéon, 6e. ☎ *01-46-33-45-30. Métro: Odéon.*

L'Eté en Pente Douce

Escape the shoulder-to-shoulder tourists on Montmartre's place du Tertre at this cute cafe. To find it, turn right after exiting the *funiculaire,* and take the first set of steps leading down. You find yourself on a leafy square facing a small park. The terrace looks out on stairs and iron lamps once painted by Montmartre artist Utrillo, and someone always performs here for a captive audience. The interior is brightly decorated with painted bor-ders of leaves and plants, mosaics, unusual *objets d'art,* and a painted ceil-ing. Between lunch and dinner, the restaurant serves tea, pastries, and sandwiches.

See map p. 160. 23 rue Muller, 18e. ☎ *01-42-64-02-67. Métro: Chateau-Rouge.*

L'Étoile Manquante

Translated as "the missing star," this is a modern, tasteful, and above all, fun cafe that plays host to all kinds of locals, artists, and writers who enjoy reasonably priced, somewhat inventive and tasty food in an atmosphere that whispers rather than shouts "cool." Little stars in the floor tiles twin-kle in the dim light from recessed round ceiling lights outlined in brown circles and from baguette-shaped sconces with artfully placed tiny holes to let the light through. The vibrant scene is reflected in the wall of rectangular mirrors in the back of the restaurant. A visit to the very dark bathrooms lit from above by "starlight" is a must.

See map p. 160. 34 rue e Vieille du Temple, 4e. ☎ *01-42-72-48-34. Métro: Hôtel de Ville or St-Paul.*

Le Sancerre

This is one of several cafes on rue des Abbesses where you can sit and watch the passing citizens of Montmartre in their hipster gear. They have great *croque monsieurs* if you're hungry, or order a *café* and contemplate your next artistic endeavor like the other people sitting at neighboring tables. Why this cafe in particular? Because it is one of the least expensive in the area, while maintaining a lively atmosphere and simple, fun décor.

See map p. 162. 35 rue des Abbesses, 18e. ☎ *01-42-58-0-20.*

Pause Café

Featured in the French film *Chacun Cherche Son Chat* (released in the United States as *When the Cat's Away*), this cafe has proved very popular with locals. It's almost always full, and if it's nighttime, the patrons are most likely stopping in for drinks on their way to a night of dancing. If you'd like to find out where these club-scene people are headed, flyers inside provide dates for upcoming events. A bright-colored, modern interior with hanging light fixtures also features found art, while outdoors is made tropical with cloth and bamboo umbrellas and potted palms. The food is fresh and tasty.

See map p. 160. 41 rue de Charonne, 11e. ☎ *01-48-06-80-33. Métro: Lédru-Rollin.*

Steeping and sipping at a tea salon (Salons de thé)

Sitting down to tea in Paris can be an elegant and refined undertaking, or a relaxing break between bouts of shopping and *musée*-hopping. The tea salons have a wide range of blends, steeped to perfection, and the pastry selections are usually excellent (Ladurée's macaroons are world-famous). Save your full meals, however, for a restaurant because tea salons tend to be expensive.

- ✔ **Angelina,** 226 rue de Rivoli, 1er; ☎ 01-42-60-82-00. Open daily from 9 a.m. to 5:45 p.m. Lunch is served from 11:45 a.m. to 3 p.m. Métro: Concorde or Tuileries; see map p. 160.

- ✔ **A Priori Thé,** 35–37 Galerie Vivienne (enter at 6 rue Vivienne, 4 rue des Petits-Champs, or 5 rue de la Banque), 2e; ☎ 01-42-97-48-75. Open Monday to Friday 9 a.m. to 6 p.m.; Saturday from 9 a.m. to 6:30 p.m., and Sunday from noon to 6:30 p.m. Métro: Bourse, Palais-Royal–Musée du Louvre, or Pyramides; see map p. 160.

- ✔ **Ladurée,** 16 rue Royale, 8e; ☎ 01-42-60-21-79. Open Monday through Saturday from 8:30 a.m. to 7:30 p.m. Métro: Concorde; see map p. 160. Also at 75 Champs-Elysées, ☎ 01-40-75-08-75, Métro:

Franklin-D-Roosevelt; and in Sainte Germain, 21 rue Bonaparte, ☎ 01-44-97-64-87.

✔ **La Fourmi Ailée,** 8 rue du Fouarre, 5e; ☎ 01-43-29-40-99. Open daily from noon to midnight. Métro: Maubert-Mutualité. See map p. 162.

✔ **Mariage Frères,** 13 rue Grands Augustins, 6e; ☎ 01-40-51-82-50. This location is open daily from noon to 7 p.m. Métro: St-Michel; see map p. 162. Another location is at 30 rue du Bourg-Tibourg, 4e; ☎ 01-42-72-28-11. Métro: Hôtel de Ville.

✔ **Salon de Thé de la Mosquée de Paris,** 39 rue Geoffroy-St-Hilaire, 5e; ☎ 01-43-31-18-14. Open daily from 10 a.m. to midnight. Métro: Place Monge. See map p. 162.

✔ **The Tea Caddy,** 14 rue St-Julien-le-Pauvre, 5e; ☎ 01-43-54-15-56. Open daily from noon to 7 p.m. Métro: St-Michel. See map p. 162.

A heady mix of wine bars

We love Paris's wine bars with their good selections of wines by the glass, and tasty light meals served all day in pleasant surroundings. The Paris wine bar is often a cozy and sophisticated alternative to the cafe.

Au Négociant

The photographer Robert Doisneau came here often (his picture is on the wall), but today a discerning crowd of regulars keep this tiny, hole-in-the-wall wine bar near Montmartre humming. The excellent pâtés and terrines are homemade and served with fresh, chewy bread.

See map p. 160. 27 rue Lambert, 18e. ☎ *01-46-06-15-11. Métro: Château-Rouge or Lamarck-Caulincourt. Mon–Fri noon–2:30 p.m.; Tues–Thurs 6:30–10:30 p.m.*

Clown Bar

It's hard to say what gets more attention here, the wine or the clowns from the nearby Cirque d'Hiver who frequent this place. The bar is decorated with a mélange of circus posters and circus-themed ceramic tiles. The wine list features an extensive selection of French offerings.

See map p. 160. 114 rue Amelot, 11e. ☎ *01-43-55-87-35. Métro: Filles du Calvaire. Mon–Sat noon–2:30 p.m. and 7 p.m.–noon*

La Cloche des Halles

This tiny bar and cafe is crowded at lunchtime with people dining on plates of ham or quiche accompanied by a bottle of wine, and maybe one of their specialty Tarte Tatin for dessert. It's convivial and fun, but very noisy and crowded, just like the rest of the quarter during the day. If you can't find a seat, you can usually stand at the bar and eat. Look closely at the exterior for the bell that once tolled the opening and closing of the vast food market for which this neighborhood was named.

See map p. 160. 28 rue Coquillière, 1er. ☎ 01-42-36-93-89. Métro: Les Halles or Palais-Royal–Musée du Louvre. Mon–Fri 8 a.m.–10 p.m.; Sat 10 a.m.–5 p.m.

La Tartine

This neighborhood wine bar is relaxed and comfortable — the head waitress will talk to you like you've known each other for years. A renovation that took place over three years ago threatened to kill the historical and well-worn atmosphere, but no worries. The same mix of working class and well heeled frequent La Tartine, and it's a great place to get a light lunch of goat cheese salad, or a pick-me-up of tartine (open-faced sandwich), cheese, or *charcuterie* (assorted sliced meats) plate and a glass of wine.

See map p. 160. 24 rue de Rivoli, 4e. ☎ 01-42-72-76-85. Métro: St-Paul. Wed–Mon noon–10 p.m.

Le Bistrot du Peintre

Painters, actors, and night crawlers hang out here nightly. The delicious and reasonably priced food, zinc bar, wood paneling, large terrace, and superb Belle Époque style would make this wine bar a highlight even if the wine selection wasn't as reasonably priced as it is.

See map p. 160. 116 av. Ledru-Rollin, 11e. ☎ 01-47-00-34-39. Métro: Ledru-Rollin. Daily 9 a.m.–2 a.m. (the kitchen closes at midnight).

L'Écluse

L'Écluse is casually chic, authentic, and conveniently located smack in the middle of in St-Germain. Have one of its 20 wines by the glass and a light bite such as *carpaccio,* salad, or soup.

See map p. 162. 15 quai des Grands-Augustins, 6e. ☎ 01-46-33-58-74. Métro: St-Michel. Daily 11:30 a.m.–1 a.m.

Le Griffonnier

The kitchen staff at Le Griffonnier deliver first-rate cuisine, and the wine cellar is superb. Sample bistro specialties such as their *confit de canard maison* (duck preserved and cooked in its own fat until it's so tender that it falls off the bone), or try a hearty plate of *charcuterie* (regional sliced meats), terrines, and cheese, usually from the Auvergne region of central France, and ask your waiter to recommend the wine. Hot meals are served only at lunchtime (until 3:30 p.m.) and on Thursday evenings.

See map p. 160. 8 rue des Saussaies, 8e. ☎ 01-42-65-17-17. Métro: Champs-Elysées–Clemenceau. Mon–Fri 8 a.m.–9 p.m.

Le Sancerre

Le Sancerre is a quiet place to relax for a light meal or glass of wine after visiting the Eiffel Tower. Loire wines are the specialty here, including, of course, Sancerre. The manager knows nothing of shyness and will discuss with you all you want to know about the wine, which plate goes well with which wine, and anything else you might want to know. Ignore his girlie-magazine pictures on the wall, as they have nothing to do with the wonderful tortes and terrines. La Sancerre serves typically French items, such as omelets of all varieties with a side of fried potatoes, and duck liver terrine. Specials change all the time, so ask as well: the last sitting included a mouth watering sun-dried tomato and emmenthal cheese torte with a homemade crust. The more adventurous can sample the ubiquitous *andouillette,* the sausage that is decidedly an acquired taste.

See map p. 162. 22 av. Rapp, 7e. ☎ *01-45-51-75-91. Métro: Alma Marceau. Mon–Fri 8 a.m.–10 p.m.; Sat 8 a.m.–4 p.m.*

Mélac

Owner Jacques Mélac has an excellent selection of wine from nearly all the regions of France, which he dispenses to a lively crowd of regulars. He's happy to give you recommendations. Usually a hot *plat du jour* is available for lunch, but you can feast on a selection of first-rate pâtés, terrines, *charcuterie* (regional sliced meats), and cheeses all day. Note the wonderful wall display of regional wines; you can't forget here that you're in a wine bar.

See map p. 160. 42 rue Léon Frot, 11e. ☎ *01-43-70-59-27. Métro: Charonne. Mon 9 a.m.–2 p.m.; Tues–Sat 9 a.m.–10:30 p.m.*

Taverne Henri IV

Although on the expensive side, the wine and food are excellent at this authentic, old-fashioned bar, where regulars, mostly male, read newspapers, discuss the news of the day, and smoke nonstop (here you may witness an older French man smoking *un ninas* [a small cigar the size of a cigarette], a dying cultural practice). The variety of wines by the glass can accompany open-faced sandwiches, pâtés, and such cheeses as Cantal and Auvergne blue.

See map p. 160. 13 place du Pont Neuf, 1er. ☎ *01-43-54-27-90. Métro: Pont-Neuf. Mon–Fri 11:30 a.m.–10 p.m.; Sat noon–6 p.m. Closed Aug.*

Willi's Wine Bar

Since 1980, an upscale crowd of professionals and tourists have sampled more than 250 different varieties of wine while seated at the polished oak bar or have dined in the high-ceilinged oak-beamed dining room from a full menu of main courses starting at 13€ ($16); the dinner three course menu is 32€ or 34€ ($38 or $41). Each year the owners commission an image relating to wine from an artist, and the colorful paintings are available for sale as prints for between 49€ and 400€ ($59–$480).

See map p. 160. 13 rue des Petits-Champs, 1er. ☎ *01-42-61-05-09. Métro: Bourse, Pyramide, or Palais Royale. Mon–Sat noon–2:30 p.m. and 7–11 p.m.; bar open Mon–Sat noon–midnight.*

Getting the scoop on Paris ice cream

If Paris doesn't have the best ice cream flavors in the world, it must run a close second. Such flavors (rhubarb, plum, cassis, honey nut . . .), such creaminess! Ask for a *cornet seule* (kor-*nay* sul; single-scoop cone) or *cornet double* (kor-*nay* doobl; double scoop) — even the cone is yummy. Parisians cite **Berthillon,** 31 rue St-Louis-en-l'Ile, 4e (☎ **01-43-54-31-61;** Métro: Cité; see map p. 160) as the best in the city, but the following establishments also put soft-serve to shame. Although Berthillon closes from July 15 through the first week in September, a note on the door directs customers to other nearby shops that sell its ice cream. **Le Flore en l'Ile,** 42 quai d'Orléans, 4e (☎ **01-43-29-88-27;** Métro: Cité), a restaurant and *salon de thé,* always has an outside station to buy Berthillon ice cream. A chain of ice cream parlors called **Amorino** (locations listed below) also boasts excellent ice cream in numerous flavors (for pure ingenuity try the grapefruit).

✔ **Amorino** 4 rue de Buci, 6e; ☎ **01-43-26-57-46;** Métro: Odéon. Other locations around the city; see map p. 162.

✔ **De Toffol Bénito,** 45 rue Mouffetard, 5e; ☎ **01-43-37-88-07;** Métro: Monge.

✔ **La Butte Glacée,** 14 rue Norvins, 18e; ☎ **01-42-23-91-58;** Métro: Abbesses; see map p. 160.

✔ **Le Bac à Glaces,** 109 rue du Bac, 7e; ☎ **01-45-48-87-65;** Métro: rue du Bac; see map p. 162.

✔ **M.P. Gourmandises,** 39 rue Harpe, 5e; ☎ **01-43-25-63-56;** Métro: Cluny-La Sorbonne; see map p. 162.

✔ **Octave,** 138 rue Mouffetard, 5e; ☎ **01-45-35-20-56;** Métro: Monge; see map p. 162.

✔ **Scoop,** 154 rue St-Honoré, 1er (behind the Louvre des Antiquaires); ☎ **01-42-60-31-84;** Métro: Louvre-Rivoli; see map p. 160.

Index of Establishments by Neighborhood

Le Marais, Ile St-Louis/Ile de la Cité (3e, 4e)

Au Bascou (Basque/Southwest, $$)
Auberge de Jarente
(Basque/Southwest, $$)
Au Bistro de la Place (Cafes, $)
Au Rendez-Vous des Amis (Cafes, $)
Bofinger (Alsatian/Brasserie, $$)
Brasserie Ile St-Louis
(Alsatian/Brasserie, $$)
Café Beaubourg (Cafes, $)
Caveau du Palais (Cafes, $$)
Chez H'anna (Vegetarian, $)
Jo Goldenberg (Central European, $–$$)
L'Ambroisie (Haute Cuisine, $$$$)
La Chaise au Plafond (Cafes, $)
La Tartine (Wine Bar, $)
Le Flore en l'Ile (Cafes, $$)
L'Étoile Manquante (Cafes, $)
Le Potager du Marais (Vegetarian, $)
Piccolo Teatro (Vegetarian, $$)
Pomme de Pain (Sandwiches, $)

Latin Quarter (5e)

Boulangerie Kayser (Boulangeries, $)
Brasserie Balzar (Alsatian/
Brasserie, $$)
Breakfast in America (American, $)
Chantairelle (Auvergne, $$)
Hédiard (Traiteurs, $)
La Contrescarpe (Cafes, $)
La Formi Ailée (Tea Salon, $)
Le Grenier de Notre-Dame
(Vegetarian, $–$$)
Le Pain Quotidien (Sandwiches, $)
Le Pot de Terre (Classic French, $)
Les 5 Saveurs d'Anada (Vegetarian, $)
M.P. Gourmandises (Ice Cream, $)
Octave (Ice Cream, $)
Restaurant Perraudin (Classic
Bistro, $$)
Salon de Thé de la Mosquée de Paris
(Tea Salon, $)
The Tea Caddy (Tea Salon, $)

St-Germain-des-Près (6e)

Amorino (Ice Cream, $)
Café de Flore (Cafes, $)
Café les Deux Magots (Cafes, $)

Café Mabillon (Cafes, $$)
Cosi (Sandwiches, $)
Jacques Cagna (Haute Cuisine, $$$)
La Bastide Odéon (Provencal, $$)
La Grande Épicerie (Traiteurs, $)
A La Petite Chaise (Classic French, $$)
La Bastide Odéon (Provencal, $$)
L'Écluse (Wine Bar, $)
Le Comptoir du Relais St-Germain
(Cafes, $$)
Lina's (Sandwiches, $)
Poilâne (Boulangeries, $)
Vagenende (Alsatian/Brasserie, $–$$)
Ze Kitchen Galerie (Modern Bistro, $$)

Eiffel Tower and Invalides (7e, 15e)

Au Bon Accueil (Modern Bistro, $$)
La Cigale (Classic Bistro, $$)
L'Atelier Joël Robuchon (Modern
Bistro, $$–$$$)
Le Bac à Glaces (Ice Cream, $)
Le Père Claude (Classic Bistro, $$)
Le Sancerre (Wine Bar, $$)
Moulin de la Vierge (Boulangeries, $)
Poujauran (Boulangeries, $)

Champs-Elysées and Ternes (8e and 17e)

BE (Boulangepicier) (Boulangeries, $)
Fouquet's (Cafes, $)
Ladurée (Tea Salon, $)
Le Cinq (Haute Cuisine, $$$$)
Le Griffonier (Wine Bar, $)
Mariage Frères (Tea Salon, $)
Michel Rostang (Classic French, $$$$)

Opéra/Gare du Nord (9e, 10e)

Chez Casimir (Classic French, $$)
Chez Michel (Breton, $$)
Lafayette Gourmet (Traiteurs, $)
16 Haussmann (Classic French, $$)

Bastille/Oberkampf (4e, 11e, 12e)

Bofinger (Alsatian/Brasserie, $$)
Café de l'Industrie (Cafes, $)
Chardenoux (Classic Bistro, $$)
Clown Bar (Wine Bar, $)
L'Ébauchoir (Classic Bistro, $$)

Le Bistrot du Peintre (Wine Bar, $)
Mélac (Wine Bar, $)
Pause Café (Cafes, $)

Montparnasse (14e)
Café de la Place (Cafes, $)
La Coupole (Cafes, $)

Trocadèro (16e)
Bonneau (Boulangeries, $)

Montmartre (18e)
Au Grain des Folies (Vegetarian, $)
Au Négociant (Wine Bar, $)
Au Poulbot Gourmet (Classic French, $–$$)
Au Progrès (Cafes, $)
Chez Marie (Classic French, $$)
La Butte Glacée (Ice Cream, $)
Le Grenier au Pain (Boulangeries, $)
Le Kokolion (Classic French, $)
L'Été en Pente Douce (Cafes, $)

Index of Establishments by Cuisine

Alsatian/Brasserie
Bofinger ($$, Bastille)
Brasserie Balzar ($$, Latin Quarter)
Brasserie Ile-Louis ($$, Ile St-Louis)
Vagenende ($–$$, St-Germain-des-Prés)
Zimmer ($$, Louvre, Les Halles)

American
Breakfast in America ($, Latin Quarter)
Sam's Bagels ($, Sentier)

Auvergne
Chantairelle ($$, Latin Quarter)

Basque/Southwest
Au Bascou ($$, Le Marais)
Auberge de Jarente ($$, Le Marais)

Boulangeries
BE (Boulangepicier) ($, Champs-Elysées)
Bonneau ($, Trocadèro)
Boulangerie Kayser ($, Latin Quarter)
Caumont ($)
Le Grenier au Pain ($, Montmartre)
Poilâne ($, St-Germain-des-Prés)
Poujauran ($, Eiffel Tower)
Moulin de la Vierge ($, Eiffel Tower)

Breton
Chez Michel ($$, Gare du Nord)

Cafes
Au Bistro de la Place ($, Le Marais)
Au Rendez-Vous des Amis ($, Le Marais)
Au Progrès ($, Montmartre)
Café Beaubourg ($, Le Marais)
Café de Flore ($, St-Germain-des-Prés)
Café de la Place ($, Montparnasse)
Café de l'Industrie ($, Bastille-Oberkampf)
Café les Deux Magots ($, St-Germain-des-Prés)
Café Mabillon ($, St-Germain-des-Prés)
Café Marly ($, Louvre)
Fouquet's ($, Champs-Elysées)
La Chaise au Plafond ($, Le Marais)
La Contrescarpe ($, Latin Quarter)
La Coupole ($, Montparnasse)
Le Comptoir du Relais St-Germain ($$, St-Germain-des-Prés, Odéon)
L'Eté en Pente Douce ($, Montmartre)
L'Étoile Manquante ($, Le Marais)
Pause Café ($, Bastille)

Central European
Jo Goldenberg ($–$$, Le Marais)

Classic Bistro
Chardenoux ($$, Bastille)
La Cigale ($$, Invalides)

La Poule au Pot ($$, Les Halles)
L'Ébauchoir ($$, Bastille)
Le Père Claude ($$, Eiffel Tower)
Restaurant Perraudin ($$, Latin Quarter)

Classic French

Au Pied de Cochon ($$, Les Halles)
Au Poulbot Gourmet ($–$$, Montmartre)
Caveau du Palais ($$, Ile de la Cité)
Chez Casimir ($$, Gare du Nord)
Chez Marie ($$, Montmartre)
A La Petite Chaise ($$, St-Germain-des-Prés)
La Tour de Montlhéry Chez Denise ($$–$$$, Les Halles)
Le Kokolion ($–$$, Montmartre)
Le Pot de Terre ($, Latin Quarter)
Michel Rostang ($$$$, Ternes)
Restaurant du Palais-Royal ($$–$$$, Louvre)
16 Haussmann ($$, Opéra)

Haute Cuisine

Jacques Cagna ($$$, St-Germain-des-Près)
L'Ambroisie ($$$$, Le Marais)
Le Cinq ($$$$, Champs-Elysées)

Ice Cream

Amorino ($, St-Germain-des-Près)
Berthillon ($, Ile de la Cité)
La Butte Glacée ($, Montmartre)
Le Bac à Glaces ($, Eiffel Tower)
Le Flore en l'Ile ($$, Ile St-Louis)
M.P. Gourmandises ($, Latin Quarter)
Octave ($, Latin Quarter)
Scoop ($, Louvre)

Modern Bistro

Au Bon Accueil ($$, Eiffel Tower)
L'Atelier Joël Robuchon ($$–$$$, Eiffel Tower)
Georges ($$–$$$, Les Halles)
Ze Kitchen Galerie ($$, St-Germain-des-Près)

Provençal

La Bastide Odéon ($$, St-Germain-des-Prés)

Sandwiches

Cosi ($, St-Germain-des-Près)
Le Pain Quotidien ($, Latin Quarter)
Lina's ($, St-Germain-des-Près)
Pomme de Pain ($,Marais)

Tea Salons

Angelina ($, Louvre)
A Priori Thé ($, Sentier)
Ladurée ($, Champs-Elysées)
La Formi Ailée ($, Latin Quarter)
Mariage Frères ($, Champs-Elysées)
Salon de Thé à la Mosquée de Paris ($, Latin Quarter)
The Tea Caddy ($, Latin Quarter)

Traiteurs

Fauchon ($, Louvre)
Hédiard ($, Latin Quarter)
La Grande Épicerie ($, St-Germain-des-Près)
Lafayette Gourmet ($, Opèra)

Vegetarian

Au Grain des Folies ($, Montmartre)
Chez H'anna ($, Marais)
Le Grenier de Notre-Dame ($–$$, Latin Quarter)
Les 5 Saveurs d'Anada ($, Latin Quarter)
Le Potager du Marais ($, Marais)
Piccolo Teatro ($$, Marais)

Wine Bars

Au Négociant ($, Montmartre)
Clown Bar ($, Bastille)
La Cloche des Halles ($, Louvre/Les Halles)
La Tartine ($, Marais)
L'Écluse ($, St-Germain-des-Près)

Le Bistrot du Peintre ($, Bastille)
Le Griffonier ($, Champs-Elysées)
Le Sancerre ($$, Eiffel Tower)

Mélac ($, Bastille)
Taverne Henri IV ($, Louvre)
Willi's Wine Bar ($, Louvre)

Index of Establishments by Price

$

Angelina (Tea Salon, Louvre)
A Priori Thé (Tea Salon, Sentier)
Amorino (Ice Cream, St-Germain-des-Près)
Au Bistro de la Place (Cafes, Le Marais)
Au Grain de Folies (Vegetarian, Montmartre)
Au Négociant (Wine Bar, Montmartre)
Au Poulbot Gourmet (Classic French, Montmartre)
Au Progrès (Cafes, Montmartre)
Au Rendez-Vous des Amis (Cafes, Marais)
BE (boulangepicier) (Boulangeries, Champs-Elysées)
Bonneau (Boulangeries, Trocadèro)
Boulangerie Kayser (Boulangereis, Latin Quarter)
Breakfast in America (American, Latin Quarter)
Café Beaubourg (Cafes, Le Marais)
Café de Flore (Cafes, St-Germain-des-Près)
Café de la Place (Cafes, Montparnasse)
Café de l'Industrie (Cafes, Bastille-Oberkampf)
Café les Deux Magots (Cafes, St-Germain-des-Près)
Café Mabillon (Cafes, St-Germain-des-Près)
Café Marly (Cafes, Louvre)
Caumont
Chez H'anna (Vegetarian, Marais)
Clown Bar (Wine Bar, Bastille/Oberkampf)
Cosi (Sandwiches, St-Germain-des-Près)
Fauchon (Traiteurs, Louvre)
Fouquet's (Cafes, Champs-Elysées)
Hédiard (Traiteurs, Latin Quarter)

Jo Goldenberg (Central European, Le Marais)
La Butte Glacée (Ice Cream, Montmartre)
La Chaise au Plafond (Cafes, Le Marais)
La Cloche des Halles (Wine Bar, Louvre/Les Halles)
La Contrescarpe (Cafes, Latin Quarter)
La Coupole (Cafes, Montparnasse)
Ladurée (Tea Salon, Champs-Elysées)
Lafayette Gourmet (Traiteurs, Opèra)
La Fourmi Ailée (Tea Salon, Latin Quarter)
La Grande Épicerie (Traiteurs, St-Germain-des-Près)
La Tartine (Wine Bar, Le Marais)
Le Bac à Glaces (Ice Cream, Eiffel Tower)
Le Bistrot du Peintre (Wine Bar, Bastille/Oberkampf)
La Butte Glacée (Ice Cream, Montmartre)
L'Écluse (Wine Bar, St-Germain-des-Près)
Le Grenier de Notre-Dame (Vegetarian, Latin Quarter)
Le Grenier au Pain (Boulangeries, Montmartre)
Le Griffonier (Wine Bar, Champs-Elysées)
Le Kokodion (Classic French, Montmartre)
Le Pain Quotidien (Sandwiches, Latin Quarter)
Le Pot de Terre (Classic French, Latin Quarter)
Le Potager du Marais (Vegetarian, Marais)
Les 5 Saveurs d'Anada (Vegetarian, Latin Quarter)
L'Été en Pente Douce (Cafes, Montmartre)

L'Étoile Manquante (Cafes, Le Marais)

Lina's (Sandwiches, St-Germain-des-Près)

Mariage Frères (Tea Salon, Champs-Elysées)

Mélac (Wine Bar, Bastille/Oberkampf)

Moulin de la Vierge (Boulangeries, Eiffel Tower)

M.P. Gourmandises (Ice Cream, Latin Quarter)

Octave (Ice Cream, Latin Quarter)

Pause Café (Cafes, Bastille-Oberkampf)

Poilâne (Boulangeries, St-Germain-des-Près)

Pomme de Pain (Sandwiches, Le Marais)

Poujauran (Boulangeries, Eiffel Tower)

Salon de thé de la Mosquée de Paris (Tea Salon, Latin Quarter)

Sam's Bagels (Boulangeries, Sentier)

Scoop (Ice Cream, Louvre)

Taverne Henri IV (Wine Bar, Louvre)

The Tea Caddy (Tea Salon, Latin Quarter)

Vagenende (Alsatian/Brasserie, St-Germain-des-Prés)

Willi's Wine Bar (Wine Bar, Louvre)

$$

Au Bascou (Basque/Southwest, Le Marais)

Auberge de Jarente (Basque/Southwest, Le Marais)

Au Bon Accueil (Modern Bistro, Eiffel Tower)

Au Pied de Cochon (Classic French, Les Halles)

Au Poulbot Gourmet (Classic French, Montmartre)

Brasserie Balzar (Alsatian/Brasserie, Latin Quarter)

Brasserie Ile St-Louis (Alsatian/Brasserie, Ile St-Louis)

Caveau du Palais (Cafes, Ile de la Cité)

Chantairelle (Auvergne, Latin Quarter)

Chardenoux (Classic Bistro, Bastille)

Chez Casimir (Classic French, Gare du Nord)

Chez Marie (Classic French, Montmartre)

Chez Michel (Breton, Gare du Nord)

Georges (Modern Bistro, Les Halles)

Jo Goldenberg (Central European, Le Marais)

La Bastide Odéon (Provencal, St-Germain-des-Prés)

La Cigale (Classic Bistro, Invalides)

La Petite Chaise (Classic French, St-Germain-des-Prés)

La Poule au Pot (Classic Bistro, Les Halles)

L'Atelier Joël Robuchon (Modern Bistro, Eiffel Tower)

La Tour de Montlhéry Chez Denise (Classic French, Les Halles)

L'Ébauchoir (Classic Bistro, Bastille)

Le Comptoir du Relais St-Germain (Cafes, St-Germain-des-Près)

Le Flore en l'Ile (Cafes, Ile Saint-Louis)

Le Grenier de Notre-Dame (Vegetarian, Latin Quarter)

Le Kokolion (Classic French, Montmartre)

Le Père Claude (Classic Bistro, Eiffel Tower)

Le Sancerre (Wine Bar, Eiffel Tower)

Piccolo Teatro (Vegetarian, Marais)

Restaurant du Palais-Royal (Classic French, Louvre)

Restaurant Perraudin (Classic Bistro, Latin Quarter)

16 Haussmann (Classic French, Opéra)

Vegenende (Alsatian/Brasserie, St-Germin-des-Près)

Ze Kitchen Galerie (Modern Bistro, St-Germain-des-Prés)

Zimmer (Alsatian/Brasserie, Louvre, Les Halles)

$$$

Jacques Cagna (Haute Cuisine, St-Germain-des-Prés)

L'Atelier Joël Robuchon (Modern Bistro, Eiffel Tower)

La Tour de Montlhéry Chez Denise (Classic French, Les Halles)
Georges (Modern Bistro, Les Halles)
Restaurant du Palais-Royal (Classic French, Louvre)

$$$$
Michel Rostang (Classic French, Ternes)
L'Ambroisie (Classic French, Le Marais)
Le Cinq (Haute Cuisine, Champs-Elysées)

Part IV
Exploring Paris

The 5ᵗʰ Wave
By Rich Tennant

"Now THAT was a great meal! Beautiful presentation, an imaginative use of ingredients, and a sauce with nuance and depth. The French really know how to make a 'Happy Meal.'"

In this part . . .

So many things to see in Paris . . . what do you do first . . . and how long will it take? Chapter 11 tells you a bit about what's worth seeing; lists some more cool things to see and do for kids, teens, history buffs, and art and literature lovers; and suggests gardens and parks to relax in after visiting all those museums. You also find here guided-tour options, from buses to bicycles! Chapter 12 describes today's shopping scene in Paris, previews four great shopping neighborhoods, covers the outdoor markets, and provides reviews of local shops of interest. In Chapter 13, you have the chance to discover Paris in four itineraries and on a walking tour. And just when you're getting used to Paris, Chapter 14 sends you away on one of five popular day trips in the Ile-de-France region.

Chapter 11

Discovering Paris's Best Attractions

*P*aris is synonymous with the Eiffel Tower, Arc de Triomphe, and the Louvre museum, and one of the major reasons you go to Paris is to see its celebrated sights. This chapter starts you off with a succinct review of 20 of the city's top attractions, giving you the lowdown on when to go, how to get there, and why to visit it in the first place. A word of advice: Figure out which sights you would be heartbroken to miss, and plan to do those first. After that, if you have the flexibility, improvise! There's so much to see that you'll reorder your itinerary daily.

Before you leave, log onto www.weather.com and print out the extended forecast for Paris. Or when you arrive, pick up a copy of the *International Herald Tribune* or *USA Today*'s international edition for extended weather forecasts and save museum visits for rainy days. (Keep in mind that most museums close on Mon or Tues and admission is free the first Sun of the month at national museums.) For a list of suggestions of what else to do on rainy days in Paris, see Chapter 17 in the Part of Tens.

Paris's Top Sights

In Paris, you're never at a loss for something to see. In this section, we give you a list of some of the city's best sights.

Paris's Top Attractions

Arc de Triomphe **1**
Cathédral de Notre-Dame **18**
Centre Georges Pompidou **13**
Champs-Elysées **3**
Eiffel Tower **4**
Hôtel des Invalides
  (Napoléon's Tomb) **7**
Jardin des Tuileries **5**
Jardin du Palais-Royal **11**
Jardin et Palais du Luxembourg **19**
Montmartre **9**
Musée d'Orsay **6**
Musée du Louvre **12**
Musée Jacquemart André **2**
Musée Nationale d'Auguste Rodin **8**
Musée Picasso **14**
Panthéon **20**
Père-Lachaise Cemetery **15**
Place des Vosges **16**
Sacré-Coeur **10**
Sainte-Chapelle **17**

Saving on seeing the sights

One of the best bargains for tourists visiting Paris is the *Paris Museum Pass,* which offers free and unlimited admission to 60 of the top sights of Paris and the Ile-de-France. The card also promises no waiting in admission lines, but you still have to stand in line for security checkpoints at the museums that have them. *Note:* The pass is *not* accepted at the Eiffel Tower.

A two-day pass is 30€ ($36), a four-consecutive-day pass costs 45€ ($54), and a six-consecutive-day pass is 60€ ($72). The length of your stay will determine which of these passes you may want to purchase; the more monuments and museums you visit, the more you will get your money's worth. And if you end up breaking even after the purchase of your pass, you will have definitely saved time by skipping the lines to vastly popular monuments, such as the Arc de Triomphe. You can buy the pass at one of the branches of the Office de Tourisme de Paris — try the branch right near the Louvre in the Carrousel du Louvre, beneath the Pyramides, 99, rue de Rivoli, 1er, open daily 10 a.m. to 7 p.m. (Métro: Palais Royal/Musée du Louvre); or in principal Métro stations (such as Charles du Gaule–Etoil, Châtelet, and Gare St-Lazare); or at the 60 museums and monuments that accept it; or at Fnac ticket branches.

Arc de Triomphe
Champs-Elysées (8e)

The panoramic view is the real attraction for visitors to the Arc de Triomphe where joyous French citizens have celebrated everything from the end of World War II and their liberation to winning the World (soccer) Cup in 1998. From the top, 49m (162 ft.) up, you can see in a straight line the Champs-Elysées, the obelisk in the place de la Concorde, and the Louvre. That big cube at the far end is the Grande Arche de la Défense in St-Denis, built to be the modern equivalent to this arch. Every year, the last day of the Tour de France sees the racers riding up the Champs and around the Arc in a series of laps before the victor is declared. The Arc de Triomphe represents victory to the French, although it has also witnessed the agony of defeat, as in 1871 when Paris was seized by the Prussians during the Franco-Prussian War, and in 1940 when Nazi armies marched victoriously through the arch and down the Champs-Elysées. Napoléon commissioned the Arc to honor his army and its 128 victorious battles. Today it houses the Tomb of the Unknown Soldier, which was dedicated in 1921 to honor the 1,500,000 French soldiers who died during World War 1. An eternal flame beneath the Arc pays tribute to the lost soldiers and is symbolically relit every evening at 6:30 p.m. Allow an hour to visit, an hour and a half in high summer.

Don't try to cross to the Arc de Triomphe on surface streets! Attempting to dodge the warp-speed traffic zooming around the Arc will likely get you seriously hurt. Instead, use one of the clearly marked entrances to the underpass beneath the Arc, which you find on surrounding streets.

Buy your ticket at the end of the underpass from a clerk in a small booth, and then climb the stairs to find yourself standing at the base of the Arc near the Tomb of the Unknown Soldier. You have two choices to reach the top: by a set of more than 250 winding steps or by an elevator. The line for the stairs is always shorter. Both stairs and elevator lead to the small interior museum and store on the Arc's top floor. To get to the outdoor viewing platform you need to climb another flight of narrow steps; the viewing platform is *not* wheelchair accessible.

Keep in mind that on busy days, there will be a line of people in the underpass waiting to buy tickets. Go early if you're visiting during the height of tourist season.

See map p. 186. Place Charles-de-Gaulle. ☎ *01-55-37-73-77. Métro: Charles-de-Gaulle–Étoile. Bus: 22, 30, 31, 52, 73, 92. Admission: 6.40€ ($7.70) adults, 3.60€ ($4.30) ages 12–25, free for children younger than 12. Open: Apr–Sept 9:30 a.m.–11 p.m.; Nov–Mar 10 a.m.–10:30 p.m. Closed major holidays.*

Cathédral de Notre-Dame
Ile de la Cité (4e)

This Gothic church dominates the Seine and the Ile de la Cité, as well as the history of Paris. A circular bronze plaque in the cathedral marks Kilomètre Zéro, from which all distances in France have been measured since 1768. And in many ways, Notre-Dame *is* the center of France. Crusaders prayed here before leaving for the holy wars. Napoléon crowned himself emperor here, and then crowned his wife Josephine empress. When Paris was liberated during World War II, General de Gaulle rushed to this cathedral to give thanks.

Construction of Notre-Dame (see the nearby "Notre-Dame de Paris" map) started in 1163 when Pope Alexander III laid the cornerstone and was completed in 1330. Built in an age of illiteracy, the cathedral windows tell the stories of the Bible in its portals, paintings, and stained glass. Angry citizens pillaged Notre-Dame during the French Revolution, mistaking religious statues above the portals on the west front for representations of kings and beheading them. (To see the statues removed by revolutionaries visit the Cluny Museum. See the write-up below.)

Nearly 100 years later, after Notre-Dame had been turned into a barn, writer Victor Hugo and other artists called attention to its dangerous state of disrepair and architect Viollet-le-Duc began the much-needed restoration. He designed Notre-Dame's spire, a new feature, and Baron Haussmann (Napoléon III's urban planner) tore down the houses cluttering the views of the cathedral.

Before entering, walk around to the east end of the church to appreciate the spectacular flying buttresses. Visit on a sunny morning to catch the giant rose windows — which retain some of their 13th-century stained glass — in all their glory. The highlight for kids will undoubtedly be climbing the 387 narrow and winding steps to the top of one of the towers for a fabulously Quasimodo view of the gargoyles and of Paris. Our advice: If

Notre-Dame de Paris

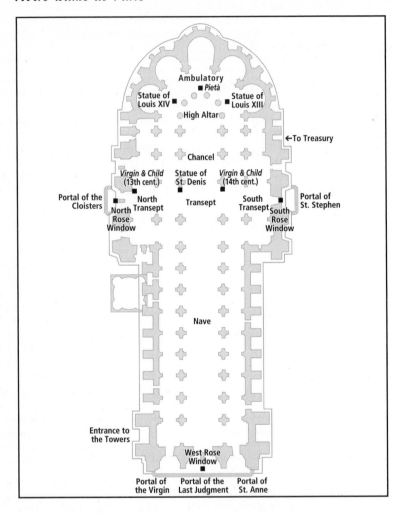

Ambulatory
■ *Pietà*
Statue of Louis XIV ■
Statue of Louis XIII ■
○ ○
High Altar ○ ○
←To Treasury
Chancel
Virgin & Child (13th cent.)
Statue of St. Denis
Virgin & Child (14th cent.)
Portal of the Cloisters
North Transept
Transept
South Transept
Portal of St. Stephen
North Rose Window
South Rose Window
Nave
Entrance to the Towers
West Rose Window
Portal of the Virgin
Portal of the Last Judgment
Portal of St. Anne

you plan to visit the tower, go early in the morning! Lines stretch down the square in front of the cathedral during the summer. Of interest to history buffs will be the Cathedral's Treasury (on the Seine side of the building), which houses such valuable items as gold and jeweled chalices and other items from Notre-Dame's long history.

See map p. 186. 6 Parvis Notre-Dame. ☎ 01-42-34-56-10. Métro: Cité or St-Michel. RER: St-Michel. Bus: 21, 24, 38, 47, 85, 96. Admission: Church free; tower 7.50€ ($9) adults, 5€ ($6) ages 18–26 and seniors, free for youth younger than 18. Open: Cathedral and tower daily 8 a.m.–6 p.m. Treasury Mon–Sat 9:30 a.m.–5 p.m. Six *masses celebrated on Sun, four on weekdays, one on Sat. Free guided visits in English Wed and Thurs at noon, and Sat at 2:30 p.m.*

Centre Georges Pompidou
Le Marais (4e)

Brightly colored escalators, elevators, air-conditioning, and tubular passages run along this building's facade, but the inside is a wonderfully spacious haven in which to view, touch, or listen to modern art and artists. British architect Richard Rogers and Italian architect Renzo Piano designed this building in the late 1960s as part of a redevelopment plan for the neighborhood, and since its opening in 1966, the Centre National d'Art et de Culture Georges Pompidou has been a surprisingly popular attraction — so popular that the wear and tear of about 160 million visitors caused the building to begin crumbling. In 1997, it closed for three years, undergoing a renovation that cost more than $100 million. It reopened with a celebration that also kicked off the new millennium on January 1, 2000. The newer of Paris's two modern art museums, the Centre Georges Pompidou includes two floors of work from the Musée National d'Art Moderne, France's national collection of modern art. The Centre Pompidou also houses a cinema, a huge public library, spaces for modern dance and music, temporary exhibits that often include video and computer works, and nearly 150 drawings, paintings, and other works by Romanian sculptor Constantin Brancusi in the Brancusi Atelier, a small building near the Pompidou's entrance. The 2006–2007 season saw an exhibit dedicated to the history and artistic importance of film and moving images, called *le Mouvement des Images* (the Movement of Images): The main hallway and projection rooms were dedicated to short clips and features that ranged from minimalist to shocking. Plan on spending at least two hours to do the works.

Sadly, taking a free escalator ride to the top for the breathtaking panoramic view of Paris is no more; you must purchase admission to the museum. However, if all you're interested in is the view, consider stopping at the Pompidou's ultrahip top-floor restaurant Georges. For the same price as an adult's full-package admission to the museum (10€/$12), you can relax with a glass of wine and enjoy the view from indoors.

As a bonus, visit the nearby Igor Stravinsky fountain (informally *la Fontaine des automats*), which is free. Its animated sculptures by Jean Tinguely and Niki de Saint Phalle include red lips spitting water, a multicolored treble clef symbol, a mermaid squirting water from strategic body parts, and a twirling grinning skull, all representations of Stravinsky's compositions.

See map p. 186. Place Georges-Pompidou. ☎ *01-44-78-12-33.* www.centrepompidou. fr. *Métro: Rambuteau, Hôtel-de-Ville, Châtelet. Bus: 21, 29, 38, 47, 58, 69, 70, 72, 74, 75, 76, 81, 85, 86. Admission: A one-day package to all exhibits — the National Museum of Modern Art, the museum gallery, the graphic arts gallery, the children's gallery, the 6th-floor panoramic view of Paris, and to Espace 315 — costs 10€ ($12) adults, 8€ ($9.60) ages 6–18, free for children younger than 6; the Brancusi Atelier is free at all opening times. Free the first Sun of the month. Museum and exhibitions* *open: Wed–Mon 11 a.m.–10 p.m., Thurs open until 11 p.m. for certain exhibitions. Closed May 1; ticket counters close at 8 p.m. and 10 p.m. on Thurs night exhibitions.*

Champs-Elysées
Champs-Elysées (8e)

This is the avenue where the military march on Bastille Day, where cinephiles line up for French and American movies playing in the many theaters, where tourists wander the broad sidewalks and browse some of the same stores that can be found back home, where the Tour de France crowns the winner. But this isn't just a boulevard; if you were in Paris when the French won the World and Euro Cup soccer championships (1998 and 2000, respectively), you understand what the Champs-Elysées means to the French. The come here to celebrate victory and freedom. When close to a million singing, flag-waving Parisians spilled into the avenue, it was said that the country hadn't experienced such group euphoria since the days following the Liberation of Paris by the Allies in 1944. The Champs also overlooked the city's biggest New Year's party; in 2000, crowds of people gathered here to watch astonishing fireworks and cheer in the new century. The scene on France's most famous street is liveliest at night, with people lining up for the numerous cinemas (see English-language films here by looking for *v.o.* for *version originale* on schedules and movie posters) and floodlights illuminating the Arc de Triomphe and place de la Concorde. Restaurants consist mainly of standard chain cafes (Chez Clément, Hippo) and American-style fast-food (McDonald's, Planet Hollywood,), although good restaurants abound on the streets surrounding the avenue (see Chapter 10). You can shop at reasonably priced stores, such as Zara, get good deals on T-shirts at Petit Bateau, pick up what all of Europe is listening to at Fnac or Virgin, wander the very luxe (Louis Vuitton, whose flagship "cultural space" and store opened in 2006), and pass chain stores that you'd see in any American mall (the Disney Store, Quiksilver). Some of the stores are open on Sunday. Allow an hour to walk from top to bottom, longer if you want to shop, eat, or dawdle.

See map p. 186. Métro: Concorde, Champs-Elysées Clémenceau, Franklin-D-Roosevelt, George V, Charles-de-Gaulle–Étoile. Bus: Many lines cross it, but only the 73 travels its entire length.

Eiffel Tower (La Tour Eiffel)
Eiffel Tower/Les Invalides (7e)

Did you know that the Eiffel Tower has its own post office? Whenever you mail anything from the town, it is postmarked with an Eiffel Tower stamp. Gustave Eiffel beat out 699 others in a contest to design what was supposed to be a temporary monument for the 1889 Exposition Universelle (World's Fair). His designs for the tower spanned 5,017m (16,460 ft.) of paper. Praised by some and criticized by others, the tower created as much controversy in its time as did I.M. Pei's pyramid at the Louvre 100 years later. Upon completion, the Eiffel Tower was the tallest human-built structure in the world, and the Prince of Wales (later Edward VII) and his family were invited to ascend it first. People have climbed it, bungee-jumped from it, and cycled down the tower's steps. Since 2003, 20,000 lights sparkle for ten minutes an hour each evening until 2 a.m. in summer and 1 a.m. in winter. Parisians often comment that the final lighting hour is the best one, because the yellow ambient lighting on the tower's structure is turned off, and only the sparkling white lights can be seen.

You can fill an entire page with trivia about Paris's most famous symbol, which weighs 7,000 tons, soars 317m (1,056 ft.), and is held together with 2.5 million rivets. But what you really want to know are the practicalities: *Do I have to climb stairs? Do elevators go to the top? Are there bathrooms? Do they have snacks? Can I ascend in a wheelchair?* The answers: The Tower has three levels that are accessible by elevator. No elevator goes directly from ground level to the top; you must change elevators at the second level. Although you can take stairs from the ground to the first and second levels, you can't take stairs from the second level to the top. Most likely you'll wait for elevators on the first and second levels in specially roped-off lines. In high season, the wait sometimes is as long an hour for each line. Restrooms are located on each level, and snack bars and souvenir stands are on the first and second levels. The tower is wheelchair accessible to the second level but not to the top.

Some advice: Six million people visit the Eiffel Tower each year. To avoid loonnnggg lines, go early in the morning or in the off-season. If this isn't possible, allow at least three hours for your visit: one hour to line up for tickets and another two just to access the elevators on levels one and two.

Food is available at the Altitude 95 restaurant on the first floor, which is simply gorgeous, but overpriced for the quality of its meals. A first-floor snack bar and second-floor cafeteria are open, but again, they're not the best values. The best food at the Eiffel Tower is also its most expensive, without a doubt: The Michelin-starred Jules Verne, one of Paris's most celebrated restaurants, is on the Eiffel Tower's second level. (One of the pluses of dining here is that you get your own private elevator to the restaurant.)

If you have the patience to wait until sunset, the Eiffel Tower at night is recommended! Its lights frame the lacy steelwork beneath you in a way that daylight doesn't, and the Seine reflects it all.

See map p. 186. Parc du Champ de Mars. ☎ *01-44-11-23-23.* www.tour-eiffel.fr. *Métro: Trocadéro, Bir-Hakeim, École-Militaire. RER: Champs-de-Mars. Bus: 42, 69, 72, 82, 87. Admission: To highest level 11€ ($12), adults, 6€ ($7.20) ages 3–11; second level 7.70€ ($8.40) adults, 4.20€ ($6.55) ages 3–11; first level 4.20€ ($6.55) adults, 2.30€ ($2.76) ages 3–11; stairs to first and second levels 3.80€ ($4.56). Under 25 years old climb the stairs for 3 euro (3.60), and children younger than 3 are free. Open: Jan 1–June 15 daily 9:30 a.m.–11:45 p.m., stairs close at 6 p.m.; June 16–Sept 2 daily 9 a.m.–12:45 a.m., stairs close at midnight; Sept 3–Dec 31 daily 9 a.m.–11:45 p.m. Closed major holidays.*

Keeping an eye on your wallet while eyeing the goods

You won't be able to avoid pesky (and illegal) vendors trying to cajole you into buying everything from Eiffel Tower key chains to postcards to mechanical butterflies; they constantly approach tourists standing in line for Eiffel Tower admission tickets. Be very attentive — some of these vendors work in tandem with pickpockets who will rip you off while you're busy looking at the displays. As for the quality of the merchandise — it's pretty bad. Buy your souvenirs from shops and licensed vendors. (See Chapter 4 for advice on what to do if you get pickpocketed.)

Hôtel des Invalides (Napoléon's Tomb)
Eiffel Tower/Les Invalides (7e)

Louis XIV, who liked war and waged many, built Invalides, one of Europe's architectural masterpieces, as a hospital and home for all veteran officers and soldiers "whether maimed or old or frail." It still has offices for departments of the French armed forces, and part of it is still a hospital. The best way to get the sense of the awe that the Hôtel des Invalides inspires is to walk to it by crossing the Alexander III bridge. The dome of the **Église du Dôme** (gilded with 12 kilograms of real gold), is one of the high points of classical art, with a skylight rising 107 meters from the ground. Sixteen green copper cannons point outward in a powerful display.

Enemy flags captured during the military campaigns of the 19th and 20th centuries hang from the rafters in two impressive rows at the **Église de St-Louis,** known as the Church of the Soldiers, but most visitors come to see the **Tomb of Napoléon,** where the emperor is buried in six coffins, one inside the other, under the great dome. The first coffin is iron, the second mahogany, the third and fourth lead, the fifth ebony, and the outermost oak. The emperor's remains were transferred here 20 years after his death in 1820 on the island of St. Helena, where he was exiled following his defeat at Waterloo. Buried along with Napoléon in smaller tombs are the emperor's two brothers, his son Napoléon II of France, Claude Rouget de Lisle (author of *La Marseillaise,* the French national anthem), and Henri de la Tour d'Auvergne, Viscount de Turenne — one of France's greatest military leaders. He was so respected that even the 1793 extremist revolutionaries, who scattered the remains of the other deceased French leaders interred at St. Denis, preserved his bones until their final resting place in les Invalides. A must-see is the **Musée de l'Armée,** one of the world's greatest military museums; admission is included when you buy your ticket for Napoléon's tomb. It features thousands of weapons from prehistory to World War II including spearheads, arrowheads, maces, cannons, and guns in addition to battle flags, booty, suits of armor, and uniforms from around the world. The DeGaulle wing tells the story of World War II on video touch screens, a decoding machine, and other artifacts. Set aside two hours for a complete visit or a half-hour to see only the tomb.

See map p. 186. Place des Invalides. ☎ *01-44-42-38-77*. Métro: La Tour Maubourg, Invalides, or Varenne. Bus: 28, 49, 63, 69, 92, 83, 87, 92. Admission 7.50€ ($9) adults; 5.50€ ($6.60) seniors and students 18–26; free for children younger than 18. Open: Oct–March daily 10 a.m.–5 p.m.; Apr–Sept daily 10 a.m.–6 p.m. Tomb of Napoléon open until 7 p.m. June 15–Sept 15. Closed the first Mon of every month, Christmas day, and the Jan 1, May, and Nov.

Jardin des Tuileries
Louvre (1er)

Come for a stroll here either before or after visiting the Louvre. Once a fashionable carriageway, today the Tuileries is Paris's most visited park and a great place to rest your feet and catch some rays on conveniently placed wrought-iron chairs surrounding the garden's fountains. In keeping with the French style of parks, trees are planted according to an orderly design and the sandy paths are arrow straight. Spread out across 25 hectare (63 acres), the gardens were originally laid out in the 1560s for Queen Mother Catherine de Medici in front of the Tuileries Palace, which was burned down during the 1871 Paris Commune. The Orangerie (which has finally reopened! — see below) and the Jeu de Paume are at the garden's western edge, and to the east you'll find 40 beautiful Maillol bronzes scattered among the trees, as well as four sculptures by Rodin, and works by Jean Dubuffet, Alberto Giacometti, David Smith, Max Ernst, Henry Moore, and Henri Laurens. You can sit down for a light snack at one of the outdoor cafes. During the summer, a carnival features an enormous Ferris wheel (with great views of the city), a log flume, fun house, arcade-style games, snacks, and machine-made soft ice cream (but we find the best ice cream in the Tuileries is the homemade ice cream sold from a stand right beyond the Arc de Triomphe du Carrousel at the entrance to the Tuileries).

See map p. 186. Quai des Tuileries. Entrances on rue de Rivoli and place de la Concorde, 1er. ☎ *01-30-20-90-43*. Métro: Concorde or Tuileries. Bus: 24, 42, 69, 72, 73, 84, 94. Admission: Free. Open: Daily 7:30 a.m.–7:30 p.m. in the winter, till 9 p.m. in the summer.

Jardin du Palais-Royal
Louvre (1er)

In past centuries, gamblers and those seeking more lascivious pleasures flocked to this garden where Cardinal Richelieu ordered the Royal Palace built in 1630 as his personal residence, complete with grounds landscaped by the royal gardener. Today the palace is no longer open to the public, but its statue-filled gardens, including Daniel Buren's wonderful prison-striped columns of staggered heights built in 1986 (which make for a great photo op), remain one of the most restful places in the city. The square is also ringed by restaurants, art galleries, and specialty boutiques, and it's home to the Comédie-Française.

See map p. 186. Entrances on rue de Rivoli and place de la Concorde. ☎ *01-47-03-92-16. Métro: Concorde or Tuileries. Bus: 21, 49, 42, 48, 67 68, 69, 72, 81, 95. Admission: Free. Open: Daily 7:30 a.m.–8:30 p.m.*

Jardin et Palais du Luxembourg
St-Germain-des-Prés (6e)

No matter which entrance you walk through, you will fall in love with this beloved park not far from the Sorbonne and just south of the Latin Quarter. It's the 6e arrondissement's **Jardin du Luxembourg,** one of Paris's most beloved parks. Children love it for its playground, pony rides, puppet theater, and the Fontaine de Médicis (the central Médici Fountain) where they can sail toy boats and watch the ducks. Besides pools, fountains, and statues of queens and poets, there are tennis and *boules* courts (*boule* means ball; in this game, players compete to see who can roll their small steel ball closest to a larger steel ball that lies farther down the court). In recent years, art has been exhibited on the wrought-iron fence at the garden's northwestern entrance near boulevard St-Michel and rue de Médicis.

The park was commissioned by King Henri IV's queen, Marie de Medici, who also had the **Palais du Luxembourg** built at the northern edge of the park. The Palais resembles the Palazzo Pitti in Florence, where Marie spent her childhood and for which she was homesick. When the queen was banished in 1630, the palace was abandoned until the Revolution in 1789, when it was used as a prison. Now the seat of the French Senate, it is not open to the public.

Orchards in the park's southwest corner contain 360 varieties of apples, 270 kinds of pears, and various grapevines. Members of the French Senate get to eat the fruit, but leftovers go to a soup kitchen. Walk north and you come across a bevy of beehives behind a low fence. A beekeeping course is taught here on weekends. See whether you can find the Statue of Liberty tucked away nearby.

See map p. 186. Main entrance at the corner of bd. St-Michel and rue des Médicis. ☎ *01-43-29-12-78. Métro: Odéon. RER: Luxembourg, Port-Royal. Bus: 38, 82, 84, 85, 89. Admission: Free. Open: Daily dawn–dusk.*

Montmartre
On the Right Bank

This neighborhood/village is for anyone who admires the work of Toulouse-Lautrec, is interested in one of Picasso's earliest studios, or loved the films *Le Destin Fabuleux d'Amélie Poulain* or *Moulin Rouge.* You can get to Montmartre by taking the Métro to the Anvers or Abbesses stop, the entrance of which is graced by a fabulous Art Nouveau Métro sign. You can either walk to the top of the *butte* (hill) or take the *funiculaire* (outdoor small railway) up. (To take the *funiculaire,* walk from the Anvers Métro station the short distance from rue Steinkerque and turn left onto rue Tardieu, where, for a Métro ticket, the *funiculaire* whisks you from the base of the Montmartre butte to the road right beneath Sacré-Coeur.) After visiting

Sacré-Coeur and the touristy but fun place du Tertre, a square with over-priced restaurants and artists clamoring to sketch your portrait, wander down the hill where you eventually stumble across Paris from another era — surprisingly unspoiled lanes, quiet squares, ivy-clad shuttered houses with gardens, and even Paris's only vineyard. Altogether, it creates a sense of the rustic village it once was. (**Note:** See Chapter 13 for a detailed walking itinerary through Montmartre.)

Musée d'Orsay
Eiffel Tower/Les Invalides (7e)

This is one museum that won't overwhelm! A brilliantly renovated train station that opened to the public in 1986, the Musée d'Orsay is one of the world's greatest museums of 19th century art, with an unsurpassed collection of Impressionist masterpieces. There are three floors of exhibits. On the ground floor are Ingres's *La Source,* Millet's *L'Angelus,* the Barbizon school, Manet's *Olympia,* and other works of early impressionism. Impressionism continues on the top level, with Renoir's *Le Moulin de la Galette,* Manet's *Déjeuner sur l'Herbe,* Degas's *Racing at Longchamps,* Monet's cathedrals, van Gogh's *Self-Portrait,* and Whistler's *Portrait of the Artist's Mother.* Works by Gauguin and the Pont-Aven school, Toulouse-Lautrec, Pissarro, Cézanne, and Seurat also are exhibited. Symbolism, naturalism, and Art Nouveau are represented on the middle level; the international Art Nouveau exhibit is worth a look for its wonderful furniture and *objets d'art* as well as Koloman Moser's *Paradise,* a beautiful design for stained glass. Give yourself three hours, including a lunch break in the museum's gorgeous, turn-of-the-20th-century Musée d'Orsay restaurant on the middle level. For less expensive and quicker light bites, the Café des Hauteurs is on the fifth floor (it has a great view of the Seine through its clock window) and a snack bar is on the mezzanine.

See map p. 186. 62 rue de Lille/1 rue Bellechasse. ☎ *01-40-49-48-14, or 01-40-49-48-48 for the information desk.* www.musee-orsay.fr. *Métro: Solférino. RER: Musée-d'Orsay. Bus: 24, 63, 68, 69, 73, 83, 84, 94. Admission (may cost more to include major temporary exhibits): 7€ ($8.40) adults; 5€ ($6) ages 18–24 and seniors and on Sun; free for children younger than 18. Free the first Sun of every month. Open: Tues–Wed and Fri–Sun 9:30 a.m.–6 p.m.; Thurs 9:30 a.m.–9:45 p.m. Closed Jan 1, May 1, and Christmas.*

The Louvre

Musée du Louvre
Louvre (1er)

The three steps to an enjoyable Louvre experience are to:

1. Buy your tickets in advance. Visitors from the United States and Canada can purchase tickets online from www.ticketweb.com and have them delivered to their homes before departure. Visitors from other countries can use www.fnac.com or www.ticketnet.com. If you are already in France upon reading this, some Métro stations have tickets for sale at the window.

Paris's top attraction:
The Seine river cruise

One of the most romantic and beautiful ways to see Paris is to take a sightseeing cruise up and down the Seine. Ignore too-expensive lunch or dinner cruises: the food won't even be very good. Instead, opt for an evening cruise. With its dramatically lit monuments and romantic bridges, Paris is truly breathtaking at night.

Three companies offer similar tours in the same price range with recorded commentaries. Perhaps the most well known are the **Bateaux-Mouches** that sail from the Right Bank and have huge floodlit boats. **Bateaux-Parisiens** sail from the Left Bank, while **Vedettes Pont Neuf** sail from the Ile de la Cité. Vedettes boats are smaller, more intimate, and not all of them are covered.

For a boat ride without commentary, take one of the **Bat-o-bus** shuttles that stop every 25 minutes between 10 a.m. and 4, 7, or 9:30 p.m. depending on the season. A one-day ticket costs 11€ ($13) adults, 5€ ($6) for children under 16, and you can jump off and on when you want.

Bateaux les Vedettes du Pont Neuf, square du Vert-Galant, 1er. ☎ 01-46-33-98-38. Métro: Pont-Neuf, sail from the riverside where the Pont Neuf crosses the Ile de la Cité. Departures: March to October at 10 a.m., 11:15 a.m., noon and then every half-hour from 1:30 p.m. to 10:30 p.m.; November to February every 45 minutes Monday through Thursday from 10:30 a.m. to noon and 2 to 6:30 p.m., and at 8 p.m. and 10 p.m. Saturday and Sunday tours leave every 45 minutes from 10:30 a.m. to noon, every half hour from 2 p.m. to 6:30 p.m., and at 8 p.m., and every half hour from 9 p.m. to 10:30 p.m. Rates: 10€ ($12) adults, 5€ ($6) children under 12. Tickets purchased on the Internet are subject to a 2€ ($2.40) discount, for adult fare only.

Bateaux-Mouches, pont de l'Alma, Right Bank, 8e. ☎ 01-42-25-96-10; www.bateaux-mouches.fr. Métro: Alma Marceau. Departures: In summer high season (approx Apr–Oct) every 30 minutes from 10 a.m. to 11 p.m.; in winter (Oct–Mar) departures leave from 11 a.m. to 9 p.m. Rates: 8€ ($9.60) for adults, 4€ ($4.80) for children 4 to 12 and adults older than 65; children younger than 4 ride free.

Bateaux-Parisiens Tour Eiffel, port de la Bourdonnais, Left Bank, 7e. ☎ 01-44-11-33-44. Métro: Bir-Hakeim. Departures: From April through September every half-hour from 10 a.m. to 11 p.m.; from October through March every hour from 10 a.m. to 10 p.m. No tours at 1:30 p.m. Rates: 10€ ($12) adults; 5€ ($6) children under 12. Free under age 3.

2. Grab a free map of the Louvre at the Information Desk under the Pyramid or get a free guide. The Louvre bookstore in the Carrousel du Louvre sells many comprehensive guides and maps in English; you can also grab brochures for "Visitors in a Hurry," or a guide-book, *The Louvre, First Visit.*

3. Take a guided tour. You can try a 90-minute tour by a museum guide (☎ **01-40-20-52-63**) that covers the most popular works and gives you a quick orientation to the museum's layout. Times and prices vary, generally a tour of the most celebrated works is 6.50€ for adults and 4.50€ for students under 26 years of age ($8 and $5). If you prefer to set your own pace, a four-hour audiotour (5€/$6) can be rented at the entrance to any of the wings.

 I.M. Pei's glass pyramid is the main entrance to the museum; pregnant women, visitors with children in strollers and the disabled have priority. Avoid this entrance and its long lines by using the **99 rue de Rivoli/ Carrousel du Louvre** entrance, or take the stairs at the **Porte des Lions** near the Arc du Triomphe du Carrousel (the arch resembling a smaller Arc de Triomphe). Those who already have tickets or have the Carte Musées et Monuments can use the special entrance to the Louvre at the **passage Richelieu** between rue de Rivoli and the courtyard.

 Tickets are valid all day so you can enter and exit the museum as many times as you prefer. Admission is reduced after 6 p.m. on Wednesday and Friday, and free the first Sunday of each month.

The Louvre didn't need Dan Brown's bestseller *The Da Vinci Code* to attract large crowds, but the attention certainly hasn't hurt. At press time, the book, and the movie starring Tom Hanks and Audrey Tautou, which starts off with an off-hours murder of the Louvre's curator and focuses on the painting by Da Vinci of The Last Supper (which is in the convent of Santa Maria delle Grazie in Milan), was still drawing crowds to all the venues mentioned in it. There is even a two-and-a-half hour private "Cracking the *Da Vinci Code*" tour of the Louvre given by Paris Muse for 110€ ($132) for an individual tour, or 95€ ($114) per person for a party of two or more (www.parismuse.com).

The Louvre palace (see "The Louvre" map nearby) evolved during several centuries, first built as the Château du Louvre in 1190 by Philip Augustus. It first opened as a museum in 1793, and it would take you a month of visits to see the more than 30,000 treasures it now houses. But a visit to the Louvre doesn't have to be overwhelming. The Louvre is organized in three wings — Sully, Denon, and Richelieu — over four floors exhibiting art and antiquities from Oriental, Islamic, Egyptian, Greek, Etruscan, Roman, Oceanic, European, and North and South American civilizations, and sculp-ture, *objets d'art,* paintings, prints, drawings, and the moats and dungeon of the medieval Louvre fortress.

When you're in a hurry, but want to do the Louvre on your own, do a quick, "best of the Louvre" tour on either Wednesday or Friday when the museum is open until 9:45 p.m. Start with Leonardo da Vinci's *Mona Lisa* (Denon

The Louvre

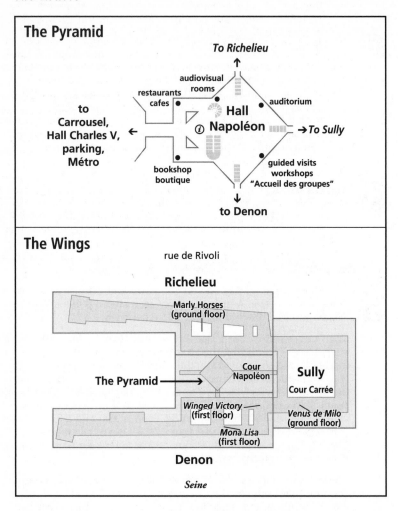

The Pyramid

To Richelieu

audiovisual rooms

restaurants cafes

Hall Napoléon

auditorium

to Carrousel, Hall Charles V, parking, Métro

→To Sully

bookshop boutique

guided visits workshops "Accueil des groupes"

to Denon

The Wings

rue de Rivoli

Richelieu

Marly Horses (ground floor)

The Pyramid

Cour Napoléon

Sully

Cour Carrée

Winged Victory (first floor)

Venus de Milo (ground floor)

Mona Lisa (first floor)

Denon

Seine

wing, first floor); on the same floor nearby are two of the Louvre's most famous French paintings, Géricault's *The Raft of Medusa* and Delacroix's *Liberty Guiding the People.* Next, visit the *Winged Victory* and Michelangelo's *Slaves* (both Denon wing, ground floor) before seeing the *Venus de Milo* (Sully wing, ground floor). After that, let your own interests guide you. Consider that only Florence's Uffizi Gallery rivals the Denon wing for its Italian Renaissance collection, which includes Raphael's *Portrait of Balthazar Castiglione* and Titian's *Man with a Glove.* And the revamped Egyptian antiquities department is the largest exhibition of Egyptian antiquities outside Cairo.

 If you want to purchase tickets in advance while in Paris, you can order tickets by phone from Fnac ☎ **08-92-68-36-22** (0.35€/40¢ per min.), and pick them up at any Fnac store (except Fnac photo shops). A 1.50€ ($1.80) commission is charged by Fnac. A nearby branch is at Forum des Halles, 1 rue Pierre Lescure.

See map p. 186. Rue de Rivoli. ☎ 01-40-20-55-55 for recorded message, 01-40-20-53-17 for information desk. www.louvre.fr. *Métro: Palais-Royal–Musée du Louvre. Admission: 8.50€ ($10) adults; 6€ ($7) after 6 p.m. on Wed and Fri; free first Sun of month, Bastille Day (July 14) for disabled visitors and for children younger than 18. Open: Fri and Wed 9 a.m.–9:45 p.m.; Thurs–Mon 9 a.m.–6 p.m. Closed Tues, Jan 1, May 1, Aug 15, and Christmas.*

Mange with Mona Lisa

There are plenty of places to refuel at the Louvre from the gastronomic Le Grand Louvre to a cafeteria serving plenty of ethnic eats. Note: The museum and its restaurants are closed Tuesdays.

Beneath the Pyramid:

✔ **Café du Louvre:** Open 9 a.m. to 7 p.m. Thursday to Sunday, until 9:30 p.m. Friday and Wednesday.

✔ **Café Napoléon:** Open Wednesday to Monday 10 a.m. to 6 p.m.

✔ **Cafétéria:** Open Wednesday to Monday 11:30 a.m. to 3 p.m.

✔ **Le Grand Louvre** (☎ **01-40-20-53-41**): Open Wednesday to Monday noon to 3 p.m. and 7 p.m. to 10 p.m. Friday and Wednesday.

In the Denon Wing:

✔ **Café Denon** (mezzanine): Open Thursday to Sunday 9 a.m. to 5 p.m.; open until 7:30 p.m. Friday and Wednesday.

✔ **Café Mollien** (first floor): Open Thursday to Sunday 10:30 a.m. to 5 p.m.; open until 9 p.m. Friday and Wednesday.

In the Richelieu Wing:

✔ **Café Richelieu** (first floor): Open Thursday to Monday 10:30 a.m. to 5 p.m.; open until 9:30 p.m. Wednesday.

In the Cour de Napoléon (facing the Pyramid):

✔ **Café Marly** (☎ **01-49-26-06-60**): Open daily 8 a.m. to 2 a.m.

See Chapter 10 for restaurant reviews.

Musée Jacquemart André
Champs-Elysées (8e)

Talk about a match made in art heaven: Edouard André, the heir of a prominent banking family, and his wife, Nélie Jacquemart, a well-known portraitist, commissioned architect Henri Parent to build their "house," then traveled the world to find French, Flemish, and Italian paintings, furniture, and tapestries to fill it. They had no children, so Nélie willed the house and its treasures to the French government, giving the city of Paris one of its best museums. This is very much worth a visit for the Italian and Flemish masterpieces by Bellini, Botticelli, Carpaccio, Uccello, Rubens, Rembrandt, and van Eyck and to see how very rich Parisians lived in the 19th century. Highlights of the collection include Rembrandt's *Docteur Tholinx,* Van Dyck's *Time Cuts the Wings of Love,* a fresco by Jean Baptiste Tiepolo, Domenico Ghirlandaio's naturalistic *Portrait d'un Vieillard,* and a portrait of *Catherine Skavronskaia* by Elisabeth Vigée-Lebrun, one of Marie Antoinette's favorite artists, and a fascinating person in her own right. As you wander the ornate gilt-ridden rooms, pause in the "winter garden," a tour de force of marble and mirrors flanking an unusual double staircase. For kids, the museum has organized a special activity: at the beginning of the visit kids receive a free booklet with word mysteries. The kids use the contents of the museum to solve the puzzles, aided by clues spread throughout the museum and find out the "secret letters." It is all worthwhile, especially for the surprise! Take advantage of the free interactive audio that guides you through the mansion with fascinating narrative. Visit at 11 a.m., allow at least an hour, then take a break in what was Madame Jacquemart's lofty-ceilinged dining room, now a pretty tearoom serving light lunches (the salads are all named for artists) and snacks.

See map p. 186. 158 bd. Haussmann. ☎ *01-45-62-11-59. Métro: Miromesnil. Bus: 22, 28, 43, 52, 54, 80, 83, 84, 93. Admission: 9.50€ ($11) adults; 7€ ($8.40) students and children from 7–17; free for ages 7 and younger. A special offer is made to members of the same family: for every three family members, be they adult or child, a free children's ticket is awarded. Open: Daily (including Dec 25) 10 a.m.–6 p.m.; Le Café is open 11:45–5:30 p.m.*

Musée Nationale d'Auguste Rodin
Eiffel Tower/Les Invalides (7e)

This is one of Paris's more relaxing museums, a large house with just 16 rooms, surrounded by bucolic gardens. Auguste Rodin, often regarded as the greatest sculptor of all time, lived and worked here from 1908 until his death in 1917, an era when his legendary sculptures were labeled obscene. This collection includes all of his greatest works. In the courtyard, *Burghers of Calais* is a harrowing commemoration of the siege of Calais in 1347, after which the triumphant Edward III of England kept the town's six richest burghers as servants. Also in the courtyard is *The Thinker.* The *Gates of Hell* is a portrayal of Dante's *Inferno.* Intended for the Musée des Arts Decoratifs, the massive bronze doors were not completed until seven years after Rodin's death. Inside the most popular attraction is *Le Baiser*

(The Kiss) which immortalizes in white marble the passion of doomed 13th-century lovers Paolo Malatesta and Francesca da Rimini. Studies done by Rodin before he executed his sculptures take up some of the 16 rooms. Particularly interesting is the evolution of his controversial nude of Balzac rising from a tree trunk. Don't miss the works of Camille Claudel, a top-rated artist and Rodin's student and lover for many years. The museum is in the 18th-century Hôtel Biron, which was a convent before it became a residence for such writers and artists as Matisse, Jean Cocteau and the poet, Rainer Maria Rilke. Count on spending at least an hour and a half in the museum.

If you don't have much time or money, pay the 1€ ($1.20) admission to visit just the gardens, where Rodin's works stand among 2,000 rosebushes. Allow at least an hour to visit the garden, longer if you want to break for coffee in the garden cafe. The 2005 addition of a glass wing housing temporary exhibits and some of the permanent collection allows for a wonderful view of the gardens. In 2006 the temporary exhibitions were closed for a short time due to security reasons: it is best to check online or call the museum to see which collections are available.

See map p. 186. Hôtel Biron, 77 rue de Varenne. ☎ *01-44-18-61-10.* www.musee-rodin.fr. *Métro: Varenne. Bus: 69, 82, 87, 92. Admission: Adults 7€ ($8.40) for entry including temporary exhibits, 6€ for just the garden and permanent collection; 5€ ($6) ages 18–24 and seniors for the full visit, 4€ ($4.80) for the permanent collection and gardens; 1€ ($1.20) for garden only; free for children younger than 18. Open: Apr–Sept Tues–Sun 9:30 a.m.–5:45 p.m.; Oct–Mar Tues–Sun 9:30 a.m.–4:45 p.m. Garden closes at 6:45 p.m. in summer, 5 p.m. in winter, last admittance one hour before closing.*

Musée Picasso
Le Marais (3e)

This mansion in the Marais houses the world's largest collection of Spanish master Pablo Picasso's art, and you can pay a visit here on each trip to Paris and see something different each time because the works are constantly rotated. Located in the renovated Hôtel Salé, which was built in the mid-17th century for a salt tax collector (hence the name which translates as the salted mansion). The museum was created in 1973 by Picasso's heirs, who donated his personal art collection to the state in lieu of paying outrageous inheritance taxes after his death. The spectacular collection includes more than 200 paintings, nearly 160 sculptures, 88 ceramics, and more than 3,000 prints and drawings. Every phase of Picasso's prolific 75-year career is represented. Works can be viewed chronologically; particularly interesting is seeing how his paintings were influenced by the women he loved at the time: his first wife, Olga; Marie-Thérèse Walter, mother of his daughter, Maya; Françoise Gilot, mother of Paloma and Paul, and Dora Maar, among others. Budget at least two hours here, if not more. It is best to go early in the morning, as the narrow corridors in parts of the museum get particularly crowded during the afternoon (they need the wall space to exhibit this enormous collection). The museum also displays works by other artists collected by Picasso, including Corot, Cézanne, Braque, Rousseau, Matisse, and Renoir. This museum is worth every minute!

See map p. 186. Hôtel Salé, 5 rue de Thorigny. ☎ **01-42-71-25-21.** www.musee-picasso.fr. Métro: Chemin-Vert, St-Paul, or Filles du Calvaire. Bus: 29, 69, 75, 96. Admission: 6.50€ ($7.80) adults; 4.50€ ($5.40) ages 18–25 and on Sun; free for children younger than 18and for all first Sun of each month. Open: Apr–Sept Wed–Mon 9:30 a.m.–6 p.m.; Oct–Mar Wed–Mon 9:30 a.m.–5:30 p.m.

Panthéon
Latin Quarter (5e)

Is it a church? Is it a museum? Is it a tomb? Perhaps the best description would be: the Panthéon is to France what Westminster Abbey is to England — a final resting place for many of the nation's greatest men and one woman, Marie Curie. Few other monuments in Paris have had as versatile a career as the neoclassical Panthéon, whose huge dome is one of the landmarks of the Left Bank. Inside the domed church's barrel-vaulted crypt are the tombs of Voltaire, Rousseau, Hugo, Braille, and Zola. French writer, politician, and adventurer André Malraux was the last to be entombed here in 1996. Louis XV originally built the Panthéon as a church in thanksgiving to St-Geneviève after his recovery from gout. Construction started in 1755, but after the French Revolution, the church was renamed the Panthéon, in remembrance of ancient Rome's Pantheon, and rededicated as a burying ground for France's heroes. All Christian elements were removed and windows were blocked. From 1806 to 1884, officials turned the Panthéon back into a church two more times before finally declaring it what it is today. Along with historical information of the great figures buried here, a small wing is devoted to explanation of the scientific theories and experiments discovered by Pierre and Marie Curie. A pendulum suspended from the central dome recreates Jean-Bernard Foucault's 1851 demonstration proving the rotation of the earth. The views from the top here are some of the best in Paris.

See map p. 186. Place du Panthéon. ☎ **01-44-32-18-00.** Métro: Cardinal-Lemoine or Maubert-Mutualité. Bus: 21, 27, 83, 84, 85, 89. Admission: 6.50€ ($8) adults; 3.95€ ($4.75) ages 18–25; free for children younger than 18. Open: Apr–Sept daily 9:30 a.m.–6:30 p.m. (Oct–Mar until 6:15 p.m.).

Père-Lachaise Cemetery
Montmartre and beyond (20e)

Chopin, Bizet, Proust, Balzac, Corot, Delacroix, Pissarro, Modigliani, Molière, Oscar Wilde, Isadora Duncan, Simone Signoret, Yves Montand, and of course, Jim Morrison (framed pictures of him grace the walls of neighboring brasseries, but his bust has been removed due to vandalism) have been laid to rest in this famous cemetery cresting above a high hill overlooking Paris. This, the world's most visited cemetery, is more outdoor museum than place of mourning. No wonder Parisians have always come here to stroll and reflect; with its winding, cobbled streets, park benches, and street signs, the 44-hectare (110-acre) Père-Lachaise is a minicity unto itself. Many visitors leave flowers or notes scrawled on Métro tickets for their favorite celebrity residents. The tombs are artistic works, decorated with exquisite marble and stone statuettes or chiseled around diminutive stained-glass windows.

Legends abound. The 18th-century bronze tomb of murdered journalist Victor Noir is reputed to make women fertile when rubbed (the polished sheen of certain parts of his statue is testament to its lore!). Oscar Wilde's impressive tomb here, carved by Sir Jacob Epstein, is covered with lipstick-spots from the kisses of his admirers. The tragic love story of Abélard and Héloïse (she was his student and her uncle castrated him when he found out about their affair) has faded, but in the 19th century, their tombs were magnets for disappointed lovers. You can obtain a free map from the gate-keeper at the main entrance, but the better map is one sold outside the entrance for 2€ ($2.40). Or you can just use the "Père-Lachaise Cemetery" map provided in this chapter. Allow at the very least two hours to visit.

See map p. 186. 16 rue du Repos. Main entrance on bd. du Ménilmontant. Métro: Père-Lachaise. Bus: 61, 69, 102. Admission: Free. Open: Mar 16–Nov 5 Mon–Fri 8 a.m.–6 p.m., Sat 8:30 a.m.–6 p.m., Sun and holidays 9 a.m.–6 p.m.; Nov 6–Mar 15 Mon–Fri 8 a.m.–5:30 p.m., Sat 8:30 a.m.–5:30 p.m., Sun and holidays 9 a.m.–6 p.m. Last entry to the cemetery is allowed 15 minutes before closing time.

Place des Vosges
Le Marais (3e)

The place des Vosges sits right in the middle of Le Marais — a symmetrical block of 36 rose-colored town houses, 9 on each side, with handsome slate roofs and dormer windows. At ground level is a lovely arcaded walkway that's now home to galleries, cafes, antiques dealers, and smart boutiques. In the early 17th century, Henri IV transformed this area into the most prestigious neighborhood in France, putting his royal palace here, and the square quickly became the center of courtly parades and festivities. After the Revolution, it became place de l'Indivisibilité. Victor Hugo lived at No. 6 for 16 years (see "Finding More Fun Things to See and Do" later in this chapter). This is one of the places in Paris where you can sit on the grass, enjoy a sandwich, and catch some rays alongside local students and older residents Allow 30 minutes to walk all the way around the square under the arcades and a brief stroll in the park.

See map p. 186. Métro: St-Paul. Bus: 20, 29, 69, 76, 96.

Sacré-Coeur
Montmartre (18e)

The white Byzantine-Romanesque basilica dominating Paris's highest hill — the one that you can see from all around the city — is Basilique du Sacré-Coeur. Built from 1876 (after France's defeat in the Franco-Prussian War) to 1919, the church's interior is not as striking as its exterior and is, in fact, vaguely depressing. The best reason to come here is for the city-spanning views from its Dome — visibility is 48km (30 miles) across the rooftops of Paris on a clear day. Conserve your pre-Dome climbing energy by using the *funiculaire* to take you to Sacré-Coeur. Simply take the Métro to the Anvers station, and then ride the elevator to exit the station. Walk

Père-Lachaise Cemetery

avenue Circulaire

Mur des
Fédérés

39

38

0   100 yds

0   100 m

94
avenue Transversale No. 3

97

37

36

avenue Greffulhe

avenue Pacthod

95
avenue Transversale No. 2

96

35

avenue Circulaire

76

92

34

42

41

40

35

38

33

43

31 **32**

33

28

34

37

36

avenue des Acacias

25

26

27

29

chemin du Dragon

19

30

31

75

18

17

32

30

Carrefour du
Grand-Rond

16

15

29

74

28

13

14

avenue Casimir-Perrier

6

5

73

8

Ancienne
Séperation
du Cimetière
Israélite

27

25 **26**

7

*Père-Lachaise
Cemetery* ■

Seine

P A R I S

Abélard & Héloïse **27**
Guillaume Apollinaire **5**
Pierre-Auguste
  Beaumarchais **34**
Hans Bellmer **24**
Sarah Bernhardt **9**
Georges Bizet **17**
Maria Callas **3**
Frédéric Chopin **28**
Colette **23**
Auguste Comte **30**
Jean Baptiste Camille
  Corot **11**
Honoré Daumier **10**
Jaques-Louis David **19**
Honoré de Balzac **16**
Eugène Delacroix **15**
Gustave Doré **14**
Isadora Duncan **6**
Paul Eluard **38**
Max Ernst **2**
Théodore Géricault **20**
Jean-Auguste-Dominique
  Ingres **13**
Jean La Fontaine **31**
René Lalique **12**
Lefebvre Masséna **35**
Amedeo Modigliani **36**
Molière **32**
Jim Morrison **29**
Alfred de Musset **21**
Edith Piaf **27**
Camille Pissarro **26**
Marcel Proust **4**
Gioacchio Antonio
  Rossini **22**
Rothschild family plot **25**
Henri de Saint-Simon **33**
Georges Seurat **18**
Simone Signoret &
  Yves Montand **8**
Gertrude Stein &
  Alice B. Toklas **39**
Oscar Wilde **1**
Richard Wright **7**

the short distance from rue Steinkerque and turn left onto rue Tardieu, where, for the price of a Métro ticket, the *funiculaire* whisks you from the base of the Montmartre butte to an area right below the church.

To reach the dome and crypt, face the church and walk around to its left side, following signs for the Dome and Crypte. You walk down a set of stairs and follow a walkway about 15m (50 ft.) to an iron gate. The entrance and ticket machine are on your right.

The climb from church floor to dome is up a flight of nail-bitingly steep corkscrew steps.

On the other side of Sacré-Coeur is the **place du Tertre,** where Vincent van Gogh once lived; he used it as a scene for one of his paintings. The place is usually swamped by tourists and quick-sketch artists in the spring and summer. Don't let the artists push you around too much: their sketched likenesses of you or your companions may leave something to be desired, especially at their prices. Following any street downhill from the place du Tertre leads you to the quiet side of Montmartre. The steps in front of the church come alive around dusk, when street musicians entertain the crowd that gathers to watch the city's lights come on. Be alert: Pickpockets love Montmartre. Young men often hang around Sacre Coeur and try to sell made-on-the-spot bracelets to tourists, tied directly on to your wrist — this is a classic way of partially incapacitating you while they rifle through the pockets of you or your fellow travelers. Don't stop for them; just give them a polite "non merci."

See map p. 186. Place du Parvis du Sacré Coeur. ☎ *01-53-41-89-00. Métro: Anvers. Take elevator to surface and follow signs to funiculaire, which runs to the church (fare: one Métro ticket). Bus: The only bus that goes to the top of the hill is the local Montmartrobus. Admission: Basilica free; dome and crypt 5€ ($6). Open: Basilica daily 6:45 a.m.–10:30 p.m.; dome and crypt daily 10 a.m.–5:45 p.m.*

Sainte-Chapelle
Ile de la Cité (4e)

Save Sainte-Chapelle for the early afternoon on a sunny day, because the effect of its 15 perfect stained-glass windows soaring 15m (50 ft.) high to a star-studded vaulted ceiling is purely kaleidoscopic. Louis IX, the only French king to become a saint, had Sainte-Chapelle, the "Holy Chapel," built as a shrine to house relics of the crucifixion, including the Crown of Thorns that Louis bought from the Emperor of Constantinople. Building Sainte-Chapelle certainly cost less than the outrageously expensive Crown of Thorns, which was said to have been acquired at the crucifixion. (Louis purchased the Crown from his cousin, Emperor Baldwin II of Constantinople, at a sum of 135,000 *livres tournois* — meanwhile Sainte-Chapelle cost only 40,000 to construct.) The Crown now resides in the vault at Notre-Dame.

Built between 1246 and 1248, Sainte-Chapelle actually consists of two chapels, one on top of the other. Palace servants used the *chapelle basse* ("lower chapel"), ornamented with fleur-de-lis designs. The *chapelle haute* ("upper chapel," accessed by 30 winding steps) is one of the highest achievements of Gothic art. If you spend the time (which can take hours or even a day!), you can see that the 1,134 scenes in the stained glass windows trace the Biblical story from the Garden of Eden to the Apocalypse. St. Louis is shown several times. Some evenings, when the upper chapel becomes a venue for classical-music concerts, the effect of its chandelier lights dancing off the windows is magical.

See map p. 186. 4 bd. du Palais, Palais de Justice. ☎ *01-53-73-78-51. Métro: Cité or St-Michel. RER: St-Michel. Bus: 21, 27, 38, 85, 96. Admission: 5.50€ ($7) adults; 3.50€ ($4.70) students over 18 and seniors; free for children younger than 18. Open: Apr–Sept daily 9:30 a.m.–6:30 p.m., Oct–Mar 10 a.m.–5 p.m. Closed major holidays.*

More Fun Things to See and Do

After you hit all of the city's top attractions, you may want to search out some of its lesser known but still captivating sights. This section introduces you to some of those spots. Organized with specific interests in mind, it gives you ideas about how to make Paris truly your own. The "More Fun Things to Do in Paris" map can help you locate the fun zones.

Especially for kids

You can have a fabulous time with your kids in Paris just seeing the traditional sights. But there are so many more things to do and see, from zoos and boat rides to puppet shows and magic museums! Steep them in the Parisian tradition of *les guignols* (puppet shows). Even though the shows are in French, it's pretty easy to figure out what's going on. You can find the shows in the Jardin du Luxembourg, the Champ de Mars, and the Jardin des Tuileries. All Parisian parks, in fact, are wonderful for children, even without the puppet shows; one of the best is the **Bois de Vincennes,** located at the most eastern edge of the city. You can rent a boat for a leisurely row on the lake, or a bike to ride on the park's miles of bike paths, or visit the great zoo with 1,200 animals. Wander the wonderful maze at the more centrally located **Jardin des Enfants des Halles,** 105 rue Rambuteau (☎ **01-45-08-07-18;** access is free, generally open from 10 a.m.–4 or 6 p.m.; Métro: Châtelet). The French love well-behaved children and are happy to welcome them, especially in the following locations which have been designed with kids in mind

Aquarium Tropical de la Porte Dorée

This is a fascinating place to visit either before or after a visit to the nearby parc Zoologique de Paris (see the last entry in this section). Aquatic life is grouped by theme and by oceanographic region in 80 aquariums. Your kids will love the circular aquarium where the Nile crocodiles live. A recent exhibit displayed piranhas in a re-creation of their natural habitat in the rapid rivers of Guyana. Allow at least an hour and a half.

See map p. 210. 293 av. Dausmenil, 12e. ☎ *01-44-74-84-80. Métro: Porte Dorée. Admission: 5.70€ ($6.80) adult, 4.20€ ($5) ages 4–25, free for children younger than 4. Open: Wed–Mon 9 a.m.–5:15 p.m.*

More Fun Things to Do in Paris

Cité des Sciences et de l'Industrie/Parc de la Villette

This enormous, modern science complex with interactive exhibits on everything from outer space to genetically manipulated plants is incredibly cool! With a planetarium, movie cinemas, ten themed gardens, and an aquarium, as well as an adventure playground designed specifically for 3- to 12-year-olds, it's hard to decide what to do first. On the complex's east side is **Explora,** which features exhibits, models, robots, and interactive games, demonstrates scientific techniques, and presents subjects that include the universe, the earth, the environment, space, computer science, and health (in one experiment, you can test your sense of smell). The **Children's City** is divided into exhibits for 3- to 5-year-olds and 6- to 12-year-olds, including: Machines and Mechanisms, the Living Species, You and Others (kids learn about how their own bodies work), and Techniques of Communications (in one demonstration, kids can be part of a weather broadcast). A separate exhibit on electricity will stand your kids' hair on end. A small section of the Children's City is reserved for 3- to 5-year-olds. Organized around a stream, children learn about themselves in relation to the world around them (in one activity, they get to wear a tortoise shell and climb into a kangaroo pouch; in another they don hard hats and learn how to build a house). The gigantic **Géode** sphere, on the complex's south side, is a wonder, with a huge hemispheric IMAX screen on which six or so films are shown daily. Another theater, the **Cinaxe,** is a simulator that projects movies on a screen while accelerating and moving the audience in different directions (children younger than 3, pregnant women, and the disabled are not allowed). Kids can climb aboard an actual submarine in the **l'Argonaute** exhibit (on the complex's south side next to Géode) and participate in technology demonstrations at the **Science Actualités (Science Today).**

After the visit, let your kids run wild in the expansive, green **parc de la Villette** where they can play in one of the ten gardens — especially neat is the **Garden of Childhood Terrors,** a blue spruce and silver birch "forest" where eerie music plays and the **Dragon Garden** where kids and adults can cruise down the tongue of a dragon, an enormous slide. There are restaurants in the complex and food stands in the park. This could easily be an all-day visit. The Cité des Sciences et l'Industrie is bordered by the La Villette canal basin. Directly across is another smaller complex, the **Cité de la Musique,** accessible by a bridge. Its exhibits, museums, and concerts are also worth a stop.

See map p. 210. 30 av. Corentin-Cariou, 19e. ☎ 01-40-05-80-00. www.cite-sciences.fr. *Métro: Porte-de-la-Villette. Admission: Explora exhibitions 7.50€ ($9) adults, 5.50€ ($6.60) seniors and students under 25, free for children younger than 7. Admission to Cité des Enfants 5€ ($6); to Géode 9€ ($11) adults, 7€ ($6.30) 25 and under and per person in large families or groups; to Cinaxe Theater 5.40€ ($6), or combined with another ticket (Explora or Géode) 4.80€ ($5.75) (children must be older that 3 to enter Cinaxe); the Argonaute submarine is 3€ ($3.60) for all. Check Web site for special combination tickets and seasonal deals. Open: Tues–Sat 10 a.m.– 6 p.m.; Sun 10 a.m.–7 p.m.*

Jardin de l'Acclimatation Bois de Boulogne

After a half-day at this 10-hectare (25-acre) amusement park, your children will sleep well! The park's layout is simple: Just follow its circular road in either direction, and it eventually gets you back to where you started. Attractions include a house of mirrors, an archery range, a miniature golf course, a petting zoo and farm, an American-style bowling alley, a playground, pony rides, paddle boats, and a "City of Merry-Go-Rounds," where young "citizens" can drive cars, fire trucks, and planes, try their hand at carnival games, and ride the carousel. The park also has an "enchanted river," a lake bordered by a bright blue-topped Korean pavilion, a restaurant, and snack and ice cream stands. The most fun way to get here is to take the Pétit Train from the Métro's Porte Maillot exit (5.20€/$6.20 adults round-trip, 3.85€/$4.60 kids round-trip.)

See map p. 210. 16e. ☎ 01-40-67-90-82. Métro: Les Sablons, exit on rue d'Orléans, entrance is about 150m (500 ft.) away. Bus: 43, 73, 82, or 174. Or take the open-air Pétit Train from the Bois de Boulogne's Porte Maillot exit; 5.20€ ($6.25) round-trip adults, 3.85€ ($4.60) round-trip children and students. Admission to the Jardin d'Acclimatation: 2.70€ ($3.20) adults and children ages 3 and older. Free for children younger than 3. Open: June–Sept daily 10 a.m.–7 p.m.; Oct–May daily 10 a.m.–6 p.m.

Jardin des Plantes/Museums of Natural History

Children will stare in awe at the bugs, bones, minerals, meteorites, dinosaurs, fossils, and endangered species in the galleries of the Jardin's Musée National d'Histoire Naturelle on the site of the former royal medicine garden. Here, the Grand Gallery of Evolution traces life and humankind's relationship to nature. Don't miss the endangered and extinct species room, which displays (stuffed versions of) Gabonese monkeys, Sumatran tigers, lemurs of Madagascar, and a mock-up of the dodo bird. English explanations of some exhibits are available. Also part of the natural history museum in separate buildings are the Mineralogical Gallery (1,800 minerals, meteorites, and precious stones), the Entomological Gallery (1,500 insect specimens for bug-loving kids), and the Paleobotanical Gallery (plant evolution and specimens of fossil plants). Walk outside amid rows of trees, beds of herbs and flowers, a 17th-century maze, carousel, greenhouses, zoo, and specialized gardens Save for last the medium-sized *ménagerie* (zoo), one of the oldest in the world, containing live bears, buffalo, big cats, apes, antelope, reptiles (including an alligator found in a room at the Hôtel de Paris), tortoises, and birds. Don't overlook the Vivarium — the spiders and insects are remarkable, especially the bugs that look like living tree branches! — or the Microzoo, where kids use microscopes to get a look at the life of the tiniest animals. A small restaurant on the zoo's premises offers pick-me-ups for the tired and cranky — and their children. Allow at least two hours.

See map p. 210. 57 rue Cuvier, 5e. ☎ 01-40-79-30-00. Métro: Gare d'Austerlitz (exit from the rue Buffon side; you're right next to the Gallery of Anatomy and Paleontology) or Jussieu (walk up rue Geoffroy St-Hilaire to the Grande Galerie de l'Evolution). Admission: Grande Galerie 8€ ($9.60) adults, 6€ ($7.20) students, seniors, and children 5 and under; other galleries 6€ ($7.20) adults, 4€ ($3.60) students, seniors, and *children; ménagerie (zoo) 6€ ($7.20) adults, 3.50€ ($.20) students, seniors, and children. Admission to gardens is free. Open: Park dawn–dusk; Grand Gallery weekdays 10 a.m.–6 p.m., Sat until 8 p.m.; other galleries weekdays 10 a.m.–5 p.m., 6 p.m. on weekends; Ménagerie daily 9 a.m.–6 p.m., Sun till 6:30 p.m.*

La Grande Arche de la Défense

The Grand Arche de la Défense is the centerpiece of a very futuristic Paris suburb rife with glass and chrome skyscrapers lending their height to surreal sculptures. Built in 1989 to commemorate France's bicentennial, the arch completes a continuous line of perspective running from the Arc de Triomphe du Carrousel in the courtyard of the Louvre, down the Champs-Elysées, and through the Arc de Triomphe to the suburb of La Défense. As well, there's a full overview of the Bois de Bologne. The netting you see here is for catching any pieces of the facade that may fall down — several chunks have already. This is a popular destination with about 500,000 visitors a year, and kids will love the cool outdoor elevator to the top. There is a restaurant on the premises, but we suggest bringing snacks to stave off any hunger pangs and enjoying a better meal back in Paris. Allow about two hours for the round-trip journey from central Paris, including the climb to the top.

See map p. 210. 1 parvis de la Défense, 92040 Paris-La Défense. ☎ 01-49-07-27-27. Métro and RER: Grande Arche de la Défense. Admission: 7.50€ ($9) adults, 6€ ($7.20) ages students and seniors, free for children younger than 6. Open: Daily Apr–Sept 10 a.m.–8 p.m., Oct–Mar until 7 p.m.

Musée de la Curiosité et de la Magie

Who amongst you is brave enough to stick his hand in the open mouth of a lion and see if it really is an illusion? You can do it here in this easy-to-miss small museum (look up for a sign reading Académie de Magie). Bona fide magicians escort you through vaulted rooms containing a collection of trick mirrors, animated paintings, talking genies, and the history of illusion in general. While they won't disclose any secrets, you and your kids will have your senses tickled through many interactive displays. Live magic shows performed throughout the afternoon are also highly entertaining. The museum shop sells all the tools your kids need to cast (benevolent) spells back home.

See map p. 210. 11 rue St-Paul, 4e. ☎ 01-42-72-13-26. Métro: St-Paul. Admission: 7€ ($8.40) adults, 5€ ($6) children younger than 13. Open: Wed and Sat–Sun 2–7 p.m. and national school holidays.

Palais de la Découverte

Within the Art Nouveau metal and glass confines of the Grand Palais, the Palais de la Découverte is a full funhouse of science brought to life for kids. Here, you can explore a planetarium, a room devoted to the earth's geology from its beginnings to the future, a mathematics atelier that promises a fun experience, and lots of live experiments on weekends. Your hair will stand on end in the electrostatics room; kids can light up displays, test their muscle reactions on special machines, see experiments about electromagnetism in an annex off the Electricity Room and learn about DNA in the Life Sciences wing. Count on spending at least two hours here.

See map p. 210. Grand Palais Av. Franklin-D-Roosevelt, 8e. ☎ 01-56-43-20-21. Métro: Franklin-D-Roosevelt. Admission: 6.50€ ($7.80) adults, 4€ ($4.80) students and children 5–17. Planetarium supplement 3.50€ ($4.20). Some workshops may cost an additional 1.50€ ($2.15) per person. Open: Tues–Sat 9:30 a.m.–6 p.m.; Sun 10 a.m.–7 p.m. Closed major holidays.

Parc Zoologique de Paris

Most animals live in settings that closely resemble their natural habitats in this modern zoo big enough (1,200 animals) to keep your kids occupied for an afternoon. A cool climbing tower *(Le Grand Rocher)* offers a great view of the lions, tigers, bears, elephant, and more, and you can even watch while some are fed lunch (bears at 11:30 a.m., pelicans at 2:15 p.m., seals and sea lions at 4 p.m. — you may be surprised that the French would allow their animals to eat after normal lunchtime is over, at 2 p.m., and you, yourself, might have some problems locating lunch in Paris at 4 p.m.). The zoo has picnic areas on-site as well as a snack bar. It's located in the middle of the Bois de Vincennes, on Paris's far eastern side. Note: Due to the closing of certain exhibits at the time of this writing, the zoo reduced its admission to a single rate, which may be subject to change. For the time being, a double-entry ticket for both the *Ménagerie* at the Jardin des Plantes and the Parc Zoologique can be purchased at either location for 10€ ($12).

See map p. 210. 53 av. de St-Maurice, Bois de Vincennes, 12e. ☎ 01-44-75-20-10. Fax: 01-43-43-54-73. Métro: Porte Dorée. (Take av. Daumesnil past the Square des Combattants Indochine to av. de St-Maurice and turn right; it's a five- to ten-minute walk.) Admission: 5€ ($6) all ages, free for children younger than 4. Open: Daily 9 a.m.–6 p.m.; Sun till 6:30 p.m.

Especially for teens

The kid-friendly sights in the previous section are appropriate for teenagers, as well. But here are a few more suggestions for kids who are a bit older.

Aquaboulevard

If could happen: Your teens say they're bored. Send them to Aquaboulevard. It may not be the beach, but its seven water slides, wave pool, against-the-current river, indoor and outdoor pools, spas and Jacuzzis, whirlpool, geysers, water cannons, walls of water, waterbed with bubbles, and waterfall make it a fun substitute, and it's safer than swimming in the Seine. A McDonald's, an Oh! Poivrier!, a pizza place, a Hippopotamus, and a first-run movie theater are located on the premises as well.

See map p. 210. 4 rue Louis-Armand, 15e. ☎ 01-40-60-10-00. Métro: Balard (head down av. de la Porte de Sèvres; just after you walk under the overpass, you will see Aquaboulevard straight ahead). Admission: 20€ ($24) people ages 12 and older, 10€

($12) children 3–11, who must be accompanied by an adult. Open: Mon–Thurs 9 a.m.–11 p.m., Fri–Sat 8 a.m.–midnight, Sun 8 a.m.–11 p.m. Children under three are not admitted.

Champs-Elysées

If it's the mall they're missing, your teens can shop to their hearts' content on Paris's most famous street in such clothing stores as O'Neill, Quiksilver, Zara, Naf Naf, and Kookaï, and music stores Virgin and Fnac. They can catch movies in French or English (look for "v.o.," for *version originale,* on the marquee or in newspaper listings for U.S. releases that aren't dubbed into French) in one of the many movie theaters and eat familiar fast food at McDonald's or KFC. Many of the stores on this street are open Sunday, and plenty of teens — both residents and tourists — hang out here.

See map p. 210. Métro: Concorde, Champs-Elysées, Clémenceau, Franklin-D-Roosevelt, George V, Charles-de-Gaulle–Étoile. Many bus lines cross the Champs, but only the 73 travels its entire length.

Les Catacombes (The Catacombs)

"Arrête, c'est ici l'Empire de la Mort" (Stop, here is the empire of death) reads the inscription over the door of Paris's most macabre attraction. Les Catacombes are truly not for the faint-hearted, and are thus perfect for hardy kids older than ten, because the tunnels are dark, damp, and spooky. A former quarry, Les Catacombes began housing bones in 1785 from the Cimetière des Innocents and an assortment of other overstocked Parisian cemeteries. Now Les Catacombes are the final resting place for about 6 million skulls and skeletons stacked in thousands of yards of tunnels (a visit is bound to provoke at least a little bit of fear, even among the bravest adults).

Those prone to claustrophobia should think twice about entering. The deep, dark tunnels close in rapidly and tightly. Equip yourself with a flashlight to navigate the poorly lit corridors and read the inscriptions, and wear proper shoes (such as hiking boots) to avoid a misstep on the rocky, often slippery passageways. Wear a hood to protect yourself from the water dripping overhead. Les Catacombes earned the nickname *place d'Enfer* ("Hell Square"), which later became *place Denfert-Rochereau,* and you can take Métro line 4 or 6, or RER B to the stop of the same name.

See map p. 210. 1 place Denfert-Rochereau, 14e. ☎ 01-43-22-47-63. Métro: Denfert-Rochereau. The entrance is an unassuming small door where a plate reads ENTRÉE DES CATACOMBES. Admission: 5€ ($6) adults; 3.30€ ($3.95) ages 8–26 and seniors; free for children younger than 8. Open: Tues–Sun 10 a.m.–5 p.m. (last entry at 4 p.m.).

Les Égouts

It sounds hard to believe, but the tour of the Paris's sewers is so popular that you sometimes have to wait as long as a half-hour in line. The tour starts with a short film about the history of sewers: The tunnels here were laid out in the 1850s during the reign of Napoléon III, at the same time that Haussmann was designing the grands boulevards, but the history of the sewers goes all the way back to Roman times. The film is followed by a visit to a small museum, and finally a short trip through the maze. Paris's sewers are laid out like an underground city, with streets clearly labeled and each branch pipe bearing the name of the building to which it's connected. Don't worry; you won't trudge through anything *dégoutant* (disgusting), but the visit may leave your clothes smelling a bit ripe. Make this the last of the day's attractions, and wear something you don't plan to wear again until after the next wash day. The ceiling occasionally drips water, but the tour guides insist that it is only condensation, and thus, clean. Guided tours are free, and most are in French, but English and also Spanish are available. Towards the end, a long montage of the evolution of the city's drainage system also gives a beautiful timeline of the entire city's development as a whole, from the pre-Roman period until present day. Plan on spending an hour and a half to two hours.

See map p. 210. 7e. ☎ *01-53-68-27-81. Métro: Alma-Marceau, then walk across the bridge to the Left Bank. RER: Pont de l'Alma. The entrance is a stairway on the Seine side of the Quai d'Orsay, facing no. 93; look for a free-standing ticket booth. Admission: 4€ ($4.80) adults; 3.20€ ($3.85) for ages 5–16; free for children younger than 5. Open: May–Sept Sat–Wed 11 a.m.–5 p.m.; Oct–Apr 11 a.m.–4 p.m. Closed three weeks in Jan.*

Especially for history buffs

Paris resounds with history. Blue plaques on buildings tell you the names of famous people and the dates that that they lived there. Brown-and-orange signs in French give you an overview of an area's particular story (for those who have learned some French for the voyage, don't despair if you don't recognize some of the verb-endings in these signs! Any historical writing makes use of a nonspoken literary past tense, the *passé simple.* It is used to make people think of the described events as truly historical, although personally it seems a bit pretentious!). The city is filled with wonderful museums to satisfy even the pickiest buff's thirst for knowledge. This section lists a few of the particularly good ones.

Cabinet des Médailles

Treasure hunters, pirates, this museum is for you. Housed in France's original national library, still referred to as the Bibliothèque Nationale de France, are an impressive display of archaeological objects, cameos, bronzes, medals, and money originally amassed by French kings. Among the more exceptional objects are the Treasure of Berthouville, a collection of Gallo-Roman money; the Cameo of Sainte-Chapelle, a huge multicolored cameo dating from the first century; and the Treasure of Childéric, one of the oldest remnants of the French monarchy. Take a peek into the Salle Labrouste, a lovely reading room built in 1868, which now echoes sadly without its book collection (ten million books were removed in 1998 to the Bibliothèque

Nationale de France in the 13e). The garden, a virtual mini-Versailles, also merits a stop. Security is tight here. Plan to spend at least an hour.

See map p. 210. Bibliothèque Nationale de France, 58 rue de Richelieu, 2e (between rue des Filles St-Thomas and rue Colbert). ☎ *01-53-79-83-30. Métro: Palais-Royal–Musée du Louvre or Bourse. Bus: 20, 29, 39, 48, 67, 74, 85, 95. Admission: Free. Open: Mon–Fri 1–5:45 p.m.; Sat 1–4:45 p.m.; Sun noon–6 p.m.*

Cluny Museum

This is one of the jewels of Paris museums, home to the famous tapestry series *The Lady and the Unicorn* (with a great gift shop to boot!). Officially called the Musée National du Moyen Age/Thermes de Cluny, it houses ancient Roman hot and cold baths, the original statues that furious revolutionaries tore from Notre-Dame in 1790 (thinking they represented royalty), and one of the most beautiful tapestry series in the world. You also find remnants of clothing that royalty wore in the Middle Ages, coins, leatherwork, and gothic furniture, as well as church art — jeweled crosses, statues, sculptures, clothing, tapestries, and paintings of saints.

In the 19th century, the Hôtel de Cluny belonged to a collector of medieval art; upon his death in the 1840s, the government acquired the house and its contents. You enter through a medieval cobblestone courtyard, the *Cour d'Honneur* (Courtyard of Honor) — be sure to take in the turreted building and its gargoyles; this is one of the only medieval residences left in Paris. After paying for admission in the tiny lobby, turn left past the gift shop (save it until last) and try to take it all in. The fascinating Roman baths and the Notre-Dame statues are one floor down; one floor up is *The Lady and the Unicorn.* The tapestries hang in a dimly lit room by themselves. You can sit in one of the cushioned seats and try to figure out the meaning of the sixth tapestry. (The first five are an allegory representing the five senses; the meaning of the sixth tapestry remains a mystery.) In one of the medieval-period chambers being renovated, one can find a detailed miniature model of the Cluny hotel, which anyone can touch — it was placed there to give blind visitors the opportunity to feel the shapes and construction used in the medieval architecture. The gift shop is a wonderful place for souvenirs, and the renovated gardens are an oasis of calm off one of the Latin Quarter's busiest streets. Every plant (except two) in *The Lady and the Unicorn* tapestries was extensively researched and tracked down to be planted here.

See map p. 210. 6 place Paul-Painlevé, 5e (between rue du Sommerard and rue des Écoles). ☎ *01-53-73-78-00. Métro: Cluny-Sorbonne. Admission: 6.50€ ($7.80) adults; 4.50€ ($5.60) ages 18–26, seniors older than 60, and for all on Sun; free for children younger than 18 and for all first Sun of month. An addition 1.20€ ($1.45) is added to the entrance for temporary exhibits. Open: Wed–Mon 9:15 a.m.–5:45 p.m. Closed Christmas, New Year's Day, and May 1.*

Conciergerie

Built in the 14th century as part of the administrative offices of the crown, the Conciergerie was turned into a prison in the 15th century, and it is probably most famous for its days as a prison during The Terror years of the French Revolution, when 4,164 "enemies of the people," including Marie Antoinette and her husband, Louis VXI, resided here before meeting their fate. Visitors pass through the Tour d'Argent (the Silver Tower), where the crown jewels were once stored, and the Tour César to the Salle des Gardes (Guard Room) entrance. Probably the most popular exhibit is Marie Antoinette's 1-sq.-m (11-sq.-ft.) cell. More than 4,000 of those imprisoned here headed for the guillotine on the place de la Révolution (now the place de la Concorde), including revolutionary ringleaders Danton and Robespierre, assassin Charlotte Corday, and the poet André Chenier. The far western tower, the Tour Bonbec, came to be known facetiously as the Tower of Babel because of the frequent screams from the many prisoners tortured there. Marie Antoinette's cell is now a chapel, and the other cells have been transformed with exhibits and mementos designed to convey a sense of prison life in a brutal era. Plan on spending two hours both here and in Sainte-Chapelle, the high-Gothic chapel and one of Paris's top sights (mentioned earlier this chapter) with 15 spectacular stained glass windows that are simply awe-inspiring.

See map p. 210. Palais de Justice, Ile de la Cité, 1er. ☎ *01-53-73-78-50. Métro: Cité, Châtelet–Les Halles, or St-Michel. (Exit the Métro at Cité, which is between rue de la Cité and bd. du Palais; the Palais is directly across bd. du Palais.) RER: St-Michel. Admission: 6.50€ ($7.80) adults; 4.50€ ($5.40) ages 18–25; free for children younger than 18. The better deal is the combined Sainte-Chapelle and Conciergerie ticket for 10€ ($12). Open: Mar–Oct daily 9:30 a.m.–6 p.m.; Nov–Feb daily 9 a.m.–5 p.m. Closed Christmas, New Year's Day, and May 1.*

La Crypte Archéologique

Descend into the crypt to find yourself at the Ile de la Cité's original level. In 1965, excavations for a new parking lot under the parvis (a portico in front of the church) of Notre-Dame revealed Gallo-Roman ramparts, third-century Gallo-Roman rooms heated by an underground furnace system called a *hypocaust,* and cellars of medieval houses. The parking lot project was abandoned, and the excavations were turned into this neat archaeological museum. Over the centuries, builders erected new structures over the ruins of previous settlements, raising the island about 7m (23 ft.). To help you visualize the buildings that once stood here, scale models show how Paris grew from a small settlement to a Roman city, and photographs show the pre-Haussmann parvis. Allow about 45 minutes, longer if you're a history buff.

See map p. 210. Place du parvis Notre-Dame, 4e (about 60m/200 ft. directly in front of Notre-Dame, accessed by downward-leading stairs). ☎ *01-55-42-50-10. Métro: Cité. RER: St-Michel-Notre-Dame. Admission: 3.30€ ($4) adults; 1.60€ ($2) ages 26 and younger. Open: Daily 10 a.m.–6 p.m.*

Musée Carnavalet

Housed inside two beautiful Renaissance mansions, Paris history comes alive here through an incredible selection of paintings, reassembled rooms in all their period glory, and other items from daily life long ago. The blue-and-yellow rooms of Louis XV and Louis XVI are here in all their ornately furnished glory. The chess pieces that Louis XVI played with while awaiting his beheading are here, as are Napoléon's cradle and a replica of Marcel Proust's cork-lined bedroom. The *Cabinet Doré de l'hotel La Rivière* room has a spectacular gilded, ceiling painting of Apollo and Aurora by Charles Le Brun; his other ceiling painting is of Psyche with the Muses. Many salons depict events related to the Revolution, and the paintings of what Paris used to look like are fascinating. Numerous models of the Bastille prison are represented, including one depicting the peasant revolt itself. In 2000, the museum opened a 1.6-million-dollar wing devoted to the archaeology of Paris's earliest settlements (some artifacts, such as the fishing boats used by settlers, date back to between 2200 and 4400 B.C.). Visitors can even touch some of the exhibits here. Temporary exhibitions are often eclectic, related to both art and Parisian history; in 2006 the contemporary sculpture artist Deverne had his work, which is found all over Ile-de-France, represented, as well as photographs of Parisian architecture taken by photographer and airplane pilot Roger Henrard. You may want to buy an English-language guidebook in the museum's gift shop, because audio guides are in French.

See map p. 210. 23 rue de Sévigné, 3e. ☎ *01-44-59-58-58. Métro: St-Paul. (Turn left on rue de Sévigné.) Admission: Free for permanent collections; temporary exhibits 7€ ($8.40) adults, 3.50€ ($4.20) students. Open: Tues–Sun 10 a.m.–6 p.m.*

Musée d'Art et d'Histoire du Judaïsme

The beautiful 17th-century mansion Hôtel de St-Aignan houses this enormous collection tracing the development of Jewish culture in France and Europe, from life in the Middle Ages to the 20th century. In addition to beautifully crafted religious objects, including several copies of the Torah, with breastplates, crowns, and cloth coverings from different Jewish communities throughout the world, there are shofars, menorahs, ark curtains, and spectacular velvet cloaks reflecting both the Sephardic and Ashkenazi traditions throughout Europe and North Africa, the museum has medieval gravestones and 20th-century paintings and sculptures. The museum also presents very thoroughly the newly available documents relating to the Dreyfus affair, the notorious scandal that falsely accused a Jewish army captain of providing secret military information to the German government in 1894. The free audio tour is very informative. The exhibits end with a collection of works by Jewish artists, including paintings by Modigliani, Soutine, Zadkine, and Chagall. A recent exhibition here included stunning portraits Polish artist Zber (Fiszel Zylberberg) painted in the French internment camp Beaune-la-Rolande where he was held for three months in 1942 before his deportation to Auschwitz. He died there on October 26th. Allow at least two hours. Security is tight here; you will have to pass through metal detectors.

See map p. 210. 71 rue du Temple, 3e (between rue Rambuteau and rue de Braque). ☎ *01-53-01-86-60.* www.mahj.org; *Métro: Rambuteau, Hôtel de Ville. Bus: 29, 38, 47, 75. Admission: 6.80€ ($8.16) adults; 4.50€ ($5.40) ages 18–26 and seniors; free for children younger than 18. Open: Mon–Fri 11 a.m.–6 p.m.; Sun 10 a.m.–6 p.m.*

Musée de l'Histoire de France/Archives Nationales

This museum displays some of the most important documents that pertain to the country's history, as well as personal papers of some famous French citizens. In 1808, Napoléon ordered the acquisition of the Rohan-Soubise estate to house Empire archives; the palace also contains the National Archives. Exhibits include Henry IV's Edict of Nantes (a document that guaranteed religious liberty); the wills of Louis XIV, Louis XVI (along with his diary), and Napoléon; the Declaration of Human Rights; Marie Antoinette's last letter; and the French constitution. Rooms are devoted to the Middle Ages, the French Revolution, and other themes.

See map p. 210. Hôtel de Rohan, 87 rue Vieille du Temple, 3e. ☎ *01-53-79-83-30. Métro: Rambuteau. Bus: 29, 75, 96. Admission: Museum 3.05€ ($3.65) adults; 2.30€ ($2.75) ages 18–25; free for children younger than 18. Open: Mon–Fri 1–5:45 p.m.; Sat 1 p.m.–4:45 p.m., and Sun noon–6 p.m.*

Place de la Bastille

Ignore the traffic and try to imagine the place de la Bastille just more than 200 years ago, when it contained eight towers rising 30m (100 ft.). It was here, on July 14, 1789 (now commemorated in France as Bastille Day), that a mob attacked the old prison, launching the French Revolution. Although the Bastille had long since fallen into disuse, it symbolized the arbitrary power of a king who could imprison anyone for any reason, while the citizenry paid high taxes for his follies. Prisoners of means could buy a spacious cell and even host dinner parties, but the poor disappeared within the prison's recesses and sometimes drowned when the Seine overflowed its banks. The attack on the prison was therefore a direct assault on royal power. The Bastille was razed in 1792. In its place stands the Colonne de Juillet, a 51m (171-ft.) bronze column built between 1830 and 1849 to commemorate Parisians killed in civil uprisings in 1830 and 1848.

11e. Métro: Bastille. (The Colonne de Juillet is across from the Métro.)

Especially for art lovers

Art in Paris is not merely French art. Many French movements began or developed here, but generations of artists from all parts of the world have thrived in Paris, and the city's museums and galleries hold enough art for several lifetimes of daily viewing. From galleries in the Marais, Bastille, St-Germain-des-Prés, and near the Champs-Elysées, through Egyptian, Assyrian, and Greco-Roman art at the Louvre, realism, Impressionism, and Art Nouveau at the Musée d'Orsay, to the modern international masters at the Centre Pompidou, it is an understatement to say that Paris offers a vast wealth of art.

Each October, Paris also presents the enormous *Foire Internationale d'Art Contemporain* (www.fiac-online.com), one of the largest contemporary art fairs in the world with stands from more than 150 galleries, half of them foreign. The following museums are often less crowded than their larger and more famous counterparts, but each has plenty of wonders in store.

Fondation Cartier pour l'Art Contemporain

This trendy museum has been known for displaying works that reflect the main trends of contemporary art since the 1980s. Supported by Cartier, the luxury jeweler and watchmaker, even the building where the art is displayed itself is a gorgeous and flashy work. Designed by architect Jean Nouvel it is too striking to miss: a glass-and-metal screen stands between the street and the glass-and-metal building, creating an optical illusion that makes the courtyard greenery appear as if it is growing indoors. The offices for the Cartier jewelry empire are upstairs (their watches average several thousand dollars a pop), and most of the first-rate contemporary art exhibits that the foundation hosts are in the basement. Exhibitions at the time of writing included moving image and sound works of video-artist and poet Gary Hill; also the moving-image works of Japanese artist Tabaimo. The permanent collection is built around large groups of work by living artists and includes paintings by artists such as Vija Celmins, Sam Francis, and Matthew Barney, as well as photography, sculpture, huge installations, and video works. Reservations are necessary for the très cool performance art and music of Les Soirees Nomades (Nomadic Evenings) on some Sundays, Wednesdays, and every Thursday night, starting from 5 p.m. to 9 p.m. Check the Web site for details about these events. Plan to spend at least an hour and a half here.

See map p. 210. 261 bd. Raspail, 14e (200 meters from the Raspail Métro stop, past Passage d'Enfer and rue Boissonade). ☎ *01-42-18-56-50, or 01-42-18-56-72 for Nomadic Evenings reservations.* www.fondation.cartier.fr. *Métro: Raspail. Admission to exhibits and Nomadic Nights: 6.50€ ($8) adults; 4.50€ ($5.40) students younger than 25; free for children younger than 10. Open: Tues–Sun noon–8 p.m.*

Maison Européenne de la Photographie

This museum's goal is to make the three fundamental mediums of photography — exhibition prints, the printed page, and film — accessible to all, and it succeeds on all fronts. A first-floor gallery exhibits original period prints (see Irving Penn's photo of Colette), the vaulted 18th-century basement displays cutting-edge photography, film projections, and installations. There is a space for young photographers to show their work, and the Roméo Martinez library displays some 12,000 titles spanning the last 50 years of photography. Martinez was editor-in-chief of *Camera* magazine for 20 years. There are permanent collections of Polaroid art and an excellent video library that allows you to look up thousands of photographs. The museum was created from two restored 18th-century mansions. Allow at least an hour and a half including a pick-me-up in the cozy vaulted 18th-century basement cafe. (*Note:* This cafe closes at 5 p.m. on Wednesdays; all other opening days it is open until 7 p.m.)

See map p. 210. 5–7 rue de Fourcy, 4e. ☎ *01-44-78-75-00.* www.mep-fr.org. *Métro: St-Paul or Pont-Marie. Bus: 67, 69, 96, 76. Admission: 6€ ($7.20) adults; 3€ ($3.60) ages 8–26 and older than 60; free for children younger than 8; free for all Wed 5–8 p.m. Free guided tours are available on certain dates, which can be verified by calling or visiting the Web site; reservations necessary. Open: Wed–Sun 11 a.m.–8 p.m.*

Musée Cognacq-Jay

La Samaritaine department store founder Ernest Cognacq and his wife Marie-Louise Jay amassed at the turn of the 20th century this collection of 18th-century rococo art that features works by François Boucher, Jean-Honoré Fragonard, Peter Paul Rubens, Louis-Michel van Loo, Jean-Antoine Watteau, Elisabeth Vigée-LeBrun, and Giambattista Tiepolo displayed in elegant Louis XV and Louis XVI paneled rooms. There is a collection of everyday objects, such as dance cards, and snuff and candy boxes, shelves of porcelain and porcelain figures, rich wood cabinets, and furniture. The building housing it all is the beautifully preserved Hôtel Donon, built in the 16th century. You can walk through a little manicured garden, open May to September, to enjoy sunny days. Temporary exhibits are presented two to three times a year. In 2006 one of the exhibitions included the history of the big department stores *(grands magasins)*, and the artwork associated with them, and how their invention elevated the couple for whom the museum is named.

See map p. 210. 8 rue Elzévir, 3e (between rue des Francs Bourgeois and rue Barbette). ☎ *01-40-27-07-21. Métro: St-Paul. Admission: Permanent collections free; temporary exhibits vary in fee from 3.30€–9€ ($3.95–$11), half-priced for youth from 14–26; free for children younger than 14. Open: Tues–Sun 10 a.m.–6 p.m.*

Musée de la Sculpture en Plein Air

On the banks of the Seine between the Institut du Monde Arabe and the Jardin des Plantes are displayed the sculptures of 29 artists, including César, Ossip Zadkine, and Stagio Stahly. You may pass by these sculptures on one of your strolls without realizing that this graceful waterside park is really a museum.

Quai St-Bernard, 5e (on the quay of the Seine between the Institut du Monde Arabe and the Jardin des Plantes). Métro: Sully-Morland or Gare d'Austerlitz. Admission: Free. If you go on a summer Thurs evening around 8 p.m., you can see outdoor dancing nearby.

Musée de l'Orangerie des Tuileries

Finally! Since the spring of 2006, visitors are delighting in the newly renovated and beautifully presented *Musée de l'Orangerie,* closed for renovations for close to a decade. The highlight of the Orangerie is most definitely its two oval rooms wrapped nearly 360 degrees with Monet's *Nymphéas,* the water lily series he painted especially for the Orangerie, and these rooms were the primary focus of the renovations. The immense and awe inspiring murals simply pop from their spotless cream-white walls, lit brightly enough to accentuate all of the beautifully emotional colors. While the rounded corners of the two oval rooms give admirers of Monet's works a calm and pleasant space to enjoy the art. Since 1984, the museum has also housed the remarkable John Walter and Paul Guillaume art collection, comprising works by Cézanne, Renoir, Rousseau, Matisse, Modigliani, Dérain, Picasso, and Soutine, among other artists.

See map p. 210. Jardin des Tuileries, 1er. ☎ 01-44-77-80-07. Métro: Concorde. Admission: 6.50€ ($7.80) for adults, 4.50€ ($5.40) for students under 26 years of age; free for all first Sun of month. Open: Wed–Mon 12:30–7 p.m., until 9 p.m. on Fri. Closed on May 1 and Christmas.

Musée Gustave Moreau

The teacher of Henri Matisse, Gustave Moreau was a symbolist painter influenced by the English pre-Raphaelites. He created fantasies of a mythological world, embracing the bizarre and painting mythological subjects and scenes in a sensuous, romantic style that look to be encrusted with jewels. The work is not to everyone's taste. The artist himself established and designed this duplex museum studio so that his symbolist work could be displayed the way he wanted long after his death. More than 6,000 of Moreau's works can be found here. Among them are *The Pretenders, The Life of Humanity, The Apparition, Orpheus by the Tomb of Eurydice,* and *Jupiter and Semele.* Moreau taught at the École des Beaux-Arts; his museum's first curator, Georges Rouault, was his favorite student, among other famous artists such as Henri Matisse. The artist's apartment is also preserved here. An hour and a half should be plenty.

See map p. 210. 14 rue de la Rochefoucault, 9e (between rue la Bruyère and rue St-Lazare). ☎ 01-48-74-38-50. Métro: Trinité d'Estienne d'Orves. Bus: 32, 43, 49, 68, or 74. Admission: 4€ ($4.80) adults; 2.60€ ($3.10) students, ages 18–25, seniors older than 60, and for adults on Sun; free for children younger than 18. Open: Wed–Mon 10 a.m.–12:45 p.m. and 2–5:15 p.m.

Musée Maillol

Curvaceous, bold, and graceful bronze statues of Aristide Maillol's favorite model, Dina Vierny, are on vibrant display as well as the works of Impressionist and Postimpressionist artists in this renovated 18th-century convent. Outside is the sculpted fountain of the four seasons by Edme Bouchardon. But it is the important modern art collection inside that rightly draws the most notice. The elegant upper floors of the museum display crayon and pastel sketches of Vierny, who Maillol discovered when she was only 15 years old. He believed her voluptuous figure was the personification of femininity and she served as his exclusive model for ten years. Maillol's personal collection includes the work of his friends, Matisse and Bonnard, as well as two sculptures by Rodin, works by Gauguin, Dégas, Rousseau, Odilon Redon, Maurice Denis, Kandinsky, and Renoir. Vierny, who collected art most of her life, has an important collection of modern primitives that include Douanier, Rousseau, and Camille Bombois, as well as drawings by Suzanne Valadon, Dégas, Picasso, and Foujita. The museum features splendid temporary exhibits; a recent exhibit was an ensemble of 59 photographs taken by Bert Stern in 1962 of the striking and fragile Marilyn Monroe.

See map p. 210. 61 rue de Grenelle, 7e. ☎ 01-42-22-59-58. www.museemaillol. com. *Métro: Rue du Bac. Admission: 8€ ($9.60) adults; 6€ ($7.20) students 16–26; free for children younger than 16. Open: Wed–Mon 11 a.m.–6 p.m. (last ticket sold at 5:15 p.m.).*

Musée Marmottan Monet

This is an exquisite museum devoted to the works of Claude Monet and contains an outstanding collection of his water lily paintings, as well as his more abstract representations of the Japanese Bridge at Giverny. The painting *Impression: Sunrise,* is located here; it was from this painting that the term *Impressionism* was coined to describe the painting style and subsequent artistic movement. Also on hand is Monet's personal collection, which includes works by his contemporaries Pissarro, Manet, Morisot, and Renoir.

The museum, located in a beautiful area between the Ranelagh garden and the Bois de Boulogne, is in a 19th-century mansion that belonged to the art historian Paul Marmottan. He donated the mansion and his collection of Empire furniture and Napoleonic art to the Académie des Beaux-Arts upon his death in 1932.

Donations have expanded the collection to include more Impressionist paintings and the stunning Wildenstein collection of late medieval French, Italian, English, and Flemish illuminated manuscripts. Allow at least an hour and a half for a visit.

See map p. 210. 2 rue Louis-Boilly, 16e. ☎ *01-42-24-07-02.* www.marmottan.com. *Métro: La-Muette. Admission: 8€ ($9.60) adults; 4.50€ ($5.40) ages 8–25; free for children younger than 8. Open: Tues–Sun 10 a.m.–6 p.m. Closed Christmas, New Year's Day, and May 1.*

Le Musée du Quai Branly

This stunning museum, is the newest art museum in Paris, just a block from the Eiffel Tower, and opened in June 2006 to much fanfare (it's not often that new art museums open up here, after all). Designed by Jean Nouvel, who also designed the Fondation Cartier and the Institut du Monde Arabe, there is plenty of glass to let in the light. Housed in four spectacular buildings with a garden walled off from the quai Branly, are the art, sculpture, and cultural materials of a vast range of non-Western civilizations, separating into different sections that represent the traditional cultures of Africa, East and Southeast Asia, Oceania, Australia, the Americas, and New Zealand. The pieces here come from the now defunct Musée des Arts Africains et Océaniens, from the Louvre and the Musée de l'Homme. Temporary exhibits are shown off in boxes all along the 180m (600-ft.) exhibition hall. Incredible masterpieces are on display made by some very advanced traditional civilizations: some of the most impressive exhibits present tribal masks of different cultures, some of which are so lifelike and emotional in their creation that you can feel the fear and elation involved in their use, which is well documented in descriptions in French and English. Allow two hours for a full visit; also take a stroll in their carefully manicured garden, or have a cafe in their small cafeteria across from the main building. There are numerous entrances to the museum grounds from the area near the Eiffel tower, the main entrance is on quai Branly.

See map p. 210. 27 or 37 quai Branly and 206 or 218 rue de l'Université, 7e. ☎ *01-56-61-70-00. Métro: Alma-Marceau, cross le pont d'Alma, turn right, and follow along* *the Seine until you come across a large glass-paneled wall, which among other things, will say "Musée du Quai Branly." RER: Pont d'Alma. Admission: 8.50€ ($10) adults, 6€ ($7.20) for students 18–26 and seniors; free for children under 18. Open: Tues–Sun 10 a.m.–6:30 p.m., Thurs till 9:30 p.m.; ticket counters close at 5:45 p.m.*

Musée Zadkine

This small museum is a delightful short distance from the Jardin du Luxembourg and is the definition of Zen. If you have time to spare after wandering in the Jardin du Luxembourg, exit the garden's west side and head approximately a block south on rue d'Assas to this serene place, the perfect spot to view the works of Belarorussian sculptor Ossip Zadkine. The small sculpture garden is sheltered within walls of Virginia creeper, and Japanese cherry, maple, and birch trees lend shade to the garden's changing sculptures. The garden and museum are free, and the temporary exhibits don't cost much more, and it's worth a visit if you like contemporary sculpture or you are familiar with the artist's work. Zadkine moved to Paris around 1909 and lived and worked in this house and studio from 1928 until his death in 1967. His art, books, tools, and furniture are all on display, as well as many of his works in brass, wood, and stone. His bronze, *Destroyed City* (1953) is considered a masterpiece; the model is exhibited here (the original is in Rotterdam). The museum is accessed through an alleyway. (*Note:* Although open at this time, the museum is scheduled to go through several phases of renovation. It is best to call ahead to make sure it is open for visits.)

See map p. 210. 100 bis rue d'Assas, 6e. ☎ 01-55-42-77-20. Métro: Notre-Dame-des-Champs or Vavin. Bus: 38, 82, 83, 91. Admission: Free for permanent exhibits; temporary exhibits 4€ ($4.80) adults; 3€ ($3.60) children and students ages 7–26 and seniors older than 60; 2€ ($2.40) for children younger than 7. Open: Tues–Sun 10 a.m.–6 p.m.

Especially for the literary

Paris's literary landmarks aren't all connected to Ernest Hemingway, F. Scott Fitzgerald, and the "Lost Generation," though it sure seems that way sometimes.

Brasserie de l'Île St-Louis

If you're a fan of *From Here to Eternity* or *The Thin Red Line,* pay a visit to this brasserie (see also Chapter 10 for a review of the food), where novelist and regular customer James Jones kept his own *chope* (mug) at the bar. Not only is the location excellent — the building is situated directly off the footbridge from Ile de la Cité to Ile St-Louis with an unparalleled view of the eastern tip of Ile de la Cité (including the back of Notre-Dame) — but this eatery is one of the last remaining independent brasseries in Paris. Jones lived with his family around the corner on Ile de la Cité, and the film about their lives, *A Soldier's Daughter Never Cries,* was filmed in the neighborhood.

See map p. 210. 55 quai de Bourbon. ☎ 01-43-54-02-59. Métro: Pont Marie. Main courses: 15€–30€ ($18–$36) lunch and dinner. V. Open: Thurs–Tues noon–12 a.m.

Brasserie Lipp and Café les Deux Magots

You can't talk about literary Paris without mentioning Ernest Hemingway, and two of his favorite hangouts are just across the street from each other on boulevard St-Germain-des-Prés. Brasserie Lipp is where Hemingway lovingly recalls eating potato salad in *A Moveable Feast,* and the Café les Deux Magots is where Jake Barnes meets Lady Brett in *The Sun Also Rises.* Tourism has driven up prices, so just go for a glass of wine or a coffee (and remember that it's cheaper standing up at the bar than sitting down at a table). The people watching will undoubtedly be good — the outfits some people wear around here are one of a kind!

See map p. 210. Brasserie Lipp: 151 bd. St-Germain, 6e. ☎ *01-45-48-53-91. Open: Daily 9–1 a.m. Café les Deux Magots: 170 bd. St-Germain, 6e.* ☎ *01-45-48-55-25. Open: Daily 7:30–1:30 a.m. Both are less than 46m (151 ft.) from the St-Germain-des-Prés Métro stop.*

Café de Flore

Next door to Les Deux Magots is this other infamous St-Germain-des-Près cafe. Sartre is said to have written *Les Chemins de la Liberté (The Roads to Freedom)* at his table here, and he and Simone de Beauvoir saw people by appointment here. Other regulars included André Malraux and Guillaume Apollinaire.

See map p. 210. 172 bd. St-Germain, 6e. ☎ *01-45-48-55-26. Métro: St-Germain-des-Prés.*

Harry's New York Bar

This place is still going strong all these years after — guess who? — Ernest Hemingway and F. Scott Fitzgerald went on a few famous benders. Unfortunately, Harry's has pretty high prices, so peek in for the ambience and maybe one drink. They do make great martinis and it's said that the Bloody Mary was invented here.

See map p. 210. 5 rue Danou, 2e. ☎ *01-42-61-71-14. Métro: Opéra; head down the rue de la Paix and take the first left. Open: Daily 10:30 a.m.–4 a.m.*

La Closerie de Lilas

Even though author John Dos Passos and painter Pablo Picasso hung out here, and Soviet revolutionary Leon Trotsky played chess here, the Cloiserie's true claim to fame is that Hemingway completed *The Sun Also Rises* on the terrace here in just six weeks. Much of the novel also takes place at Closerie des Lilas, which means "the courtyard of lilacs." Lilac bushes still bloom here, and the place is just as crowded as it was in the 1930s, although its high, high prices are geared toward an American tourist crowd.

See map p. 210. 171 bd. du Montparnasse, 6e. ☎ *01-40-51-34-50. Métro: Vavin, or RER: Line B to Port-Royal. Exit onto bd. du Port-Royal and walk west. Cross av. de l'Observatoire. Boulevard du Port-Royal turns into bd. du Montparnasse. The restaurant is on the north corner of av. de l'Observatoire and bd. du Montparnasse. Open: Daily noon–1 a.m.*

Maison de Balzac

The very modest Honoré de Balzac lived in this rustic cabin in this very posh residential Passy neighborhood from 1840 to 1847 under a false name to avoid creditors, only allowing entrance to those who knew the password. He wrote some of his most famous novels here, including those that make up his *La Comédie Humaine (The Human Comedy)*. His study is preserved, and portraits, books, letters, and manuscripts are on display. You can also see his jewel-encrusted cane (why spend on bills when you can have jewels?) and the Limoges coffeepot that bears his initials in mulberry pink. Expect to spend about 45 minutes here.

See map p. 210. 47 rue Raynouard, 16e. ☎ 01-55-74-41-80. Métro: Line 6 to Passy; walk 1 block away from the river and turn left into rue Raynouard. Bus: 32, 50, 70, 72. Admission: Permanent collections free; temporary exhibits 4€ ($4.80) adults, 3€ ($3.60) seniors, 2€ ($2.40) students to age 26, free for children 13 and younger. Open: Tues–Sun 10 a.m.–6 p.m. Closed holidays.

Maison de Victor Hugo

Here's your chance to explore one of those gorgeous place des Vosges apartments! Of course, if you or your kids have read *The Hunchback of Notre-Dame* or *Les Miserables,* you may want to visit here anyway. Victor Hugo lived on the second floor of this town house (built in 1610) from 1832 to 1848. The museum was designed to reflect the way Hugo structured his life: Before Exile, During Exile, and After Exile. (He fled the country after an unsuccessful revolt against President Louis Napoléon [who later became Napoléon III], and returned to Paris 16 years later after the collapse of the Second Empire.) You can see some of his furniture, samples of his handwriting, his inkwell, first editions of his works, and a painting of his 1885 funeral procession at the Arc de Triomphe. Portraits of his family adorn the walls, and the fantastic Chinese salon from Hugo's house on Guernsey (where he was exiled) is reassembled here. The highlight is more than 450 of Hugo's drawings, illustrating scenes from his own works. Ask the various caretakers standing around for information about the apartment, they are bursting with knowledge and will be glad to practice their English. Plan to spend an hour here.

See map p. 210. 6 place des Vosges, 4e (between rue des Tournelles and rue de Turenne, nearer to rue de Turenne). ☎ 01-42-72-10-16. Métro: St-Paul. Bus: 20, 29, 65, 69, 96. Admission: Free. Open: Tues–Sun 10 a.m.–6 p.m. (ticket window closes at 5:15 p.m.). Note: Though admission is free, you still must stand in line for a ticket from the cashier in the gift shop (enter on the right).

Shakespeare and Company Bookstore

This is *not* the original Shakespeare and Company, even though it looks old and dusty enough to be. The original opened in 1919 at 6 rue Dupuytren (take the Métro to Odéon, walk through the square there, and turn left) by Sylvia Beach. Two years later, Beach moved the shop to 12 rue de l'Odéon (the building is no longer there) and stayed until the United

States entered into World War II (in German-occupied Paris, Beach was considered an enemy alien and was forced to abandon shop). The newest of the Shakespeares was opened by George Whitman in the mid-1960s and named in honor of Beach (as is his daughter, Sylvia Beach Whitman, who shares the management of the place with her father). It serves as a haven for Americans and English speakers, playing the dual role of gathering place and bookstore. A chubby black and white cat is always asleep somewhere in the upstairs of the shop. Don't be afraid to pet him: His reaction will most likely be to sleep some more. Poetry readings take place on Sunday nights, and Whitman will give lodging to a (debatably) lucky few writers or poets in exchange for work in the store.

See map p. 210. 37 rue de la Bûcherie, 5e. ☎ 01-43-26-96-50. Métro or RER: St-Michel.

Especially for nature lovers

Most parks are open until sunset, unless otherwise noted. Count on spending at least one hour (much of that relaxing in the beautiful surroundings).

Bois de Boulogne

This huge park on the west side of Paris was once a royal forest and hunting ground. Napoléon III donated it to the city and Baron Haussmann transformed it, using London's Hyde Park as his model. Today the Bois is a vast reserve of more than 880 hectares (2,200 acres) with jogging paths, bridle trails, bicycling (bike rental available Apr–Oct near the Les Sablons entrance to the park), and boating on its Lac Inférieur and Lac Supérieur (boat rental available at the northern edge of the Lac Inférieur). Also here are the **parc de la Bagatelle** (see the listing later in this section); the famous **Longchamp** and **Auteuil** racecourses; the **Stade Roland Garros,** where the French Open is held; the **Musée National de des Arts et Traditions Populaire** (documents French everyday life from the year 1000 to the present); and the beautiful **Pré Catalan,** a lovely park in which it is said the copper beech here has a span wider than any other tree in Paris. The Pré Catalan contains the **Jardin Shakespeare** in which you can find many of the plants and herbs mentioned in Shakespeare's plays and the Pré Catalan restaurant, one of Paris's prettiest and most expensive restaurants. The **Jardin d'Acclimatation** (see "Especially for Kids" earlier in this chapter) is one of Parisian children's favorite amusement parks. **Les Serres d'Auteuil,** at the southeastern edge of the Bois, are the municipal greenhouses and gardens that supply Paris with its flowers and plants. Open to the public, the greenhouses are especially nice to visit in winter; they provide a taste of the Caribbean with orchids, tropical plants, and palm trees. As the sun sets, prostitutes in parked cars and vans line the road on each side of the Porte Dauphine entrance, so the Bois is best enjoyed in daylight. This park is so big that you can spend an entire afternoon here.

See map p. 186. 16e. Métro: Porte Dauphine or Les Sablons.

Bois de Vincennes

Once a hunting ground for kings, this is the largest green space in Paris. You can rent a boat at the two lakes here: **Lac Daumesnil,** on the west side of the park has two islands connected by a bridge; **Lac des Minimes** is located on the northwestern edge of the Bois. The Bois de Vincennes is home to the **parc Zoologique** (see "Especially for kids" earlier in this chapter); a **Buddhist center** right next to the bridge at Lac Daumesnil, complete with temple and Buddha effigy; and the **Château de Vincennes,** in which early monarchs Charles V and Henri III sought refuge from war and where Mata Hari was executed in 1917. The Bois de Vincennes houses the spectacular **parc Floral de Paris** (see the next listing), the **Hippodrome de Vincennes** for harness racing, and the **Aquarium Tropicale de la Porte Dorée** (see the "Especially for kids" section). This is also a big park you can spend an entire afternoon enjoying.

12e. Métro: Porte Doree or Chateau de Vincennes.

The Center for Nature Discovery, Garden in Memory of Diana, Princess of Wales

Diana fans now bring their messages and bouquets here instead of to the flame at place de l'Alma (Métro: Alma-Marceau), near the entrance to the tunnel where the princess, her friend Dodi Fayed, and driver Henri Paul were killed in an automobile accident on August 31, 1997. In this small park that opened in 2002, children discover how to grow flowers, vegetables, and decorative plants and learn about nature. Plan on spending at least a half-hour here.

21 rue des Blancs-Manteaux, 3e. Métro: Rambuteau.

Parc de Belleville

This park is a tranquil place to watch the sun set over western Paris and has one of the best panoramic views of the city — without the lines. Topped by the Maison de l'Air, a museum with displays devoted to the air that we breathe, you can enjoy fountains, a children's play area, and an open-air theater with many concerts during the summer. Rock formations and grottoes evoke the days when the hill was a strategic point for fighting enemies such as Attila the Hun. Access the park by taking the rue Piat off rue de Belleville and enter through an iron gate spelling out the words Villa Ottoz. A curved path leads you to tree-lined promenades (more than 500 trees are here), with the first of the magnificent Left Bank views peeping through the spaces between pretty houses. Beds of roses and other seasonal flowers line walks, and views of the city's Left Bank become more pronounced the higher up the terraced pathways you go.

20e. Métro: Pyrénées (walk down rue de Belleville and turn left onto rue Piat where you see arched iron gates leading into the park) or Courrones (cross bd. de Belleville and turn left onto rue Julien Lacroix to find another entrance).

Parc de la Bagatelle

Contained in the Bois de Boulogne, the parc de la Bagatelle is known for its rose gardens and the thematic gardens that reveal the art of gardening through the centuries. A water lily pond pays homage to a certain famous painter (think Monet) because the park was designed by Monet's friend, Jean-Claude-Nicolas Forestier, whose claim to fame was as designer of the Champs-de-Mars and other gardens. Forestier was inspired by the Impressionists and their way of showing flowers by species and emphasizing the effects of mass planting. The rose garden here remains his major work with 10,000 roses of 1,200 varieties, most of them peaking in June. You can also enjoy bulbed plants (tulips, hyacinths, and so on) in March, peonies, clematis, and irises in May, water lilies in June, dahlias and autumn foliage in October; and winter-flowering trees, shrubs, and snowdrops during the cold months. The Orangerie here is home to the Festival Chopin à Paris from mid-June to mid-July (in 2006 each concert at this festival also featured a Mozart piece, commemorating his 250th anniversary; fans of Chopin were not upset as the Polish composer followed in the footsteps of Mozart, and even requested that the Mozart *Requiem* be played at his funeral). The château, which you can view from the outside only, was built by the Comte d'Artois in 1775, after he made a bet with his sister-in-law, Marie Antoinette, that he could do it in less than 90 days. It took 66 days. Under Napoléon, it was used as a hunting lodge.

16e. Métro: Porte Maillot. Exit at av. Neuilly. Bus: 244 to the Bagatelle-Pré Catalan stop.

Parc de la Villette

This modern park has a series of themed gardens, including an exotic bamboo garden and one featuring steam and water jets. Scattered throughout the park are playgrounds and other attractions. (See "Especially for Kids" earlier in this chapter.) In the summer, you can catch an outdoor movie or listen to a concert, and your kids can play on a giant dragon slide. You can also visit the children's museum, the Cité des Sciences et de l'Industrie, and the Musée de la Musique, which are all located on the grounds separated by the La Villette canal basin.

You can get to the parc de la Villette by Métro, but a fun, alternative route worth trying is the guided canal trip to the park from Pont l'Arsenal or Musée d'Orsay with **Paris Canal** (☎ 01-42-40-96-97; Métro: Bastille) or with **Canauxrama** (☎ 01-42-39-15-00; Métro: Jaurés). See "Seeing Paris by Guided Tour" later in this chapter.

19e. Métro: Porte de la Villette.

Parc des Buttes-Chaumont

Featuring cliffs, a suspension bridge, waterfalls, a lake, and a cave topped by a temple, this former gypsum quarry and centuries-old dump is one of four man-made parks Napoléon III commissioned to resemble the English gardens he grew to love during his exile in England. The waterfall cave is musty, but romantic — it is listed in *Où S'Embrasser à Paris* (Where to Kiss in Paris) as one of the top hidden make-out spots in the city (in the mornings you may even have it to yourselves.) This is worth a stop if you're in the area.

See map p. 186. 19e. Métro: Buttes-Chaumont. (The station is located within the park.)

Parc Floral de Paris

The Bois de Vincennes houses the spectacular parc Floral de Paris, with a butterfly garden, library, and miniature golf course, as well as the parc Zoologique de Paris. You can rent bikes here and ride around the extensive grounds, or row a rented canoe around a winding pond. (You can even rent quadricycles — bicycles built for four — for around 10€/$12).

12e. ☎ 01-55-94-20-20. Métro: Château de Vincennes. Exit at cours des Maréchaux and walk south; the chateau is on the right. Cross av. des Minimes into the park. Admission: 1€ ($1.20) before noon and after 6 p.m., 3€ ($3.60) after noon for adults; 0.50€ (60¢) and 1.50€ ($1.80) seniors and students 7–26. Opens at 9:30 a.m.–dusk.

Parc Monceau

A Dutch windmill, a Roman temple, a covered bridge, waterfall, farm, medieval ruins, and a pagoda, all designed by Carmontelle are some of the oddities in this park in Paris's ritzy 8th. It was a favorite place for Marcel Proust to stroll, and it contains what is said to be Paris's largest tree, an Oriental plane tree with a circumference of almost 7m (23 ft.). Have a picnic on a bench here with supplies from the rue de Levis (open Tues–Sun; Métro: Villiers) and watch the English nannies from the nearby palatial apartment buildings stroll with their charges.

See map p. 186. Boulevard de Coucelles, 8e. Métro: Monceau. (The Métro station is at the edge of the park.)

Promenade Plantée

This old railroad bridge was converted into a clever 5-km-long (3-mile) garden that begins behind the Opéra Bastille, runs along the length of avenue Daumesnil, the Reuilly Garden, and the Porte Dorée to the Bois de Vincennes (it makes a great jogging path). Beneath the promenade, artisans have built boutiques and studios into the bridge, collectively known as the Viaduc des Arts. Check them out for eclectic, unusual gifts.

12e. Métro: Bel Air or Dugommier. Walk from the Métro to av. Daumesnil. The elevated railroad bridge above av. Daumesnil is the Promenade Plantée.

Houses of the holy

Paris has had a tradition of worship since the first settlers on the Isle of Parisii in the third century B.C. In fact, many of Paris's churches were built on the ruins of pagan temples. Today Paris's churches are treasure troves of fine art, stained glass, and architecture. Included here are some of those worth a visit.

Église St-Etienne du Mont

Standing directly behind place du Panthéon, this is one of Paris's most extraordinary churches. Completed and consecrated in the 17th century, on the site of a 13th-century abbey, the church is a unique blend of late Gothic and Renaissance styles. Preserved near the chancel and set in an ornate copper-trimmed shrine is the sarcophagus stone for Paris's patron saint Geneviève, who saved the city from the Huns in the fifth century. The most impressive attraction here, however, is the 16th-century rood screen, embraced by twin spiraling marble staircases — a stunning display of Renaissance design. The tombs of Pascal and Racine are also here.

1 place St-Geneviève, 5e. ☎ *01-43-54-11-79. Métro: Cardinal Lemoine. Open: Daily Sept–June Mon–Sat 8:30 a.m.–noon and 2–7 p.m., Sun 9 a.m.–noon and 3:30–7:30 p.m.; July–Aug Tues–Sun 10 a.m.–noon and 4–7:15 p.m.*

Église St-Eustache

This massive church at the heart of Les Halles was built between 1532 and 1637, combining a Gothic structure with Renaissance decoration. Molière and Mme. de Pompadour were baptized here, and Molière's funeral was held here in 1673. This was the first church to contain the tombs of celebrated Parisians, most notably Louis XIV's finance minister, Colbert. The organ is one of the finest in Paris and has been entirely restored and modernized. Franz Liszt used to play the organ here, and there is a free concert every Sunday at 5:30 p.m. There are also free jazz and piano concerts from time to time.

2 Impasse St-Eustache, 1er. ☎ *01-42-36-31-05.* www.saint-eustache.org. *Métro: Les Halles. Open: Mon–Fri 9:30 a.m.–7:30 p.m.,*

Église St-Germain-des-Près

This is the most famous church in the 6th and one of the most important Romanesque monuments in France. Built in the 11th century, St-Germain-des-Près was an important abbey and center of learning during the Middle Ages. At the time of the French Revolution, the monks were expelled and the church was vandalized. But much still remains, including the large tower, the oldest in Paris. King John Casimir of Poland is buried at the church, as is the heart of René Descartes. A small square at the corner of place St-Germain-des-Près and rue de l'Abbaye contains Picasso's small sculpture of the head of poet Guillaume Apollinaire.

3 place St-Germain-des-Près, 6e. ☎ *01-55-42-81-33. Métro: St-Germain-des-Près. Open: Daily 8 a.m.–8 p.m.*

Église St-Julien le Pauvre

One of the oldest churches in Paris, this small example of Gothic splendor sits in the lovely square René Viviani. Originally constructed in the 12th century, it lies on the original pilgrimage route of St-Jacques de Compostelle to Spain. The oldest tree in Paris, an acacia reputedly planted in 1602, still stands in its garden. The church contains a stunning wooden screen, which encloses a beautiful chancel. Many classical concerts take place here throughout the year.

79 rue Galande, 5e. ☎ *01-43-54-52-16. Métro: St-Michel. Open Mon–Sun 9:30 a.m.– 1 p.m.*

Église St-Roch

This 17th-century church has the richest trove of painting and sculpture in Paris outside a museum. Beginning on the right aisle, notice the bust of *Maréchal François de Créqui* by Geneviève, *Cardinal Dubois and Priests* by Coustou and paintings by Louis Boulanger in the fourth chapel. The celebrated statue by Falconet, *Le Christ au Jardin des Oliviers* is at the entrance to the choir, and other highlights include *La Nativité* by Anguier (on the altar), the bust of Le Nôtre by Coysevox, and the monument to the painter Mignard by Girardon (both on the left side). Classical music concerts are played here on Tuesdays, often featuring compositions by Bach and Vivaldi, starting around 12:30 p.m.

296 rue St-Honoré, 1er. ☎ *01-42-44-13-20. Métro: Tuileries or Palais-Royal-Musée du Louvre. Open: Mon–Sat 8 a.m.–7:30 p.m., Sun 8:30 a.m.–7:30 p.m.*

Église St-Severin

A religious building has stood here since the sixth century. The current building, begun in the 13th century, is in flamboyant Gothic style. The west portal came from the church of St-Pierre-aux-Boeufs on the Ile de la Cité before it was demolished in 1837. The dramatic palm-tree shaped vaulting only serves to enhance the brilliant stained glass windows behind the altar depicting the seven sacraments. Also notable is the chapel to the right of the altar, which was designed by Mansart and contains an intensely moving series of etchings by Georges Rouault and an extraordinary rendering of the crucifixion by G. Schneider.

1 rue des Prêtres-St-Severin, 5e. ☎ *01-42-34-93-50. Métro: St-Michel. Open: Mon–Sat 11 a.m.–7:30 p.m., Sun 9 a.m.–8:30 p.m.*

Église St-Sulpice

This church, unfinished since the funds ran out in the mid-18th century, houses three of Eugène Delacroix's greatest masterpieces: *Jacob Wrestling with the Angel, Heliodorus Driven from the Temple,* and *St. Michael Vanquishing the Devil.* And that's not all: during both equinoxes and at the midday winter solstice, sunlight hits the bronze meridian line running along the north-south transept, climbs the obelisk to the globe on top and lights the cross. The organ here is one of the grandest in Paris, built in 1781. More recently, and to the chagrin of the church caretakers, St-Sulpice has become a tourist hot spot due to its feature in Dan Brown's *The DaVinci Code.* Among other things, the book suggests that the church had been built on the site of a round pagan temple, with the meridian line as the original outline of its boundaries. This is all untrue; however it does not make this beautiful and grand church any less interesting to visit.

Place St-Sulpice, 6e. ☎ *01-42-34-59-65. Métro: St-Sulpice. Open: Daily 7 a.m.–
7:30 p.m.*

La Madeleine

Resembling a Roman temple, the Madeleine is one of Paris's minor landmarks. Although construction started in 1806, the Madeleine wasn't consecrated as a church until 1842. The building was originally intended as a
temple to the glory of the Grande Armée (Napoléon's idea, of course).
Climb the 28 steps leading to the facade and look back: You'll be able to see
rue Royale, place de la Concorde and the obelisk, and, across the Seine,
the dome of Invalides. Inside, Rude's *Le Baptême du Christ* is on the left as
you enter.

Place de la Madeleine, 8e. ☎ *01-44-51-69-00. Métro: Madeleine. Open: Daily 7 a.m.–
7 p.m., closed Sun from 1:30–3:30 p.m.*

La Mosquée de Paris

Built from 1922 to 1926 in the Hispano-Moorish style and overlooked by a
green and white minaret, this is one of the newer religious establishments
in Paris. The complex is divided into three sections for study, leisure, and
worship. At the heart is a patio surrounded by finely carved arcades, modeled on the Alhambra in Granada, Spain. The Salon du Thé here is a lovely
place for refreshment, as popular for its Arabian Nights décor as it is for
its mint teas and baklava. Fountains, North African music, plush banquettes, and mosaics create an exotic but casual hangout for the local student population. The *hammam* (steam baths) are a popular place with
trendy types who get massaged and exfoliated here (I hear it's pretty
painful!).

39 rue Geoffroy-St-Hilaire, 5e. ☎ *01-43-31-18-14. Métro: Monge. Open: Daily 10 a.m.–
10 p.m.*

Paris's Bridges

When you buy Métro tickets, have a look at the logo. What looks like the
profile of a woman in a circle is actually an artistic rendering of the Seine
as it meanders through Paris. What the spanning the river. Here are just
a few.

Pont des Arts

The Pont des Arts is one of Paris's prettiest bridges. This seven-arched
pedestrian-only footbridge connecting the Louvre and the Académie
Française was opened in 1804, the first iron bridge on the Seine. It suffered
much bomb damage during World Wars I and II, and barges often ran into
it. It finally collapsed in 1979 and was replaced with this steel version in
1984. You see plenty of artists painting the views of the northern tip of Ile
de la Cité, the Louvre, and the Académie Française, as well as pedestrians

navigating the potted plants on their way to the Louvre. During the warm seasons it becomes a popular picnic spot. Art exhibits are occasionally displayed; summer 2006 saw larger-than-life sized photographs of children from impoverished countries.

Pont Neuf

The 12-arched Pont Neuf (New Bridge) is probably Paris's most famous bridge, and its design marks the end of the Middle Ages. Started in 1578, it was finally completed in 1603 and opened to the public by Henri IV in 1603. A statue of Henri IV astride a horse divides the bridge into its two spans, which are anchored on the tip of Ile de la Cité.

Métro: Pont Neuf.

Petit Pont

The Petit Pont (Little Bridge) crosses the Seine from the Left Bank to the Isle de la Cité. The current one-arched bridge was constructed in 1853 but a bridge has spanned the Seine here since the times of Julius Caesar, who wrote about one in his Commentaries. The Petit Pont crosses the Seine from the Left Bank to the Isle de la Cité. This current incarnation dates from 1853.

Pont St-Michel

The Pont St-Michel has three arches and is decorated with a large letter N which causes some to mistake it for the Pont Neuf. The N in fact refers to Napoléon III who had it built in 1857 to replace the crumbling bridge that preceded it that, up until 1808, still had people living in houses on the bridge.

Métro: St-Michel.

Paris by Guided Tour

If you're a newcomer to the wonders of Paris, an orientation tour can help you understand the city's geography. But even if you've been coming to Paris for ten years or more, one of the various tours can introduce you to sides of the city you never knew existed. As you see in this chapter, you have many good reasons for taking a guided tour. In fact, being shown around by guides whose enthusiasm makes the city come to life, can be the high point of your entire trip.

Embarking on a bus

Paris is the perfect city to explore on your own, but if time is a priority, or your energy is at low ebb, consider taking an introductory bus tour. The biggest company is **Cityrama** (4 place des Pyramides, 1er; ☎ 01-44-55-61-00; www.cityrama.fr; Métro: Palais-Royal–Musée du Louvre). The one and a half hour orientation tour is 17€ ($20), 8.50€ ($10) for children aged 4 to 11 (children younger than 11 ride for free). Also available are full-day art or history tours (the major artistic and historic sights including a Seine cruise) for 76€ ($91) adults, 38€ ($46) children. Tours to Versailles (from 39€/$47 adults, 20€/$55 children) and to Chartres (55€/$66 adults, 28€/$33 children) are a better bargain because they take the hassle out of visiting these monuments. Nighttime illumination tours include a Seine boat cruise and start at 32€ ($38) for adults, 16€ ($19) for children.

Paris L'OpenTour, 13 rue Auber, 9e (☎ **01-42-66-56-56;** www.paris-open tour.com; Métro: Havre-Caumartin), from Paris's public transportation system (the RATP), has quickly come to rival Cityrama. Its bright yellow and green convertible double-decker buses take you to four different areas, and you listen to recorded commentary in English through a set of headphones given to you when you board. The *Paris Grand Tour* covers Paris's most central sights, minus the Islands: the Madeleine, Opéra, the Louvre, Notre-Dame, St-Germain-des-Près, Musée d'Orsay, place de la Concorde, Champs-Elysées, Arc de Triomphe, Trocadéro, Eiffel Tower, and Invalides. The *Montmartre-Grands Boulevards* tour goes to the Montmartre funiculaire (but not up the Montmartre hill), the Gare du Nord, Gare de l'Est, and the Grands Boulevards. The *Bastille-Bercy tour* goes east to Notre-Dame, the *Bibliothèque Nationale de François Mitterrand,* Gare de Lyon, and parc Bercy. The *Montparnasse–St-Germain-des-Près* tour goes to the Jardin du Luxembourg, the Observatory, the Tour Montparnasse, the Catacombes, Invalides, and St-Germain-des-Près.

L'OpenTour makes its stops at regular city bus stops marked with the L'OpenTour logo. You can board at any of these stops and buy a pass right on the bus. The pass is also on sale at any branch of the Paris Tourist Office, L'OpenTour kiosks near the Malesherbes (8e) and Anvers (9e) bus stops, the RATP office at place de la Madeleine (8e), the Montmartre tourist office (21 place du Tertre), the main Batobus docks on the Seine, and the offices of Paris l'Open Tour at 13 rue Auber (9e), and even the Cityrama office (address above). Your hotel may also have the passes for sale, ask at the reception desk.

A one-day pass costs 25€ ($30), 12€ ($14) for children aged 4 to 11; a two-day pass costs 28€ ($34) for adults, 12€ ($14) for children 4 to 11, and 20€ ($24) for holders of the Paris Visite pass. You can get on or off the bus as many times as you want, which, in our opinion, makes this the more worthwhile tour. The buses run daily every 15 to 30 minutes throughout the year from about 9:15 a.m. to 6:30 p.m.

The **RATP** also runs the **Balabus** (☎ **01-58-76-16-16**), a fleet of orange-and-white buses that only runs on Sundays and holidays, 12:30 to 8 p.m. from April to September. Routes run between the Gare de Lyon and the Grand Arche de La Défense, in both directions, and cost just one Métro ticket. Look for the *Bb* symbol across the side of the bus and on signs posted along the route.

Touring by boat

One of the most beautiful ways to see Paris is by taking a sightseeing boat cruise up and down Paris's waterways. In addition to the Seine River cruises (see the "Paris's top attraction: The Seine river cruise" sidebar earlier this chapter), try a longer and more unusual tour with **Paris Canal** (☎ 01-42-40-96-97; www.pariscanal.com; Métro: Bastille). Its three-hour cruises leave the Musée d'Orsay at 9:30 a.m. and end at parc de la Villette. The boat passes under the Bastille and enters the Canal St-Martin for a lazy journey along the tree-lined quai Jemmapes. You cruise under bridges and through many locks. The boat leaves the parc de la Villette at 2:30 p.m. for the same voyage in reverse, in front of the sign that says "Folie des Visites du Parc." Reservations are essential. The trip costs 16€ ($19) for adults, 13€ ($16) for ages 12 to 25 and older than 60, and 9€ ($11) for children 4 to 11.

If you have restless young children, the wait for the water to rise at each lock may prove too long. You may want to consider one of the shorter Seine boat trips mentioned in Chapter 17.

Canauxrama (☎ 01-42-39-15-00; www.canauxrama.com; Métro: Jaurès) offers two-and-a-half-hour tours similar to Paris Canal's at 9:45 a.m. and 2:30 p.m., leaving from Port l'Arsenal in the 12e and ending at the parc de la Villette in the 19e. The cost is 14€ ($17) for adults, 11€ ($13) for ages 12 to 25, 8€ ($10) for children 6 to 11, and free for children younger than 6. Reservations are required.

Horsing around — a guided tour at two horsepower

The Citroën 2CV (meaning two *chevaux,* or two horsepower) was to France what the VW Beetle was to the United States, and it was France's most popular car from its debut before World War II up to 1990, when Citroën stopped production. Now you can tour Paris in its best-loved car with **4 Roues Sous 1 Parapluie** (Four Wheels Under an Umbrella, ☎ 08-00-80-06-31 inside France; outside France 06-67-32-26-68; www. 4roues-sous-1parapluie.com). Run by 20-something Florent Dargnies, one to three people can choose from numerous tours, organized into three main themes around the City of Light. *Paris eternal* presents the essential monuments such as the Eiffel Tower, Notre-Dame, and the Place de la Concorde. *Paris méconnu* (unknown Paris) presents plazas and sites not normally frequented by tourists, but that are still very much a part of the city's charm. *Paris thématique* offers different themed tours, including a *DaVinci Code* tour, a tour of different gardens throughout the city, and a shopping tour. You can even make your own custom excursion with the help of the staff at the *4 roues* (Note: The price per person decreases significantly if you have more than one person in the car). There are two classifications of tours: a *virée* (54€–158€ or $65–$190 per person) lasts an hour and a half and leaves every two hours starting from 9 a.m. to 3 p.m., with two more tours available starting at 8 p.m.; a *flânerie* (84€–238€ or $101–$285 per person) lasts three hours and start at 9:30 a.m., 1:30 p.m., and 8:30 p.m. The extended tours simply pack in more sites. The chauffeur/tour guides are very funny and full of knowledge, and each speaks English and French. These are not big cars and a three-hour three-person (adult) tour could get uncomfortable. Reservations required telephone or contact them online through their secure server.

Walking your way across Paris

Paris Walks (☎ 01-48-09-21-40; www.paris-walks.com) was founded by Peter and Oriel Caine and has become a popular English-language outfit whose two-hour guided walks cost 10€ ($12) for adults, 8€ ($8.05) for students younger than 21, and 5€ ($5.75) for children under 15. Specific tours concentrate on a single neighborhood *(The Village of Montmartre, The Historic Marais, St-Germain-des-Près)*, a particular theme *(Hemingway's Paris)*, or perhaps a single sight *(Les Invalides, the Paris Sewers)*. Private tours are also available. Check the Web site or call for the designated meeting place.

Paris à Pied (☎ 800-594-9535 in the United States; www.parisapied. com) has three three-hour tours geared to first-time visitors to Paris. Tours cost $59 (they prefer to be paid in dollars) and are made up of no more than six people. Tours take in the heart of Old Paris, the Latin Quarter, Montmartre, and the Marais.

French Links (☎ 01-45-77-01-63; www.frenchlinks.com) is run by Rachel Kaplan, the author of numerous guidebooks about living in Paris, such as *Best Buys to French Chic in Paris,* as well as the continuously updated *Paris Insider Guides,* who lets you customize your tour from a two-hour walking tour, to a full-day cultural tour. Trained, experienced guides with degrees in art and history lead you on such walks as *Paris in a Basket: Gourmet Market Tour, Parisian Art Nouveau, The Liberation of Paris, Photographer's Walking Tour,* and many others. And they're happy to help you design your own tour. The talks are entertaining and fun, geared to everyone from high-school and college-age students to retirees. Tours start at $375 for one to six people for two and a half hours. All tours must be prebooked and prepaid with a U.S. bank check or by credit card (MasterCard, Visa, or AmEx) using their secure server.

Seeing Paris by bike

The banks of the Seine are closed to cars and opened to pedestrians and cyclists March to November each Sunday from 10 a.m. to 5 p.m. It may not make much of a dent in the air quality, but bicycling is a fun and healthy way to do some sightseeing. For a bike map of Paris, pick up the *Plan Vert* from one of the branches of the Paris tourist office.

The RATP (which runs the city's buses and subways) in partnership with the mayor's office rents bikes through its *Roue Libre* program. To rent a bike, you need to put down a 200€ ($240) deposit per bike by traveler's check or with cash and show a passport or driver's license, or you can leave your passport or drivers license with the office as a guarantee of returning the bike. Without reservations you can show up to the office and rent a bike for one hour at a rate of 4€ ($4.80) or for four hours at a rate of 10€ ($12). Costs of reservations made ahead of time are 10€ ($12) per weekday, 15€ ($18) per day during the weekend (rental period is from 9 a.m.–7 p.m.); night rental starting between 5 to 6 p.m. until 10 to 11 a.m. the following day is 6€ ($7); a weekend package from 9 a.m. Saturday to 11 a.m. Monday is 27€ ($32); a week rental from 9 a.m. Monday to 7 p.m. Friday is 22€ ($26), and a eight-day rental is 32€ ($38). A Roue Libre location is at 1 passage Mondétour, in front of 120 de la rue Rambuteau, 1er (☎ 01-44-76-08-60-43; Métro: Les Halles); open daily 9 a.m. to 7 p.m. Roue Libre also gives 25€ (or 20€ for those under 26; $30 or $24, respectively) three-hour guided tours of Paris.

It's not just bike tours you can take with **Fat Tire Bike Tours** (24 rue Edgar Faure, 15e; ☎ 01-56-58-10-54; www.fattirebiketoursparis. com), formerly Mike's Bike Tours. This American-accented outfit conducts tours on the Segway scooter, the first of its kind in Paris (70€/$81 for a four-hour day or night tour). Check the separate Web site, (www.citysegwaytours.com) for details; the company and contact information remain the same. Day tours leave daily February 15 through November 30 at 10:30 a.m. Night tours run from April 1 through October 31 at 6:30 p.m. There are no tours on the final day of the Tour de France, and no night tours on June 21 and July 14.

Look for the yellow meeting-point sign in front of the Pilier Sud (South Pillar) of the Eiffel Tower (*Pilier Sud* is spelled out above the ticket booth) for the bike tour; look for the guide on the Segway in the same place for the Segway tour. Friendly guides take you on day or night bike tours of the city (22€/$26 day students, 24€/$29 adults; night tours are 26€/$31 students, 28€/$34 adults, 44€/$51 and 48€/$55 both tours). The tours last three to four hours. Day tours are at 11 a.m. and 3 p.m. April 15 through October 15, and 11 a.m. only February 15 through March 31 and October 16 through November 30. Night tours, which are beautiful (especially the ride past the Grand Pyramid through the courtyard at the Louvre), take place at 7 p.m. nightly April 1 through November 15, and at 7 p.m. Saturday, Sunday, Tuesday, and Thursday in March and from the November 16 to November 30. Reservations are optional for day tours but required for night and Segway tours. Bike rental is available at 2€ ($2.40) per hour, 15€ ($18) for 24 hours, 25€ ($30) for a weekend, and 50€ ($60) per week. Cash, check, or credit card (250€ per bike) deposit is required.

Paris à Vélo C'est Sympa (☎ 01-48-87-60-01; www.parisvelosympa. com; Métro: Richard Lenoir; meeting place 22 rue A Baudin, 11e) has three-hour *Heart of Paris* tours of Paris at 10 a.m. Friday through Monday from April to October, and Saturday and Sunday at 10 a.m. from November to March. Reservations are required, and most tours are in French (call or stop in to find out times of English-speaking tours). The company also has night *(nocturne)* bike tours Saturday at 8:30 p.m. May to September. Other tours include *Paris Contrasts, Unusual Paris, Paris at Dawn* (starting at 6 a.m.), and the *Youth Special.* Prices for all tours are 34€ ($41) for adults, 28€ ($34) for ages 12 to 26, and 18€ ($22) for children under age 12. Children must be a minimum of 4½ ft. to use the bicycles. Daylong tours for groups can also be arranged; call for information. Bike rental is available at 13€ ($16) a day (from either 9 a.m.–7 p.m. or from 7 p.m.– 9 a.m. the next day), 10€ ($12) for a half-day, 17€ ($20) for a 24-hour period, 25€ ($30) for the weekend, and 60€ for an entire week. Tandem bike rentals are 26€ ($31) a day, 20€ ($24) for a half-day, 34€ ($41) for 24 hours, 50€ ($60) for a weekend, and 120€ ($144) for the week. A 250€ ($300) deposit is required for bike rentals, 600€ ($720) deposit for tandem bikes (you can also leave your passport as a deposit, if you feel comfortable with this). Day rentals are available on Mondays, Wednesdays, Thursdays, and Fridays.

Chapter 12

Shopping the Local Stores

* *

In This Chapter

▶ Getting an overview of Paris's shopping scene
▶ Understanding Customs and the VAT
▶ Finding the best department stores, street markets, and bargain shops
▶ Searching the prime shopping neighborhoods

* *

*E*very first-time visitor to Paris should set aside a little time for shopping in one of the best shopping cities in the world! Even the window-shopping is exquisite: Enticing goods are arranged just so in windows — and the prices are listed! Believe it or not, bargains *do* exist here. From the toniest haute couture shop to the hidden *dépot-vente* (resale shop) selling last year's Yves Saint Laurent at fabulously reduced prices, even nonshoppers find something. This chapter gives you an overview of the Parisian shopping scene, providing hints about where to find the bargains, how to get it all home, and even how to get some of your money back.

Surveying the Scene

The cost of shopping in Paris isn't always astronomical. If you plan only to buy haute couture clothing, then yes, you'll pay top prices. However, Paris has many stores that sell clothing and goods at prices comparable to what you'd pay in the United States. And some items in Paris are cheaper even than they are in your hometown, including some French and European brands of perfume and cosmetics, shoes, clothing from French-based companies such as Petit Bateau and Lacoste, and French-made porcelain, cookware, and glassware. You'll obviously pay more for any name brand imported from the United States, such as Donna Karan and Calvin Klein, and for any souvenirs in areas heavily frequented by tourists.

 Keep in mind that a 19.6 percent value-added tax (VAT) is tacked on to the price of most products, which means that most things cost less at home. (For details on getting a VAT refund, see the next section "Getting the VAT back.") Appliances, paper products, housewares, computer supplies, electronics, and CDs are notoriously expensive in France, but checking out prices of French products before your trip can help you recognize a bargain.

Probably the best time to find a bargain in Paris is during the government-mandated twice-annual sales _(soldes)_ in January and July when merchandise gets marked down 30 percent to 50 percent or more. You will often see lines of Parisians outside their favorite stores the first days of the sales. If you can brave the crowds, you just may find the perfect designer outfit at a fraction of its retail price.

Generally, store hours are Monday through Saturday from 9:30 a.m. (sometimes 10 a.m.) to 7 p.m., and later on Thursday evenings, without a break for lunch. Some smaller stores are closed Monday or Monday mornings, and break for lunch for one to three hours, beginning at around 1 p.m., but this schedule is becoming increasingly rare. Small stores also may be closed for all or part of August and on some days around Christmas and Easter. Sunday shopping is gradually making inroads in Paris but is limited mostly to tourist areas; try the Carrousel du Louvre at the Louvre, rue de Rivoli across from the Louvre, rue des Francs-Bourgeois in the Marais, and the Champs-Elysées. The department stores are open the five Sundays before Christmas, and occasionally one or two Sundays during the annual sales.

 Politeness is imperative when you shop in Paris. Always greet salespeople at smaller stores with _"Bonjour, madame"_ or _"Bonjour, monsieur"_ when you arrive (the Glossary in Appendix B can help with pronunciation). And regardless of whether you buy anything, say, _"Merci, au revoir"_ (Thank you, goodbye) when you leave.

Clothing sizes are different around the world. In French men's trousers, for example, add 10 to the waist size you wear in U.S. clothing to get the French size. To determine what size you need to look for, check out Table 12-1, which lists conversions for U.S. and Continental sizes.

Table 12-1   **The Right Fit: Size Conversions**

U.S.	Continental	U.S.	Continental
Women's Clothes		_Women's Shoes_	
4	36	5	36
6	38	6	37
8	40	7	38
10	42	8	39
12	44	9	40
14	46	10	41

(continued)

Table 12-1 *(continued)*

U.S.	Continental	U.S.	Continental
Men's Shirts		**Men's Shoes**	
14½	37	7	39½
15	38	8	41
15½	39	9	42
16	41	10	43
16½	42	11	44f½
17	43	12	46

Getting the VAT back

Whenever you spend more than 175€ to 182€ ($210–$218) in a single store, you're entitled to a partial refund on the value-added tax (VAT), also referred to in France as TVA. The refund, however, isn't automatic. Food, wine, and tobacco don't count, and the refund is granted only on purchases that you take out of the country — not on merchandise that you ship home. The amount of the refund varies; it's 12 percent in Galeries Lafayette and Printemps, and it may be anywhere from 15 percent to 18 percent at smaller boutiques.

When applying for a refund, you must show the store clerk your passport to prove your eligibility. You're then given an export sales document (in triplicate — two pink sheets and a green one), which you must sign, and usually an envelope addressed to the store.

Two private tax refund companies operate in Paris, the bigger **Global Refund** (www.globalrefund.com) and **Premier Tax Free** (www.premier taxfree.com).

When you send more than 175€ ($210) in a store that participates in Global Refund's Europe Tax-Free shopping program (indicated by the *Tax-Free* sticker in the store's windows), you're given a Tax-Free Shopping Cheque that shows the amount of refund owed to you when you leave the country. Have this check stamped by a customs officer in the airport, and then take it to the special Global Refund counter for an instant refund. Global Refund offices are located within department store Galeries Lafayette and in the men's boutique, Madelios, at 23 bd. de la Madeleine, 1er (Métro: Madeleine), in Charles de Gaulle airport at Terminal 1 departures level, Gate 26; Terminal 2A, Gate 5; Terminal 2B, Gate 7; Terminal 2C, Gate 5; Terminal 2F, Gate 11; and in Terminal 3 on the Departures level. In Orly Airport, there is only one Global Refund office in Orly South near the international baggage claim on the departures level.

It works the same way with Premier Tax Free. Look for Premier Tax Free stickers in the windows of stores participating in this program, and spend more than 175€ ($210) to get your refund. Premier Tax Free offices are located at American Express, 11 rue Scribe, 9e (Métro: Opéra); Travelex Opéra, 45 av. de l' Opéra (Métro: Opéra); at two Travelex Champs-Elysées locations: 73 and 125 (Métro: Franklin D. Roosevelt and Charles de Gaulle-Étoile respectively), in Charles de Gaulle Airport Terminal 1, Gate 26; and in Orly South on the departures level.

Department stores that cater to foreign visitors, such as Au Printemps and Galeries Lafayette, have special *détaxe* areas where clerks prepare your invoices for you. You must present your passport. Otherwise, when you leave the country, bring all documents to the airport's *détaxe* booth and have a Customs official stamps them. Enclose the appropriate document (the pink one) in the store envelope the clerk provided when you bought your merchandise and mail it from the airport from which you are leaving the European Union. The wait for a refund is anywhere from one to six months. Travelers leaving from Charles-de-Gaulle Airport can visit the *détaxe* refund point in Terminal 1 on the departure level between Gate 14 and 16; in Terminal 2, Hall B between Doors 6 and 7 near the baggage claim area; or in Hall A between Doors 5 and 6; and in Terminal T9, near the departure gates. At Orly, the *détaxe* booth is in Orly West between Halls 3 and 4 on the departure level.

Whenever you're claiming a tax refund, try to arrive at the airport as early as possible because you must show everything you're declaring to a Customs official, and you may have to wait in line. Plus, after you finish with *détaxe,* you must stand in line again to check your luggage.

If you're traveling by train, go to the *détaxe* area in the station before boarding because you can't have your refund documents processed on the train. Give the three sheets to the Customs official, who stamps them and returns a pink and a green copy to you. Keep the green copy and mail the pink copy to the store.

Your reimbursement is either mailed as a check (in euro) or credited to your credit-card account, which is better, as you may find it difficult to cash a check for euro in your own country. If you don't receive your tax refund within six months, write to the store, giving the date of purchase, and the location where the forms were given to Customs officials. Include a photocopy of your green refund sheet.

Getting your goodies through Customs

Returning **U.S. citizens,** who've been away for 48 hours or more, are allowed to bring back, once every 30 days, $800 worth of merchandise duty-free (a *duty* is a tax). You're charged a flat duty of 3 percent on the next $1,000 worth of purchases; on gifts, the duty-free limit is $100 (any item that costs more than $100 is subject to the full tax). You can't bring fresh food into the United States (ignore what the people in the Paris

Paris Shopping

Gibert Joseph **82**
H&M **65**
Hédiard **22**
Jacadi **13**
Jamin Puech **59**
JSFP Traiteur **85**
Kazana **60**
La Cave des Martyrs **33**
La Chaise Longue **57**
La City **34**
La Clef des Marques **95**
Lafayette Gourmet **35**
La Grande Epicerie de Paris
  (at Le Bon Marché) **11**
La Maison du Chocolat **26**
La Maison du Miel **25**
La Maison Ivre **86**
La Marelle **44**
La Samaritaine **67**
La Vaissellerie **74**
Le Bon Marché **11**
Le Dépôt-Vente de
  Buci Bourbon **64**
Le Drugstore **16**
Legrand Filles et Fils **45**
Le Louvre des
  Antiquaires **49**
Le Mouton à Cinq Pattes **9**
Le Village St-Paul **78**
Les Caves Augé **19**
Librarie La Hune **88**
Lumicristal **38**
Madelios **30**
Mango **70**
Marché aux Puces de la
  Porte de St-Ouen **31**
Masculin Direct **61**
Mi-prix **5**
Mona Lisait **54**
Monic **75**
Morgan **83**
Natalys **16**
Nicolas **29**
Nip' Shop **3**
1-2-3 **50**
Passage Brady **40**
Passage Choiseul **47**
Passage des Panoramas **42**
Passage du Caire **43**
Passage du Grand Cerf **53**
Passage Jouffroy **41**
Passage Verdeau **36**
Petit Bateau **14**
Porte de Vanves **7**
Pylones **79**
Réciproque **2**
The Red Wheelbarrow **77**
Rodier **14**
Rue d'Alésia **6**
Rue Paradis **37**
Rue St-Placide **10**
Saint James **91**
S.D. Spontini **55**
Shakespeare and
  Company **80**
Shoe Bizz **93**
Tartine et Chocolat **17**
Tati **71**
Ted Baker **56**
Verrerie des Halles **51**
Viaduc des Arts **76**
Village Voice **90**
Zara **66**

Alessi **24**
Anna Lowe **18**
Annexe des Créateurs **21**
Antoine et Lili **39**
Au Nain Bleu **27**
Au Printemps **20**
Baccarat **37**
BHV **72**
Biche de Bère **69**
Bijoux Burma **15**
Bonpoint **87**
Boulevard de
  Rochechouart **32**
Cacharel **92**
Cedre Rouge **12**
Celio **8**
Colette **48**

Comptoir des Cotonniers **58**
Conforama **68**
Cop-Copine **58**
Déhillerin **52**
Du Pareil au Même **62**
Eric et Lydie **69**
Etam **82**
Façonnable **23**
Fauchon **28**
Fnac Eveil & Jeux **94**
Forum des Halles **54**
France Ma Douce **74**
Franck et Fils **4**
Galerie Colbert **44**
Galerie Vivienne **46**
Galeries Lafayette **35**
Gelati **84**

duty-free stores tell you; fresh meats and cheeses are *not* allowed); canned foods, however, are allowed.

Citizens of the United Kingdom and **Ireland** who are returning from a European Union (EU) country have no limit on what they can bring back from an EU country, as long as the items are for personal use (including gifts), and the necessary duty and taxes have been paid. Limits are set at: 3,200 cigarettes, 200 cigars, 3kg (6.6 lbs.) smoking tobacco, 10 liters of spirits, 90 liters of wine, and 110 liters of beer.

Canada allows its citizens a once-a-year C$750 exemption after spending seven days out of the country, and you're allowed to bring back duty-free: 200 cigarettes, 1.5 liters of wine or 1.14 liters of liquor, and 50 cigars. In addition, you can mail gifts to Canada from abroad at the value of up to C$60 a day, provided they're unsolicited and don't contain alcohol, or tobacco, or advertising matter. Write on the package *Unsolicited gift, under $60 value.* All valuables need to be declared on the Y-38 form before your departure from Canada, including serial numbers of valuables you already own, such as expensive foreign cameras.

The duty-free allowance in **Australia** is A$900 or A$450 for those younger than 18 and does not include tobacco or alcohol. Upon returning to Australia, citizens can bring in 250 cigarettes or 250 grams of loose tobacco, and 1.125 liters of alcohol. If you're returning with valuable goods that you already own, such as foreign-made cameras, you need to file form B263.

The duty-free allowance for **New Zealand** is NZ$700. Citizens older than 17 can bring in 250 cigarettes or 250 grams of tobacco or cigars, plus 2.25 liters of alcohol.

Checking Out the Big Names

Two of Paris's major department stores, Au Printemps and Galeries Lafayette, offer visitors a 10 percent discount coupon, good in most departments. If your hotel or travel agent doesn't give you one of these coupons (they're sometimes attached to a city map), you can ask for them at the stores' welcome desks; the clerks speak English.

Check out the "Paris Shopping" map for the locations of the stores listed here.

Au Printemps

Au Printemps is one of Paris's largest department stores, and a recent renovation costing millions of euro has made it one of Paris's best. Merchandise is sold in three different buildings: Printemps de l'Homme (menswear), Printemps de la Maison (furniture and accessories), and Printemps de la Mode (women and children's fashion). Designers include (but are certainly not limited to) Dolce & Gabbana, Armani, and Burberry.

Fashion shows take place under the 1920s glass dome (seventh floor) at 10 a.m. every Tuesday year-round, and every Friday from March to October. You can easily spend a day here, and there are eight restaurants scattered throughout the three buildings. The beauty department in the main building is, according to Printemps, the largest in the world. There is a fabulous selection of lingerie in the basement level of the main building, as well. Détaxe is offered at 12 percent here.

64 bd. Haussmann, 9e. ☎ *01-42-82-50-00. Métro: Havre-Caumartin. Open: Mon–Sat 9:35 a.m.–7 p.m.; open until 10 p.m. Thurs.*

BHV

Near the Marais, BHV *(Bazar de l'Hôtel de Ville)* sells the usual clothing, cosmetics, luggage, and leather ware at decent prices, but it's really worth a visit because of its giant basement-level hardware store with everything you need to fix up your home. The upper levels feature furniture and bedding, plus Café les Bricollations, decorated like your grandfather's old workshop and serving light lunches and snacks.

52 rue de Rivoli, 1er. ☎ *01-42-74-90-00. Métro: Hôtel de Ville.*

Forum des Halles

This was the site of the original wholesale market of Paris, where merchants would come from kilometers away to set up tables of fruits, vegetables, dairy products, and so forth. In 1971 the market was formally moved to a suburb outside the city limits, and a major RER and Métro stop — "les Halles" — and a mall complex were built. The forum is the closest thing to a "mall" shopping center that one can find in Paris. In the place where once stood fish-mongers and butchers of Emile Zola's *Le Ventre de Paris* (les Halles market is a centerpiece of the story) one can go clothes shopping in the Gap, Celio, and H&M, buy CDs and DVDs at Fnac, buy furniture at Habitat, get lunch, and even see a movie at the UGC theatres on the lowest underground level. Beware that it can be seedy later on at night.

101 Porte Berger, 1er. ☎ *01-44-76-96-56. Access from numerous doors surrounding the complex, on rue Rambateau, rue Berger, and rue de Pierre Lescot; or enter directly from Métro station. Open: Sun. Métro: Les Halles*

Galeries Lafayette

Of the three major Paris department stores, Galeries Lafayette is probably the most-visited by a hair due to its prolific advertising. Merchandise here ranges from good to excellent with lots of deals during the sales. Look for women's clothing from Sonia Rykiel, Comptoir des Cotonniers, and agnès b. And check out the gourmet grocery store, Lafayette Gourmet, in the men's store. Main store restaurants include: Häagen-Dazs, Lina's gourmet sandwiches, Fauchon tea room and restaurant, McDonald's, Café Sushi, and Lafayette Café on the sixth floor, which has great views of Paris (it's a self-serve cafeteria and my personal favorite). If you don't already have one, ask at the front desk for the 10 percent discount coupon, good in most departments. All the advertising has only benefited Galeries Lafayette: this store gets downright crowded, and if you visit during the sales, pace yourself or you can become thoroughly fatigued. Détaxe is 12 percent here.

40 bd. Haussmann, 9e. ☎ *01-42-82-34-56. Métro: Opéra or Chaussée-d'Antin. Open: Mon–Sat 9:30 a.m.–7:30 p.m.*

La Samaritaine

Alas! Parisians have been upset for over a year now at the temporary closing of their beloved shopping destination, arguably perfect rooftop view of Paris, and important 1920's architectural monument. The store closed in June 2005 after its president announced that the building had become, in its advanced age, a serious fire risk. It will remain closed for around five more years (estimates and official announcements dance around 4–6 years); all of the electrical systems, plumbing, and fire systems will be completely renovated. The owner of La Samaritaine (LVMH, the Möet-Hennessy Louis Vuitton luxury group) has plans to relaunch the store as an outlet for luxury brand clothing and other items, not unlike Harrods of London fame. Located between the Louvre and the Pont Neuf, La Samaritaine is housed in four buildings with Art Nouveau touches, and has an Art Deco facade on quai du Louvre. Named after a hydraulic pump originally installed near the Pont Neuf in 1609, la Samaritaine will return, but for now enjoy the view of Paris from the top of the Pompidou center, and its chic restaurant, Georges (see Chapter 10).

19 rue de la Monnaie, 1er. ☎ *0800-010-015 for a free phone call for any questions or updated information (Mon–Fri 10 a.m.–6 p.m.). Métro: Pont-Neuf or Châtelet–Les Halles.*

Le Bon Marché

This is Paris's only Left Bank department store, and it's a wonderful respite from the multibuilding, crowded shopping experience of Au Printemps and Galeries Lafayette. Elegant, but small enough to be manageable, much of the store's merchandise is exquisite and includes designers such as Sonia Rykiel, Bensimon, Vivienne Westwood, Burberry, and Yohji Yamamoto. The main store's third floor is particularly renowned for its large shoe selection and grand lingerie department (where dressing rooms have phones to summon your salesperson). The basement features a beautiful bookstore and upscale toys as well. Nothing here is cheap. Make sure to visit Le Grand Épicerie next door (is there anything you can't get at Le Bon Marché?), where you can buy everything from toilet paper to truffles. A cafe, Delicabar, above Le Grand Épicerie, has a menu divided into tasty sweet and salty offerings, while the Café de la Grand Épicerie on the second floor in the Home Décor section, features selections chosen by the gourmet grocery store's food, wine, and pastry professionals.

24 rue de Sèvres, 7e. ☎ *01-44-39-80-00. Métro: Sèvres-Babylone.*

Le Drugstore

Though not a department store (it's more a minimall), Le Drugstore is included here because it was once an important part of Parisian culture in the 1960s, and its owner, ad giant Publicis, is hoping to regain that status with a stunningly modern glass renovation that cost millions of euro. Inside is a brasserie run by a disciple of multistarred French chef Alain Ducasse (waitstaff is clothed by French designer Jean-Charles Castelbajac), an invitation-only restaurant, Privé Marcel, an international newsstand, gift shop, a drug store (naturally), gourmet food, wine and cigar stores, and a Shu Uemura beauty products shop. Also here are movie theaters and a cool bar with a terrace overlooking the Champs and the Arc de Triomphe. Owned by Publicis since the late '50s, Le Drugstore was the height of cool in the 1960s when it was one of the few places in Paris you could pick up a pack of cigarettes or a magazine at 2 a.m. (and in a sense, it still is since most *tabacs* are closed by 11 p.m. at the latest, not to mention newsstands). Has its new revamping made it the hip place it once was while helping to push the Champs-Elysées into the 21st century? The jury is still out.

131 av du Champs-Elysées, 8e. ☎ 01-44-43-79-00. Métro: Georges V, Charles-de Gaulle-Étoile. Open: Daily 10 a.m.–2 a.m.

Monoprix

These Target-like stores are Paris's best-kept secret, where you can find wonderful clothing, much of it fashion-forward, at reasonable prices along with accessories, low-priced cosmetics, lingerie, and housewares. Many locations also have large grocery stores. The Champs-Elysées branch at no. 52 is open until midnight Monday to Saturday.

Various locations. ☎ 08-10-08-40-00.

Tati

For the most part, Tati is frankly tacky, but where else can you find the occasional funky top for 2€ ($2.40)? Or wear-for-one-season shoes at 10€ ($12)? In fact, you never know what you may find here if you dig; the occasional gem rewards those who are persistent. Tati also has a jewelry branch called Tati Or (see "Gifts and Jewelry" later in this chapter, eyewear (Tati Optic), and a travel agency (Tati Vacances). Despite rumors of closing and the near-buyout of its Barbès-Rochechouart location, business has bounced back and cheap clothing and accessory items abound! Expect crowds.

4 bd. Rochechouart, 18e. ☎ 01-55-29-50-00. Métro: Barbès-Rochechouart. Other branches are located at 68 av. du Maine (☎ 01-43-57-92-80; Métro: Gaîté), 30 av. d'Italie (☎ 01-56-80-06-80; Métro: Place d'Italie), and 76 av. Clichy, 17e (☎ 01-58-22-28-90; Métro: La Fourche).

Taking It to the Street (Markets)

The huge **Marché aux Puces de la Porte de St-Ouen,** 18e, purportedly the largest flea market in the world, is a real shopping adventure and although you probably won't snag a bargain, it's still well worth the visit! Open Saturday, Sunday, and Monday, it features several thousand stalls, carts, shops, and vendors selling everything from vintage clothing (see if you can find the vendor whose specialty is wearing her merchandise from the mid-1800s) to antique chandeliers, paintings, furniture, and toys. You need to arrive early to snag the deals — if you can find any. The best times for bargains are right at opening time and just before closing time. To reach the market, take the Métro to the Porte de Clignancourt stop; exit onto avenue de la Porte de Clignancourt. (You can also exit onto bd. Omano, which turns into avenue de la Porte de Clignancourt.) Head north a block and cross beneath an underpass; the markets begin on your left. Open Saturday through Monday 9 a.m. to 8 p.m.

Starting at the underpass just past the Clignancourt Métro stop, you'll see stalls selling cheap junk, but don't stop here! Turn left onto rue des Rosiers, the market's main street. Be alert; pickpockets roam the markets, especially the stalls on the periphery.

Don't pay the ticketed price or the price the vendor first quotes you; always haggle. You can usually get at least 10 percent off.

Visitors to Paris usually choose the Clignancourt market over the convivial market at **Porte de Vanves,** 14e, a gem still waiting to be discovered. Probably the smallest of the fleas, it's nevertheless a good place to browse among friendly dealers. To reach the market, take the Métro to the Porte de Vanves stop; exit at boulevard Brune; follow it east to avenue Georges Lafenestre, and turn right. Open Saturday and Sunday 8:30 a.m. to 1:00 p.m. A cheap clothing market takes its place after 1 p.m. Other flea markets include one at **Porte Montreuil** (Métro: Porte de Montreuil) and another at **place d'Aligre,** 14e (Métro: Ledru-Rollin, open 9 a.m.–noon). Much more downscale, these markets give the term "junk" a whole new meaning.

Scoring Bargains in Paris

The savvy Parisian waits for sales, knows the addresses of discounters, and knows that some of the best fashion deals are found in resale shops that deal directly with designer showrooms for half-price designer clothing that has been worn on a runway or used in a fashion shoot. And four words are the key to her world: *soldes* (sales), *dégriffés* (designerwear with the labels cut out), *stock* (overstock), and *dépot-vente* (resale). Most *depôts-vente* are on the Right Bank in the 8e, 16e, and 17e arrondissements. If you're itching for a bargain after shopping for full-price items, visit one of the streets where discount stores abound:

✔ **Rue d'Alésia,** 14e (Métro: Alésia), is filled with French designer discount outlets selling last year's overstock at up to 70 percent below retail. These stock boutiques are more downscale than their sister shops; be prepared to rifle through the racks to find the gems. Outlets include **Chevignon** at no. 122, **Darjeeling** (a French lingerie brand) at no. 68, **Cacharel** at no. 114, **Georges Rech** at no. 100, **Tout Compte Fait** at no. 101bis, **Via Veneto** at no. 72 (for Dior, Armani, and other designer menswear), **Jacadi** at no. 116, and **Naf Naf** at no. 143.

✔ **Rue Paradis,** 10e (Métro: Poissonnière), is filled with wholesale china and porcelain stores such as **Paradis Porcelaine** at no. 56 and **La Tisanière Porcelaine** at no. 21.

✔ **Rue St-Placide,** 6e (Métro: Sèvres-Babylone), is also a street of dreams with many discount stores, including **Le Mouton à Cinq Pattes** (8 rue St-Placide) and **Kookaï Le Stock** (15 Ter). Discounted no-name shoes and housewares are also sold here. This street, perpendicular to Le Bon Marché, is quite a relief on the pocketbook after perusing the wares at the luxury department store.

✔ **Boulevard de Rochechouart,** 18e (Métro: Anvers or Barbès-Rochechouart), is certainly not the prettiest of Paris's boulevards and can get awfully crowded. But for those who care about bargains, is a street of deep discounts with multiple branches of **Tati** (at 4 and 18), and a **Celio Stock** at no. 15, among others. If you have time to spare after visiting Sacré-Coeur, head south from the cathedral down rue Steinkerque or rue Seveste and make a left onto boulevard de Rochechouart.

You can also try these discount stores spread throughout the city.

Anna Lowe

The sales pitch here is "big brands at small prices," and if you consider only the very best designers, this store is for you. It carries Yves Saint Laurent, Chanel, and Giorgio Armani at a steep discount — at least 50 percent. The clothes may be overstock or last year's models with samples from the runway. Most of the staff speaks English.

104 rue du Faubourg-St-Honoré, 8e. ☎ *01-42-66-11-32 or 01-40-06-02-42. Métro: Miromesnil or St-Phillippe-de-Roule.*

Annexe des Créateurs

This is made up of two stores — one devoted to selling gently worn designer daywear, the other to barely worn evening wear. If you don't mind wearing resale togs, you could save yourself between 40 percent and 75 percent off the retail price of the items. The store has been described as an Ali Baba's cave entirely devoted to luxury, and the description is apt. You find names like Chanel, Dior, Thierry Mugler, Louis Vuitton, Hermès, Vivienne Westwood, and Jean-Paul Gaultier.

19 rue Godot de Mauroy, 9e. ☎ *01-42-65-46-40. Métro: Hauvre-Caumartin or Madeleine.*

Bonpoint

These exquisite children's clothes with such touches as hand-smocking, lace collars, and velvet usually come with a steep price. However, this Bonpoint branch sells end-of-season clothes at reduced prices; it's particularly good during the yearly sales in January and July.

42 rue de l'Université, 7e. ☎ *01-40-20-10-55. Métro: Rue-du-Bac.*

La Clef des Marques

This large, somewhat drab store sells baby clothes, shoes, lingerie, sports clothes and end-of-series couture items. Racks are overfull so you have to hunt a bit for a bargain.

124 bd. Raspail, 6e. ☎ *01-45-49-31-00. Métro: Notre-Dame des Champs.*

La Marelle

Located in the wonderful Galerie Vivienne, this store resells clothing from some of the top designers in very good condition.

21 Galerie Vivienne, 2e. ☎ *01-42-60-08-19. Métro: Palais Royal.*

Le Depôt-Vente de Buci Bourbon

This resale store is actually two shops right next to each other with vintage and not-so-old clothing and accessories for men and women along with gently used furniture.

4 and 6 rue Bourbon Le Chateau, 6e. ☎ *01-46-34-45-05 and 01-46-34-28-28. Métro: St-Germain-des Prés or Mabillon.*

Le Mouton à Cinq Pattes

Visit "the sheep with five legs" when you're feeling energetic — racks at this "dégriffe" store are simply packed and the store is often crowded. It carries extremely well-known designer names (most of the tags are ripped out) on women's, men's, and children's clothing, shoes, and accessories. The stock changes constantly, so if you see something you like, grab it; it won't be there the next time.

8 and 18 rue St-Placide, 6e. ☎ *01-45-48-86-26 for all stores. Métro: Sèvres-Babylone. Another branch is located at 138 bd. St-Germain (☎ 01-43-26-49-25).*

Masculin Direct

This sizeable men's store, located directly behind the BHV, carries all sorts of a sports and evening wear made by Pierre Cardin, Bayard, and Guy Laroche, all at discounted prices. During the sales you can go mad here, but the rest of the time the store is yours, with shopkeepers that only make you feel comfortable as you browse for that perfect-color shirt.

18 rue des Archives, 4e. ☎ *01-42-77-16-56. Métro: Hôtel de Ville.*

Mi-prix

This store, though far from the center of the city in the 15e, is worth the long trip: Karl Lagerfeld, Missoni, and Gianfranco Ferré are just some of the labels that are steeply discounted in this men's discount store.

27 bd. Victor, 15e. ☎ *01-48-28-42-48. Métro: Balard or Porte de Versailles.*

Nip' Shop

Yves Saint Laurent, Sonia Rykiel, and Guy Laroche are big labels here, but lesser-known designers are also represented. It's in the same neighborhood as Réciproque (see the next listing), but much more intimate. Ask the smiling woman who runs this shop for suggestions and advice; she knows her wares and will find the item that has been waiting for you all along.

6 rue Edmond-About, 16e. ☎ *01-45-04-66-19. Métro: Rue de la Pompe.*

Réciproque

This series of *depôt-ventes* (resale shops) on rue de la Pompe is the largest in Paris for men, women, and children. Exhaust yourself among the jewelry, furs, belts, antiques, scarves, and designer purses (Hermès, Dior, Gucci, and Vuitton are just a few of the names we've seen). This store is for shoppers willing to spend upwards of $1,000 on a gently-worn Chanel suit, less for other designers (a careful search can result in Hermès scarves and ties at a third of their normal price!). Mid-range labels are also well represented.

88, 89, 92, 93, 95, and 101 rue de la Pompe, 16e. ☎ *01-47-04-30-28. No. 88 is a "gift shop" with small accessories and jewels, nos. 89–95 are the different categories of women's clothing and shoes, and the men's shop is exclusively at no. 101. Métro: Rue de la Pompe. Closed Mon.*

Hitting the Great Shopping Neighborhoods

You don't need beaucoup bucks to afford to shop in Paris (except for certain stores in the 8e!). Great deals for every taste and dollar amount can be found. Read this section to get a significant head start in the hunt for that perfect item.

The land of luxe: The 8e

Head for the 8e to see why people around the world in need of a luxury shopping spree jet to Paris. Nearly every French designer is based on two streets — **avenue Montaigne** (Métro: Alma-Marceau, Franklin-D-Roosevelt) and **rue du Faubourg St-Honoré** (Métro: Concorde) — where prices of more than 1,000€ ($1,200) are normal, and snooty sales clerks are par for the course. You can still have a good time window-shopping here (and get an idea for what's in style), even if you don't have a platinum card.

Although avenue Montaigne and rue du Faubourg St-Honor boast some of the same big designer names, they are completely different in temperament. Avenue Montaigne is wide, graceful, lined with chestnut trees, and undeniably hip, attracting the likes of **Dolce & Gabbana** at no. 22 (☎ 01-42-25-68-78) and **Prada** at no. 10 (☎ 01-53-23-99-40). Other designers on this street include **Céline,** 36 avenue Montaigne (☎ 01-56-89-07-92); **Chanel,** 42 avenue Montaigne (☎ 01-47-23-74-12); **Christian Dior,** 30 avenue Montaigne (☎ 01-40-73-73-73); **Escada,** 53 avenue Montaigne (☎ 01-42-89-83-45); **Ferragamo,** 45 avenue Montaigne (☎ 01-47-23-36-37); **Gucci,** 60 avenue Montaigne (☎ 01-56-69-80-80); **Ungaro,** 2 avenue Montaigne (☎ 01-53-57-00-00); and **Valentino,** 17 avenue Montaigne (☎ 01-47-23-64-61).

Rue du Faubourg St-Honoré is jammed with shoppers walking along the small, narrow sidewalks. Begin at the rue Royale intersection and head west. **Prada** is located at no. 6 (☎ 01-58-18-63-30); **Yves St-Laurent** for women is at no. 38 (☎ 01-42-65-74-59), men at no. 32 (☎ 01-53-05-80-80). Other designer stores you run across here include **Ferragamo,** 46 rue du Faubourg St-Honoré (☎ 01-43-12-96-96); **Gianni Versace,** 54 rue du Faubourg St-Honoré (☎ 01-47-42-55-31); **La Perla,** 20 rue du Faubourg St-Honoré (☎ 01-43-12-33-60); **Chloé,** 56 rue du Faubourg St-Honoré (☎ 01-44-94-33-00); **Sonia Rykiel,** 70 rue du Faubourg St-Honoré (☎ 01-42-65-20-81); **Pierre Cardin,** 59 rue du Faubourg St-Honoré (☎ 01-42-66-92-25), and **Missoni,** 1 rue du Faubourg-St-Honoré (☎ 01-44-51-96-96).

Arty and individual: The 3e and 4e

There's something for everyone in the Marais: Divide your time between culture (15 museums are here alone) and commercialism in this beautiful neighborhood crammed with magnificent Renaissance mansions, artists' studios, secret courtyards, and some of the most original shops in the city. **Rue des Francs-Bourgeois** (Métro: St-Paul or Rambuteau), the highlight of the area, is full of small shops selling everything from fashion to jewels. And its stores are open on Sunday! **Rue des Rosiers** (Métro: St-Paul) is a fashion destination in its own right, with hot designers standing shoulder-to-shoulder with Jewish delis. Everything is really close in the Marais, so don't be afraid to ramble down the tiniest lane whenever whim dictates. Part of the fun of this neighborhood is that it's such a mixed (shopping) bag.

Marais highlights include **Paule Ka,** 20 rue Mahler (☎ **01-40-29-96-03**), for the sort of 1960s clothing made famous by Grace Kelly, Jackie Onassis, and Audrey Hepburn; **Jacenko/Seducteur,** 38 rue de Poitou (☎ **01-42-71-80-38**) for unique menswear, mostly cotton or cotton blend materials that are beautifully tailored and soft to the touch (fitted sport jackets, shirts, and sweaters by the British cotton experts of John Smedle are just some items); **Autour du Monde,** 12 rue des Francs-Bourgeois (☎ **01-42-77-16-18**), a clothing/housewares store with everything from relaxed and sporty cotton dresses by Bensimon to delicate linen sheets and inventive tableware; and **Antik Batik,** 8 rue Foin (☎ **01-48-87-95-95**), a French company just making inroads in the U.S. and featuring clothes inspired by numerous cultures. You can find African prints and wood beaded shirts and necklaces, as well as Chinese silk outfits and Indian-inspired scarves and long-shirt and pants ensembles; **Issey Miyake,** 3 place des Vosges (☎ **01-48-87-01-86**), for loose, structured clothing that screams "artist." **Jean-Claude Monderer,** 22 rue des Francs Bourgeois (☎ **01-48-04-51-41**) sells stylish men's and women's sneakers, loafers, and sleek and often-pointy going out shoes for both sexes (pointed shoes have been *à la mode* in Paris in the last few years). Also check out **Zadig et Voltaire,** 16 rue Pavée (☎ **01-44-59-39-06**), for casual clothes with a flair from new and established European designers.

BCBG chic: The 6e

Stylish young professionals with old family (called *Bon Chic Bon Genr* or BCBG) and call this, one of the prettiest areas in Paris, home. Here you can shop with the BCBG amid bookstores, art and antiques galleries, high-end designer clothing shops, decently priced shoe and accessories stores, and sophisticated and trendy boutiques. You won't go thirsty with famed literary hangouts such as **Café de Flore, Les Deux Magots,** and **Brasserie Lipp** nearby, and you may not even go broke — all price ranges are represented here.

Louis Vuitton has a huge store behind Les Deux Magots on 6 place St-Germain (☎ 01-45-49-62-32), and **Christian Dior** is nearby at 16–18 rue de l'Abbaye (☎ 01-56-24-90-53). **Giorgio Armani** is at 149 bd. St-Germain (☎ 01-45-48-62-15); **Céline,** 58 rue de Rennes, (☎ 01-45-48-58-55); **Christian Lacroix,** 2 place St-Sulpice (☎ 01-46-33-48-95); or **Prada,** 5 rue de Grenelle (☎ 01-45-48-53-14). Much more pleasing price-wise are **Stefanel,** 54 rue de Rennes (☎ 01-45-44-06-07), **Comptoir des Cotonniers,** 59T rue de Bonaparte (☎ 01-43-26-07-56), and **Et Vous,** 69 rue de Rennes (☎ 01-40-49-05-10), and **Tara Jarmon,** 18 rue de Four, (☎ 01-46-33-26-60). If you love things of the sea, check out **Blanc et Bleu,** 28 rue Bonaparte (☎ 01-44-07-38-54); their fairly expensive but unique clothing evokes the yacht club and sailing for anyone who loves boats.

Gap and other international chain stores have taken up residence in the Marché St-Germain at 14 rue Lobineau, a modern shopping mall that's a bit out of place in a neighborhood known for bookstores and upscale boutiques. Visit if you need to experience air-conditioning and use the restrooms; otherwise don't waste your time — prices are higher, and the styles are the same at home.

Young and branché: The 2e

Branché means "plugged in" or "hip" to Paris's younger fashion crowd, and the 2e is where you head if you are. The area sells a mix of high fashion and discount, with Jean-Paul Gaultier in the pretty **Galerie Vivienne** on one end and Kookaï Le Stock on the other. The cheapest shopping is in the **Sentier area,** around the Sentier Métro stop, which is Paris's garment district, overlapping parts of the 3e and 1er. The best — but not the cheapest — shops are found within a square formed on the south by rue Rambuteau, on the west by rue du Louvre, on the north by rue Réamur, and on the east by rue St-Martin. This area is where you can find hip secondhand clothes, funky club wear, and *stock boutiques* selling last season's designs at a discount.

 The neighborhood is considered a chic and wealthy neighborhood, but prostitutes still frequent the area later in the afternoon and evening, especially rue St Denis.

For last year's unsold stock of women's and teen's clothing, visit **Kookaï Le Stock,** 82 rue Réamur, 2e (☎ 01-45-08-93-69). **Kiliwatch,** 64 rue Tique-tonne, 2e (☎ 01-42-21-17-37), sells the cool looks of up-and-coming designers mixed in with vintage clothing, though none of it is a bargain in this large and spread-out space, while the Paris branch of London store **Kokon To Zai,** 48 rue Tiquetonne, 2e (☎ 01-42-36-92-41), sells funky designer wear in a small store that dazzles with mirrors and neon. **Le Shop,** 3 rue d'Argout, 2e (☎ 01-40-28-18-38), sells two floors of club wear, skateboards, and CDs — all to tunes spun by a DJ. Those with a more sophisticated palate can go to **Barbara Bui,** 23 rue Etienne-Marcel, 1er (☎ 01-40-26-43-65), for elegant, contemporary fashion. Youthful and fresh, but still respectably fashionable for men is **Chevignon,** 26 rue Etienne Marcel, 1e (☎ 01-42-33-60-20). For sophistication with an edge, head to **Jean-Paul Gaultier,** 6 rue Vivienne (☎ 01-42-86-05-05). Find men's, women's, and children's clothes at **agnès b** at 2, 3, 6, and 19, rue du Jour (☎ 01-40-39-96-88, 01-42-33-04-13, 01-45-08-56-56, and 01-42-33-27-34, respectively). The stores are minimalist and designs are timelessly chic with plenty of black clothes for the whole family (the men's store is at no. 3, children's at no. 2, women's at no. 6, and accessories at no. 19).

Bohemia: the 18th

Some would say the Marais and Montmartre have the same kind of funky aesthetic; while they're not entirely wrong, les Montmartrois (citizens of Montmartre) truly recall, with their offbeat outfits and offbeat jobs (artists, musicians, writers), fashion that seems to come from another era. Thus a lot of the stores around here feature chunky but organic jewelry or dangling Indian metal decoratives. You see soft leathers and tweed pants alongside ballooning linen trousers and funky, often incredibly-shaped hats. It is possible get much better clothing bargains than you would find in the Marais. The window shopping here shouldn't be missed: Be sure to check out rue d'Orsel (one of the consignment shops features a snow-white cat, sleeping on the shoes you might buy!), rue Lépic, and rue des Abbesses.

Passé Devant, 62 rue d'Orsel (☎ 01-42-54-75-15) is a *depot-vente* or con-signment shop that sells women's attire from couture lines or from tal-ented but discontinued boutique designers. Bargains are hit or miss. You can get to **Heaven,** 83 rue des Martyrs (☎ 01-44-92-92-92) easily: they sell men and women's items that are simply divine! **Jo.** at 47 rue d'Orsel (☎ 01-55-79-99-16) carries chic and slim-cut menswear from Emile Lafaurie; **Jérémie Barthod,** 7 rue des Trois Frères (☎ 01-42-62-54-50) features unique costume jewelry — if twisted metal and glass beads could grow naturally out of the ground, this is how they would look. **Le Diable et Moi,** 29 rue des Abbesses (☎ **01-42-55-40-43**) has chic and somewhat expensive funny print T-shirts and short skirts, primarily for hipster chicks, and **Colline,** 21 rue des Abbesses (☎ **01-42-58-54-63**) is the place to get cashmere sweaters, plush velour jackets, and dresses and blouses with beautifully detailed, colorful, and unique prints.

The arcades

In the 19th century, people, horses, and carriages crowded unpaved, dirty, badly lit streets. When it rained, everything turned to mud. Imagine shopping in these conditions! But one 19th-century shopkeeper looking for innovative ways to draw crowds to his store proposed displaying wares in pretty covered passageways with other merchants. And thus, the first malls were born. These days, the charming iron and glass arcades are still shopping havens, and the 2e has Paris's greatest concentration, each with its own character.

✔ **Passage Choiseul,** 44 rue des Petits-Champs (Métro: Quatre-Septembre), dates from 1827 and is the longest and most colorful arcade selling discount shoes and clothing and used books. French writer Céline grew up here and included it in his books *Journey to the End of Night* and *Death on the Installment Plan.*

✔ **Passage des Panoramas,** 11 bd. Montmartre and 10 rue St-Marc (Métro: Grands Boulevards), opened in 1800 and was enlarged with the addition of galleries Variétés, St-Marc, Montmartre, and Feydeau in 1834. Its stores sell stamps, clothes, and gifts, and it's the passage with the largest choice of dining options: Korean food, a cafeteria, tea salons, and bistros.

✔ **Passage Jouffroy,** across the street at 10 bd. Montmartre (Métro: Grands Boulevards), was built between 1845 and 1846. It became an instant hit as Paris's first heated gallery. After an extensive restoration of its tile floors, the gallery now houses a variety of arty boutiques, including a dollhouse store, and an Italian cafe that sells fancy kitchen gizmos such as espresso machines and vacuum-pump wine stoppers.

✔ **Passage Verdeau,** 31 bis rue du Faubourg-Montmartre (Métro: Le Peletier), was built at the same time as its neighbor, Passage Jouffroy. You can find old prints, movie stills, books, and postcards here.

✔ **Galerie Vivienne,** 4 place des Petits-Champs, 5 rue de la Banque, or 6 rue Vivienne (Métro: Bourse), is hands down the most gorgeous of all the arcades. Its classical friezes, mosaic floors, and graceful arches have been beautifully restored. Built in 1823, this neoclassical arcade is now a national monument that attracts upscale art galleries, hair salons, and boutiques, including Jean-Paul Gaultier.

✔ **Galerie Colbert** is linked to the adjoining Galerie Vivienne. It was built with a large rotunda and decorated in Pompeian style in 1826 to capitalize on the success of Galerie Vivienne.

(continued)

(continued)

> ✔ The pretty **Passage du Grand Cerf,** 10 rue Dussoubs (Métro: Etienne-Marcel), has more of a modern bent, with jewelry designers, trendy clothing stores, furniture stores with funky, "ethnic-inspired" pieces, decorative tchotchkes, and an ad agency.
>
> For a complete change of pace, head over to the following arcades, but keep in mind that the neighborhoods aren't the nicest. The **Passage Brady,** 46 rue du Faubourg St-Denis (Métro: Strasbourg St-Denis), has become an exotic bazaar where Indian restaurants and spice shops scent the air. The passage opened in 1828. The **Passage du Caire,** 2 place du Caire (Métro: Sentier), is one of the oldest arcades built in 1798 to commemorate Napoléon's triumphant entry into Cairo. It reflects the Egyptomania of the time with fake columns and death masks of pharaohs on its exterior. In the heart of Paris's Sentier garment district, it's home to clothing wholesalers and manufacturers.

Shopping in Paris from A (ntiques) to W (ine)

Listed here are some of the best stores representing both economy and first-class shopping in the City of Light.

Antiques

Le Louvre des Antiquaires

This enormous mall is filled with all kinds of shops selling everything from silverware to sketches by famous artists to Louis XIV furniture. Items are pricey, but rumors have it that some good deals exist here. A cafe and toilets are located on the second floor.

2 place du Palais-Royal, 1er. ☎ *01-42-97-27-27. Métro: Palais-Royal-Musée du Louvre.*

Le Village St-Paul

This indoor-outdoor arts and antiques fair was once a 17th-century village. Its shops display paintings, antiques, and other items, both inside and in the courtyard. It's easy to walk past the entrances, so look for the signs just inside the narrow passageways between the houses on rue St-Paul, rue Jardins St-Paul, and rue Charlemagne. Keep in mind that this is a very popular destination on the weekend. Closed Tuesday and Wednesday.'

23–27 rue St-Paul, 4e. No telephone. Métro: St-Paul.

Bookstores

Gibert Joseph

Gibert Joseph is *the* Parisian students' bookstore, selling new and second-hand books, records, videos, and stationery on several floors and in several branches on boulevard St-Michel. If you're looking to learn some basic French vocabulary or grammar, there are small practice textbooks for English-speakers at rock-bottom prices. Late September, when students at some of the nearby colleges buy their textbooks, it can get very crowded.

26 and 30 bd. St-Michel, 6e. ☎ *01-44-41-88-88. Métro: Odéon or Cluny-Sorbonne.*

Librarie La Hune

Sandwiched between cafes Les Deux Magots and de Flore, this bookstore has been a center for Left Bank intellectuals since 1945 when Sartre was among its clients. Most books are in French. It's open until midnight every night except Sunday.

170 bd. St-Germain, 6e. ☎ *01-45-48-35-85. Métro: St-Germain.*

Shakespeare and Company

No, this *isn't* the original (that was on rue l'Odéon), but English-speaking residents of Paris and backpackers still gather in this wonderfully dark and cluttered store, named after Sylvia Beach's legendary literary lair and run more and more these days by owner George Whitman's daughter, Sylvia Beach Whitman. There is a selection of new books, but most books are used. Backpackers and willing travelers can sleep in beds among the stacks, while working during the day to pay for a good night's sleep. A fat black cat lives there as well and has been sleeping on the same desk on the second level each time we visited — you can pet him, he's friendly. **Note:** Poetry readings are held on Sundays.

37 rue de la Bûcherie, 5e. ☎ *01-43-25-40-93. Métro or RER: St-Michel.*

Village Voice

Quality fiction in English is the highlight of this small two-level store in St-Germain-des-Prés, along with an excellent selection of poetry, plays, non-fiction, and literary magazines. Owner Odile Hellier has been hosting free poetry and prose readings with celebrated authors and poets since 1982, and this is a wonderful place to attend an English-language reading. (Check *Paris Free Voice* for readings.)

6 rue Princesse, 6e. ☎ *01-46-33-36-47. Métro: Mabillon or St-Germain.*

Mona Lisait

The French hold very dear their independent lifestyle, and chain bookstores don't play a big part of the culture. Mona Lisait (a play-on-words of the famous painting by Da Vinci, it translates as "Mona was reading") is one of the chains, but one we find acceptable because its stores always have a great number of used books available — and the new ones are often on sale. Some of the used books are barely touched and you're sure to find a bargain on some beautiful editions of famous works.

9 rue Saint Martin, 4e. ☎ *01-42-74-03-02. Métro: Rambuteau. Other locations at 7 bd. Bonne Nouvelle, 2e,* ☎ *01-42-33-69-27, Métro: Bonne Nouvelle; and 39 rue Jussieu, 5e,* ☎ *01-40-51-81-22, Métro: Jussieu.*

The Red Wheelbarrow

Founded by Canadian bookseller, Penelope Fletcher Le Masson in 2001, this cozy English-language bookstore not far from Le Village St. Paul (see Antiques above) stocks primarily contemporary and classic literature, with novels translated from French, general nonfiction, including a wide range of Paris- and France-related titles, and an extensive children's section. They also carry some French-English bilingual books and stories set in France.

22 rue St. Paul, 4e. ☎ *01-48-04-75-08. Métro: St. Paul.*

Ceramics, china, and glass

Baccarat

This famous crystal production house and museum used to be located at a landmark building at 30 rue de Paradis. However the museum and general quarters have moved to place des Etats-Unis in the 16e, a much more chic location. Several other boutiques throughout Paris sell this famous brand of crystal, for which one will pay dearly.

30 rue de Paradis, 10e. ☎ *01-47-70-64-30 or 01-40-22-11-00. Métro: Boissière. Other boutiques can be found at 17 rue de la Paix, 2e,* ☎ *01-42-4418-45; and 11 place de la Madeleine, 8e,* ☎ *01-42-65-36-26.*

La Maison Ivre

The Left Bank between St-Germain-des-Prés and the Seine is the unofficial antiques and art gallery district, and this store sits right in the district's heart. It carries an excellent selection of handmade pottery from across France, emphasis on the Provence region, and ceramics from southern France. You can purchase beautiful, well-made pieces of ovenware, bowls, platters, plates, pitchers, mugs, and vases.

11 place des Etats-Unis, 16e. ☎ *01-40-22-11-10. Métro: St-Germain-des-Prés.*

Lumicristal

For discounted crystal by Daum, Limoges, and Baccarat, Lumicristal is the place to shop.

22 bis rue de Paradis, 10e. ☎ *01-47-70-27-97 or* ☎ *01-42-46-96-25. www.lumicristal. com. Métro: Château-d'Eau, Poissonnière, or Gare-de-l'Est.*

Clothing for children

Du Pareil au Même

Du Pareil au Même is *the* place to buy clothes for every child on your list — clothes are practical, *très mignons* (very cute), and very reasonably priced.

1 rue St-Denis, 1er ☎ *01-42-36-07-57.* www.dpam.com. *Métro: Châtelet. Many branches are located throughout the city,*

Jacadi

When BCBG women (see the "BCBG Chic: The 6e" section earlier in this chapter) have children, Jacadi is where they buy their very proper children's clothes that feature rich fabrics and such gorgeous touches as hand-done smocking and pretty fabrics.

256 bd. St-Germain, 7e. ☎ *01-42-84-30-40.* www.jacadi.com. *Métro: Suferino. Many branches are located throughout the city.*

Natalys

Part of a French chain with a dozen stores in Paris, Natalys sells children's wear, maternity wear, and related products.

74 rue de Rivoli, 1er. ☎ *01-40-29-46-35. Métro: Hôtel de Ville. Other branches include 69 rue de Clichy, 9e,* ☎ *01-48-74-07-44; and 47 rue de Sèvres, 6e,* ☎ *01-45-48-77-12.*

Petit Bateau

For years, women in the know have been stocking up on t-shirts at the teenage end of the spectrum from this very cute (and somewhat expensive) brand of clothing that uses simple patterns and color pairings to give a sense of delightful and well-made simplicity. The signature "little boat" icons either grace the front of their t-shirts shirts or attach via little side-labels — anyone can feel like a small French kid chasing pigeons through the Jardins de Luxembourg while munching on hand-made French pastries. We say *anyone* because Petit Bateau, originally designed with infants, toddlers, and young children in mind, now carries the same fun little-kid styles sized for adults!

24 rue Cler, 7e. ☎ *01-47-05-18-51. www.petit-bateau.com. Métro: La Tour Maubourg. Another branch can be found at 116 av. des Champs-Elysées, 8e.* ☎ *01-40-74-02-03. Métro: George V.*

Tartine et Chocolat

This store features more typically French, precious, and pricey clothes.

105 rue du Faubourg-St-Honoré, 8e. ☎ *01-45-62-44-04. Métro: Concorde. Another branch is located at 266 bd. St-Germain, 7e.* ☎ *01-45-56-10-45.*

Clothing for men

Celio

Dressing like a youthful Parisian man doesn't have to kill your wallet. We often call Celio "the French Gap," which refers to their prices and their menswear — shirts, polos, button-down pants, belts, jackets, etc. — basically everything that Gap sells but with a specifically French twist of small details and a bit more flair than the Gap would sell (the pants are tighter, for starters). Celio has over twenty locations in Paris, but some carry limited lines of their wares. Listed below are some of the bigger ones.

66 bd. du Montparnasse, 14e. ☎ *01-45-38-90-03. Other boutiques are found at 65 rue de Rivoli, 1e,* ☎ *01-42-21-18-04; and 4 rue Halèvy, 9e,* ☎ *01-42-68-30-60.*

Façonnable

For quality shirts in nearly every color and casual pants, in addition to jackets, suits, and other men's finery (all a bit on the conservative side), Façonnable is the place. In the United States, Nordstrom carries some of Façonnable's fashions, but this store has the entire line.

9 rue du Faubourg-St-Honoré, 8e. ☎ *01-47-42-72-60. Métro: Madeleine or Concorde. Another branch is located at 174 bd. St-Germain, 6e.* ☎ *01-40-49-02-47.*

Madelios

This huge store offers one-stop shopping for men, selling everything from overcoats to lighters to luggage. If companions get bored waiting, the store is part of a small mall that has some nice stores for browsing.

23 bd. de la Madeleine, 1er. ☎ *01-53-45-00-00. Métro: Madeleine.*

Saint James

If you've ever dreamed of wearing the horizontal-striped sweaters of a virile French sailor, then this is the store where you buy that sweater. Saint James is the place for the sailor-at-heart: All of the sweaters, slacks, jackets, and shirts available are both beautifully tailored and rugged. They can be very functional clothes for outdoor movement, but they make also a fashion statement — "I love France," or also "I love the ocean." They also outfit women, children, and infants.

66 rue de Rennes, 6e. ☎ *01-53-45-00-00. Métro: St-Germain-des-Prés.*

S.D. Spontini

Looking like the urbane, ultra-Parisian man doesn't have to be difficult: S.D. Spontini has several boutiques throughout the city and has reasonable prices for very fashionable menswear. These boutiques sport funky button-down shirts worn going clubbing or sitting around in a cafe; as well as fitted pants; shiny, somewhat pointed shoes; belts; and those rib-textured sweaters that 20-something (or 20-something-spirited) French men wear at almost any time of the year. Regarded as fashionably unconservative and casual, you can dress up for a night on the town in these beautiful clothes, or dress down for a leisurely walk or lunch in Paris.

29 rue des Francs Bourgeois, 4e. ☎ *01-44-78-70-71. Métro: St-Paul.*

Ted Baker

This is the Paris branch of the London designer and sells relaxed dressy and casual clothes with little details (like large French cuffs or a wild pattern lining the collar) that set this brand apart.

20 rue des Francs Bourgeois, 3e. ☎ *01-44-54-02-98. Métro: St-Paul.*

Clothing for teens and the young-at-heart

Antoine et Lili

If you're strolling the quays of the hip Canal St-Martin, have a peek into this candy-colored store selling youngish bohemian-style clothes and accessories, and decorations that look great in dorm rooms. Some fun items include picture frames made from colorful scrap metal, or funky notebooks bound with hand-made paper. A garden and small canteen also are located here.

95 quai Valmy, 10e. ☎ *01-40-37-41-55. Métro: Gare de l'Est. Other branches are at 51 rue des Francs Bourgeois, 4e,* ☎ *01-42-72-26-60; and 90 rue des Martyrs, 18e,* ☎ *01-42-58-10-22.*

Cop-Copine

Cutting-edge and flattering, Cop-Copine makes great youthful clothes that enhance your good parts and disguise your not-as-good ones.

80 rue Rambuteau, 2e. ☎ *01-40-28-49-72. Métro: Les Halles. RER: Châtelet-Les Halles. Another branch is located at 37 rue Etienne-Marcel.* ☎ *01-53-00-94-80.*

H&M

Hennes & Mauritz, the Swedish "IKEA of fashion," has a large selection of up-to-the-minute men and women's fashion at very low prices. This is where you run to get the latest Prada copy — the store markets to the fashion conscious. In 2004 Fashion guru Karl Lagerfeld designed an exclusive collection marketed at their usual low prices, which incidentally sold out around the world within hours. In 2005, the "couture charitable design" came from Stella McCartney, again selling out within hours. H&M's clothes will not hold together as well as the real couture stuff, but you can get at least a year of solid wear out of them. The clothes bought at H&M stores outside Europe have a slightly different cut than the ones in Europe.

120 rue de Rivoli, 1er. ☎ *01-55-34-96-86. Métro: Hôtel-de-Ville or Louvre-Rivoli.*

Mango

With locations throughout the city, this store is popular with young Parisian women for its inexpensive, fashion-conscious, body-hugging (sometimes tacky) clothes.

82 rue de Rivoli, 1er. ☎ *01-44-59-80-37. Métro: Hôtel-de-Ville or Louvre-Rivoli.*

Morgan

Form-fitting suits, dresses, and casual wear in synthetics and blends can be found at low prices for young women here.

92 av. Champs-Elysées, 6e. ☎ *01-43-59-83-72. Métro: George V.*

Zara

Zara offers well-made copies of today's hottest styles for women, men, and children at extremely low prices. Expect bargains galore during the January and July sales.

128 rue de Rivoli, 1er. ☎ *01-44-54-20-42. Métro: Hôtel-de-Ville or Louvre-Rivoli. Locations all over the place, including 44 av. Champs-Elysées, 6e,* ☎ *01-45-61-52-81; and 45 rue de Rennes, 6e,* ☎ *01-44-39-03-50.*

Clothing for women

Cacharel

Beautiful women's, children's, and men's clothes are featured at Cacharel, some in pretty Liberty-flower printed fabrics. A Cacharel overstock boutique is at 114 rue Alésia, 14e (☎ **01-45-42-53-04**).

64 rue Bonaparte, 6e. ☎ *01-40-46-00-45. Métro: Saint-Sulpice.*

Colette

This is Paris's most cutting-edge clothing store, and everything from designer clothes to cameras to beauty products is on sale here arranged in *très* artistic displays. You can also find artsy tchotchkes, art magazines, avant-garde coffee table books, and art exhibits. Even if you don't buy (the prices are astronomical), just looking is fun and you can break for a snack or drink from one of the extensive selection of waters at the basement Water Bar.

213 rue St-Honoré, 1er. ☎ *01-55-35-33-95. Métro: Tuileries.*

Comptoir des Cotonniers

This reasonably-priced designer has branches in the major department stores as well as its own boutiques scattered around the city. Clothes are fashionable without being too cutting-edge and made well from cotton, wool, or silk. Their numerous boutiques market to women from young to middle aged. Styles, though not timeless, will last a few seasons at home.

33 rue des Francs-Bourgeois, 4e. ☎ *01-42-76-95-33.* www.comptoirdescotonniers. com. *Métro: St-Paul. Over 20 additional locations throughout the city.*

Etam

Women's clothing at Etam is made mostly from synthetic or synthetic-blend fabrics, but the fashions are recent, and the stores are simply *everywhere*. Etam's lingerie, sold in regular Etam stores and separately at Etam

Lingerie, has the best deals on pretty and affordable nightclothes and underwear.

67 rue de Rivoli, 1er. ☎ *01-44-76-73-73. Métro: Pont Neuf. There's an Etam Lingerie at 135 rue de Rennes, 6e.* ☎ *01-45-44-16-88.*

Franck et Fils

Franck et Fils is not a simple boutique: it is a mini department store of truly high-class fashion, located in the snobby-chic 16e arrondissement village of Passy. Catering to women only, one can pick up here such luxuries as Chanel suits, new couture creations, fur-lined gloves, and beautiful hair accessories, as well as elaborate hats, feather headbands, handbags, and more. A staple shopping destination for chic Parisians.

80 rue de Passy, 16e. ☎ *01-44-14-38-00. Métro: La Muette.*

Gelati

Paris is home to exquisite shoe designers such as Christian Louboutin, Robert Clergerie, and Maude Frizon, but if you can't afford their high, high prices, come to this fun shoe store that carries styles inspired by top designers but doesn't reflect their couture prices.

6 rue St-Sulpice, 6e. ☎ *01-43-25-67-44. Métro: Mabillon.*

Jamin Puech

This boutique sells very unique and avant-garde handbags, made from plush materials such as satin and beautiful beige velvets: each bag is hand-made with personal touches (some are made to look like a piece of antique furniture). Although not cheap, considering how much handbags can run in this town, you might find something truly original that's more worth the price.

68 rue Vieille du Temple, 3e. ☎ *01-48-87-84-87. Métro: Rambateau.*

La City

The clothes sold here are perfect for work or for going out to dinner, and young women are the target audience. Although everything is synthetic, the prices are reasonable.

37 rue Chaussée d'Antin, 9e. ☎ *01-48-74-41-00. Métro: Chaussée d'Antin. Other branches are located in the les Halles shopping mall, 1e,* ☎ *01-40-13-00-83; and 5 bis rue St-Placide, 6e,* ☎ *01-42-84-32-84.*

1-2-3

Like La City, 1-2-3 targets young women looking for stylish suits, blouses, and sweaters to wear to work and après (after). Most clothes are synthetics or synthetic blends; clothing and accessories are sold at moderate prices.

146 rue de Rivoli, 1er. ☎ 01-40-20-97-01. Métro: Louvre-Rivoli. Other branches around the city.

Rodier

For quality, stylish knitwear, Rodier is the upscale choice. Prices are high for ready-to-wear, but you can often find good bargains during the sales.

52 av. Ternes, 17e. ☎ 01-58-05-09-06. Métro: Ternes. Other branches include 27 rue Tronchet, 8e. ☎ 01-45-01-79-88.

Shoe Bizz

Here you will find the latest well-made fashions for your feet at budget-friendly prices.

42 rue Dragon, 6e. ☎ 01-45-44-91-70. Métro: Ternes. Another branch is at 48 rue de Beaubourg, 3e. ☎ 01-48-87-12-73.

Crafts

Viaduc des Arts

When the elevated railroad cutting across the 12e was transformed into the Promenade Plantée, the space beneath was redesigned to accommodate a long stretch of artisan shops, galleries, furniture stores, and craft boutiques. Some of the glasswork artists here are absolutely superb. If you plan to visit the Bois de Vincennes via the Promenade Plantée, duck in for a look on any day except Sunday, when it's closed. The Viaduc Café here (43 av. Daumensil) is a pleasant place for a light bite or a glass of wine.

9–147 av. Daumensil, 12e. Métro: Bastille, Lédru-Rollin, Reuilly-Diderot, or Gare-de Lyon.

Food

Fauchon

Paris's original gourmet store is still going strong, opening small branches all over the city. This is its flagship store, and here the signature pink-labeled cans of coffee, caviar, foie gras, biscuits, wines, oils, candy, and pastries fight for beautifully organized shelf space. If you're in the area, take a peek inside if only for its long history. Split into two parts, one section carries the many prepackaged gourmet delights, clearly meant to be gifts; the other carries staples. But save your shopping for other, cheaper grocery stores that may stock, incidentally, some of Fauchon's products. Its tea salon is next door.

26 place Madeleine, 8e. ☎ 01-70-39-38-00. Métro: Madeleine.

Hédiard

Across the street from rival Fauchon is Hédiard, a gourmet food shop that sells most of the same products as Fauchon, but packaged in red and black stripes. Hédiard is slightly cheaper than Fauchon and has good prepared hot and cold food. If you must have fois gras with your baguette, then Hédiard is one of the places you can count on finding it. Branches are located throughout the city.

21 place de la Madeleine, 8e. ☎ *01-43-12-88-88. Métro: Madeleine.*

JSFP Traiteur

If you're visiting the rue de Buci market, have a look inside this store (originally known as Jacques Papin) if only to salivate over some of the most exquisite foods you may ever see, including trout in aspic, fine pâtés and salads, lobsters, and smoked salmon. The name has changed, but the quality remains the same in this busy pedestrian street in the Latin Quarter.

8 rue de Buci, 6e. ☎ *01-43-26-86-09. Métro: Odéon.*

Lafayette Gourmet

They keep this large, well-stocked supermarket well hidden in the men's building at Galeries Lafayette. Once you find it, you'll discover it's a terrific spot to browse for gifts or for yourself. It has a good selection of wines, and the house-brand merchandise, often cheaper than other labels, is of very good quality. Eat at the prepared-food counters or sit at the small bar for a glass of wine.

40 bd. Haussmann, 9e. (Enter through the men's dept. of Galeries Lafayette. It's on the mezzanine level, accessed by an escalator.) ☎ *01-42-82-34-56. Métro: Chaussée-d'Antin.*

La Grande Epicerie de Paris (at Le Bon Marché)

This is one of the best luxury (meaning it's not cheap) supermarkets in Paris and a great place to look for gourmet gifts, such as olive oils, homemade chocolates, fresh pastas, and wine. Food is artfully arranged in glass cases, and the produce is some of the freshest around. It makes for wonderful one-stop picnic shopping, too, offering a wide array of prepared foods and cheeses and terrific snack food, some of it from the U.S.(!), too.

38 rue de Sèvres, 7e. ☎ *01-44-39-81-00. Métro: Sèvres-Babylone.*

La Maison du Chocolat

Each candy here is made from a blend of as many as six kinds of South American and African chocolate, flavored with just about everything imaginable. The salespeople here know everything there is about mixing chocolate taste with fillings; ask them to help you with an assortment if you think you can contain yourself from stuffing them in your mouth all at once! All the merchandise is made on the premises. If the smell doesn't lure you in, the windows will. Possibly the classiest chocolate shop ever, the man selling ice cream at the exterior of the shop wears a full suit, even during mid-July.

225 rue du Faubourg-St-Honoré, 8e. ☎ *01-42-27-39-44. Métro: Ternes. Another branch is at 52 rue François Premier, 8e.* ☎ *01-47-23-38-25.*

La Maison du Miel

For an unusual but very welcome gift, try bringing back some French honey from this little shop. It has more than 40 varieties of honey you never dreamed possible (pine tree or lavender), identified according to the flower to which the bees were exposed. Honey being the favored refreshments of the Greek gods, Zeus would have approved of this fine shop!

24 rue Vignon, 9e. ☎ *01-47-42-26-70. Métro: Madeleine or Havre-Caumartin.*

Gifts and jewelry

Biche de Bère

Chunky and unusual jewelry in sterling silver and gold plate can be found here.

15 rue des Innocents, 1er. ☎ *01-40-28-94-47. Métro: Châtelet.*

Bijoux Burma

To make others whisper "Are they real or aren't they?", visit Bijoux Burma for some of the best costume jewelry in the city. (You can always reply: "They're real and they're *fabulous!*")

50 rue François 1er, 8e. ☎ *01-47-23-70-93. Métro: Franklin-D-Roosevelt. Other branches are at 8 bd. des Capucines, 9e,* ☎ *01-42-66-27-09; and 249 rue St. Honoré 1er* ☎ *01-42-60-06-27.*

Eric et Lydie

This shop in the arty Passage du Grand Cerf contains unusual, beautiful, and often reasonably priced costume jewelry, hair ornaments, and other accessories.

7 passage du Grand Cerf, 2e. ☎ *01-40-26-52-59. Métro: Etienne-Marcel.*

France Ma Douce

This cute boutique in the Marais features specially made items from the "four corners" of France. A diverse assortment of gifts are available: Espadrilles from the Basque country, Provençal napkins from the southeast, striped sailor shorts from Brittany, lavender soaps and oils, truffles, olive oil, books on regional delicacy, and even cheese. The staff speaks perfect English and is happy to assist you.

27 rue du Bourg Tibourg, 4e. ☎ *01-44-59-38-03. Métro: Hôtel de Ville.*

Kazana

For the funky, big-earring wearing, fashionable pseudo-hippie in your life, Kazana will undoubtedly provide something fun and colorful. This small chain carries fashion accessories including colorful scarves (some hand made in Central America), a huge assortment of oversized and small dangly earrings made from wood, metal, and shiny seashells, bracelets, and bead necklaces, as well as decorated pocketbook mirrors and other hand-luggage sized gifts, all wrapped in happy fuchsia and magenta-colored packaging. It's surprisingly inexpensive.

15 rue Vielle du Temple, 4e. ☎ 01-42-78-20-38. Métro: Hôtel de Ville. Another boutique can be found at 8–10 rue Steinkerque, 18e. ☎ 01-42-57-16-73. Métro: Abbesses.

La Chaise Longue

This bilevel gift shop is open on Sunday (when it gets very crowded) and is simply bursting at the seams with cool gifts such as dinnerware, designer teapots, three-dimensional picture frames, patterned drinking glasses, children's straw hats with a cat face and ears, bath towels with fun prints, among many, many other things. It's very reasonably priced and definitely worth a visit — this is one of those stores where you find something you didn't know existed but cannot live without.

20 rue des Francs Borgeois, 3e. ☎ 01-48-04-36-37. Métro: St-Paul. Another location is at 8 rue Princesse, 6e. ☎ 01-43-29-62-39. Métro: St Michel.

Monic

There's so much to look at in this store in the Marais — open Sunday afternoons — that it's overwhelming! Here awaits a wide range of afford-able costume jewelry and designer creations, many at discount prices.

5 rue des Francs-Bourgeois, 4e. ☎ 01-42-72-39-15. Métro: St-Paul. Another location can be found at 14 rue de l'Ancienne-comédie, 6e. ☎ 01-43-25-36-61. Métro: Odéon.

Pylones

These boutiques sell Simpsons and Tintin collectibles, children's umbrel-las that stand on their own, bicycle bells shaped like ladybugs, pastel col-ored toasters, back massagers shaped like octopi, and a variety of other unusual and brightly-colored gift items. It's a fun place to browse.

57 rue de St-Louis-en-l'Ile, 4e. ☎ 01-46-34-05-02. Métro: Cité. Branches at 7 rue Tardieu, 18e, ☎ 01-46-06-37-00; 13 rue Ste-Croix de la Brètonnerie, 4e, ☎ 01-48-04-80-10; and 98 rue du Bac, 7e, ☎ 01-42-84-37-37. Métro: Rue du Bac.

Home and housewares

Alessi

Alessi offers bright and affordable kitchen implements, such as magnet-ized salt and pepper shakers and dish scrubbers that look a bit *human*. You can find some cutlery, dishes, and linens, too. Check out the Mr. Suicide drain plug — a yellow man chained to a blue stopper that floats to the surface when you take a bath.

31 rue Boissy d'Anglas, 8e. ☎ 01-42-66-14-61. Métro: Madéleine or Concorde.

Cedre Rouge

Cedre Rouge sells that urban rustic look made with natural materials for the garden or terrace, apartment or country home. It isn't cheap, but you can find some unusual gifts (like cute, but tiny, snail candleholders for 20€/$24). Finds include Tuscan pottery, Irish linen tablecloths and napkins, Murano glass, teak and wicker furniture, beeswax candles, and surprisingly lifelike synthetic plants.

116 rue du Bac, 6e. ☎ *01-42-84-84-00. Métro: Sèvres-Babylone or Rue du Bac. Another branch is at 22 av. Victoria, 1e.* ☎ *01-45-24-62-62.*

Conforama

This huge store sells everything for your home at reasonable prices: furniture, appliances, garden tools and accessories, and everyday china and glass. Check out their selection of kitchen tools: It always boggles our minds how many different gadgets the French have available for making delicious food.

2 rue de Pont-Neuf, 1er. ☎ *01-42-33-37-09. Métro: Pont Neuf.*

Déhillerin

Filled with high-quality copper cookware, glasses, dishes, china, gadgets, utensils, ramekins, pots, and kitchen appliances, this place makes cooks go wild — especially because the prices are discounted. With the current rate of exchange, don't be surprised when you find out how much a discounted price still turns out to be!

18–20 rue Coquillière, 1er. ☎ *01-42-36-53-13.* www.e-dehillerin.fr. *Métro: Les Halles.*

La Vaissellerie

These boutiques are always crammed full of very cute and inexpensive white porcelain tableware, as well as clever postcards, placemats, and tablecloths in check-patterns or simple Provençal designs (think yellow and blue borders with pictures of olives and jugs), not to mention spice containers, labeled jars for *farine* and *sucre* (flour and sugar) — essentially anything you could need for your kitchen. We suggest as a gift a set of espresso-cups because they are easily portable and have unique designs.

92 rue St-Antoine, 4e. ☎ *01-49-80-06-57. Métro: St-Paul. Another location is at 85 rue de Rennes, 6e.* ☎ *01-42-22-51-49. Métro: Rennes or Montparnasse Bienvenue.*

Verrerie des Halles

The restaurant industry buys its china, glassware, furniture, and other supplies here, and you can, too, at discount prices.

15 rue du Louvre, 1er. ☎ *01-42-36-80-60. Métro: Louvre-Rivoli.*

Toys

Au Nain Bleu

F.A.O. Schwartz in Manhattan emulated this, the world's fanciest toy store. Translated as "at the blue dwarf's," for more than 150 years Au Nain Bleu has been selling toy soldiers, stuffed animals, games, and puppets in a gorgeous space. More modern toys are also on hand, including airplanes and model cars. However, at the time of this writing, the store had been closed for renovations with no notice of a time frame for reopening. Call the number listed below to get the latest information. Obviously, this would be a terrific place to bring your kids!

5 bd. Malesherbes, 8e. ☎ *01-42-65-20-00. Métro: Madeleine.*

Fnac Eveil & Jeux

An outpost of the Fnac chain, Fnac Eveil & Jeux sells books, videos, and music for children, and has story hours and other activities for its young guests.

19 rue Vavin, 6e. ☎ *01-56-24-03-46. Métro: Vavin.*

Galeries Lafayette

Floor 4 of the Galeries Lafayette main store is devoted to toys and children's clothing, and there's a play area kids love.

40 bd. Haussmann, 9e. ☎ *01-56-24-03-46. Métro: Havre-Caumartin, Chaussée-d'Antin-La Fayette, Opéra, or Trinité.*

Wine

Legrand Filles et Fils

In addition to fine wines, this store stocks brandies, chocolates, coffees, and oenophile (wine-lover) paraphernalia. It also conducts wine tastings one night a week.

1 rue de la Banque, 2e. ☎ *01-42-60-07-12. Métro: Bourse.*

Les Caves Augé

This is the oldest wine shop in Paris with a sommelier (wine steward) on site who can advise you on the vintage French and international wines this store carries. If you're looking for something delightful, you'll be very pleased; if you're looking for delightfully inexpensive, you may have a bit of trouble.

116 bd. Haussmann, 8e. ☎ *01-45-22-16-97. Métro: St-Augustin.*

Nicolas

This Nicolas is the flagship store of the almost 125-year old wine chain that has more than 110 branches in and around Paris. It offers good prices for bottles you may not be able to find in the United States. Look for the maroon or wine-colored facade with yellow-lettering; if you're going on a picnic, you can always depend on Nicolas.

31 place de la Madeleine, 8e. ☎ *01-42-68-00-16. Métro: Madeleine.*

La Cave des Martyrs

Written on the window of this store is *Les Cavistes Pas Ordinaires* which is akin to "not your ordinary caviste" or wine-vendor. The friendly staff members here have an extensive knowledge of wine and are not shy at all with customers. Definitely ask them for help because they will pick you out something fantastic; they can do it at any price range and succeed with flying colors. They also carry spirits, liquors, and champagne, of course.

39 rue des Martyrs, 9e. ☎ *01-40-16-80-27. Métro: Notre-Dame de Lorette.*

Chapter 13

Following an Itinerary

In This Chapter
▶ Visiting for three days
▶ Staying for five days
▶ Taking a tour of Montmartre

*W*hen you're short on time or have young children with you, you want to maximize your opportunities to see the best Paris has to offer in the most efficient way possible. The itineraries in this chapter help you figure out where to start and what to do. But branch out and explore those interesting alleyways and pretty green spaces you encounter all around you. That is what is so much fun about Paris: It reveals itself in all kinds of ways, making the trips of each individual visitor different — and special.

Making the Most of Paris in Three Days

On **Day One,** start early by having coffee and croissants at a cafe or pick up a pastry at a *boulangerie* near your hotel to eat on the run. Then begin at the true center of Paris: **Notre-Dame** on the **Ile de la Cité.** The cathedral is *the* starting point for any tour, and it's Paris's starting point, as well; you're at Kilometre Zéro, from which all distances in France are measured. From there, take a short walk west to the island's other Gothic masterpiece — **Sainte-Chapelle** in the **Palais de Justice.** After-ward, cross the Seine to the **Louvre** on the Right Bank. Select just a few rooms in a particular collection for your first visit. The Louvre is one of the world's largest and finest museums, and it would take months to see everything. Take a well-deserved lunch break in the museum's comfort-able **Café Marly** overlooking I.M. Pei's pyramid (see Chapter 10 for a description).

From the museum, stroll west through the beautiful **Jardin des Tuileries** to the **place de la Concorde,** with its Egyptian obelisk and fountains. Continue west up the **Champs-Elysées,** browsing the stores (**Fnac** and **Virgin Megastore** are good places to buy music, and each has a cafe on the premises for a break; **Zara** is good for the latest fashion at low prices) on either side of the avenue until you come to the **Arc de Triomphe.** Pay it a visit, then find avenue Marceau on the south side of the Arc and walk south or take bus 92 to Alma Marceau and board the **Bateaux-Mouches** for a **Seine boat ride** (see Chapter 11). After you disembark, have dinner at the friendly and reasonably priced **L'Assiette Lyonnaise,** 21 rue Marbeuf, 8e (from Pont L'Alma walk down av. George V to rue Marbeuf and make a right; L'Assiette Lyonnaise is on your right).

Explore the **Left Bank** on **Day Two.** Take the Métro to LaMotte-Picquet-Grenelle and stop into **Monoprix** just across the street for cheap picnic food from its grocery store. Walk north up avenue de Suffren until you reach the **École-Militaire.** Facing it is the **Eiffel Tower** and its front lawn, the **Champs-de-Mars,** where you can spread out to have a picnic after visiting the tower. After you climb the tower (and have lunch), head east on the quai Branly and pay a quick visit to the new **Musée de quai Branly** if you'd like to experience the art of traditional cultures of Africa, East and Southeast Asia, Oceania, Australia and New Zealand, and the American continents. Afterward head east on quai Branly (which turns into quai d'Orsay) until you reach the grounds of Invalides and visit the gold-topped **Église du Dôme** (which contains the **Tomb of Napoléon**). Admission also includes entrance to the **Musée de l'Armée.** Across boulevard des Invalides is the **Musée Rodin,** where you can enjoy a slow walk around the beautiful gardens before gazing at the artwork inside. Still have energy? Great! Hop on the Métro at Varenne, at the corner of boulevard des Invalides and Varenne, change to RER Line C, and arrive at Musée d'Orsay. Afterward, walk over to the Métro's **Assemblée Nationale** station at the intersection of boulevard St-Germain and rue de Lille. Take the Métro two stops to rue du Bac and exit onto boulevard St-Germain, making sure to walk in the direction traffic is heading, all the while browsing in upscale shops and art galleries. At place St-Germain-des-Prés, look for one of the famous cafes, **Café de Flore, Les Deux Magots** (see Chapter 10), or **Brasserie Lipp** and have a well-deserved drink. When you finish, take rue Bonaparte (which intersects St-Germain-des-Prés) south to Parisians' favorite park, the **Jardin du Luxembourg.** Stroll through the park and exit at the boulevard St-Michel gates on the park's east side. Walk north on boulevard St-Michel toward the river. You'll be in the **Latin Quarter.** The **Panthéon** is at the top of the hill on rue Soufflot. You can enjoy a nice meal at one of the many inexpensive restaurants located behind the Panthéon on rue Mouffetard.

On **Day Three,** get up early and hop on the Métro to St-Paul, in the heart of the **Marais.** Head east on rue St-Antoine, then turn north onto rue de Birague which will take you right to Paris's oldest square, the aristo-cratic **place des Vosges,** bordered by 17th-century town houses. Exit on rue des Francs-Bourgeois, then turn north onto rue Vieille du Temple until you see the **Musée Picasso.** Try to arrive when it opens at 9:30 a.m., and allow two hours for your visit. Afterward double back on rue du Vieille du Temple to rue des Rosiers and pick up lunch from **Jo Goldenberg.** Browse the stores here and head west on rue des Francs Bourgeois, which turns into rue Rambuteau. Follow rue Rambuteau west to rue Beaubourg, where you'll face the back of the wonderful **Centre Georges Pompidou.** Spend two hours exploring it. Afterward, jump on the Métro

at the Rambuteau station and head for Père-Lachaise. Spend the afternoon searching out **Cimitière Père-Lachaise**'s famous residents with the
2€ ($2.40) map (it's the best one) sold outside the gates on boulevard de
Ménilmontant. Afterward, take the Métro's Line 2 to the Anvers station.
Walk north on rue Tardieu to the base of **Sacré-Coeur.** Take the funicular
(one Métro ticket) to the top and then spend 15 to 20 minutes inside
Sacré-Coeur before climbing to its dome. After climbing down, head
behind the church to the **place du Tertre,** which still looks like an
old-fashioned Parisian square, despite artists begging to paint your picture (some can be quite persuasive, but they're too expensive, and it's
better to just politely tell them *"non, merci"*). Even though the cafes are
picturesque — and more expensive — save your appetite for **Au Poulbot
Gourmet,** 39 rue Lamarck (follow rue Lamarck down the hill to no. 39)
for dinner.

Planning a Five-Day Visit

Spend the first three days as outlined in the "Making the Most of Paris in
Three Days" itinerary. Add the **Conciergerie** to your tour of Ile de la Cité
on Day One; the entrance is on the Seine side of the Palais de Justice.

On **Day Four,** visit **Versailles.** On **Day Five,** take the Métro to Opéra to
visit the stunning **Opéra Garnier** with its mural by Marc Chagall. If
you're carrying traveler's checks, cash the last of them at nearby
American Express on rue Scribe and then head north to boulevard
Haussmann to shop the rest of the afternoon away at department
stores **Au Printemps** and **Galeries Lafayette.** The sixth-floor cafeteria
at Galeries Lafayette offers plenty of lunch or dinner choices — from a
salad bar to grilled steaks and dessert.

Take a Stroll through a Parisian Village

In recent years **Montmartre** has been revitalized by tourist visits, and
the quarter itself has recently become fashionable and hip again. Its
twisted streets and ivied walls are still just as charming as the days
before it was incorporated into the city, when it was a village known for
its cheap wines and artistic inhabitants (many artists left Paris proper
for Montmartre at night precisely because of the cheap drinks). The
twisting streets here can sometimes mean very confused voyagers, but
fear not! This half-day's tour of Montmartre will have you walking around
like a local in no time.

 Bring a map that has a good rendering of the 18th arrondissement.
Though getting lost is part of the fun of Montmartre, it's getting out that
can get a bit frustrating.

✔ **Scoping Abbesses, Part One:** Start out at Place Blanche, where you'll be greeted by the infamous **Moulin Rouge.** Take the requisite picture (lit up at night, it is most impressive!), and walk up **rue Lepic.** Open during the day are great cheese shops and small produce shops. At no. 12 is **Lux-Bar,** which opened a century ago and continues to give locals a place to soothe their palates. Across the street at no. 15 is **Café des Deux Moulins** of Amélie fame. The interior remains mostly the same, with the glass "toilettes" sign and the copper-topped bar (the cigarette counter was removed a while ago for more space). A big poster of Amélie graces the back wall. Turn right and walk down **rue des Abbesses.** Here is some great shopping (**Colline** at no. 20 and **Le Diable et Moi** at no. 29 bis). You will also pass fantastic *boulangerie* **Le Grenier du Pain,** at no. 38, and a good people-watching cafe, **Le Sancerre,** at no. 35, eventually ending up in place des Abbesses. Here you will see the **Eglise St-Jean-de-Montmartre,** which was built in 1904, and also the beautiful art-deco entrance to the Abbesses stop, designed by Hector Guimard. It is one of the last two original Métro entrances left in the city.

A good place to have a picnic lunch if you buy your sandwich from Le Grenier à Pain is next to the "I love you wall" located in the Square Jehan Rictus (just off of place des Abbesses, on the other side of the Métro entrance and the merry-go-round). In this small green space is a wall with the words "I love you" (*Je t'aime* in French) written in over a hundred different languages. *Comme c'est romantique!*

✔ **Scoping Abbesses, Part Two:** The next part of the tour leads up to everyone's favorite Montmartre landmark: Sacre Coeur! However, the streets leading up to it are quite important — especially if you like shopping! Walk along rue des Abbesses until you cross **rue des Martyrs.** You'll see an **Antoine et Lili** at no. 90, a shop perfect for interesting little gifts for the college crowd. Then, take a quick left and right onto rue Yvonne le Tac. At no. 9 you pass the entrance to the chapel built on the supposed spot of the beheading of St. Denis, for whom all of Montmartre is named. At no. 8 is a lovely ivied building, while around the corner you pass the local cafe **Au Progrès** at 7 rue des Trois Frères, a great place to sit and order a light meal. It's perfectly situated in a four-way crossroads, the ideal panoramic view of Parisian streets. Make another right and go up and down rue d'Orsel. You'll pass two women's *depot ventes* (second-hand shops) which have fantastic used couture, such as Chanel, at reasonable prices (**Passé Devant,** no. 62, and the terrific nameless store at 47 bis — the stubborn owner refuses to name it — made infamous by the beautiful white cat lounging in the window). Also on rue d'Orsel are some art galleries, an antique bookstore, and some really ugly modern furniture shops. If it's later at night, a great restaurant on this street is **le Koklion,** at no. 62. For menswear, go to **Jo.,** at no. 47, and **S.D. Spontinini,** just up the street at 1 rue de Trois Frères. If you were to follow this street up any farther, you might find great costume jewelry, at **Jérémie Bertole,** or a real circus supply store (fun gift ideas!), at **Bonjour l'Artiste,** at no. 35.

✔ **Sacre Coeur and Place du Tertre:** And now the part you've all been waiting for! Climb the lamppost-divided stairs famously depicted in the photograph by Brassaï, or take the funicular. Enjoy the fantastic, free view for which you don't have to wait in line, or pay 5€ ($6) to go to the top of Sacre-Coeur for a much more spectacular view. Work started on this basilica in the 1870s and the building is a pastiche of Romanesque and Byzantine styles. Renoir, Picasso, Seurat, Degas, Van Gogh, and Zola all hung out in Pigalle and Montmartre. And there was no keeping Toulouse-Lautrec away, of course. Follow around the western side of the basilica, passing the dwarfed Église St Pierre du Montmartre, and wander around Place du Tertre without letting yourself get too abused by the painters dying to paint your picture. Here you can truly see how this place was once its own village, with adorable houses, old paned windows, and tiny cobblestone passageways (not to mention some of the highest rents in the city). Walk around the edges of the Place du Tertre area to the **Espace Dalí** at 11 rue Poulbot, a small museum dedicated to Dalí's work, of which there is a plethora to see (and hear — his voice plays over eerie ambient music). Then wander up rue des Saules, passing the famous cabaret **Au Lapin Agile** at no. 22, a famous haunt of artists Picasso, Modigliani, and Utrillo (they still have music shows here, but they are vastly overpriced). Around the corner is the **Musée de Montmartre,** at 12 rue Cortot, where you can learn all about the history and art associated with this beloved part of Paris.

✔ **There and back again:** Once you've had enough of the hilltop, make your way down through place Jean Baptiste Clément and down rue de la Mire to rue Ravignan, where you can see a beautiful house (built in 1911), located right across the street from 49 rue Gabrielle, where Picasso had his first studio in Paris. On this street are more art studios and funny narrow passages, as well as the very fairly priced **Chez Marie** (no. 27; see Chapter 10 for the review). Continue east to the upper portion of rue Lepic, where you can catch a glimpse of the oldest and only remaining windmill in Montmartre, **Le Moulin de la Galette** (unfortunately, you can't visit it). Descend further past rue Berthe and onto rue Androuet, where you will find the Collignon grocery from Amélie — she really did live in Montmartre! You are again on rue des Trois Frères. Follow it along and you will shortly pick up rue Ravignan again. Here you can find the **Bateau Lavoir,** another studio haunted by the likes of Picasso and Modigliani, at 11 bis place Emile Godeau. In this spot, there are benches where you can rest before you end up back at Abbesses, enjoying another quick view of the Paris skyline.

Chapter 14

Going Beyond Paris: Five Day Trips

*T*he daytrips outlined in this chapter are well-worth tearing yourself away from Paris, even though it may be difficult to tear yourself away from the City of Light. Don't worry; you'll be back in the city in time to enjoy a nightcap in a cafe. The "Daytrips from Paris" map can help you plan your excursions.

The Château de Versailles

Press time was just weeks before Sophia Coppola's movie version of the life of Marie Antoinette, "teen queen," hit the world's theaters. Whether attendance at Versailles will spike as a result remains to be seen. Even if you haven't seen the film, you will discover that there's more to Versailles (☎ **01-30-83-77-88**; www.chateauversailles.fr) than its incredible château, of which the words "awe-inspiring" don't begin to do justice. This is a small city on more than 800 hectares (2,000 acres) that houses formal and fanciful gardens, meadows (with sheep), a mile-long Grand Canal modeled on the one in Venice, the Grand and Petit Trianon mansions, a hamlet (The Hameau) where Marie Antoinette played peasant, the restored royal stables, a coach museum, fountains, and woods. All this attests to the power royalty once had and to one king who truly believed he deserved it: Louis XIV. The king hired the best to build Versailles: Louis Le Vau and Jules Hardouin-Mansart, France's premier architects; André Le Nôtre, designer of the Tuileries gardens; and Charles Le Brun, head of the Royal Academy of Painting and Sculpture, who fashioned the interior. Construction got underway in 1661.

Daytrips from Paris

In 1682, Louis XIV transferred the court to Versailles to live with him and thus prevent plots against him. Historians estimate that anywhere from 3,000 to 10,000 people, including servants, lived at Versailles in the 100 years between the rules of Louis XIV and Louis XVI, and court etiquette grew to be absurd. (Sometimes attendants engaged in power struggles about who ranked high enough to dress Marie Antoinette while the young queen waited, shivering. And Versailles's female royalty gave birth before a live audience; the higher the rank, the better the seat.) When you see all this over-the-top magnificence and try to estimate the cost, you may have a better understanding of the anger of the revolutionaries a century later.

Versailles

Louis XIV enjoyed an incredibly long reign of 72 years (though he was just a boy when he inherited the title). When he died in 1715, he was succeeded by his great-grandson, Louis XV, who continued the outrageous pomp and ceremony and made interior renovations and redecorations until lack of funds forced him to stop. Louis XV's son and daughter-in-law, Louis XVI and Marie Antoinette made no major changes at Versailles, but by then it was too late. On October 6, 1789, a mob voicing the feelings of the average French citizen sick of bearing the brunt of the costs of royalty's foibles, marched on the palace and forced the royal couple to return to Paris. This was the beginning of the French Revolution. The royal family eventually lost their lives, save one daughter (though some report that the young *dauphin,* or heir to the throne, never really died in prison, but was spirited away from the country), and Versailles ceased to be a royal residence.

The monarchy was reinstated in 1830, and Louis-Philippe, who reigned from 1830 to 1848 and succeeded Louis XVIII, prevented Versailles's destruction by donating his own money to convert it into a museum dedicated to the glory of France. In the mid-20th century, John D. Rocke-feller also contributed to the restoration of Versailles, and the work from that contribution continues to this day. The nearby "Versailles" map shows the current configuration.

Getting there

Catch the **RER line C** to Versailles from one of the stops at the Gare d'Austerlitz, St-Michel, Musée d'Orsay, Invalides, Ponte d'Alma, Champ de Mars, or Javel and take it to the Versailles Rive Gauche station (take "direction Versailles-rive-gauche-château), from which there's a shuttle bus to the château. Or, you can take the 15-minute walk through the pretty town itself. Round-trip tickets cost 5.40€ ($6.50) and the trip takes about 35 minutes. Eurailpass holders travel free on the RER but must show their Eurailpass at the kiosk near any RER entrance to receive a ticket that opens the turnstile leading to and from the RER platforms.

An alternative method of reaching Versailles from central Paris involves regular **SNCF trains,** which make frequent runs from two rail-way stations — Gare St-Lazare and Gare Montparnasse — to Versailles. Trains departing from Gare St-Lazare arrive at the Versailles Rive Droit railway station; trains departing from Gare Montparnasse arrive at Versailles Chantiers. Both stations lie within a ten-minute walk of the château, which is a wonderful way to orient yourself with the town, its geography, its scale, and its architecture. If you can't or don't want to walk, you can take bus B, bus H, or (in midsummer) a shuttle bus marked *Château* from any of the three stations directly to the château for a fee of 2.50€ ($2.90) each way per person. Because of the vagaries of the bus schedules, it may be easier to walk. Directions to the château are clearly signposted from each railway station.

To reach Versailles by car, drive west on the A13 highway from Porte d'Auteuil toward Rouen. Take the Versailles-Château exit, about 23km (14 miles) from Paris. Park in the visitors' parking lot at place d'Armes for 4.50€ ($5.15) Monday through Friday, 5.50€ ($6.30) on weekends. The drive takes about a half-hour, though in traffic it can take more than an hour.

You can also take advantage of the Versailles "**Passeport**" (☎ 01-30-83-77-88), a one-day pass to visit the entire Chateau de Versailles and all of the surrounding attractions within the city. This includes audio guided tours in the chateau, the Chapel and opera house, the King and Queen's

Grand Apartments, the Dauphin's (Crown Prince) Apartments, and the "Appartements de Mesdames" (ladies-in-waiting, only open on weekends). After this massive opulent castle visit, you have free reign of the parks, gardens and forest groves, **Domaine de Marie-Antoinette** (Marie-Antoinette's private fields), and all of the temporary exhibits. If you use the Passeport during the high season, the **Musée des Carrosses** (the Coach museum of Louis-Philippe, see below) and the spectacle of Les **Grands Eaux Musicales** (see below) are also included. The tickets cost 25€ ($30) during high season and 16€ ($19) during low season — keep in mind that seeing each attraction separately requires purchasing your ticket at an Fnac or SNCF ticket booth.

Don't want the hassle of getting to Versailles yourself? You can also take a tour bus there. **Cityrama,** 2 place des Pyramides, 1er (☎ **01-44-55-61-00;** www.cityrama.fr), has different trips to Versailles ranging from 39€ to 92€ ($47–$110) for adults, 20€ to 43€ ($23–$51) children (the higher-priced tickets also include trips to Fontainebleau and Barbizon). **Paris Vision,** 214 rue de Rivoli, 1er (☎ **01-42-60-30-01;** www.parisvision.com), offers bus excursions starting from 39€ to 145€ ($47–$174); it's half price for ages 4 to 11.

Exploring Versailles

Two words of advice — arrive early! More than three million tourists visit Versailles each year, and you'll want to have as much of a head start as possible.

The first rooms you see in the palace are the six Louis XIV–style **Grand Appartements,** which kings used for ceremonial events, and the **Petit Appartements,** where they lived with their families. Louis XV stashed his mistresses, Madame du Barry and Madame de Pompadour, in his second-floor apartment, which you can visit only with a guide. Attempts have been made to restore the original décor of the Queen's bedchamber, which Marie Antoinette renovated with a huge four-poster bed and silks in patterns of lilacs, her favorite flower, and peacock feathers. Look for the secret door through which she attempted to escape.

Other magnificent rooms include the **Salons of War and Peace,** which flank the palace's most famous room, the 71m-long (236-ft.) **Hall of Mirrors.** Hardouin-Mansart began work on the hall in 1678, and Le Brun added 17 large windows and corresponding mirrors. The ceiling paintings represent the accomplishments of Louis XIV's government. Jacques-Ange Gabriel designed the **Library** with its delicately carved panels. The **Clock Room** contains Passement's astronomical clock, which took 20 years to make; it's encased in gilded bronze.

Gabriel also designed the **Royal Opéra** for Louis XV. Try to imagine it the way it used to be during a concert — bearskin rugs under foot and the light of 3,000 powerful candles. Hardouin-Mansart built the gold-and-white **Royal Chapel** between 1699 and 1710. After his father's death,

Louis XVI and Marie Antoinette prayed for guidance here, fearing they were too young to run the country.

After you see the château, plan to spend at least an hour strolling through the **Formal Gardens,** spread across 100 hectares (250 acres). Here Le Nôtre created a Garden of Eden, using ornamental lakes and canals, geometrically designed flowerbeds, and avenues bordered with statuary. Louis XV, imagining he was in Venice, would take gondola rides with his lover of the moment on the mile-long Grand Canal. The restored vegetable gardens *(le Potager de Roi)* are here, as well. If you visit on a weekend in the summer, try to take in **The Grands Eaux Musicales,** a show in which the fountains move in time to the classical music of Bach, Mozart, or Berlioz. Cost is 7€ ($8.40) adults, 5.50€ ($6.60) ages 10 to 26 and seniors, children younger than ten are free. Another spectacle is **Les Fêtes de Nuit de Versailles,** a breathtaking sound-and-light show with fireworks held seven times a year between June and September. Cost is 17€ ($20) adults, 15€ ($17) ages 10 to 26 and seniors, children younger than ten are free. (For reservations to either show, call ☎ **0-892-68-36-22;** 0.35€/40¢ per min.)

Because of the crowds and long lines, most guests are content to visit only the château and gardens, but you can see much more at Versailles if you have the stamina. The most important of the remaining sights are the **Grand Trianon** and the **Petit Trianon.** *Trianon* was the name of the town that Louis bought and then razed in order to construct a mansion, le Grand Trianon, where he could eat light meals away from the palace. Designed in 1687, again by Hardouin-Mansart, the Grand Trianon has traditionally served as a residence for the country's important guests, although former President Charles de Gaulle wanted to turn it into a weekend retreat for himself. Napoléon I spent the night here, and U.S. President Richard Nixon slept in the room where Madame de Pompadour (Louis XV's mistress) died. Gabriel, the designer of the place de la Concorde, built the Petit Trianon in 1768 for Louis XV, who used it for trysts with Madame du Barry, his mistress after La Pompadour. Marie Antoinette adopted it as her favorite residence, where she could escape the constraints of palace life.

Behind the Petit Trianon is the **Hamlet,** a collection of small thatched farmhouses and a water mill, a setting where Marie Antoinette pretended she was back at her family's country retreat in Austria. Near the Hamlet is the **Temple of Love,** built in 1775 by Richard Mique, Marie Antoinette's favorite architect. In the center of its Corinthian colonnade is a reproduction of Bouchardon's Cupid shaping a bow from the club of Hercules.

Louis XIV's stables, **Le Grande Ecurie,** are newly restored and open to the public. Also designed by Hardouin-Mansart, the stables held as many as 600 horses owned by the king. These days, you'll see 20 ivory-colored Lusitano horses from Portugal. A morning tour here includes a dressage demonstration with riders in costume on horses performing to music. Near the stables is the entrance to the **Coach Museum,** which houses coaches from the 18th and 19th centuries, among them one used at the coronation of Charles X and another used at the wedding of Napoléon I and his second wife, Marie-Louise. One sleigh rests on tortoiseshell runners. A ticket to the Petit Trianon also admits you to this museum.

Admission to Le Grande Ecurie is 7.50€ ($8.60) adults, 3€ ($3.60) 17 and under. Open Tuesday to Friday 9 a.m. to 1 p.m., weekends 11 a.m. to 3 p.m. Admission to the coach museum is 2€ ($2.40), free for children younger than 18. It's open every weekend from April to October 9 a.m. to 6:30 p.m. and the first two weekends in November 12:30 to 5:30 p.m.

Admission to the palace is 14€ ($17) for adults, 10€ ($12) for ages 18 to 24 and over 60. It's free for those younger than 18 and for all on Sunday. Combined admission to the Grand and Petit Trianons is 9€ ($11) for adults during the high season, and 5€ ($6) during low season; children younger than 18 are free. Admission to the gardens is free except for the days of Grands Eaux Musicales (see above for prices).

One-hour audio tours of the King's Chambers are 14€ ($17), which includes admission to the chateau, and free for those under age 18. Lecturer-led one-hour tours of the palace are admission price plus 4€ ($4.80), 3€ (3.60) ages 10 to 17 and seniors; one-and-a-half-hour tours are admission plus 6€ ($7.20), 4.50€ ($5.40) ages 11 to 17 and seniors; two-hour tours are admission plus 8€ ($9.60) for adults, 6€ ($7.20) ages 10 to 17. Tours are free for children younger than ten.

From May to September, the palace is open Tuesday through Sunday from 9 a.m. to 6:30 p.m. The rest of the year, the palace is open Tuesday through Sunday from 9 a.m. to 5:30 p.m. From May through September the Grand Trianon and Petit Trianon are open daily noon to 6:30 p.m.; from October to April, the Grand Trianon and Petit Trianon are open daily noon to 5:30 p.m. The park and the gardens are open every day, except in bad weather, from 7 a.m. in summer and 8 a.m. in winter until sunset (between 5:30 and 9:30 p.m. depending on the season).

Dining options

The town of Versailles has no shortage of places where you can break for lunch, but after you're on palace grounds, you may find it infinitely more convenient just to stay put — otherwise you have to hike back into town and back out to the palace again. In the château, you can eat at Le Café, a snack bar just off the Cour de la Chapelle. In the Formal Gardens is an informal restaurant, **La Flotille,** on Petite Venise. (To get there from the château, walk directly back through the gardens to where the canal starts. Petite Venise and the restaurant are to your right.) There is La Petite Venise, a wood-beamed restaurant, brasserie and tea room with outdoor seating between the Grand Canal and the Apollo Fountain. Finally, several **snack bars** and fresh-squeezed orange juice stands are located in the gardens near the Quinconce du Midi and the Grand Trianon.

Note: For those with limited mobility, electric cars are available at the south entrance (☎ **01-39-66-97-66**).

The Palais de Fontainebleau

You can combine culture and outdoor activities at Fontainebleau, a terrific day trip from Paris: After you tour the castle, you can hike the trails or rent bikes to ride in the 16,800-hectare (42,000-acre) Forêt (forest) de Fontainebleau. The palace (☎ **01-60-71-50-75**; check out the nearby "Fontainebleau" map) is probably most famous as the site of Napoléon's farewell to his imperial guard before he went into exile. It also contains more than 700 years of royal history from the enthronement of Louis VII in 1137 to the fall of the Second Empire in 1873. And Leonardo Da Vinci played a small role in its history.

Getting there

To reach Fontainebleau by train, take the SNCF Montargie line to Fontainebleau Avon station; it departs hourly from the Gare de Lyon in Paris. The trip takes 35 to 60 minutes and costs about 9€ ($11). Fontainebleau Avon station is just outside the town in Avon, a suburb of Paris. From the station, the town bus (direction Château) makes the 3km (2-mile) trip to the château every 10 to 15 minutes on weekdays and every 30 minutes on Saturdays and Sundays.

You can also reach Fontainebleau on a tour bus. **Cityrama,** 4 place des Pyramides, 1er (☎ **01-44-55-61-00**; www.cityrama.fr), combines both Fontainebleau and the nearby artist's village of Barbizon for 61€ ($73) adult, 31€ ($37) child.

Exploring Fontainebleau

Fontainebleau was built for love. François I transformed a run-down royal palace into Fontainebleau in 1528 for his mistress, and his successor, Henri II, left a beautiful memorial to the woman he loved — a **ballroom** decorated with the intertwined initials of his mistress, Diane de Poitiers, and himself.

The Mona Lisa once hung here, and it is said that its creator, Leonardo da Vinci personally brought the painting to its buyer, his friend François I. The Mona Lisa remained in the royal family for years before it was gifted to the Louvre. Stucco-framed paintings now hanging in the **Gallery of François I** include *The Rape of Europa* and depict mythological and allegorical scenes related to the king's life. Make sure to see the racy ceiling paintings above the **Louis XV Staircase,** which was originally painted for the bedroom of a duchess. The stairway's architect simply ripped out the bedroom floor, using its ceiling to cover the stairway. One fresco depicts the Queen of the Amazons climbing into Alexander the Great's bed.

Fontainebleau

When Louis XIV ascended the throne, Fontainebleau was largely neglected because of his preoccupation with Versailles, but it found renewed glory under Napoléon I. You can walk around much of the palace on your own, but most of the Napoleonic rooms are accessible only on guided tours, which are in French. Napoléon had two bedchambers; mirrors adorn either side of his bed in the grander chamber (look for his symbol, a bee), while a small bed is housed in the aptly named **Small Bedchamber.** A red-and-gold throne with the initial "N" is displayed in the **Throne Room.** You can also see Napoléon's **offices,** where the emperor signed his abdication; however, the document on exhibit is only a copy. Minor apartments include those once occupied by Madame De Maintenon, the second wife of Louis XIV; those of Pope Pius VII, whom Napoléon kept a virtual prisoner; still another was Marie Antoinette's.

After a visit to the palace, wander through the gardens, paying special attention to the lovely, bucolic carp pond, and take caution while walking by some of the fearless swans. If you'd like to promenade in the forest, a detailed map of its paths is available from the **Office de**

Tourisme, 4 rue Royale, near the palace (☎ **01-60-74-99-99;** www.fontainebleau-tourisme.com). You can also rent bikes nearby from **À la Petite Reine,** 32 rue des Sablons (☎ **01-60-74-57-57**), for about 5€ ($6) an hour, 15€ ($18) a half day, 19€ ($23) a full day, with a credit-card deposit. The **Tour Denencourt,** about 5km (3 miles) north of the palace, makes a nice ride and has a pretty view. Other mapped-out walking and bike tours of the city and environs can be downloaded from the Tourist Office Web site.

The Palais de Fontainebleau (☎ **01-60-71-50-60**) is open Wednesday through Monday, and is closed on New Years Day, Christmas Day, and the first of May. The opening hours October through May are from 9 a.m. to 5 p.m.; from June to September the hours are 9 a.m. to 6 p.m. Admission to the Grand Appartements is 6.50€ ($7.80) for adults, 4.50€ ($5.60) for ages 18 to 26 and older than 60, free for those under age 18. Free for all on the first Sunday of the month.

Dining options

If you're arriving by train and plan to visit only Fontainebleau, consider bringing a picnic from Paris. In fine weather, the château's gardens and nearby forest beckon. If you have a car, however, save your appetite for Barbizon (see below).

On the western edge of France's finest forest lies the village of **Barbizon,** home to a number of noted landscape artists — Corot, Millet, Rousseau, and Daumier. The colorful town has a lively mix of good restaurants, boutiques, and antiques shops — the perfect place to while away an afternoon. For lunch, try the **Relais de Barbizon,** 2 av. Charles de Gaulle (☎ **01-60-66-40-28**). The three prix-fixe menus at 19€, 30€, and 64€ ($22, $36, and $77) may feature such hearty home-style dishes as duckling in wild cherry sauce and a *tarte au citron* (lemon pie). The restaurant is open Thursday through Monday noon to 2:30 p.m. and 8 to 10 p.m. (Only lunch is served on Tues.)

If you stay in Fontainebleau for lunch, try **Le Table des Maréchaux** (in the Hôtel Napoléon, 9 rue Grande (☎ **01-60-39-50-50**). Its 35€ ($42) three-course Ménu de l'Empereur may include goat cheese and gorgonzola profiteroles sprinkled with almond, or a wildfowl terrine with a sun-dried tomato and onion spread to accompany. You can then move on to main courses of roasted pork served with pan-fried fennel in curry sauce, or a breast of duckling served with honey and dried fruits. Finish up with a puff pastry of honey ice cream and chestnut cream, or French toast in ice cream made with *pain d'épices* (spiced bread). In warm weather, diners can eat on the outdoor terrace.

The Cathedral at Chartres

It survived the French Revolution, even though it was scheduled for demolition. It withstood two world wars, when volunteers took down all

Notre-Dame de Chartres

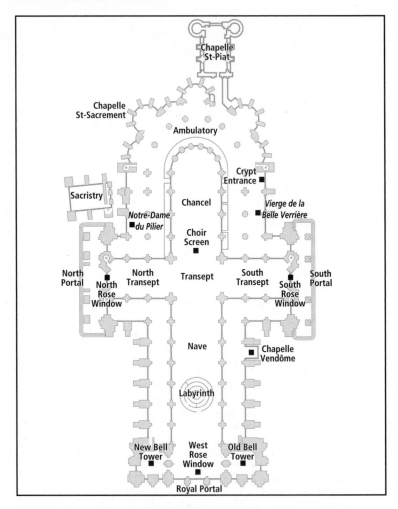

of its 12th- and 13th-century stained glass piece by piece. But for a majority of its visitors, the Cathédrale de Notre-Dame de Chartres (☎ 02-37-21-59-08; see the nearby "Notre-Dame de Chartres" map), one of the world's greatest Gothic cathedrals and one of the finest creations of the Middle Ages, comes second in importance to a small scrap of material housed inside. Known as the *Sancta Camisia,* it is said that it was worn by the Virgin Mary when she gave birth to Jesus — and that's the biggest draw here. This sacred scarf was supposedly a gift from the Empress Irene of Byzantium to Charlemagne, and has been resting in the cathedral of Chartres since 876 C.E. (*Note:* this refers to a different or earlier construction than the Chartres cathedral that we know today).

Getting there

Pick up one of the hourly SNCF trains from Paris's Gare Montparnasse to the town of Chartres. A round-trip ticket costs about 23€ ($28); the trip takes an hour.

If you'd like to drive to Chartres, take the A10/A11 highway from Porte d'Orléans and follow the signs to Le Mans and Chartres. The drive takes about 75 minutes.

Traveling to Chartres by tour bus is another option. **Cityrama,** 4 place des Pyramides, 1er (**☎ 01-44-55-61-00;** www.cityrama.fr), offers five-hour excursions leaving from Paris every Tuesday, Thursday, and Saturday for 58€ ($70) adult, 39€ ($47) child. **Paris Vision,** 214 rue de Rivoli, 1er (**☎ 01-42-60-30-01;** www.parisvision.com), also has a tour that departs the same days for the same amount.

Exploring the cathedral

Take one of Malcolm Miller's excellent 75-minute guided tours of Chartres Cathedral. Miller, an Englishman who has made the study of the cathedral his life's work, has published such books as *Chartres Cathedral* (Riverside Books Co.) and *Chartres Stained Glass* (Jarrold Publishing) and has been giving fascinating tours of the cathedral for 45 years. Tours are Monday through Saturday at 11 a.m. and 2:45 p.m. from Easter to November (although he is sometimes available in winter, too). Cost is 10€ ($12). Call **☎ 02-37-28-15-58,** fax at **☎** 02-37-28-33-03, or E-mail millerchartres@aol.com.

If you can't get in touch with Malcolm Miller, call the cathedral Welcome Center at **☎ 02-37-21-75-02.** Guided Crypt visits are available, but in French only. They meet outside of the cathedral at the "La Crypte" store from April 1 to October 31 at 11 a.m., 2:15 p.m., 3:15, and 4:15 (excluding Sun and holidays). From November to March the tours leaves from the cafe gift shop in the North tower, at 11 a.m. and 4:15 p.m. Call **☎ 02-37-21-75-02** for the gift shop. Visits of the North tower take place May to August from 9:30 a.m. to 12:30 p.m., and then from 2 to 5 p.m. (Sun only from 2–5 p.m.). Admission to the tower is about 4€ ($4.80) for adults, 3€ ($3.60) for seniors and students; children younger than 12 are admitted free. Roof structure tours (this is a great way to learn about how intricate gothic architecture is) are at 3 p.m. May through August, and in September through April on Saturdays and Sundays, not counting school holidays, they start as late as 5 p.m.

Sunday afternoons are a terrific time to visit, when free organ concerts (4:45–5:45 p.m.) and the filtered light coming in from the western windows make the church come wonderfully alive.

The cathedral that you see today dates principally from the 13th century, when it was built with the combined efforts and contributions of kings, princes, church officials, and pilgrims from across Europe. This Notre-Dame was among the first to use flying buttresses.

On your tour, begin at the very beginning — with the **entryway.** People say that Rodin sat for hours on the edge of the sidewalk, contemplating the portal, spellbound by its sculptured bodies draped in long, flowing robes with amazingly lifelike faces. Before entering, walk around to both the north and south portals, which date from the 13th century. The bays depict such biblical scenes as the expulsion of Adam and Eve from the Garden of Eden, and episodes from the life of the Virgin.

Next, just inside, are the **Clocher Vieux** (Old Tower) with its 105m (350-ft.) steeple dating from the 12th century, and the **Clocher Neuf** (New Tower). Originally built in 1134, the new tower's elaborate ornamental tower was added between 1507 and 1513 following one of the many fires that swept through the cathedral.

You can climb to the top of the Clocher Neuf, but make sure your shoes aren't slippery — parts of the tower are without a railing and are quite steep and narrow.

The cathedral is also known for its celebrated **choir screen.** Don't let the simple term fool you; this is a carved wood structure that took nearly 200 years to complete. The niches, 40 in all, contain statues illustrating scenes from the life of Mary. The screen is in the middle of the cathedral toward the altar.

Few of the rushed visitors ever notice the screen; they're transfixed by the stained-glass windows. Bring a pair of binoculars to better focus on the panes, which cover more than 2,508 square meters (26,996 square feet). The glass is unequaled anywhere in the world and is truly mystical. It was spared in both world wars, because in both wars, the glass was removed piece by piece. Currently, the Association Chartres Sanctuaire du Monde has undertaken the considerable task of raising the millions of euro necessary for the restoration of the windows, which have suffered on both sides from smoke from the cathedral's candles and from pollution.

Most of the stained glass dates from the 12th and 13th centuries. Many visitors find it difficult to single out one panel or window of particular merit; however, the oldest is the 12th-century **Notre Dame de la belle verrière** (Our Lady of the beautiful window, sometimes called the Blue Virgin) on the south side. The colors from the glass are such a vibrant, startling blue that many find it hard to believe that the window is 1,000 years old. In the **nave** (the widest in France), have a look down at the 13th-century labyrinth. It was designed for pilgrims to navigate on their hands and knees as a form of penance, all 300m (1,000 ft.) of it. These days, much of it is covered with folding chairs for Mass. The wooden **Virgin of the Pillar,** to the left of the choir, dates from the 14th century.

The **crypt** was built over a period of 200 years, beginning in the 9th century. Enshrined is **Our Lady of the Crypt,** a Madonna made in 1976 that replaced one destroyed during the Revolution. The **Sancta Camisia,** the holy relic that some people believe Mary wore during the birth of Jesus, is behind the choir screen in a chapel to the left of the church's treasury.

The cathedral is open daily April through September from 8 a.m. to 8 p.m., October through March from 7:30 a.m. to 7:00 p.m. Ask at the Chartres tourist office (☎ 02-37-18-26-26) outside the cathedral for information about tours in English and a schedule of masses open to the public.

Dining options

Restaurants, cafes, and snack bars abound around town, but just a stone's throw from the cathedral is **Le Café Serpente,** 2 Clôitre Notre-Dame (☎ 02-37-21-68-81). Facing the south side of the cathedral with outside tables, this restaurant serves traditional French fare at reasonable prices, with lunch priced between 10€ and 20€ ($12–$24) for two courses that may start with a dish of leeks and asparagus with foie gras and include a main course of *filet de rouget* (red fish filet). If you're just there for a snack or light meal, the requisite *salade composée* (large meal-salads) or some tasty omelets are available. The restaurant is open daily for lunch, and Monday through Saturday for dinner.

On the other side of the cathedral you can find the **Jardin Gourmand du Presbytère,** 21 Cloître Notre-Dame (☎ 02-37-21-27-02), a charming and inexpensive restaurant that feels positively homey and will make you feel like you're eating in someone's French kitchen with kitschy decorations. Here you can get simple entrees for 5€ ($6) such as a pea-mint soup or a spinach pastry, and for a main course they have a great pan-fried salmon with perfumed rice. Even just a coffee here is worth the stop: you face a shady and cool side of the cathedral and you can study the intricate statues and stonework as you dine. The restaurant is open Monday through Saturday at noon through 2 p.m., opening again around 7 o'clock for dinner.

For more upscale dining, take the time to wander through town where you'll discover **Le Moulin de Ponceau,** 21–23 rue de la Tannerie (☎ 02-37-35-30-05). This chic restaurant can be on the expensive side, but it's worth it from the fresh market-menu to the gorgeous scenery. Beautifully situated on the banks of the Eure river, this restaurant's terrace overlooks a stunning panorama of ancient houses, stone bridges, and weeping willows leaning into to the gently flowing water of the Eure, which is more of a stream than river at this juncture. A la carte you can order fois gras raviolis stuffed with black truffles for 29€ ($35) and calf sweetbread roasted with morels at 38€ ($46). Menus are at 32€ and 45€ ($38–$54) for three courses, which include a rabbit confit. If it is between the months of May and July, don't hesitate to get the menu *Le Retour du Marché* ("back from the market") at a ludicrously low 25€ ($30), which includes three courses often with such starters as provençale sardine tarts and beef carpaccio. Main courses may include asparagus risotto, a spice marinated pork, or even, believe it or not, kangaroo marinated in curry (we didn't believe it either — at which market are they shopping?). Relax, listen to the water flowing, and throw your breadcrumbs to the ducks that paddle along the current. To find rue de la Tannerie, head through old town, on rue au Lait, for example, in the direction of the Eure. The streets are very twisted and there is no perfect route. Once you end up at the bank, cross the nearest bridge — rue de la Tannerie follows along its East bank. If you have extra time, spend it by exploring the medieval cobbled streets of the **Old Town.** At the foot of the cathedral are lanes with gabled and turreted houses and humped bridges spanning the Eure River. The turreted Norman house (it's the oldest-looking one there) on rue Chantault, dates back nine centuries.

Stop in to the **Musée de Beaux-Arts de Chartres,** 29 Cloître Notre-Dame (☎ **02-37-90-45-80**), to see paintings by old masters such as Watteau, Brosamer, and Zurbarán, and admire the museum's architecture, some of which dates back to the 15th century. The museum is open Wednesday through Monday, 10 a.m. to noon and 2 to 5 p.m. (except on Sundays, when it opens only after 2 p.m.). It is closed on November 1 and 11 and Christmas day. Admission is 2.70€ ($3.25) and 1.40€ ($1.70) for children under 12 and senior citizens (students get in free).

Disneyland Paris

Disneyland Paris, known locally as *Le Parc Disneyland* (☎ **08-25-30-02-22** [0.15€/20¢ per min.]; www.disneylandparis.com), is France's number-one attraction, with more than 50 million visitors a year. When it opened in 1992 the French were dead set against it; now 40 percent of its visitors are French, and half of those are Parisian. Set on a 2,000-hectare (5,000-acre) site (about one-fifth the size of Paris) in the suburb of Marne-la-Vallée, the park incorporates the elements of its Disney predecessors but gives them a European flair. Allow at least a full day to see Disneyland Paris.

Information about hotels and packages is constantly changing, so your best bet for staying up to date is to obtain the Disneyland Resort Paris brochure from the Web site a few months in advance.

Getting there

To get to Disneyland Paris by train, take the **RER Line A** from the center of Paris (Invalides, Nation, or Châtelet–Les Halles) to Marne-la-Vallée/Chessy, a 35-minute ride. Trains run every 10 to 20 minutes, depending on the time of day. The station is at the entrance to the park.

Avoid lines at the resort by buying Disneyland passes at all RER A stations, except Marne-la-Vallée, and Métro stations including Charles-de-Gaulle–Etoile, Franklin-D-Roosevelt, Gare de Lyon, Porte Maillot, Esplanade de la Défense, Anvers, Père-Lachaise, Place de Clichy, Gallieni,

Havre-Caumartin, Villiers, Alésia, Barbès-Rochechouart, Châtelet, Denfert-Rochereau, and Gare de l'Est. The pass is good for either Disneyland Park or Walt Disney Studios but not both.

Within the park, a free shuttle bus connects the various hotels with the theme park, stopping every 6 to 15 minutes, depending on the time of year. Service begins an hour before the park opens and stops an hour after closing.

If you prefer to drive to Disneyland Paris, take the A4 highway east and exit at Park Euro Disney. Guest parking at any of the thousands of spaces costs 8€ ($9.60). A series of moving sidewalks speeds up pedestrian transit from the parking areas to the theme park entrance.

Exploring the park

The Disneyland Paris resort consists of two theme parks. The first, **Disneyland Park,** clusters together five "lands" of entertainment (Main Street, U.S.A; Frontierland; Adventureland; Fantasyland; and Discoveryland) and is where most of the massive and well-designed hotels, a nightlife center (Le Festival Disney), swimming pools, tennis courts, dozens of restaurants, shows, an aquarium, and the Manchester United Soccer School are located. If your kids are younger than 7, they'd be best suited for Main Street, U.S.A., Fantasyland, Sleeping Beauty's Castle, and the afternoon parade. Children ages 7 through 12 will most likely enjoy Frontierland, the Phantom Manor ghost house, the Big Thunder Mountain roller coaster, Adventureland, Indiana Jones and the Temple of Doom roller coaster, and the Pirates of the Caribbean ride. Discoveryland, the Space Mountain roller coaster, and the Star Tours simulated spacecraft ride should please your teens.

Walt Disney Studios Park is the newer of the two parks and is set up as a movie studio come to life, where children participate in the movie-making process. The entrance is called the Front Lot and resembles the Hollywood Disney studios — water tower, gates, and all. En Coulisse restaurant is located here, serving the kind of food kids like and Americans are known for — hamburgers, pizza, salads, and ice cream. In a film studio resembling a street, kids can become a part of the filming of impromptu comedy sketches as they walk around the park; later in the day, they get to see themselves on screen. In the Animation Courtyard, cartoon characters come to life via black light and mirrors, and children can play at being animators at interactive displays. The French Disney Channel has its studios here, in the Production Courtyard; kids get to see how a TV studio really works and may be asked to serve as extras. An international buffet, Rendez-Vous des Stars, is located here. The Back Lot features the Backlot Express Restaurant, serving sandwiches and other quick fare, and the Rock-n-Roller Coaster, a very fast and very loud ride (120 speakers playing Aerosmith) that whips you through an Aerosmith rock video. Calm down afterward by watching the stunt show spectacular, which is highlighted by a high-speed car chase. Food kiosks sell popcorn, ice cream, hot dogs, and so on throughout the park.

A guide for visitors in wheelchairs gives important information about access to rides and other attractions all around the park. You can pick up a copy at City Hall in the Disneyland Park or call to have a copy sent to you (☎ 01-60-30-60-30).

Admission (subject to change) to **either** Disneyland Park or the Walt Disney Studios Park for one day is 43€ ($52) for visitors 12 and older, 35€ ($42) for children ages 3 to 11 years, and free for children younger than 3. Admission for a one-day Everywhere Pass (called the *Passe-Partout*) good for unlimited access to **both** the theme park and the studios park costs 53€ ($64) for adults, 45€ ($54) ages 3 to 11; a two-day Pass is 96€ ($115) for adults and 79€ ($95) ages 3 to 11, the three-day pass is 115€ ($138) for adults and 95€ ($114) for children ages 3 to 11. Entrance to Le Festival Disney (a consortium of shops, dance clubs, and restaurants) is free; there's usually a cover charge for the dance clubs.

Disneyland Paris is open all year. Hours vary. From January to March the parks are open Monday to Friday 10 a.m. to 8 p.m. and weekends 9 a.m. to 8 p.m. From March to May the parks are open daily 9 a.m. to 8 p.m., and from the middle of June to the end of August daily from 9 a.m. to 11 p.m. From September to December, the scheduling hours become erratic during certain weekends due to various school holidays, and they also vary with the weather. Definitely call or check online before you go at the Web site and phone number listed in the first paragraph of this section.

Avoid waiting in long lines with the free **FASTPASS.** After presenting the pass at the ride you want, you're given a time frame for when to come back and board the ride first upon your return. Ask for it at the ticket booth or City Hall.

Staying at Disneyland

If you want to stay at Disneyland overnight or for a few days, you need to book well in advance. Plenty of hotels are available at different price levels, and you can explore the options and book accommodations on the park's Web site at www.disneylandparis.com.

Monet's Gardens at Giverny

Monet moved to Giverny (☎ 02-32-51-28-21; www.fondation-monet.com for Fondation Claude Monet, which runs the museum) in 1883, and the water lilies beneath the Japanese bridge in the garden and the flower garden became his regular subjects until his death in 1926. In 1966, the Monet family donated Giverny to the Académie des Beaux-Arts in Paris, perhaps the most prestigious fine-arts school in France, which subsequently opened the site to the public. Giverny has since become one of the most popular attractions in France, inspiring millions with its landscape and Provençal-themed house, but even the crowds can't completely overwhelm the magic.

Getting there

Catch an SNCF train at the Gare St-Lazare in Paris approximately every hour for the 45-minute trip to Vernon, the town nearest the Monet gardens. The round-trip fare is about 23€ ($28). From the station, buses make the 5km (3-mile) trip to the museum for 2€ ($2.40); a taxi ride will cost 5€ to 8€ ($6–$9.60); you can rent a bike in Vernon, or even go on foot — the route along the Seine makes for a nice walk.

If you're driving to Giverny, take the A13 highway from the Porte d'Auteuil to Bonnières, then D201 to Giverny. The whole trip takes about an hour.

Traveling to Giverny by tour bus is another option. **Cityrama,** 4 place des Pyramides, 1er (☎ **01-44-55-61-00;** www.cityrama.com), has two trips to Giverny: a five-hour trip on Tuesday through Saturday for 63€ ($76) adults, 32€ ($38) children 4 to 11 (children under age 4 ride free); and an all-day Giverny–Auvers-sur-Oise trip on Sunday or Wednesday for 105€ ($126) for adults, 95€ ($114) for children, which includes lunch at the American Museum. Call for specific dates. **Paris Vision,** 214 rue de Rivoli, 1er (☎ **01-42-60-30-01;** www.parisvision.com), offers two trips: a Versailles-Giverny all-day trip on Tuesday, Thursday, and Saturday that includes lunch at the **Moulin de Fourges** and a visit to the American Art Museum for 152€ ($183) for adults, 109€ ($132) for children; and a trip without the museum and lunch in the city of Versailles on Tuesday through Sunday for 116€ ($139) for adults and 85€ ($108) for children.

Exploring the gardens

Even before you arrive at Giverny, you probably have some idea of what you're going to see — but nothing prepares you for the spectacular beauty of seeing the gardens up close. The gardens are usually at their best in May, June, and July. Should you yearn to have them almost to yourself, plan to be at the gates when the gardens open, or go on a rainy day (June is probably the busiest month, although they will all be busy). You'll probably spend at least a half-day at Giverny, longer if you plan to eat lunch and visit the American Museum.

The gardens are open from April to November Tuesday through Sunday from 9:30 a.m. to 6 p.m., as well as Easter Monday and Whit Monday (51 days after Easter). Admission to the house and gardens is 6.60€ ($8) for adults, 4€ ($4.80) for students, and 3€ ($3.60) for ages 7 to 12 (children under age 7 get in free); admission to only the gardens is 4€ (4.80), and admission to only the house is 1.50€ ($1.80). No advance tickets are sold.

Some say Monet's influence was responsible for the influx of American artists into the village of Giverny in the late 1880s. Others say that Monet had little contact with the Americans, and it was Giverny's beauty that captured the hearts of painters such as John Singer Sargent and William Metcalf, who began spending their summers there. In any case, at one point, more than 50 American artists lived in Giverny with their

A calendar of flowers

Check the month corresponding to that of your visit (if it falls between Apr–Oct when Monet's gardens are open), and see the blooms in store.

✔ **April:** Tulips, pansies, forget-me-nots, narcissi, daffodils, cherry, and crabapple, lilacs

✔ **May:** Irises, peonies, rhododendrons, geraniums, wisteria

✔ **June:** Roses, poppies, clematis, tamaris

✔ **July:** Roses, rhododendrons, zinnias, dahlias, verbena, salvias, gladioli, beginning of water lilies, sunflowers, hollyhocks

✔ **August:** Dahlias, cosmos, hibiscus, end of water lilies

✔ **September:** Nasturtiums, asters, dahlias, cosmos

✔ **October:** Dahlias

families. You can see much of their work at the **Musée d'Art Américain Giverny** (☎ 02-32-51-94-65), just 91m (299 ft.) from Monet's house and gardens.

The museum is open April 1 through October 31, Tuesday through Sunday from 10 a.m. to 6 p.m., as well as Easter Monday and Whit Monday (51 days after Easter). Admission is 5.50€ ($6.60) for adults, 4€ ($4.80) for students and seniors, 3€ ($3.60) for ages 12 to 18, and free for children younger than 12. Admission is free for all on the first Sunday of every month.

Dining options

Your entry ticket is no longer valid once you leave Monet's home, so think ahead about whether you want to eat lunch before or after your visit. Most people arrive in early afternoon to have a better chance of avoiding the crowds in the morning.

The square directly across from Monet's house and the adjacent street have many little cafes and crêperies. But a short walk from the gardens is **Les Jardins de Giverny,** 5 Chemin du Roy (☎ 02-32-21-60-80). This beautiful and tranquil restaurant opens its doors onto a rose garden in warm weather and serves delicious regional specialties. A *trou Normand* (cider and Calvados sorbet) aids digestion between courses that may include an asparagus-filled puff pastry and warm oysters cooked in *beurre blanc* and cider with a frothy sorell *sabayon* (sauce made of whipped eggs and wine), or baby duck filet prepared with in-season fruits. Main courses cost between 19€ and 28€ ($23–$35). The 27€ ($32) and 37€ ($44) menus are better deals. Open Tuesday to Sunday noon to 3 p.m. and 7:30 to 10 p.m. Closed in winter.

Another good restaurant in town is **Le Relais Normand** (☎ **02-32-21-16-12**) in the Hôtel d'Evreux, an old Norman manor house with a fireplace and terrace. It serves such delicious dishes as roasted Normandy oysters with a nut and mushroom filling, beef filet with Livarot cream cheese, and duck filet with caramelized red fruit. The three prix-fixe menus cost 22€, 28€, and 32€ ($26, $34, and $38). The restaurant is open for lunch Tuesday through Sunday from noon to 3 p.m.

Part V
Living It Up After Dark: Paris Nightlife

The 5th Wave   By Rich Tennant

In this part . . .

Paris may not be a city that never sleeps, but it's just as fabulous after the sun sets as it is during the day. There is so much to do! Take your pick of French-language, English-language, or avant-garde theater, ballet, opera, symphony, and even cabaret spectacles like Moulin Rouge. But beware! Events can sell out quickly. Chapter 15 gives you the lowdown on Paris's vibrant theater scene and previews the symphony, opera, and ballet. Chapter 16 hits the bars and clubs, jumping jazz spots, live-music venues, classy cocktail joints, and those naughty cabarets.

Chapter 15

Applauding the Cultural Scene

● ●

In This Chapter

▶ Getting the inside scoop on the performing arts scene

▶ Finding out what's playing and getting tickets

▶ Taking in plays, symphony, opera, and dance in Paris

● ●

*T*his is the city that nurtured expats James Joyce, Eugene Ionescu, and Samuel Beckett; gave the world playwrights Molière, Victor Hugo, Pierre Corneille, and Jean Racine; and produced actors Sarah Bernhardt and Antonin Artaud. Fortunately for visitors, you don't need to understand French to take in an evening of culture here. Paris has a world-class orchestra, opera, ballet companies — and wonderful venues that house them. There's a flourishing English-language theater scene, and cutting-edge theater productions with scope and visuals that make language secondary!

This chapter helps you find out what's going on and then gets you there.

Getting the Inside Scoop

Paris is one of *the* places in the world to see top-tier ballet and listen to world-renowned symphonies. Unlike New York City, where theaters are located in the area around Broadway and 42nd streets, and serious music and ballet happen at Carnegie Hall and Lincoln Center, in Paris cultural offerings are scattered around the city, from the **Opéra Bastille** in the 12th to **Théâtre National de la Colline** in the 20th. The Opéra Bastille's director is **Gérard Mortier,** known for being cutting edge. A 2007 highlight here is: Verdi's Un Bal Masqué. The **Palais Garnier** presents in 2007 the French national ballet company's run of *Don Quixote,* following the choreography of the late monumental Russian ballet artist Rudolf Nuryev. In other spectacles, the Opéra Nationale will perform a several week run of *The Tales of Hoffman,* a widely appreciated opera by Jacques Offenbach featuring Grammy-nominated tenor Rolando Villazon, who sang in the 2005–06 season of *La Bohème* in the same theater.

Paris is home to a growing *early music* scene (music of the Middle Ages, Renaissance, baroque, rococo, and the early classical eras) led by the early music group **Les Arts Florissants,** which has performed operas in Paris's biggest venues. Check out the Web site of the Paris Convention and Visitors' Bureau (www.parisinfo.com) for venues and pricing.

The musical is a hot ticket here: Paris audiences were wild for *Le Petit Prince,* from the book by Antoine de Saint-Exupéry, and it was staged for a second season through 2004. This is an especially good run for a show in France: The concept of musical theater is different than in English-language theater, with a band in place of a full orchestra and a four-month run is considered successful. Songs from musicals are especially popular and mainstream in France, sometimes selling albums before the show even opens. If you see a show, don't be surprised to hear some of its music on the radio. At press time, *Le Comte de Monte-Cristo* was all the rage. Other upcoming musicals include *le Roi Soleil,* a historical fiction of France set to music and dance at the Palais des Sports, and a French adaptation of *Cabaret,* directed by Sam Mendes at the Folies Bergère.

On any given day, close to 100 theatrical productions may be going on in Paris and the surrounding area. Because Paris is just a three-and-a-half-hour Eurostar ride from London, some of that city's finest actors have found their way across the Channel and into the city's English-language theater community, where they joined up with American, Australian, and even some bilingual French *confrères* (colleagues). Productions in English may not be plentiful, but quality is high, and a wide range of styles is offered.

Arrive early to performances. On the reverse side of some Paris theater tickets may be written: *Les spectateurs retardaires ne peuvant à être placés que lors d'une interruption du spectacle et en fonction de l'accessibilité.* In other words, late arrivals cannot be seated until there is an interruption (intermission) in the play, if they are seated at all. Others may say *Pour bien garantir votre place, nous vous remercions en avance d'arriver un quart d'heure avant l'ouvrerture de la spectacle.* This means if you show up to the theater exactly at curtain-opening (instead of 15 minutes in advance), your seat may have been already given away depending on the popularity of the show. Opera tickets say: *Les spectateurs retardaires ne peuvent à être placés qu'à la fin du premier tableau, du premier acte de l'ouvrage ou à l'entracte,* meaning that late arrivals cannot be seated until the end of the first scene, the first act or between acts. Some theaters will not even seat those who arrive after the curtain rises, in many cases because the plays being performed are short with no intermission. You want to arrive at the theater or opera early anyway; the bars in these locations are generally very good and are relaxing places to unwind before the shows.

A *placeuse* (an usher, usually female) wearing a small purse around her neck will show you to your seats. Yes, that purse is for tips, which are expected; generally tip 1€ or 2€ ($1.20–$2.40) per person.

Dinner and a show

Because performances tend to start around 8 p.m. and French restaurants tend to open at 7 p.m., with dining lasting anywhere from one and a half to three hours and more, what's a hungry show-goer to do? Have a snack before the show, and feast afterward at one of the many cafes or brasseries open late. The following are listed in Chapter 10, and plenty more can be found around the city.

✔ **Au Pied de Cochon,** in the 1er, is open 24 hours.

✔ **Bofinger,** in the 4e, is open until 1 a.m.

✔ The Latin Quarter's infamous **Brasserie Balzar,** 5e, stays open until 11:45 p.m.

✔ **Brasserie Ile St-Louis,** on the tip of Ile St-Louis right across from Notre-Dame, is open until 1 a.m.

✔ **Café Marly,** 1er, in the Louvre's courtyard is open until 2 a.m.

✔ You can order food at showy **Fouquet's,** 8e, on the Champs-Elysées until 11:30 p.m.

✔ **La Coupole** on boulevard du Montparnasse, 14e, is open until 1:00 a.m., 1:30 a.m. on weekends.

✔ **La Tour de Monthélery/Chez Denise** is centrally located in the 1er and open 24 hours.

✔ **Le Mondrian,** 6e, serves snacks until dawn.

✔ **Le Zimmer,** 1er, at place du Châtelet, serves food until 12:30 a.m.

✔ Trendy **Man Ray,** in the 8e, serves food until midnight.

✔ St-Germain's **Vagenende,** 6e, stays open until 1 a.m.

 Paris audiences tend to dress up for performances, in nice jewelry and dressy pants or skirts for the women, jackets for the men. Generally, the nicer the venue, the dressier the look. Thus, for men a tie and jacket are recommended at the Palais Garnier, whereas an open collar under a stylish jacket would be the look for a performance at Bouffes du Nord.

Finding Out What's Playing and Getting Tickets

Several local publications provide up-to-the-minute listings of performances and other evening entertainment. *Pariscope: Une Semaine de Paris* (0.40€/48¢) is a weekly guide with thorough listings of movies, plays, ballet, art exhibits, clubs, and more. It can be found at any newsstand. *L'Officiel des Spectacles* (0.35€/42¢) is another weekly guide in French. *Paris Nuit* (3.05€/$3.65) is a French monthly that contains good articles

Saving money on tickets

For half-price theater tickets for national theaters and other venues, go to the **Kiosque-Théâtre** at the northwest corner of the Madeleine Church (directly across from no. 15 place de la Madeleine; Métro: Madeleine) to buy tickets for same-day performances. The panels all around the kiosk indicate sold-out shows with a little red man; a little green man tells you that tickets are still available. The Kiosque-Théâtre is open Tuesday through Saturday from 12:30 to 8 p.m., Sunday from 12:30 to 4 p.m. A second branch of the discount-ticket counter is located on the esplanade between the Tour Montparnasse and the Gare Montparnasse. Try to arrive no later than noon, because lines are usually long.

and listings. You can pick up the free music monthlies, *La Terrasse* and *Cadences,* outside concert venues. The *Paris Free Voice* is a free monthly publication that spotlights events of interest to English speakers, including poetry readings, plays, and literary evenings at English-language bookstores and libraries. You can find it at cybercafes and English-language bookstores or at www.parisvoice.com.

You can also get information on the Web from the **French Government Tourist Office** (www.francetourism.com), the **Paris Convention and Visitors' Bureau** (www.parisinfo.com), and the **Maison de la France** (www.franceguide.com). Likewise, try **Culture Kiosque** (www.culture kiosque.com) for excellent magazine-style sites about opera and dance, including schedules, reviews, and phone numbers for ordering tickets. The *Paris Free Voice* also has a Web site (www.parisvoice.com), featuring an events calendar and reviews of current opera, dance, and theater.

Ticket prices in this chapter are approximate; costs vary, depending on who is performing what on which day of the week. Call the theaters for information, or consult *Pariscope* and other entertainment listings. Many concert, theater, and dance tickets are sold through **Fnac** department stores and at the box office. You can find a dozen or so Fnac outlets throughout Paris; the most prominent is 74 av. des Champs-Elysées (Métro: George V). You can also reserve by phone at Fnac (☎ **08-92-68-36-22;** 0.45€/55¢ per min.) Monday through Friday from 9 a.m. to 8 p.m., Saturday from 10 a.m. to 5 p.m. Easier is **TicketNet** (www.ticketnet. fr), in French and English (look for the teeny, tiny British flag to the right of the Contact tab at the top of the welcome page), which allows you to buy tickets to cultural events online.

Raising the Curtain on the Performing Arts

The theaters listed here are national theaters supported by the government, but many private ones also exist. For full listings, consult *Pariscope:*

Une Semaine de Paris (.40€/48¢), a weekly guide with thorough listings of movies, plays, ballet, art exhibits, and clubs sold at all newsstands.

Attending the theater

A good mix of modern and classic tragedies and comedies comes alive in breathtaking performances in the **Salle Richelieu** of the **Comédie-Française,** 2 rue de Richelieu, 1er (☎ 01-44-58-15-15; www.comedie-francaise.fr; Métro: Palais-Royal–Musée du Louvre). Performances are in French. Tickets cost 11€ to 35€ ($13–$42). Last-minute seats are on sale one hour before the start of the performance; for ages 28 and older, one can purchase a section C ticket for 50 percent off, sometimes costing as low as 5€ ($6); and for people 27 and younger, an empty seat in sections A and B costs 10€ ($12). To purchase tickets up to 14 days in advance, phone daily from 11 a.m. to 6:30 p.m. (except Mar 24 and 25, May 1, and July 14, and the last Mon–first Fri of Sept). For those who want to buy tickets at the theater, the ticket window is open daily 11 a.m. to 6 p.m. To order tickets 15 days to two months in advance, fax information to ☎ 01-44-58-15-00 or purchase online (no phone reservations are accepted). *Note:* The Web site is in French with some English; pricing and other practical information is in French.

Also a part of the Comédie-Française, the **Théâtre du Vieux Colombier,** 21 rue Vieux Colombier, 6e (☎ 01-44-39-87-00/01; Métro: St-Sulpice), is an intimate 300-seat venue where mostly modern works are performed. Tickets cost 8€ to 28€ ($9.60–$34) for adults, 6€ to 13€ ($7.20–$16) for people under 27, and 6€ to 21€ ($7.20–$25) for seniors. To purchase tickets up to 14 days in advance, call daily 11 a.m. to 6:30 p.m. To order tickets 15 days to two months in advance, fax information to ☎ 01-44-39-87-02 or purchase online (no phone reservations are accepted).

The Comédie-Française also has a workshop in the **Carrousel du Louvre Studio-Théâtre,** where actors perform one-hour plays and readings. Video projections of plays and films are also shown here. Tickets are sold at the ticket window one hour before the performance and cost 7€ to 16€ ($8.40–$19) for adults, 5€ to 12€ ($6–$14) for seniors, and 4€ to 8€ ($4.80–$9.60) for people 27 and younger.

For popular, contemporary plays, the **Théâtre National de Chaillot,** 1 place du Trocadéro, 16e (☎ 01-53-65-30-00; www.theatre-chaillot.fr; Métro: Trocadéro), is your place. Part of the Art Deco Palais de Chaillot, the theater is located directly across the Seine from the Eiffel Tower. Tickets are 27€ to 33€ ($32–$40) for adults, 21€ to 27€ ($25–$32) for seniors and per person for groups of ten or larger, and 12€ to 17€ ($14–$20) for people 26 and younger. To purchase tickets by telephone, call Monday through Saturday 11 a.m. to 7 p.m. Box office hours are the same and you can also visit Sundays from 1 to 5 p.m.

The **Théâtre National de la Colline,** 15 rue Malte-Brun, 20e (☎ 01-44-62-52-52; www.colline.fr; Métro: Gambetta), has modern drama from around the world, and the **Petit Théâtre,** located upstairs, has short plays and offerings from international theater's less famous but up-and-coming playwrights. Arrive early to have a glass of wine and admire the view from the Café de la Colline in the lobby. Tickets cost 27€ ($32) for adults, 22€ ($26) for seniors, and 13€ ($16) for people younger than 30. On Tuesdays, adults and seniors pay 18€ ($22). To purchase tickets by phone, call Monday to Saturday from 11 a.m. to 6:30 p.m.; one can also visit the box office in person at these times, and sales of tickets commence 14 days before the play opens. After three years of work, one can finally see a show at the newly renovated **Odéon Théâtre de l'Europe,** 6 place de l'Odéon (☎ 01-44-85-40-00; www.theatre-odeon.fr; Métro: Odéon). During the interim, productions were housed at two locations, on 8 and 17 bd. Berthier, 17e, once home to the Opéra-Comique. Troupes will continue to perform in these wonderful Parisian spaces. Spectacles here are varied and eclectic (Lou Reed once read his poems at the Odéon). Tickets in the Berthier theatres are 26€ ($31) for adults, 20€ ($24) for seniors, and 13€ ($16) for people younger than 30. At Theatre de l'Odéon tickets range from 12€ to 30€ ($14–$36) for adults, 7.50€ to 20€ ($9–$24) for students, and 7.50€ to 22€ ($9–$26) for seniors. To purchase tickets by phone, call ☎ 01-44-85-40-40 Monday to Saturday 11 a.m. to 6:30 p.m. Tickets also go on sale at the box office at each of the theaters 90 minutes before the show.

Seeking English-language theater

Summer is a good time to catch English-language theater in Paris. The **Théâtre de Nesle,** 8 rue de Nesle, 6e (☎ 01-46-34-61-04; Métro: St-Michel), and **Les Déchargeurs,** 3 rue des Déchargeurs, 1er (☎ 01-42-36-00-02, reservations at ☎ 08-92-80-12-28; [.45€/55¢ per min.]; Métro: Châtelet), sometimes stage English-language plays. Or, for comedy in English, try **Laughing Matters,** which has recently moved to a new location in the salsa club La Java, 105 rue Faubourg du Temple, 10e (☎ 01-53-19-98-88; www.anythingmatters.com; Métro: Goncourt-Hôpital Saint-Louis). This company is thriving; the lineups are always terrific, featuring award-winning comics from the United States, the United Kingdom, Ireland, and Australia. Shows start at 8:30 p.m.; admission varies, but count on paying 20€ to 25€ ($24–$30) at the door.

Other English-language theaters include — the **International Players** (www.internationalplayers.info), a nonprofessional but still high-quality Anglophone theater company that performs musicals and plays in its space just outside of the city limits at La Salle des Arts, 3 rue de la République, St-Germain en Laye (RER: St-Germain en Laye). Past productions include *Sleeping Beauty* (2006), *The Pirates of Penzance* (2005), and *The Importance of Being Earnest* (2004). In 2007, a planned headline show was *Oklahoma!* Also, the international drama company **Drama Ties** (☎ 01-75-50-16-91), started in 1901, searches to spread theatrical expression and production, while encouraging the practice of Anglophone theater. Actors here put on their own original plays in English and use various theaters in and around Paris; last season included runs of *The Quest for the Gorgon's Head,* and *Snow White's Black Heart,* an adaptation by Hester Kamin.

And keep in mind that some theater isn't meant to be understood. In fact, sometimes *not* understanding the language can actually be a bonus. Several well-known avant-garde theater companies are located in Paris, including **Les Bouffes du Nord,** at 37Bis bd. Chapelle, 10e (☎ 01-46-07-34-50), run by the legendary Peter Brook, and **Le Théâtre du Soleil,** in the bois de Vincennes (☎ 01-43-74-24-08), known for its stunning adaptations of both classics and original works. Even though these performances are usually in French, the scope of these productions is so large, and the visuals so profound, you may not even notice that you haven't understood a single word.

Listening to classical music and the symphony

Classical music concerts occur throughout the year, and many of them are quite affordable. Look for flyers at churches announcing schedule times, prices, and locations.

More than a dozen Parisian churches regularly schedule relatively inexpensive organ recitals and concerts. The most glorious, where the music is nearly outdone by the gorgeous stained-glass windows, is **Sainte-Chapelle,** 4 bd. du Palais, 1e (☎ 01-44-07-12-38; Métro: Cité). Concerts take place every day at 7 and 8:30 p.m. You can also hear music at **St-Eustache,** 1 rue Montmartre, 1er (☎ 01-42-36-31-05; Métro: Les Halles); **St-Sulpice,** place St-Sulpice (☎ 01-46-33-21-78; Métro: St-Sulpice), which has an amazing eight-columned pipe organ concerts on most Sundays at 4 p.m.; **St-Germain-des-Prés,** place St-Germain-des-Prés (☎ 01-55-42-81-33; Métro: St-Germain-des-Prés); the **Madeleine,** place de la Madeleine (☎ 01-42-64-83-16; Métro: Madeleine); and **St-Louis en l'Ile,** 19 rue St-Louis-en-l'Ile (☎ 01-44-62-00-55; Métro: Pont-Marie). In a less magnificent setting, the Sunday concerts at the **American Church,** 65 quai d'Orsay (☎ 01-40-62-05-00; Métro: Invalides or Alma-Marceau), are friendly and inviting and take place at 5 p.m. from September to June.

Free concerts are staged occasionally in the parks and gardens. (See Chapter 3 for a calendar.) **Maison de la Radio,** 116 av. du President Kennedy, 16e (☎ 01-56-40-12-12; Métro: Kennedy-Radio France), offers free tickets to recordings of some concerts. Tickets are available on the spot an hour before the recording starts. The **Conservatoire National Superieur de Musique** at the Cité de la Musique, 209 av. Jean Jaurés, 19e (☎ 01-40-40-45-45; Métro: Porte de Pantin), stages free concerts and ballets performed by students at the conservatory, while the **Concert Hall** here (☎ 01-44-84-44-84) plays host to all types of performances, from jazz to world music.

Paris's is the **Salle Pleyel,** 252 rue du Faubourg-St-Honoré, 8e (☎ 01-42-56-13-13) is home to the Orchestre de Paris, and gives 50 concerts a year. The Radio France Philharmonic also plays about 20 concerts a year here, and the lucky traveler may catch a performance of the London Symphony orchestra, which often visits several times a season. This magnificent concert hall was closed for renovations from 2004 to 2006, and it reopened in September 2006. The hall has been acoustically fine-tuned and refurnished with more comfortable seating and promises some grand musical experiences. Reservations are best made by phone Monday to Friday 10 a.m. to 6 p.m. Senior citizens and youths under 27, take note: an hour before the show any available, last-minute tickets are offered at just 10€ ($12).

Enjoying opera and ballet

Whatever your choice of the classic arts — opera, ballet, concerts, recitals — you'll find it performed in Paris by local and international performers of the highest caliber in some of the most wonderful venues imaginable. Inaugurated in 1874, the **Châtelet, Théâtre Musical de Paris,** 1 place du Châtelet, 1er (☎ **01-40-28-28-40;** www.chatelet-theatre. com; Métro: Châtelet), is one of the top places to take in culture in Paris. Upcoming highlights include the Gabriel Fauré *Requiem,* a series of Brahms piano concertos, and the opera *Carmen,* scheduled for May 2007. Tickets range from 10€ to 120€ ($12–$144). The box office is open daily from 11 a.m. to 7 p.m. To make reservations by phone, call between 10 a.m. and 7 p.m. daily. There is a 2.50€ ($3) surcharge for Internet and phone reservations.

You can see dazzling performances by the national opera and ballet troupes at both the radiant **Palais Garnier,** place de l'Opéra, 9e (☎ **01-72-29-35-35** from abroad or **08-92-89-90-90** for reservations [.35€/45¢ per min.]; www.opera-de-paris.fr; Métro: Opéra; RER: Auber), and the ultramodern **Opéra National de Bastille** (see the next paragraph). The Palais Garnier conducts more ballet performances, and the Opéra Bastille puts on more opera. Tickets are priced from 7€ ($8.40) for seats that have little or no visibility to 300€ ($360) for the first row of the balcony. Reserve by phone up to four weeks in advance and buy at the ticket windows for performances up to 14 days in advance (including same-day tickets). Making reservations online or by phone adds a 3€ ($3.60) surcharge. The box office is open Monday through Saturday from 9 a.m. to 6 p.m.

The **Opéra National de la Bastille,** place de la Bastille, 12e (☎ **08-92-89-90-90** for reservations [35€/45¢ per min.]; www.opera-de-paris.fr; Métro: Bastille), offers first-class comfort and magnificent acoustics at each level of the auditorium, although Parisians tend to think the building is a badly designed eyesore (as with many new and modern structures, such as the Centre Pompidou and I.M. Pei's Louvre pyramid, Parisians do not always take well to very modern additions to their beloved capital; their reaction to the Eiffel tower was equally strong). The opera house is located at the place de la Bastille; at night, kids crowd the steps, showing off their skateboarding moves, talking on cellphones, and flirting. Tickets are priced between 5€ ($6) for reduced and no-visibility seats to 150€ ($180) for the front rows of orchestra and balcony seating. Reserve by phone up to four weeks in advance and buy at the ticket windows for performances up to 14 days in advance (including same-day tickets). The cheapest seats are on sale only at the box office. Making reservations online or by phone incurs a 3€ ($3.60) surcharge;

call Monday to Friday 9 a.m. to 6 p.m. and Saturday 9 a.m. to 1 p.m. to make a reservation by phone. The box office, located at 130 rue de Lyon (the side of the opera house facing the Bastille monument), is open Monday through Friday 11 a.m. to 6:30 p.m.

The other major venue for opera is the stunning Belle Époque **Opéra-Comique,** 5 rue Favart, 2e (☎ **01-42-44-45-47** for reservations; www. opera-comique.com; Métro: Richelieu-Drouot), which offers wonderful musical theater in the Salle Favart, a more intimate venue (the auditorium is so small you can hear people whispering onstage) than its opera hall counterparts. Jérome Savary, of American and French descent, is musical director; he will retire after the 2006–07 season. Tickets are priced from 7€ to 100€ ($8.40–$120) depending on the performance. The box office at place Boieldieu (front of the theater, 2e) is open Monday through Saturday from 10 a.m. to 6 p.m. and Sunday from 11 a.m. to 7 p.m.

Chapter 16

Hitting the Clubs and Bars

* *

In This Chapter

▶ Getting the lowdown on the latest hot spots
▶ Searching out your kind of music and dancing
▶ Unwinding over cocktails

* *

*W*hether you want to spend the evening talking over cocktails, chatting up the beautiful people, or dancing till you drop, Paris affords plenty of opportunities to paint the town *rouge*. Bars usually close around 2 a.m., but most clubs don't open until 11 p.m., and the music doesn't stop pumping until dawn. Check the listings (in French) in *Night Life, Nova,* or *Pariscope* magazines.

Hot Spots for Cool Jazz

You'll have a great time jitterbugging with the noisy crowd of foreigners and locals at the cozy and cavelike **Caveau de la Hûchette,** 5 rue de la Hûchette, 5e (☎ 01-43-26-65-05; Métro or RER: St-Michel), a legendary club that has been welcoming jazz bands for more than 50 years. Cover is 11€ ($13) Monday through Thursday; Friday through Sunday and the eve of a holiday it's 13€ ($16) between 9 p.m. and 1 a.m. Those under 25 pay 9€ ($11) every night. Music starts at 9:30 p.m.

Your best deal at **Le Petit Journal Saint-Michel,** 71 bd. St-Michel, 5e (☎ 01-43-26-28-59; www.petitjournalsaintmichel.com; Métro: Cluny-La-Sorbonne; RER: Luxembourg), is the 50€ ($60) menu, which includes cover charge, three-course meal, and a drink. For 45€ ($54) you can get a similar deal with two courses, or just pay a 17€ or 20€ ($20 or $24) cover for entry with a drink included (the cheaper entry is for non-alcoholic drinks). Open Monday to Saturday at 7 p.m. with concerts starting around 9:15 p.m. Check out also their sister club, **Le Petit Journal Montparnasse,** 13 rue de Commandant-Mouchotte, 14e (☎ 01-43-21-56-70; Métro: Gaîté).

Le Baiser Salé (the Dirty Kiss), 56 rue des Lombards, 1er (☎ 01-42-33-37-71; Métro: Châtelet), is a small space that gets crowded with fans of world beat. You can hear fusion jazz, funk, Brazilian, Afro-Caribbean, salsa, and merengue. The cover on Tuesday and Thursday through

Sunday varies from 13€ to 18€ ($16–$22). On Monday and Wednesday nights, admission is free. The club is open daily from 7 p.m. to 6 a.m. with concerts generally starting at 10 p.m. Just down the street is a terrific place to hear some of France's most interesting jazz. **Duc des Lombards,** 42 rue des Lombards, 1er (☎ **01-42-33-22-88;** www.ducdes lombards.com; Métro: Châtelet–Les Halles) is often crowded with casually dressed enthusiasts. A ticket to a show starts at 16€ ($19; buy tickets from their distributor at ☎ **01-42-94-97-76**). These two clubs, along with the other two Jazz clubs on rue des Lombards (**Le Sunset** and **Le Sunside,** both at no. 60, ☎ **01-40-26-46-60** and ☎ **01-40-26-21-25,** respectively) have formed an association, the "Paris Jazz Club," which allows a lover of Jazz to purchase one 20€ ($24) entry for all four places on a specific night. Call any of the above numbers or check the above Web site for details.

The best jazz musicians from around the world perform at **New Morning,** 7–9 rue des Petites-Ecuries, 10e (☎ **01-45-23-51-41;** www. newmorning.com; Métro: Château-d'Eau), one of Paris's best jazz clubs, where just a few of the illustrious players here have been Stan Getz, Miles Davis, and Wynton Marsalis. The venue opens at 8 p.m. and concerts start at 9 p.m. Cover starts at 17€ ($20), depending on the act.

The 1961 film featuring Louis Armstrong, *Paris Blues,* was shot at **Le Bilboquet,** 13 rue St-Benoit, 6e (☎ **01-45-48-81-84;** Métro: St-Germain-dès-Pres). You can eat your dinner downstairs and then ascend to the piano bar, where a copper-plated ceiling makes for some interesting acoustics. Legends such as Charlie Parker and Duke Ellington have played in this unique and classy establishment. Concerts start at 8:30 p.m. from Sunday to Thursday and at 9 p.m. on Fridays and Saturdays. There is no cover, but drinks can be expensive at the bar (around 10€/$12).

The more experimental, the better, in the cellar at **Le 7 Lézards,** 10 rue des Rosiers, 4e (☎ **01-48-87-08-97;** Métro: St-Paul). Depending on the performer, entry is free or can cost up to 16€ ($19). This is the place where jazz musicians go to wind down, and you can have a good meal in the restaurant upstairs beforehand. Check out the program on the Web at www.7lezards.com. Concerts start between 7 p.m. and 10 p.m.

Listening to Live Music

Cithéa, 114 rue Oberkampf, 11e (☎ **01-40-21-70-95;** Métro: Parmentier or Ménilmontant), is a strongly supported concert bar, whose funky patrons from this neck of Paris groove to an eclectic mix of world, jazz, and funk bands. You can catch concerts Wednesday through Saturday, and a DJ spins after midnight or whenever the bands aren't playing. Cover is free to 12€ ($14) depending on the entertainment and paid entry can include one drink. Open Tuesday to Saturday at 9 p.m., closing at 5:30 a.m. Tuesday through Thursday and 6:30 a.m. Friday and Saturday.

If you enjoy variety, or just being surprised, you may want to make the trip up to the "world's sofa," at **La Divan du Monde,** 75 rue des Martyrs, 18e (☎ 01-44-92-77-66; www.divandumonde.com; Métro: Pigalle). Truly a grand mix of styles, in short, this place is hip and the music eclectic. Concerts start anywhere from 7 to 10 p.m. Monday through Saturday and at 5 p.m. on Sunday. On weekends, a DJ spins music after the concerts until the early morning. Cover can be anywhere from free to 22€ ($26) depending on the act. Call for closing hours.

In another life, **La Flèche d'Or,** 102 bis rue de Bagnolet, 20e (☎ 01-44-64-01-02; www.flechedor.fr; Métro: Alexandre-Dumas), was the Charonne train station, but now it's a restaurant turned music venue. The club's weeknight openings vary, but you can count on its being in full-swing Thursday through Saturday from 8 p.m. until at least 2 a.m., and sometimes until 6 a.m. Cover ranges from free to 11€ ($13) depending on the act.

A little far off the beaten track, **Abracadabar,** 123 av. Jean Jaurès, 19e (☎ 01-42-03-18-04; www.abracadabar.fr; Métro: Laumière ou Ourcq), deserves a mention because it features some of the best live music in Paris in an intimate venue. Concerts and live shows range from and mix together reggae, dancehall, rock, funk and North African Arabic as well as hip hop and classic French. Best of all, the cover is never more than 3€ ($3.60) Opening at 6 p.m., concerts starting around 9 p.m., you can dance until 2 a.m. from Sunday to Wednesday, and until 5 a.m. from Thursday to Saturday.

Avril Lavigne, Dido, and Yannick Noah (once a popular French tennis player, now a popular singer) have all played at the trendy **La Scène Bastille,** 2 bis rue des Taillandiers, 11e (☎ 01-48-06-50-70; www.la-scene.com; Métro: Ledru-Rollin). There's a cozy lounge with caramel-colored padded walls, and room to dance to whatever music is playing. Nights without live bands are clubbing nights, led by a DJ. Concerts usually start at 10 p.m. and cost 10€ or 12€ ($12 or $14), nights with a DJ (check the Web site for calendar) usually cost 12€ or 14€ ($14 or $17).

Shaking Your Groove Thing at the Best Dance Clubs

You can always find someplace to dance the night away in Paris — and legions of Parisians eager to dance if not with you, then with their mirrored reflections! Paris clubs change their programming from night to night, with house *music de rigeur* at many places. Check *Pariscope* magazine for barge concert schedules. Salsa, the hottest trend a few years back, is still going strong as is techno, house, world, classic rock, or swing.

A word of advice: Some of these clubs have strict door policies and turn away those wearing sneakers, sweat suits, baseball caps, and shorts. Many nightclubs accept reservations, so if you're worried about getting past the bouncers, give your club of choice a call (or ask the concierge of your hotel to do it). To club on a budget, go out during the week when cover charges may be (officially or unofficially) waived. Yes, it's sexist, but women often get in free, especially if they're dressed in something slinky, low-cut, or short (or all three). Black clothes seem to be the rule for men and women, and the later you go — or earlier in the morning as the case may be — the more fashionable people get.

Barrio Latino, 46–48 rue du Faubourg-Saint-Antoine, 11e (☎ **01-55-78-84-75;** Métro: Bastille), is a restaurant/bar/club that delivers a terrific time — if you can get in. The lines here on weekends are enormous. It has three bars, private areas where you can see (but not be seen), a lounge complete with pool table, a second-floor restaurant serving Latino food, and energetic Latin music that sets everyone to dancing (and sweating!). Food ranges from hamburgers to Central, South American, and Caribbean specialties, each dish listed with its respective country. Open during the week from 11 a.m. to 2 a.m.; weekend club nights run until 5 a.m.

Unpretentious and *branché* all at the same time, **le Triptyque,** 142 rue Montmartre, 2e (☎ **01-40-28-05-55;** www.letriptyque.com; Métro: Grands Boulevards or Bourse) hosts clubbing nights and live music by music groups or hot and up-and-coming DJs in the American and European music scene. Unlike some snooty nightclubs in Paris, Triptyque is very much "do-your-own-thing" and no bouncers should give any trouble. Entry changes based on who is performing, but many nights are free, and paid nights are usually between 5€ to 8€ ($6–$9.60). Open on the weekends (Sun is house night) and most Wednesday nights, club nights start at 11 p.m. while concerts start at 8 p.m.

The Irish lightship **Batofar,** across from 11 quai François Mauriac, 13e (☎ **01-53-60-17-30;** Métro: Bibliothèque François Mitterand or Quai de la Gare), is a hot, sweaty, and ultimately fun time. Music can be anything from drum-and-bass to British pop, starting around 8 p.m., and the party can go on all night. Drinks, for which there is nearly always a line, are reasonable (4€–8€/$4.80–$9.60), the clientele are in their 20s and early 30s, and it can get crowded, but it's still worth it. Open daily, hours can change based on the night, but parties start no earlier than 6 p.m. and can last until to 5 a.m. Cover ranges from free to 15€ (18) depending on the band or DJ for the night. A small snack bar *(La Cantine)* is on board.

Elysée Montmartre, 72 bd. De Rochechouart, 18e (☎ **01-42-92-45-36;** Métro: Anvers), a club that serves the dual function of disco and major concert hall, is home to twice-monthly nights that pull in more than 1,000 clubbers. Moby, Björk, U2, and the Red Hot Chili Peppers are just some big musical acts that have headlined here. Check *Pariscope* for events and prices. Dances are usually held 11 p.m. to 5 a.m. Cover charges vary from 12€ to 25€ ($14–$30).

If you like house music, **Le Wax,** 15 rue Daval, 11e (☎ 01-40-21-16-16; Métro: Bastille) is the place for you. The club is the premiere place for "tek-house" and house DJs who spin it all night long. Décor here is very *Clockwork Orange,* with plastic bubbles on the walls, yellow plastic couches, and lots of crimson and orange. They even play disco on certain nights. Be warned, the bathrooms are especially psychedelic, especially after your second drink. Open Tuesday to Saturday 6 p.m. to 2 a.m. and Friday and Saturday 6 p.m. to 5 a.m. One of the best things about Le Wax is the price — it's free.

The basement dance hall at **La Coupole,** 102 bd. du Montparnasse, 14e (☎ 01-43-20-14-20; Métro: Vavin), is a retro venue with plush banquettes and old-fashioned sounds that's a big draw for locals and out-of-towners. Tuesdays and Fridays are salsa nights, with dance classes starting at 7:30 p.m. for 10€ ($12; including a drink) and lasting two hours; after this it becomes a regular salsa club. Brazilian music is played on Thursdays, and Saturday nights vary. Regular cover is 12€ ($14) on Thursdays and Saturdays. During the week, the club shuts down between 2 to 3 a.m., and Fridays and Saturdays the party lasts from midnight to 5:30 a.m.

Also in Montparnasse are possibly two of the most popular places to go clubbing; formerly L'Enfer, **Red Light,** 34 rue du Départ, 15e (☎ 01-42-79-94-53; www.enfer.fr; Métro: Montparnasse Bienvenue) is a medium-sized club that welcomes a maximum-sized crowd. With some seating and multiple raised platforms above the floor for those who dare to dance, you can see the trendiest kids in town wearing the newest fashions available. Cover can vary, usually it starts around 15€ ($18), but some nights are free: check the Web site to see if reduced or free passes can be printed out (usually you have to show up before a certain hour). Just around the corner is equally popular **Le Mix,** 24 rue de l'Arrivée (☎ 01-56-80-37-37; www.mixclub.fr; Métro: Montparnasse Bienvenue). Groove with the fashionistas at both of these clubs on Fridays and Saturdays until 5 a.m. to house and "tek-house" beats. Le Mix boasts spinning provided by music gurus Ministry of Sound and David Guetta (a holy name among Parisian clubbers). Le Mix also has a varying cover — many nights are free admission before midnight; always check on the Web beforehand. Sundays from 6 p.m. to midnight is the club's popular gay Tea Dance.

If you ever wanted to dance in a basement that is essentially under the Louvre, it doesn't get much classier than **Cab** (formerly Cabaret), 2 place du Palais Royal, 1er, (☎ 01-58-62-56-25; www.caberet.fr; Métro: Palais Royal-Musée du Louvre). Also a restaurant until 11 p.m., here you can rub shoulders with French models, businessmen and women, and the BCBG children of rich and old-name families. Dim indigo lighting illuminates black leather furniture that looks like it was grown and not assembled. There are two bars with shiny black or glass surfaces, and three different seating areas (not counting the VIP section!) Catch a seat, if you can, in the crawl-passage that runs through the club, adorned entirely in red-violet velvet. Music is usually house and electro, with various hip-hop songs and other American hits mixed in. A 20€ ($24) entry gets you in with one drink, and cocktails remain pricey, starting around 10€ ($12). The bouncers are picky and won't let you in if you're not properly dressed (women, trendy clothes with hair and makeup done, guys in shirts and trendy jeans at the least, slacks or a jacket can help; above all, no sneakers!). Open Wednesday and Friday through Sunday from 11:30 p.m. until 4:30 a.m.

Located next door to le Moulin Rouge, the huge trilevel **La Loco** (previously "La Locomotive"), 90 bd. de Clichy, 18e (☎ **01-53-41-88-89;** Métro: Blanche), is popular with American students and young people from Paris and the surrounding suburbs. Each level is devoted to house, techno, hip-hop, or raï (remixed traditional music, mostly from Algeria, but consisting of all the countries of the Mahgreb), so everyone can find their niche. The *sous-sol* (basement) is the most chilled out of the three levels, and you can even see the remnants of an old railway line (hence the name). Mixed drinks start at 9€ ($11), beer at 7€ ($8.40). Cover Monday through Thursday is 12€ ($14) without a drink and 14€ ($17) with one drink; cover on Friday is 5€ ($6) without a drink before midnight and 10€ ($12) with one drink, and 20€ ($24) with a drink after midnight (although it is not stated, women will generally get in for half-price or free). Free admission for women on Sundays until 1 a.m. Open 11 p.m. to 5 a.m.

On the outskirts of the Marais, and right next to the hoppin' Oberkampf neighborhood, is the small bar/club **Favela Chic,** 18 rue Faubourg du Temple, 11e (☎ **01-40-21-38-14;** Métro: République). Always packed, this Brazilian music venue bursts with energy. A restaurant by day, at night the long tables in the front area fill up with laughing 20 to 30 year olds of diverse backgrounds and ethnicities. The dance floor is also always packed, and big comfy couches and chairs line the best areas to dance, if you can snag one. The music is often remixed Brazilian clubbing fare, but there is also electro, hip-hop, and other eclectic selections made by the live DJs. It can get very sweaty, but drinks are reasonably priced (6€/$7 cocktails). Entry is free during the week and only 7€–10€ on weekends ($8.40–$12). Open Tuesdays through Thursdays from 7:30 p.m. to 2 a.m., on the weekends it stays open until 4 a.m.

Literally facing the door at the same address as Favela Chic is **Le Gibus** (☎ **01-47-00-78-88**), another popular dance club that is also less expensive and rocks all night. The DJs here play more popular dance music and top forties hits from the '70s to the '90s. A little less eclectic than its neighbor, it is still very popular among the diverse crowd and you will enjoy the lower-than-most 10€ ($12) cover charge that includes a drink. It occasionally hosts gay nights.

Opened in 1992 and still going strong, **Rex Club,** 5 bd. Poissonière, 2e (☎ **01-42-36-83-98;** Métro: Bonne Nouvelle), has been one of the most popular clubs for house and techno — if not *the* club — with Paris's best sound system and most popular DJs. September 2006 saw the Rex Club's reopening with a new general director. Open Wednesday to Saturday 11 p.m. to 6 a.m. Closed August. Admission averages 15€ ($18).

Stepping Out: The Gay and Lesbian Scene

Gay dance clubs and bars come and go so fast that even the magazines devoted to them, such as *Gai Pied Hebdo* and *Illico,* both distributed free in the gay bars and bookstores, have a hard time keeping up. For lesbians, try the magazines *Lesbia* or *La Dixième Muse* for club and bar listings in their classifieds section. Also look for *Gai Guide* and *Têtu,* which has a special insert section in every issue devoted to nightlife in all of France.

Amnesia Café, 42 rue Vieille-du-Temple, 4e (☎ 01-42-72-16-94; Métro: Hôtel-de-Ville), is a relaxed cafe/bar/bistro/club decorated in warm, coppery tones and furnished with comfortable leather chairs and banquettes. The cafe is open daily 10:30 a.m. to 2 a.m.; the club is open daily 8:30 p.m. to 2 a.m., later on the weekends.

Le Carré, 18 rue du Temple, 4e; (☎ 01-44-59-38-57) is a currently ultrahip bar and restaurant with modern décor. Eat dinner here until 1 a.m. on the terrace and watch all the people walk up into the depths of the Marais. Open daily until 2 a.m. weeknights; weekends can last until 4 a.m.

For clubbing before you go clubbing, head to **Mixer Bar,** 23 rue Sainte Croix de la Bretonnerie, 4e; (☎ 01-48-87-55-44; Métro: Hôtel de Ville). This multilevel bar comes with live house DJs, video and a mixed male/female crowd. Mostly lesbians handle one bar, the other is taken care of by gay men. Open daily until 2 a.m., and 5 a.m. on the weekends.

For those who thus enjoy the crowds and clubbing, **Raidd,** 23 rue du Temple, 4e (call the Open Café for details, see below; www.raiddbar.com; Métro: Hôtel de Ville) is the place for you. Dance, top-forties, and house music abound, and Raidd's a must-visit for those taking in the gay scene in Paris. Some nights have go-go dancers taking showers behind a glass wall. Open every day from 9 p.m. until 5 a.m.

The **Banana Café,** 13 rue de la Ferronerie, 1er (☎ 01-42-33-35-31; Métro: Châtelet–Les Halles), was once the most popular of gay bars in Paris. It still is very popular but the clientele has gotten less and less gay; expect to run into young drunk men looking for women. Open all night, it has a street-level bar and a dance floor *sous-sol* (in the basement) that has live piano music or a DJ. After 10 p.m., things get crazy, with go-go boys dancing on the bar (look for holiday themed costumes) or on platforms in the basement.

La Champmeslé, 4 rue Chabanais, 2e (☎ 01-42-96-85-20; Métro: Pyramides), a few blocks east of the avenue de l'Opéra, is one of the oldest lesbian bars of Paris, and features an older and more sophisticated crowd. This comfortable bar for women has cabaret singing each Thursday night, and once a month there are tarot card readings, art exhibitions, literary readings and other themed nights. Cocktails start at 8€ ($9.60), beer at 5€ ($6). Open daily noon to 2 a.m.

Bliss Kfé, 30 rue du Roi-de-Sicile (☎ **01-1/42-78-49-36;** www.bliss-kfe. com; Métro: Saint Paul or Hôtel de Ville), a former upscale *boulangerie* turned stylish, intimate lounge/bar, is a hangout for hip chicks. Although a primarily lesbian hangout, it is advertised as a mix of gay men and women. Open every day from 5 p.m. to 2 a.m.

Le Pulp, 25 bd. Poissonière, 2e (☎ **01-40-26-01-93;** Métro: Grands-Boulevards), is not only one of Paris's hippest lesbian clubs, but also a hip destination for *tout le monde* (everyone), especially on mixed Thursdays. Open Wednesday to Sunday 11p.m. to 5 a.m. Free Wednesday and Thursday, cover is 10€ ($12) Friday to Sunday.

Previously Les Scandaleuses, **le 3w Café,** 8 rue des Ecouffes, 4e (☎ **01-48-87-39-26;** Métro: St-Paul), sets a relaxed tone for a diverse mix of women, with styles running from pink-haired punk to denim and flannel. This place is simply jammed on weekends. Open daily 6 p.m. to 2 a.m.

Le Tango, 13 rue au Maire, 4e (**01-42-72-17-78;** www.boite-a-frissons. fr; Métro: Arts et Métiers) has mixed lesbian and gay parties Friday through Sunday. Truly a convivial place that doesn't play house or hard techno (disco, jazz, and French classics are played instead), here you can talk over the din easily. Sunday Tea Dance usually accompanies a drag show. Open at 11 p.m. and continuing until 4:30 a.m.

A new bar that looks very promising is **Oh Fada!** at 35 rue Ste-Croix de la Bretonnerie, 4e (☎ **01 40 29 44 40**). Started by the night club team "Follivores," (they organize gay parties throughout Paris), this bar is populated by a friendly and convivial crowd of a mixed age. Described as "atypique," it is becoming more and more popular among those who are tired of the gay-ghetto snobbism (but still want cute bartenders). Although it's on one of the most popular corners of the Marais, a sign inside reads *Ici on n'est pas dans Le Marais* ("Here you're not in the Marais").

Open Café, 17 rue des Archives, 4e (☎ **01-42-72-26-18;** Métro: Hôtel de Ville), is the classic gay watering hole of Paris, in business for years and still a favorite among locals and tourists. Basic cafe fare is served all day. Open Sunday to Thursday 11 a.m. to 2 a.m. and Friday and Saturday until around 4 a.m.

Le Vinyl (formerly le Scorp and le Scorpion), 25 bd. Poissonnière, 2e; (☎ **01-40-26-28-30;** Métro: Grands Boulevards) is an all-around popular dance club with strong gay overtones — it's so hip, straight people come here just for the good party. There are often drag shows and different nightly themes. The crowd tends to be young and two-thirds male. On Thursdays, Vinyl still hosts "Oh la la!" — a dance party with 100 percent French music ('60s to '80s pop) featuring live performances by nearly forgotten artists. Open seven days a week, usually not open before 11:30 p.m. and definitely not closed until dawn. Fridays and Saturdays are specifically gay, while the rest are equally gay-friendly.

Queen, 102 av. des Champs-Elysées, 8e (☎ 01-53-89-08-90; Métro: George V), is still one of the hottest clubs in town, with nightly crowds so thick you may find it difficult to get a drink. A walk-up balcony lets you watch the crowd from up high, and across the way is a stage suspended 6m (20 ft.) in the air, from which dancers perch and sway to the music. Monday night is "straight" night and is the most tame of the nights: weekends may include drag shows or strippers. Cover (including one drink, with or without alcohol) is 15€ ($18) Sunday and Tuesday to Thursday; Friday, Saturday, and Monday cover (including one drink, with or without alcohol) is 20€ ($24). Open daily from 11 p.m. to 7 a.m., till 8 a.m. on weekends.

For a fairly small dancing venue, **Folies Pigalle,** 11 place Pigalle, 9e; (☎ 01-48-78-25-56) is quite popular. The crowd is a genial mix of gays and straights (the gays say there are more straights, and vice versa), dancing and drinking in a former cabaretlike theater. The Sunday Tea Dance is a popular BBB night (Black, *Blanc et Beurres,* meaning black, white, and French North African Arabs, i.e. a multirace grouping). The Folies hosts a popular *afters* (after-hours party), which starts at 6 a.m. and goes on till noon.

Kicking Back with Classy Cocktails

If you're looking for a quiet, romantic place to unwind with a drink — or if you're on the prowl for where the hip, hot folks hang out — these places should fit the bill. Most bars and lounges in Paris open daily at 9 p.m., but no one arrives until after midnight. They generally close around 4 a.m.

At **Alcazar,** 62 rue Mazarine, 6e (☎ 01-53-10-19-99; Métro: Odéon), elements of traditional brasserie style, such as banquettes and mirrors, are slicked up with modern flair and mixed with innovations such as a glassed-in kitchen theatrically installed along the left wall.

Bob Cool, 15 rue des Grands Augustins, 6e (☎ 46-33-33-77; Métro: Odéon or St-Michel), enjoys a hip and down-to-earth clientele, made up of all ages of the literary St-Germain-des-Prés crowd. Aspiring writers and artists collect around the antique oak bar and open up their laptops on the tables in the front room. The back room's banquettes play host to a cool crowd, especially during the workweek Happy Hour between 5 and 9 p.m., when two drinks go for the price of one. Clientele ranges in age from 18 to 70, and all are welcome. Open Monday to Saturday 5 p.m. to 2 a.m.

You can enjoy **China Club,** 50 rue de Charenton, 12e (☎ 01-43-43-82-02; Métro: Bastille), a popular bar/restaurant near the Bastille, for its basement piano bar, its ground-floor restaurant, or best, its first-floor bar evoking an opium den of the 1930s. The atmosphere is one of hushed, Colonial-decorated elegance. All cocktails are well made (8€/$9.60), but the Chinese food is overpriced.

In the swanky neighborhood of the Champs-Elysées is **Nirvana Lounge,** 3 av. Matignon, 8e (☎ **01-53-89-18-91;** Métro: Franklin D. Roosevelt), with a bright pink entrance with flashy curves, and celebutante clientele. The lounge music playing is this place's own, released every year and sold at the bar. The food is quite good but super expensive, just like everything else here. Cocktails are great as well, if you don't mind spending more than 12€ ($14) a pop. Open every day, from 8 a.m. all the way to 2 a.m.

Founded in 1911, French locals still mingle with tourists at **Harry's New York Bar,** 5 rue Daunou, 2e (☎ **01-42-61-71-14;** Métro: Opéra or Pyramides). It's been one of Europe's most famous bars, as popular today as it was in the time of that notorious Lost Generation of writers who really knew how to ring up a bar tab. It is said that the Bloody Mary was invented here, and the selection of whiskey is amazing. Make sure you step downstairs if only to look at the 1930s Piano Bar, which resembles the inside of a cozy yacht. Open every day from 10:30 a.m. to 4 a.m.

The très delicious specialty *flammenkeuche* — large, square, thin-crusted pizzas topped with cream, herbs, and goodies such as salmon, ham, and goat cheese — draws a trendy crowd to **La Fabrique,** 53 rue du Faubourg St-Antoine, 11e (☎ **01-43-07-67-07;** Métro: Bastille). This restaurant is sleek, the bar is minimalist, and the color to wear appears to be black. Although the bar is open until around 4 a.m., depending on the crowds, food is served only until midnight. Be ready to stand in line on the weekends, and look out for private parties when the restaurant is closed to the public. Open every day from 9 a.m. to 4 a.m.

In a neighborhood juxtaposed with chic and grunge, **Café Etienne Marcel,** 34 rue Etienne Marcel, 2e (☎ **01-45-08-01-03;** Métro: Etienne Marcel) is another funky Paris hangout under the care of the experts of chic, the Costes brothers. White plastic seats and walls with bold colors and graffiti art make for a fine place to order a complicated drink. The music playing is from the yearly release of the *Hôtel Costes* CDs. Open every day from 11 a.m. to 2 a.m.

Le Bar, in the Hotel Plaza-Athénée, 25 av. Montaigne, 8e (☎ **01-53-67-66-65;** Métro: Alma-Marceau), is one of the in spots in Paris, where a crowd with champagne taste sips drinks that cost more than some bottles of wine. Unless you're somebody (or on the arm of somebody), there's no guarantee you'll get in, and when you do, be prepared to withstand the once-over you'll receive from the other fabulously-dressed folk. Service is reportedly slow at times. Drinks start at 20€ ($24).

The **Lizard Lounge,** 18 rue du Bourg-Tibourg, 4e (☎ **01-42-72-81-34;** Métro: Hôtel-de-Ville), is stylish yet easygoing and a pleasant place to hang out with an arty, international crowd. The music is loud, but the heavy-gauge steel balcony overlooking the main bar offers a chance for quieter conversation. Even the bathrooms have funky décor, with their lizard logo inlaid on some surfaces. You can also come early in the evening for a reasonably priced light meal prepared in the open kitchen.

Live bands play or a DJ spins dance music in the refurbished basement weeknights (except Mon) and all weekend.

Sit outside for fantastic people watching, or choose from three floors of funky art-covered walls and sit in one of the antique chairs at **Les Etages,** 5 rue de Buci, 6e (☎ 01-46-34-26-26). Popular among young professionals, the cocktails list here is extensive and complete: Try all sorts of champagne-mixed fruit cocktails, or trust their bartenders to mix you something stronger but with just as much flavor. You can eat as many of their fantastic honey-roasted peanuts as you want, but after two refills, they will definitely give a judgmental glare. Open every day from 11 to 2 a.m.

Don't visit **Mandala Ray** (formerly Man Ray), 34 rue Marbeuf, 8e (☎ 01-56-88-36-36; Métro: Franklin-D-Roosevelt), for dinner. Have a drink at the upstairs bar instead while listening to jazz Monday through Thursday (but do visit the enormous downstairs to see the statues of two winged Asian goddesses, who appear concerned — possibly about the food). Clubbing begins around 11 p.m. (around 20€/$24 cover) when the restaurant winds down, the music takes on a harder edge, and a sleek international crowd stands shoulder to shoulder along the curving bar. American artist and photographer Man Ray's photos adorn several walls. Celebrity owners include Sean Penn, Johnny Depp, and John Malkovich. Open from 7 p.m. to 2 a.m. during the week, and until 5 a.m. on the weekends.

A night at the Casbah

A popular trend nowadays is Arabic-themed bars, cafes, and tea salons — in these places you can get Turkish coffee, mint tea, regional sweets and dishes (and almost always, some hummus). The biggest attraction, however, are the hookah pipes filled with fruit-flavored tobaccos (smoking a hookah is referred to as smoking *shisha* or *nargila* in countless spelling and variations). Paris boasts big North African, Egyptian, Turkish, and Middle Eastern populations, many of whom enjoy a good smoke now and again, perhaps to the accompaniment of an *oud* (a Middle Eastern string instrument) player. These are not technically bars, and you usually can't get alcoholic drinks here. However, a pot of mint tea, some jasmine-flavored hookah, and some fantastic Arabic music can be a fun evening out.

✔ **Le Scarabee** (5 rue des Trois Frères, 18e; ☎ 01-42-52-05-94; Métro: Anvers) is Egyptian owned (and decorated) and boasts comfortable floor cushions and tasty honey-filled and sugary desserts, all with happy, smiling service to boot. Definitely try the mint tea here.

✔ **New Baghdad** (13 rue Monsieur le Prince, 6e; ☎ 01-40-46-99-51; Métro: Odéon) is always crowded with French North Africans and boasts — of all things — some truly delicious and thick milkshakes.

✔ **Eddar** (7 rue St-Sabin, 11e; ☎ 01-43-57-17-81; Métro: Chemin Vert) has fun décor and sometimes live music or traditional singing — in the very popular Bastille/Oberkampf area.

Spending an Evening at a French Cabaret

Parisian cabarets had a reputation for sensual naughtiness long before Josephine Baker danced bare-breasted in a G-string adorned with bananas at Folies Bergères in the 1920s. Although Edith Piaf and Maurice Chevalier were highlights at venues like the Moulin Rouge, today it's the topless can-can dancers who draw in the crowds. The dancers are often overshadowed by light shows, special effects, and tinny recorded music, but if you're expecting to see lots of flesh in today's Parisian revues, you won't be disappointed. The shows are highly overrated and very expensive but continue to be a huge attraction for tourists. The infamous Folies Bergères no longer exists as a cabaret; it's now a concert hall.

When seeing a Parisian cabaret show, have dinner somewhere else and save yourself some cash. For the money you'd spend at the cabaret, you can have an absolutely fabulous meal at one of the pricier suggestions in Chapter 10. Some of the cabarets admit children, though not kids younger than 4. Be aware that every other member of the audience may be from another country — these are some of the least Parisian experiences you can have while still being in Paris.

At the **Crazy Horse, Paris,** 12 av. George V, 8e (☎ **01-47-23-32-32;** www. lecrazyhorseparis.com; Métro: George V), one can see at this moment their celebrated show, *Taboo,* a striptease show that highlights each dancer (who have names like Vanity Starlight, Bee Bee Opaline, and Nooka Karamel). Cover and two drinks cost from 50€ ($60) at the bar (35€/$42 if you're under 26 with one drink) to 110€ ($132) in the orchestra with a half-bottle of "Grand Marque" champagne. Special dinner-show packages with restaurants De Vez, Chez Francis, and Fouquet's start at 115€ ($138). Two shows nightly at 8:30 and 11 p.m., with three shows on Saturday at 8 p.m., 10:15 p.m., and 12:15 a.m.

The **Lido,** 116 av. des Champs-Elysées, 8e (☎ **01-40-76-56-10;** www.lido. fr; Métro: George V), celebrated in 2006 its 60th anniversary by inviting couples celebrating their own 60th anniversaries and giving them a gift of a specially printed photo of the octogenarians enjoying the burlesque. Chef Philippe Lacroix runs a team of 35 sous and pastry chefs, and the turnout is pretty good, but it doesn't justify the ticket price. Its revue, *C'est Magique,* offers "flying" and "swimming" dancers, and an ascending stage that periodically delivers feathered women, fountains, and an ice rink, as well as high-tech laser lighting and video projections. The other show, *Bonheur,* features a woman singing French *chansons* (songs), and is supposedly the most expensive spectacle in Europe, The show with dinner and a half-bottle of champagne costs 140€ to 210€ ($168–$252); with just drinks, the show starts at 80€ ($96) for the later show at 11:30 p.m., and 100€ ($120) for the earlier show at 9:30 p.m.

Probably of the most famous of the cabarets, the **Moulin Rouge,** place Blanche, Montmartre, 18e (☎ **01-53-09-82-82;** www.moulinrouge.fr; Métro: place Blanche), has been packing in crowds since 1889, and its signature can-can dancers, made famous in paintings by Toulouse-Lautrec, still bare breasts in the show's finale today. Edith Piaf, Yves Montand, and Charles Aznavour made their reputations at the Moulin Rouge, and even Frank Sinatra performed here. The show *Féerie* features comedy, animal, and magic acts with the requisite scantily clad women bumping and grinding around the stage. Table seats have better views than seats at the bar. A bar seat and two drinks cost 97€ ($116) for the 9 p.m. show, 87€ ($104) for the 11 p.m. show. Dinner followed by the 9 p.m. show costs 140€ to 170€ ($168–$204); you must arrive for dinner by 7 p.m.

Probably the most French of the cabarets is the **Paradis Latin,** 28 rue Cardinal-Lemoine, 5e (☎ **01-43-25-28-28;** www.paradislatin.fr; Métro: Cardinal-Lemoine), designed by Gustave Eiffel. A genial master encourages audience participation during a show that's less gimmick-filled than the others. To save money, forgo dinner for the lower-priced Champagne Revue, which includes a half-bottle of bubbly and costs 80€ ($96); dinner (at 8 p.m.) plus show packages range from 114€ to 200€ ($137–$240). Performances are Wednesday through Monday, with a 9:30 p.m. showtime.

Part VI
The Part of Tens

The 5th Wave   By Rich Tennant

"It serves you right for requesting a lap-dance from someone doing the can-can."

In this part . . .

Okay, these little extras won't make or break your trip, but they may just make it a little more fun. In Chapter 17, we give you the inside scoop on where to find spectacular views of the city — without the other tourists. In Chapter 18, we show you where to make like Manet and have *déjeuner sur l'herbe* — in other words, the best places to go for a fabulous picnic.

Chapter 17

Ten (Well, Nine) Places to See Paris — Without the Lines

In This Chapter

▶ Finding a fantastic panorama off the beaten path

▶ Discovering some special Paris vistas

*W*ith wait times at the Eiffel Tower guaranteed to exceed an hour and sometimes two in high season (and not a whole lot less at the Arc de Triomphe) you may wish you could spend the time differently. Fortunately, there are lots of other places to observe Paris vistas without long lines, if any. Some are even free!

Galeries Lafayette

The sixth floor cafeteria of Galeries Lafayette's main store, 40 bd. Haussmann, 9e (☎ 01-42-82-34-56; Métro: Opéra or Chaussée-d'Antin), is sleek and modern and sells fresh hot and cold food. But one of the best reasons to come here is for the views over the rooftops of Paris. If you're not hungry for a meal, at least try the delicious hand-scooped ice cream from the cart here, grab a table beside a window, and enjoy!! See Chapter 12.

La Madeleine

See rue Royale, place de la Concorde and the obelisk, and, across the Seine, the dome of Invalides after climbing the 28 steps of La Madeleine church, place de la Madeleine, 8e (☎ 01-44-51-69-00; Métro: Madeleine). After taking in the view, pop inside to see Rude's *Le Baptême du Christ*, which is on the left as you enter. See Chapter 11.

Panthéon

A spectacular view of the Eiffel Tower and the surrounding neighbor-hoods is available from the Panthéon's dome, place du Panthéon, 5e (☎ 01-44-32-18-00; Métro: Cardinal-Lemoine or Maubert-Mutualité; Bus: 21, 27, 83, 84, 85, 89). This museum, once a mausoleum that was once a church built in honor of the patron saint of Paris now boasts Foucault's pendulum hanging from the domed ceiling. The hill on which the Panthéon is built is a terrific place to see fireworks on Bastille Day. See Chapter 11.

Parc de Belleville

It's off-the-beaten track, sure, but this park in the 20e offers tree-lined promenades (more than 500 trees are here) and magnificent Left Bank views peeping through the spaces between pretty houses. Beds of roses and other seasonal flowers line walks and views of the city's Left Bank become more pronounced the higher up the terraced pathways you go. (Located in the 20e; take the Métro to Pyrénées, then walk down rue de Belleville and turn left onto rue Piat where you see arched iron gates leading into the park; you can also take the Métro to Courrones, cross boulevard de Belleville and turn left onto rue Julien Lacroix where another entrance is located.) See Chapter 11.

Pont des Arts

This steel-and-wood, seven-arched, pedestrian-only footbridge connects the entrance to the Louvre on one end with the magnificent Acadèmie Français on the other. The walk across offers breathtaking views all across the river, but especially of the tree-lined tip of Ile de la Cité with the spires of Notre-Dame and Sainte-Chapelle, the turrets of the Conciergerie and the fabulous curving, white apartment and judicial buildings. (Métro: Pont Neuf; walk west along quai de Louvre or quai de la Conti. It's the bridge directly to the west of Pont Neuf.)

Restaurant Georges at the Centre Georges Pompidou

It used to be that visitors to the Centre Georges Pompidou could skip the museum entirely and ride the escalators on the outside of the build-ing (enclosed in a plastic tube like a giant gerbil habitat) to the top for breathtaking views of the city. That's no longer permitted; you need to buy a ticket for the museum first. Unless, of course, you have drinks, lunch, or dinner at the trendy Costes brothers restaurant Georges (you need a reservation to gain access to the floor). The entrance is to the left of the museum's main entrance, 19 rue Beaubourg, 4e (☎ 01-44-78-47-99; Métro: Rambuteau or Châtelet). See Chapter 11.

Sacré Coeur

To see the view from Sacré Coeur in the 18e, 25 rue du Chevalier-de-la-Barre, 18e (☎ 01-53-41-89-00; Métro: Anvers — take the elevator up and follow signs to the *funiculaire,* which runs to the church; Bus: the local Montmartrobus is the only bus that goes to the top of the hill), you have two choices: The first method is the free panorama from the wall just in front of the church (use the coin-operated viewing machines); or you can pay 5€ ($6) to visit Sacré Coeur's dome. To reach the dome, face the church and walk around to its left side, following signs for the Dome and Crypte. Walk down a set of stairs and follow a walkway about 15m (50 ft.) to an iron gate. The entrance and ticket machine are on your right. The climb from church floor to dome is up a flight of nail-bitingly steep corkscrew steps, but the view is worth it. See Chapter 11.

Tour Montparnasse

At a height of 207m (689 ft.), the Tour Montparnasse, 33 av. du Maine, 15e (that looming black skyscraper on the Left Bank; ☎ 01-45-38-52-56; Métro: Montparnasse-Bienvenüe), towers above Paris, and from its panoramic roof terrace on the 56th floor, you can see as far as 40km (nearly 25 miles) in nice weather. Right next to the Gare du Montparnasse, it's a bit pricey (9€/$11 adults, 6.50€/$8 students 16–20 years, 4€/$4.80 ages 7–15), but the views are exceptional — you've never seen Paris like this! See Chapter 12.

The Towers at Notre Dame

Climb 387 narrow and winding steps to the top of one of the towers here for Quasimodo's view of the gargoyles and of Paris below. Our advice: If you plan to visit the tower, go early in the morning! Lines stretch down the square in front of the cathedral during the summer. It's at 6 Parvis Notre-Dame, Ile de la Cité, 4e (☎ 01-42-34-56-10; Métro: Cité or St-Michel; RER: St-Michel; Bus: 21, 38, 85, 96). See Chapter 11.

Chapter 18

Ten Plus Great Places for a Picnic

In This Chapter

▶ Finding that special place to enjoy a meal in *plein air* (fresh air)

▶ Enjoying Paris like a Parisian

*P*ick up some delicious meats, sweets, and wine (see Chapter 12 for recommendations) from one of Paris's open-air markets, *traiteurs* (gourmet food shops), and grocery stores and enjoy an open-air feast without the worry of tipping or dressing to dine. Best of all, you can lay down for a snooze right after you eat.

A word of advice: Such parks as the Luxembourg Gardens or the Tuileries jealously guard their lawns; you may have to walk a bit before you find a spot where you can spread out on the grass. But chairs are everywhere — some even have reclining backs! — and you can pull a few right up to a fountain and eat amidst the spray from the water. If this seems too public, your best bet is to try the vast Bois de Vincennes or Bois de Boulogne where you can picnic nearly anywhere. Don't forget to clean up afterward.

Banks of the Seine near the Musée de Sculpture en Plein Air

Twenty-nine artists created abstract works that complement the meditative mood that the banks of the Seine inspire (kids climb all over them). Sculptures include those by French sculptor César Baldaccini and the Belarorussian Ossip Zadkine. Wander amid the sculptures before you spread out your meal in this waterside park that's really a museum (the name **Musée de Sculpture en Plein Air** translates to *Open-Air Sculpture Museum*) (Métro: Sully-Morland or Gare d'Austerlitz).

Bois de Boulogne

A former royal forest and hunting ground, this vast reserve of more than 880 hectares (2,200 acres) with jogging paths, horseback riding paths, cycling (rentals are available), and boating on two lakes. Picnic areas are abundant here. The **Longchamp** and **Auteuil racecourses** are located here, as is the **Jardin Shakespeare** in the Pré Catelan, a garden containing many of the plants and herbs mentioned in Shakespeare's plays (Métro: Porte Maillot, Porte Dauphine, or Porte Auteuil).

Bois de Vincennes

Rent canoes or bikes or visit the **parc Zoologique** (zoo) and petting zoo after you picnic on the extensive grounds at the Bois de Vincennes, which also has a Buddhist center, complete with a temple. The Chateau de Vincennes, where early monarchs such as Charles V and Henri III sought refuge from wars is also the place where Mata Hari met her demise. The **parc Floral de Paris** (☎ 01-43-43-92-95) is here with its spectacular amphitheatre (and jazz concerts on summer Sat), a butterfly garden, library, and miniature golf (Métro: Porte Dorée or Chateau de Vincennes).

Jardin des Tuileries

The Tuileries is a restful space in the center of Paris that houses the Orangerie and the Jeu de Paume at its western edge and plays home to 40 beautiful Maillol bronzes scattered among the trees to its east. This spot is the city's most formal garden, with pathways and fountains that invite you to sit on the metal chairs provided and munch on picnic treats while cooling off in the breezes off the waters.

The name means *tuiles* (tiles) — the clay here was once used to make roof tiles. The gardens were originally laid out in the 1560s for Catherine de Medici in front of the Tuileries Palace (which burned down in 1871). In the 17th century, landscape artist André Le Nôtre, creator of the gardens at Versailles, redesigned a large section (Métro: Tuileries or Concorde).

Jardin du Luxembourg

You can sit on metal chairs near the boat pond or spread out on grass open to picnickers directly across from the Palais de Luxembourg, on the park's south edge. Not far from the Sorbonne and just south of the Latin Quarter, the large park is popular with students and children, so it isn't the quietest of places. Besides pools, fountains, and statues of queens and poets, tennis and *boules* (lawn bowling) courts are available. See whether you can find the miniature Statue of Liberty (Métro: Odéon; RER: Luxembourg).

Parc de Belleville

Though the parc de Belleville is out of the way, it's still a wonderful place to visit with children, watch the sun set across western Paris, or nosh on a baguette with *saucisson sec* (cured sliced sausage, a bit like French salami). The park has fountains, a children's play area, an open-air theater with concerts during the summer, rock formations, and grottoes that evoke the long-ago days when the hill was a strategic point to fight enemies like Attila the Hun. Beds of roses and other seasonal flowers line the walks, and views of the city's Left Bank become more pronounced the higher up the terraced pathways you go.

Access the park by taking the rue Piat off rue Belleville and enter through an iron gate spelling out the words *Villa Ottoz.* A curved path leads you to tree-lined promenades (more than 500 trees are here) with the first of the magnificent Left Bank views peeping through the spaces between pretty houses. Take the Métro to Pyrénées; then walk down rue de Belleville and turn left onto rue Piat, where you see arched iron gates leading into the park. You can also take the Métro to Courrones, cross boulevard de Belleville, and turn left onto rue Julien Lacroix where another entrance is located.

Parc de la Villette

Picnic at Parc de la Villette in the summer while watching an outdoor movie or listening to a concert. Afterward, you and your kids can visit the enormous children's museum complex, the **Cité des Sciences et de l'Industrie** (Museum of Science and Industry), and the **Musée de la Musique** (Music Museum), located on the grounds. This modern park has a series of theme gardens and includes an exotic bamboo garden and a garden featuring steam and water jets. Scattered throughout the park are playgrounds and other attractions (see Chapter 13). The most fun way to get here is to take a canal trip from Pont l'Arsenal or the Musée d'Orsay (see Chapter 11). You can also take the Métro to Porte de la Villette.

Parc des Buttes-Chaumont

Parc des Buttes-Chaumont is one of the four man-made parks that Napoléon III commissioned to resemble the English gardens he grew to love during his exile in England. Built on the site of a former gypsum (a mineral used to make plaster) quarry and a centuries-old dump, it features cliffs, waterfalls, a lake, and a cave topped by a temple. You have plenty of places to lay out your picnic spread here. For a pleasurable walk to further whet your appetite, exit at Métro Danube. Walk east along rue David d'Angers until you find villa du Danube, a sloping road. Follow this through to villa de la Renaissance, and you will discover rue de Mouzaïa: along this walk and around here you can wander beautiful cobblestoned streets (all called "villa" something with houses that look nothing like the rest of Paris, sporting ivied balconies and Provençale-style roofs (Métro: Buttes-Chaumont or Danube).

Parc du Champ de Mars

Once a parade ground for French troops, parc du Champ de Mars is the vast green lawn beneath the Eiffel Tower, extending to the École Militaire (Military Academy), at its southeast end, where Napoléon was once a student. You have plenty of places to relax and contemplate the tower. If you have an evening picnic (bring wine, it's okay, everyone else does it!), you can count the hours passing by watching the blinking lights go on and off on the Eiffel tower (up until 1 a.m.); listen for cheers and "awwww"s as people admire the Parisian symbol. After your picnic, take a boat tour of the Seine from the nearby Bateaux Mouches (Métro: Bir-Hakeim).

Parc Monceau

Marcel Proust's favorite park, Monceau allegedly contains Paris's largest tree — an Oriental plane tree with a circumference of almost 7m (23 ft.). The painter Carmontelle designed several structures for parc Monceau, including a Dutch windmill, a Roman temple, a covered bridge, a water-fall, a farm, medieval ruins, and a pagoda. Garnerin, the world's first parachutist, landed here. In the mid-19th century, the park was redesigned in the English style. There is a small shop near the entrance where one can buy sweets and drinks, however, we suggest visiting a local *boulangerie* instead. Very close by are the fantastic market streets rue Poncelet and rue des Levis (Métro: Ternes).

Square du Vert Galant

This spot is one of the most romantic in Paris (and may be crowded with others depending on the time of day and year you visit. We guarantee you'll have it all to yourself in January, however.) Descend the stairs near the middle of Pont Neuf (near the Pont Neuf tour boats) to this beautiful spot commemorating Paris's favorite king, Henri IV. You're at the very tip of Ile de la Cité, in the middle of the Seine. You can spread out on a bench under the trees and enjoy the stunning views of both banks and the river stretching out ahead. The square is 7m (23 ft.) lower than the rest of the island; this was the original level of Paris during the Gallo-Roman period. At sunset, this is a popular spot for romantics (Métro: Cité).

Part VII

Appendixes

The 5th Wave   By Rich Tennant

In this part . . .

We tucked some really useful information into these appendixes. Appendix A — the yellow Quick Concierge section — gives you straight-to-the-point, bare-bones info on how to contact your embassy, find a pharmacy, cash a check, and generally take care of business. Appendix B is a glossary of some of the French terms you may need. It features pronunciation guides so you can at least attempt to sound like a native.

Appendix A

Quick Concierge

●●●

*H*ow do you use the telephones? Where can you find your embassy or consulate? This Quick Concierge offers answers to a variety of "Where do I . . . ?" and "How do I . . . ?" questions.

Fast Facts

American Express

The big Paris office, 11 rue Scribe, 9e (☎ 01-47-77-79-28; Métro: Opéra Chaussée-d'Antin or Havre-Caumartin; RER: Auber), is open weekdays from 9 a.m. to 6:30 p.m. The bank is open from 9 a.m. to 6:30 p.m. Saturday, but the mail pick-up window is closed.

ATM Locations

As in big cities in the United States, ATMs are easy to find in Paris. Most bank branches have at least one outdoor machine, and there are ATMs in major department stores and in train stations. If you want a list of ATMs that accept MasterCard or Visa cards before you leave home, ask your bank, or print out lists from www.visa.com or www.mastercard.com.

Baby-sitters

Check out Allo Maman Dépannage, 38 rue Greuze, 16e (☎ 01-47-55-15-75), or Kid Services, (☎ 0-820-00-02-30; 10€/15¢ per min.). Specify when calling that you need a sitter who speaks English. Also, try the American Church's basement bulletin board where English-speaking (often American) students post notices offering baby-sitting services. The church is located at 65 quai d'Orsay, 7e (☎ 01-45-62-05-00; Métro: Invalides).

Business Hours

The *grands magasins* (department stores) are generally open Monday through Saturday from 9:30 a.m. to 7 p.m.; smaller shops close for lunch and reopen around 2 p.m., but this practice is rarer than it used to be. Many stores stay open until 7 p.m. in summer; others are closed Monday, especially in the morning. Large offices remain open all day, but some close for lunch. Banks are normally open weekdays from 9 a.m. to noon and from 1 or 1:30 to 4:30 p.m. Some banks also open on Saturday morning. Some currency-exchange booths are open very long hours; see "Currency Exchange," later in this list.

Camera Repair

Photo Suffren, 45 av. Suffren, 7e. (☎ 01-45-67-24-25) repairs camera equipment on site at this location not far from the Eiffel Tower.

Climate

From May to September you can expect clear sunny days and temperatures in the 70s to high 80s (Fahrenheit) at the height of summer. But be prepared for rainy or searingly hot summers, too. From late October to April the weather is often gray and misty with a dampness that gets into your bones. Always bring an umbrella. Temperatures average about 45 degrees Fahrenheit in winter, and the low 60s in spring and autumn. *Note:* Ignore the song "April in Paris," and pack layers for your early spring trip to the City of Light. It is often quite chilly.

Collect Calls

For an AT&T operator: ☎ 0800-99-00-11.

Credit Cards

If you lose your Visa card, call ☎ 08-00-90-11-79; for MasterCard, call ☎ 08-00-90-13-87. To report lost American Express cards, call ☎ 08-00-99-00-11.

Currency Exchange

It is so much easier to use your ATM card to get cash in Paris — you usually get a better rate of exchange than you do at *bureaux de change* (exchange offices), hotels, restaurants, and shops. Most banks in Paris have stopped cashing travelers checks and now steer tourists to bureaux de change. If you must use travelers checks, for good rates, without fees or commissions, and quick service, try the Comptoir de Change Opéra, 9 rue Scribe, 9e (☎ 01-47-42-20-96; Métro: Opéra; RER: Auber). It is open weekdays from 9:00 a.m. to 5:30 p.m., Saturday from 9:30 a.m. to 4:00 p.m. The bureaux de change at all train stations (except Gare de Montparnasse) are open daily; those at 63 av. des Champs-Elysées, 8e (Métro: Franklin-D-Roosevelt), and 140 av. des Champs-Elysées, 8e (Métro: Charles-de-Gaulle–Étoile), keep long hours.

Despite disadvantageous exchange rates and long lines, many people prefer to exchange their money at American Express (see the "American Express" listing earlier in this Appendix).

Customs

Non-EU nationals can bring into France duty-free 200 cigarettes or 100 cigarillos or 50 cigars or 250 grams of smoking tobacco; 2 liters of wine and 1 liter of alcohol over 38.8 proof; 50 grams of perfume, one-quarter liter of toilet water; 500 grams of coffee, and 100 grams of tea. Travelers 15 years old and older can also bring in 183€ ($219) in other goods; for those 14 and younger, the limit is 91€ ($109). EU citizens may bring any amount of goods into France as long as it is for their personal use and not for resale.

Returning U.S. citizens who have been away for 48 hours or more are allowed to bring back, once every 30 days, $800 worth of merchandise duty-free. You'll be charged a flat rate of 10 percent duty on the next $1,000 worth of purchases; on gifts, the duty-free limit is $100. You can't bring fresh food into the United States; canned foods, however, are allowed.

Returning U.K. citizens have no limit on what can be brought back from an EU country as long as the items are for personal use (including gifts), and the necessary duty and tax have been paid. Guidance levels are set at: 800 cigarettes, 200 cigars, 1kg (2.2 lbs.) smoking tobacco, 10 liters of spirits, 90 liters of wine, and 110 liters of beer.

Canada allows its citizens a once-a-year C$750 exemption after seven days, and you're allowed to bring back duty-free 200 cigarettes, 1.5 liters of wine or 1.14 liters of liquor, and 50 cigars. In addition, you may mail gifts to Canada from abroad at the rate of C$60 a day, provided they're unsolicited and don't contain alcohol, tobacco, or advertising matter. Write on the package *Unsolicited gift, under $60 value.* All valuables need to be declared on the Y-38 form before departure from Canada, including serial numbers of valuables you already own, such as expensive foreign cameras.

The duty-free allowance in Australia is A$400 or, for those younger than 18, A$200. Upon returning to Australia, citizens can bring in 250 cigarettes or 250 grams of loose tobacco, and 1.125 liters of alcohol. If you're returning with valuable goods you already own, such as foreign-made cameras, you need to file form B263.

The duty-free allowance for New Zealand is NZ$700. Citizens older than 17 can bring in 200 cigarettes or 50 cigars or 250 grams of tobacco (or a mixture of all three if their combined weight doesn't exceed 250 grams), plus 4.5 liters of wine or beer or 1.125 liters of liquor.

Dentists

You can call your consulate and ask the duty officer to recommend a dentist. For dental emergencies, call SOS Urgences Stomatologique Dentaire (☎ 01-45-35-41-41) daily from 9 a.m. to midnight.

Doctors

Call your consulate (see "Embassies and Consulates" later in this list for numbers) and ask the duty officer to recommend a doctor, or call SOS Médecins (☎ 01-43-07-77-77), a 24-hour service. Most doctors and dentists speak some English. You can also call for an appointment at the Centre Médicale Europe, 44 rue d'Amsterdam (☎ 01-42-81-93-33). Consultations cost about 20€ ($24), and specialists are available.

Drugstores

Pharmacies are marked with a green cross and are often upscale, selling toiletries and cosmetics in addition to prescription drugs and over-the-counter remedies. If you're shopping for products other than drugs, buying them elsewhere, such as a *supermarché* (supermarket), is almost always cheaper.

A 24-hour pharmacy, Derhy/Pharmacie Les Champs, is conveniently located on the Champs-Elysées at 84 avenue des Champs-Elysées, 8e (☎ 01-45-62-02-41; Métro: George V).

Electricity

The French electrical system runs on 220 volts. You need adapters to convert the voltage and fit sockets. These are cheaper at home than they are in Paris. Many hotels have two-pin (in some cases, three-pin) sockets for electric razors. Asking your hotel whether you need an adapter is a good idea before plugging in any electrical appliance.

Embassies and Consulates

If you have a passport, immigration, legal, or other problem, contact your consulate. Call before you go: They often keep strange hours and observe both French and home-country holidays. Here's where to find them: Australia, 4 rue Jean-Rey, 15e (☎ 01-40-59-33-00; Métro: Bir-Hakeim); Canada, 35 av. Montaigne, 8e (☎ 01-44-43-29-00; Métro: Franklin-D-Roosevelt or Alma Marceau); New Zealand, 7 ter rue Léonard-de-Vinci, 16e (☎ 01-45-01-43-43; Métro: Victor-Hugo); Consulate of Great Britain, 18 bis rue d'Anjou, 8e (☎ 01-44-51-31-02; Métro: Madeleine); Embassy of Ireland, 4 rue Rude, 16e (☎ 01-44-17-67-00); US passports are issued at the Consulate of the United States, 2 rue St-Florentin, 1er (☎ 01-43-12-22-22; Métro: Concorde).

Emergencies

Call ☎ **17** for the police. To report a fire, dial ☎ **18**. For an ambulance, call ☎ **15**. The main police station, 7 bd. du Palais, 4e (☎ 01-53-71-53-71; Métro: Cité), is open 24 hours a day.

Hospitals

Two hospitals with English-speaking staff are the American Hospital of Paris, 63 bd.

Victor-Hugo, Neuilly-sur-Seine (☎ 01-46-41-25-25), just west of Paris proper (Métro: Les Sablons or Levallois-Perret), and the Hôpital Franco-Brittanique, 3 rue Barbes Levallois-Perret (☎ 01-46-39-22-22), just north of Neuilly, across the city line northwest of Paris (Métro: Anatole-France). Note that the American Hospital charges about $600 a day for a room, not including doctor's fees. The emergency department charges more than $60 for a visit, not including tests and X-rays.

Information

Before you go, contact the French Government Tourist Office, 444 Madison Ave., 16th floor, New York, NY 10022-6903 (☎ 212-838-7800; www.francetourism.com). When you arrive, contact the Office de Tourisme de Paris, 127 av. des Champs-Elysées, 8e (☎ 08-92-68-30-00; .35€/80¢ per min. between 9 a.m.–7 p.m.).

In addition, check the "Where to Get More Information" section later in this appendix.

Internet Access

To surf the Web or check your E-mail, open an account at a free-mail provider, such as Hotmail (www.hotmail.com) or Yahoo! Mail (www.yahoo.com), and all you need to check E-mail while you travel is a Web connection, available at Internet cafes everywhere. After logging on, just point the browser to your E-mail provider, enter your username and password, and you have access to your mail.

The following Paris Web bars, listed by arrondissement, charge modest fees (4€–7€ ($4.80–$8.40 per hour):

Cybercafé de Paris, 11 and 15 rue des Halles, 1er. ☎ 01- 42-21-11-11. Métro: Châtelet.

XS Arena St-Michel, 53 rue de la Harpe, 5e. ☎ 01-44-07-38-39. Métro: Mabillon, St-Michel.

Language

In the tourist areas of Paris, English is widely understood. As you move into more residential sections of the city, however, you will probably meet people who don't speak English. I suggest carrying a pocket-sized phrasebook such as *Berlitz Phrase Book: French,* available at all bookstores, (or use the glossary in Appendix B).

Laundry and Dry Cleaning

The more expensive your hotel, the more it costs to have your laundry or dry cleaning done there. Instead, find a laundry near you by consulting the Yellow Pages under *Laveries pour particuliers.* Take as many coins as you can. Washing and drying 6kg (13¼ lb.) usually costs 7€ ($8.40). Dry cleaning is *nettoyage à sec;* look for shop signs with the word PRESSING, and don't expect to have your clothes back within an hour; you may be able to get them back the next day if you ask nicely. The dry cleaning chain 5 à Sec has stores across Paris.

Liquor Laws

Supermarkets, grocery stores, and cafés sell alcoholic beverages. The legal drinking age is 16. Persons younger than 16 can be served an alcoholic drink in a bar or restaurant when accompanied by a parent or legal guardian. Wine and liquor are sold every day of the year. *Be warned:* The authorities are very strict about drunk-driving laws. If convicted, you face a stiff fine and a possible prison term of two months to two years.

Lost Property

Paris's Prefecture of Police runs the central Lost and Found, Objets Trouvés, 36 rue des Morillons, 15e (☎ 08-21-00-25-25;

Métro: Convention), at the corner of rue de Dantzig. The office is open Monday, Wednesday, and Friday from 8:30 a.m. to 5 p.m. and Tuesday and Thursday from 8:30 a.m. to 8:00 p.m. (except in July and Aug). For Lost and Found on the Métro, call ☎ 01-40-06-75-27.

Luggage Storage

Most hotels will store luggage for you for free, and that's your best bet, especially when you plan to return to Paris after a tour of the provinces.

Maps

Maps printed by the department stores are usually available free at hotels, and they're good for those visiting Paris for only a few days and hitting only the major attractions. But if you plan to really explore all the nooks and crannies of the city, the best maps are those of the *Plan de Paris par Arrondissement,* pocket-sized books with maps and a street index, available at most bookstores. They're extremely practical, and prices start at around 9€ ($11). You can find them in Paris bookstores, at the Target-like chain store, Monoprix, (there is one in nearly every Paris arrondissement), bookstores, *presse* stores (large versions of newsstands), and some of the bigger newsstands. Most Parisians carry a copy because they too get lost at times.

Newspapers and Magazines

Most newsstands carry the latest editions of the *International Herald Tribune,* published Monday through Saturday, and the major London papers. *Time* and *Newsweek* are readily available in Paris and so is the International edition of *USA Today.* You can also get the *New York Times* in some of the bigger English-language bookstores.

Pharmacies

See "Drugstores."

Police

Dial ☎ 17 in emergencies; otherwise, call ☎ 01-53-71-53-71.

Post Office

Large post offices are normally open weekdays from 8 a.m. to 7 p.m., Saturday from 8 a.m. to noon; small post offices may have shorter hours. Many post offices (PTT) are scattered around the city; ask anybody for the nearest one. Airmail letters and postcards to the United States cost .90€ ($1.10); within Europe .50€ (60¢); and to Australia or New Zealand, .90€ ($1.10).

The city's main post office is at 52 rue du Louvre, 1er, (☎ 01-40-28-76-00; Métro: Louvre-Rivoli). It's open 24 hours a day for urgent mail, telegrams, and telephone calls. It handles *Poste Restante mail* — sent to you in care of the post office and stored until you pick it up. Be prepared to show your passport and pay .75€ (90¢) for each letter you receive. If you don't want to use Poste Restante, you can receive mail in care of American Express. Holders of American Express cards or traveler's checks get this service free; others pay a fee.

Restrooms

Public restrooms are plentiful, but you usually have to pay for them. Every cafe has a restroom, but it's supposed to be for customers only. The best plan is to ask to use the telephone; it's usually next to the *toilette.* For a .40€ (50¢), you can use the street-side toilets, which are automatically flushed out and cleaned after every use (*Note:* These toilets do not give change for a .50€ piece. Some Métro stations have serviced restrooms; you're expected to tip the attendant .50€ (60¢).

Safety

Paris is a relatively safe city; your biggest risks are pickpockets and purse snatchers, so be particularly attentive in museum lines, popular shopping areas, around tourist attractions, on the Métro, and on crowded buses (especially in the confusion of getting on and off). Popular pickpocket tactics include someone asking you for directions or bumping into you while an accomplice takes your wallet ,and bands of children surrounding and distracting you and then making off with purchases and/or your wallet.

Women need to be on guard in crowded tourist areas and on the Métro against overly friendly men who seem to have made a specialty out of bothering unsuspecting female tourists. Tricks include asking your name and nationality and then taking advantage of your politeness by sticking like a burr to you for the rest of the day. They're usually more harassing than harmful, but if you're too nice, you may be stuck spending time with someone with whom you prefer not to. A simple *laissez-moi tranquille* (*lay*-say mwa tran-*keel;* leave me alone) usually works.

Smoking

Although restaurants are required to provide nonsmoking sections, you may find yourself next to the kitchen or the restrooms. Even there, your neighbor may light up and defy you to say something about it. Large brasseries, expensive restaurants, and places accustomed to dealing with foreigners are more likely to be accommodating.

Taxes

Watch out: You can get burned. As a member of the European Community, France routinely imposes a standard 19.6 percent value-added tax (VAT) on many goods and services. The tax on merchandise applies to clothing, appliances, liquor, leather goods, shoes, furs, jewelry, perfume, cameras, and even caviar. You can get a rebate — usually 13 percent — on

certain goods and merchandise, but not on services. The minimum purchase, depending on the store, is 180€ ($219) in the same store for nationals or residents of countries outside the European Union. Chapter 12 has more on VAT and how to deal with it.

Taxis

Alpha Taxis (☎ 01-45-85-85-85), or G7 (☎ 01-47-39-47-39). Be aware that the meter starts running as soon as you call a cab, so they're more expensive than hailed taxis. You can hail taxis in the street (look for a taxi with a white light on; an orange light means it's occupied), but most drivers won't pick you up if you're within 200m (0.12 miles) of a taxi stand (look for the blue *Taxi* sign).

Telephone/Telex/Fax

Most public phone booths take only telephone debit cards called *télécartes,* which you can buy at post offices and *tabacs* (cafes and kiosks that sell tobacco products). You insert the card into the phone and make your call; the cost is automatically deducted from the value of the card recorded on its magnetized strip. The télécarte comes in 50- and 120-unit denominations (a *unit* is a measure of time set by the phone company issuing the card — you get more units for your money if you call during off-peak hours after 7 p.m. and before 8 a.m.), costing about 7 € ($8.40) and 16€ ($19), respectively, and can be used only in a phone booth.

Cashiers almost always try to sell you a card from France Télécom, the French phone company, but cards exist that give you more talk time for the same amount of money. Instead of inserting the card into a public phone, you dial a free number and tap in a code. The cards come with directions, some in English, and can be used from public and private phones, unlike France Télécom's card, which you can use only on public phones. Look for *tabacs* that have advertisements for Delta Multimedia or Kertel, or ask for a *télécarte international avec un code.*

For placing international calls from France, dial 00 and then the country code (for the United States and Canada, 1; for Britain, 44; for Ireland, 353; for Australia, 61; for New Zealand, 64), then the area or city code, and then the local number (for example, to call New York, dial 00 + 1 + 212 + 000-0000). To place a collect call to North America, dial ☎ 00-33-11, and an English-speaking operator will assist you. Dial ☎ 00-00-11 for an American AT&T operator; MCI ☎ 0800-99-00-19; and Sprint ☎ 0800-99-00-87.

For calling from Paris to anywhere else in France (the provinces, in other words, or *province*), the country is divided into five zones with prefixes beginning 01, 02, 03, 04, and 05; check a phone directory for the code of the city you're calling.

If you're calling France from the United States, the number you dial probably looks something like this: 011-33-(0)1-00-00-00-00. You must first dial the international prefix, 011; and then the country code for France, (33); followed by city code and the rest of the number. When dialing from outside France, leave off the 0, which is often indicated in parentheses, in the city code.

Avoid making phone calls from your hotel room; many hotels charge at least .75€ (90¢) for local calls, and the markup on international calls can be staggering.

You can send telex and fax messages at the main post office in each arrondissement of Paris, but asking at your hotel or going to a neighborhood printer or copy shop is often cheaper.

Time Zone

Paris is six hours ahead of Eastern Standard Time; noon in New York is 6 p.m. in Paris.

Tipping

The custom is to tip the bellhop about 1€ coin per bag, more in expensive (splurge) hotels. If you have a lot of luggage, tip a bit more. Don't tip housekeepers unless you do something that requires extra work. Tip a few euro if a reception staff member performs extra services.

Although your *addition* (restaurant bill) or *fiche* (cafe check) bears the words *service compris* (service charge included), always leave a small tip. Generally, 5 percent is considered acceptable.

Taxi drivers appreciate a tip of .50€ to 1€ (60¢–$1.20) or whatever it costs to round up the fare to the next euro. On longer journeys, when the fare exceeds 20€ ($24), a 5 percent to 10 percent tip is appropriate. At the theater and cinema, tip 1€ ($1.20) if an usher shows you to your seat. In public toilets, a fee for using the facilities often is posted. If not, the maintenance person will expect a tip of 1€ ($1.20). Put it in the basket or on the plate at the entrance. Porters and cloakroom attendants are usually governed by set prices, which are displayed. If not, give a porter 1€ ($1.20) per suitcase, and a cloakroom attendant .50€ (60¢) per coat.

Transit Info

The telephone number for reservations on France's national railroads (SNCF) is ☎ 36-35 (.35€/80¢ per min; open daily from 7 a.m.–10 p.m.). *Remember:* You must validate your train ticket in the orange ticket *composteur* on the platform or pay a fine. For information in English about Paris subways and buses (RATP) call ☎ 08-92-68-41-14.

Water

Tap water in Paris is perfectly safe, but if you're prone to stomach problems, you may prefer to drink mineral water.

Weather updates

http://europe.cnn.com/WEATHER

www.weather.com

Toll-Free Numbers and Web Sites

Major airlines

Air Canada
☎ 888-247-2262
www.aircanada.ca

Air France
☎ 800-237-2747
www.airfrance.com

Air Tahiti Nui
☎ 877-824-4846
www.airtahitinui.com

American Airlines
☎ 800-433-7300
www.aa.com

British Airways
☎ 800-247-9297
www.british-airways.com

Continental Airlines
☎ 800-784-4444
www.continental.com

Delta Air Lines
☎ 800-221-1212
www.delta.com

Iceland Air
☎ 800-223-5500
www.icelandair.com

Northwest/KLM
☎ 800-225-2525
www.nwa.com

United Airlines
☎ 800-822-2746
www.ual.com

US Airways
☎ 800-428-4322
www.usairways.com

Virgin Atlantic
☎ 800-862-8621
www.virginatlantic.com

Major car rental agencies in Paris

Avis
Gare d'Austerlitz, 13e
☎ 08-20-61-16-29/0.12€ (16¢) per minute
www.avis.com

Hertz France
Gare de l'Est, 10e
☎ 01-42-05-50-43
www.hertz.com

National
Gare de Lyon, 12e
☎ 01-40-04-90-04
www.nationalcar.com

Europcar
60 bd. Diderot, 12e
☎ 08-25-82-54-63/0.15€ (20¢) per minute
www.europcar.fr

Where to Get More Information

The information sources listed here are the best of the bunch; dig in before you go, and you'll be well prepared for your trip.

Tourist offices

For general information about France, contact an office of the **French Government Tourist Office** at one of the following addresses:

- ✔ **In the United States: The French Government Tourist Office,** 444 Madison Ave., 16th floor, New York, NY 10022-6903 (☎ 212-838-7800; www.francetourism.com); 676 N. Michigan Ave., Chicago, IL 60611-2819 (☎ 312-751-7800).

- ✔ **In Canada: Maison de la France/French Government Tourist Office,** 1981 Ave. McGill College, Suite 490, Montréal PQ H3A 2W9 (☎ 514-845-4868).

- ✔ **In the United Kingdom: Maison de la France/French Government Tourist Office,** 178 Piccadilly, London W1V 0AL (☎ 09068-244-123).

- ✔ **In Australia: French Tourist Bureau,** 25 Bligh St. Level 20, Sydney, NSW 2000 Australia (☎ 02-231-5244; fax: 02-231-8682).

- ✔ **In New Zealand:** You won't find a representative in New Zealand; contact the Australian representative.

- ✔ **In Paris: The Office de Tourisme et des Congrès de Paris,** is no longer headquartered on the Champs-Elysées, but has branches throughout the city at the following locations *Note:* These centers are closed on May 1.

  - **The Opéra-Grands-Magasins Welcome Center,** 11 rue Scribe, 9e, open Monday through Saturday 9 a.m. to 6:30 p.m. (Métro: Chausée d'Antin or Opéra; RER: Auber).

  - **The welcome kiosk beneath the modern glass-roofed terminal of the Gare du Nord,** 8 rue de Dunkerque, 10e, open seven days a week from 8 a.m. to 6 p.m. (Métro and RER: Gare du Nord).

  - **The Gare de Lyon Welcome Center,** 20 bd. Diderot, 12e, open Monday through Saturday 8 a.m. to 6 p.m. (Métro and RER: Gare de Lyon).

  - **21 place du Tertre,** 18e, open daily 10 a.m. to 7 p.m. (Métro: Abbesses).

  - **Carrousel du Louvre, beneath the Pyramide,** 99 rue de Rivoli, 1er, open daily 10 a.m. to 10 p.m. (Métro: Palais Royal/Musée du Louvre).

  - **Pyramides Tourist Bureau,** 25 rue des Pyramides, 1er, open daily 9 a.m. to 7 p.m. (Métro: Pyramides).

Surfing the Web

You can find plenty of excellent information about Paris on the
Internet — the latest news, restaurant reviews, concert schedules,
subway maps, and more.

  ✔ **Aeroports de Paris** (www.adp.fr): Click the American flag on
    this site's home page for an English version that provides trans-
    fer information into Paris and lists terminals, maps, airlines,
    boutiques, hotels, restaurants, and accessibility information for
    travelers with disabilities.

  ✔ **Bonjour Paris** (www.bonjourparis.com): This site should be
    one of the first you browse before your trip; it's just full of useful
    information about Paris. You can find everything from cultural
    differences to shopping to restaurant reviews, all written from
    an American expatriate point of view.

  ✔ **Café de la Soul** (www.cafedelasoul.com): A sleekly designed
    Web site for African-American travelers in Paris. The site features
    articles, travelogues, and links to resources in the City of Light.

  ✔ **French Government Tourist Office** (www.francetourism.com):
    Here you can find information on planning your trip to France
    and practical tips, family activities, events, and accommodations.

  ✔ **Google Maps** (http://maps.google.com): On the Google's
    map engine, typing in a Paris address with a zip code will bring
    up a detailed map of the surrounding area, including Métro
    stops and any relevant information that Google can find on the
    business, including phone numbers, official Web pages, and
    business hours.

  ✔ **Magic Paris** (www.magicparis.com): The big attractions, such
    as the Louvre and the Eiffel Tower, are featured along with shop
    and gallery listings organized by arrondissement. Airport termi-
    nal information and click-on subway maps are also posted here.

  ✔ **Paris Digest** (www.parisdigest.com): Paris Digest selects "the
    best sights in Paris" and provides photos and links to them and
    to restaurants with views and good décor, and information
    about shopping, hotels, and things to do.

  ✔ **Paris France Guide** (www.parisfranceguide.com): This site
    has plenty of useful information about Paris, with current
    nightlife, restaurant, music, theater, and events listings. This
    guide is brought to you by the publishers of the *Living in France,*
    Study in France, and *What's on in France* guides.

  ✔ **Paris Pages** (www.paris.org): So much information is on this
    site that you won't know where to begin. Lodging reviews are
    organized by area and the monuments standing nearby, and you
    can find photo tours, shop listings, and a map of attractions
    with details. Some of the information may be out of date.

✔ **Paris Tourist Office** (www.parisinfo.com): The official site of the Paris Tourist Office provides information on the year's events, museums, accommodations, nightlife, and restaurants.

✔ **Parler Paris** (www.parlerparis.com): This site should be among the first you browse before your trip, or sign up for the biweekly newsletter. Editor Adrian Leeds really knows Paris, and Parler Paris is a true insider's guide to visiting and living in Paris. Her insightful commentary covers everything from visits to hidden Paris places to delicious budget dining.

✔ **RATP (Paris Urban Transit)** (www.ratp.fr): Find subway and bus line maps, timetables and information, and routes and times for Noctambus, Paris's night buses that run after the Métro closes. Click on the word *English* for the English-language version.

✔ **SNCF (French Rail)** (www.sncf.fr): The official Web site of the French railway system, this site sells seats online for trips through France. You can also find timetables and prices here. Click on the Union Jack on the upper-left corner of the screen for English.

✔ **Subway Navigator** (www.subwaynavigator.com): This site provides detailed subway maps for Paris and other cities around the world. You can select a city and enter your arrival and departure points, and then Subway Navigator maps out your route and estimates how long your trip will take.

Hitting the books

Most bookstores have several shelves entirely devoted to Paris-related titles, given that the city is one of the most-visited on the planet. Here are a few other books that may be useful for your trip. All Frommer's guides are published by Wiley, Inc.

✔ *Frommer's Paris,* updated every year, is an authoritative guide that covers the city and its surroundings.

✔ *Frommer's Paris Day by Day* is a four-color guide that offers travelers dozens of itineraries that show how best to see Paris in a short amount of time.

✔ *Frommer's Portable Paris* is the pocket-sized version of *Frommer's Paris.*

✔ *Frommer's Memorable Walks in Paris* is for folks who want to explore the city in depth and on foot with easy directions and descriptions of important sights.

✔ *Frommer's Irreverent Guide to Paris* is a fun guide for sophisticated travelers who want the basics without much excess.

Appendix B

A Glossary of French Words and Phrases

*W*hy **La** *Tour Eiffel* but **Le** *Tour de France?* Why **un** *cabinet* but **une** *cabine?* Simply put, in French and other Romance languages, nouns are assigned a gender. The article preceding the noun, such as *le* and *la* (which mean *the*) and *un* and *une* (which mean *a* or *one*), corresponds to that gender. *La* and *une* are feminine; *le* and *un* are masculine. Plural nouns are preceded by *les*. An extra letter is also added to the noun itself to signify feminine gender. So Dan Rather is *un journalist,* but Diane Sawyer is *une journaliste.* French schoolchildren spend years memorizing the gender of nouns; fortunately no one expects you to do the same!

Basic Vocabulary

English	French	Pronunciation
Yes/no	**Oui/non**	wee/nohn
Okay	**D'accord**	dah-*core*
Please	**S'il vous plaît**	see-voo-*play*
Thank you	**Merci**	mair-*see*
You're welcome	**De rien**	duh ree-*ehn*
Hello (during daylight hours)	**Bonjour**	bohn-*jhoor*
Good evening	**Bonsoir**	bohn-*swahr*
Goodbye	**Au revoir**	o ruh-*vwahr*
Police	**la police**	lah po-*leese*
What's your name?	**Comment vous appelez-vous?**	ko-mahn-voo-za-pel-ay-*voo*
My name is . . .	**Je m'appelle . . .**	jhuh ma-*pell*
Happy to meet you	**Enchanté(e)**	ohn-shahn-*tay*

English	French	Pronunciation
Miss	**Mademoiselle**	mad mwa-*zel*
Mr.	**Monsieur**	muh-*syuh*
Mrs.	**Madame**	ma-*dam*
How are you?	**Comment allez-vous?**	kuh-mahn-tahl-ay-*voo*
Fine, thank you, and you?	**Très bien, merci, et vous?**	tray bee-ehn, mare-see, ay *voo*
Very well, thank you	**Très bien, merci**	tray bee-ehn, mair-*see*
So-so	**Comme ci, comme ça**	kum-*see,* kum-*sah*
I'm sorry/excuse me	**Pardon**	pahr-*dohn*
I'm so very sorry	**Désolé(e)**	day-zoh-*lay*
Do you speak English?	**Parlez-vous anglais?**	Par-lay voo ahn-*glay*
I don't speak French	**Je ne parle pas français**	jhuh ne parl pah frahn-*say*
I don't understand	**Je ne comprends pas**	jhuh ne kohm-*prahn* pah
Could you speak more slowly?	**Pouvez-vous parler un peu plus lentement?**	poo-*vay* voo par-*lay* uh puh ploo lan-te-*ment*
Could you repeat that?	**Répetez, s'il vous plaît**	ray-peh-*tay,* see voo *play*
What is it?	**Qu'est-ce que c'est?**	kess-kuh-*say*
What time is it?	**Qu'elle heure est-il?**	kel uhr eh-*teel*
What?	**Quoi?**	kwah
Pardon?	**Pardons?**	par-*doh*
Help!	**Aidez-moi!**	*ay*-day moi!
How? *or* What did you say?	**Comment?**	ko-*mahn*
When?	**Quand?**	cohn
Where is . . . ?	**Où est . . . ?**	ooh-eh
Where are the toilets?	**Où sont les toilettes?**	ooh-sohn lay twah-*lets*
Who?	**Qui?**	kee
Why?	**Pourquoi?**	poor-*kwah*
Here/there	**Ici/là**	ee-*see*/lah

(continued)

Basic Vocabulary *(continued)*

English	*French*	*Pronunciation*
Left/right	**à gauche/à droite**	ah gohsh/ah drwaht
Straight ahead	**Tout droit**	too-drwah
I'm American/Canadian/British	**Je suis américain(e)/ canadien(e)/ anglais(e)**	jhe swee a-may- ree-*cah (kehn)*/canah-dee-*ahn (en)*/ahn-*glay (glaise)*
I'm going to . . .	**Je vais à . . .**	jhe vay ah
I want to get off at . . .	**Je voudrais descendre à . . .**	jhe voo-*dray* day-son-drah-ah

Health Terms

English	*French*	*Pronunciation*
I'm sick	**Je suis malade**	jhuh swee mal-*ahd*
I have a headache	**J'ai mal à la tête**	jhay mal ah la tet
I have a stomachache	**J'ai mal au ventre**	jhay mal oh *vahn*-trah
I would like to buy some aspirin	**Je voudrais acheter des aspirines**	jhe *voo*-dray *ash*-tay days as-peh-*reen*
Hospital	**l'hôpital**	low-pee-*tahl*
Insurance	**les assurances**	lez ah-sur-*ahns*

Travel Terms

English	*French*	*Pronunciation*
Airport	**l'aéroport**	lair-o-*por*
Bank	**la banque**	lah bahnk
Bridge	**pont**	pohn
Bus station	**la gare routière**	lah gar roo-tee-*air*
Bus stop	**l'arrêt de bus**	lah-*ray* duh boohss
By means of a bicycle	**en vélo/par bicyclette**	ahn *vay*-low/par bee-see-*clet*
By means of a car	**en voiture**	ahn vwa-*toor*

English	French	Pronunciation
Cashier	**la caisse**	lah *kess*
Driver's license	**permis de conduire**	per-*mee* duh con-*dweer*
Elevator	**l'ascenseur**	lah sahn *seuhr*
Entrance (to a building or a city)	**porte**	port
Exit (from a building or a freeway)	**une sortie**	oon sor-*tee*
Ground floor	**rez-de-chausée**	ray-duh-show-*say*
Highway to . . .	**la route pour . . .**	lah root por
Luggage storage	**consigne**	kohn-*seen*-yuh
A map of the city	**un plan de la ville**	uh plahn de la *veel*
Museum	**le musée**	luh mew-*zay*
No entry	**sens interdit**	sehns ahn-ter-*dee*
No smoking	**défense de fumer**	day-*fahns* duh fu-may
On foot	**à pied**	ah pee-*ay*
One-day pass	**ticket journalier**	tee-kay jhoor-nall-ee-*ay*
One-way ticket	**aller simple**	ah-*lay sam*-pluh
A phone card	**une carte téléphonique**	oon cart tay-lay-fone-*eek*
A postcard	**une carte postale**	oon carte pos-*tahl*
Round-trip ticket	**aller-retour**	ah-*lay* re-*toor*
Second floor	**premier étage**	prem-ee-*ay* ay-*taj*
Slow down	**ralentissez**	rah-lahn-tis-*ay*
Store	**le magasin**	luh ma-ga-*zehn*
Street	**la rue**	la roo
Suburb	**la banlieue**	lah bahn-*liew*
Subway	**le Métro**	luh may-tro
Telephone	**le téléphone**	luh tay-lay-*phun*

(continued)

Travel Terms *(continued)*

English	French	Pronunciation
Ticket	**un billet**	uh *bee*-yay
Ticket office	**vente de billets**	vahnt duh bee-*yay*
Toilets	**les toilettes**	lay twa-*lets*
I'd like . . .	**Je voudrais . . .**	jhe voo-*dray*
a room	**une chambre**	oon *shahm*-bruh
the key	**la clé (la clef)**	lah clay

Shopping Terms

English	French	Pronunciation
How much does it cost?	**C'est combien?/Ça coûte combien?**	say comb-bee-*ehn?*/sah coot comb-bee-*ehn*
That's expensive	**C'est cher/chère**	say share
That's inexpensive	**C'est raisonnable/C'est bon marché**	say ray-son-*ahb*-bluh/say bohn mar-*shay*
Do you take credit cards?	**Est-ce que vous acceptez les cartes de credit?**	es-kuh voo zaksep-*tay* lay kart duh creh-*dee*
I'd like to buy . . .	**Je voudrais acheter . . .**	jhe voo-dray ahsh-*tay*
Aspirin	**des aspirines**	deyz ahs-peer-*eens*
Cigarettes	**des cigarettes**	day see-ga-*ret*
Condoms	**des préservatifs**	day pray-ser-va-*teefs*
Contraceptive suppositories	**des ovules contraceptives**	days oh-*vyules* kahn-trah-cep-*teef*
A dictionary	**un dictionnaire**	uh deek-see-oh-*nare*
A gift (for someone)	**un cadeau**	uh kah-*doe*
A handbag	**un sac à main**	uh sahk ah man
A magazine	**une revue**	oon reh-*vu*
Matches	**des allumettes**	dayz a-loo-*met*
Lighter	**un briquet**	uh *bree*-kay

English	French	Pronunciation
A newspaper	**un journal**	uh zhoor-*nahl*
A road map	**une carte routière**	oon cart roo-tee-*air*
Shoes	**des chaussures**	day show-*suhr*
Soap	**du savon**	dew sah-*vohn*
Socks	**des chaussettes**	day show-*set*
A stamp	**un timbre**	uh *tam*-bruh
Writing paper	**du papier à lettres**	dew pap-pee-*ay* a *let*-ruh

Elements of Time

English	French	Pronunciation
Sunday	**dimanche**	dee-*mahnsh*
Monday	**lundi**	luhn-*dee*
Tuesday	**mardi**	mahr-*dee*
Wednesday	**mercredi**	mair-kruh-*dee*
Thursday	**jeudi**	jheu-*dee*
Friday	**vendredi**	vawn-druh-*dee*
Saturday	**samedi**	sahm-*dee*
Yesterday	**hier**	ee-*air*
Today	**aujourd'hui**	o-jhord-*dwee*
This morning	**ce matin**	suh ma-*tan*
This afternoon	**cet après-midi**	set ah-preh mee-*dee*
Tonight	**ce soir**	suh *swahr*
Tomorrow	**demain**	de-*man*
Now	**maintenant**	mant-*naw*

Index

See also separate Accommodations and Restaurant indexes at the end of this index.

BUSINESS, CAREERS & PERSONAL FINANCE

0-7645-5307-0   0-7645-5331-3 *†

Also available:
- Accounting For Dummies †
  0-7645-5314-3
- Business Plans Kit For Dummies †
  0-7645-5365-8
- Cover Letters For Dummies
  0-7645-5224-4
- Frugal Living For Dummies
  0-7645-5403-4
- Leadership For Dummies
  0-7645-5176-0
- Managing For Dummies
  0-7645-1771-6

- Marketing For Dummies
  0-7645-5600-2
- Personal Finance For Dummies *
  0-7645-2590-5
- Project Management
  For Dummies
  0-7645-5283-X
- Resumes For Dummies †
  0-7645-5471-9
- Selling For Dummies
  0-7645-5363-1
- Small Business Kit For Dummies *†
  0-7645-5093-4

HOME & BUSINESS COMPUTER BASICS

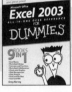

0-7645-4074-2   0-7645-3758-X

Also available:
- ACT! 6 For Dummies
  0-7645-2645-6
- iLife '04 All-in-One Desk Reference
  For Dummies
  0-7645-7347-0
- iPAQ For Dummies
  0-7645-6769-1
- Mac OS X Panther Timesaving
  Techniques For Dummies
  0-7645-5812-9
- Macs For Dummies
  0-7645-5656-8
- Microsoft Money 2004 For Dummies
  0-7645-4195-1

- Office 2003 All-in-One Desk
  Reference For Dummies
  0-7645-3883-7
- Outlook 2003 For Dummies
  0-7645-3759-8
- PCs For Dummies
  0-7645-4074-2
- TiVo For Dummies
  0-7645-6923-6
- Upgrading and Fixing PCs
  For Dummies
  0-7645-1665-5
- Windows XP Timesaving
  Techniques For Dummies
  0-7645-3748-2

FOOD, HOME, GARDEN, HOBBIES, MUSIC & PETS

0-7645-5295-3   0-7645-5232-5

Also available:
- Bass Guitar For Dummies
  0-7645-2487-9
- Diabetes Cookbook For Dummies
  0-7645-5230-9
- Gardening For Dummies *
  0-7645-5130-2
- Guitar For Dummies
  0-7645-5106-X
- Holiday Decorating For Dummies
  0-7645-2570-0
- Home Improvement All-in-One
  For Dummies
  0-7645-5680-0

- Knitting For Dummies
  0-7645-5395-X
- Piano For Dummies
  0-7645-5105-1
- Puppies For Dummies
  0-7645-5255-4
- Scrapbooking For Dummies
  0-7645-7208-3
- Senior Dogs For Dummies
  0-7645-5818-8
- Singing For Dummies
  0-7645-2475-5
- 30-Minute Meals For Dummies
  0-7645-2589-1

INTERNET & DIGITAL MEDIA

0-7645-1664-7   0-7645-6924-4

Also available:
- 2005 Online Shopping Directory
  For Dummies
  0-7645-7495-7
- CD & DVD Recording For Dummies
  0-7645-5956-7
- eBay For Dummies
  0-7645-5654-1
- Fighting Spam For Dummies
  0-7645-5965-6
- Genealogy Online For Dummies
  0-7645-5964-8
- Google For Dummies
  0-7645-4420-9

- Home Recording For Musicians
  For Dummies
  0-7645-1634-5
- The Internet For Dummies
  0-7645-4173-0
- iPod & iTunes For Dummies
  0-7645-7772-7
- Preventing Identity Theft
  For Dummies
  0-7645-7336-5
- Pro Tools All-in-One Desk
  Reference For Dummies
  0-7645-5714-9
- Roxio Easy Media Creator
  For Dummies
  0-7645-7131-1

SPORTS, FITNESS, PARENTING, RELIGION & SPIRITUALITY

0-7645-5146-9   0-7645-5418-2

Also available:
- Adoption For Dummies
  0-7645-5488-3
- Basketball For Dummies
  0-7645-5248-1
- The Bible For Dummies
  0-7645-5296-1
- Buddhism For Dummies
  0-7645-5359-3
- Catholicism For Dummies
  0-7645-5391-7
- Hockey For Dummies
  0-7645-5228-7

- Judaism For Dummies
  0-7645-5299-6
- Martial Arts For Dummies
  0-7645-5358-5
- Pilates For Dummies
  0-7645-5397-6
- Religion For Dummies
  0-7645-5264-3
- Teaching Kids to Read
  For Dummies
  0-7645-4043-2
- Weight Training For Dummies
  0-7645-5168-X
- Yoga For Dummies
  0-7645-5117-5

TRAVEL

 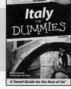

0-7645-5438-7   0-7645-5453-0

Also available:
- Alaska For Dummies
  0-7645-1761-9
- Arizona For Dummies
  0-7645-6938-4
- Cancún and the Yucatán
  For Dummies
  0-7645-2437-2
- Cruise Vacations For Dummies
  0-7645-6941-4
- Europe For Dummies
  0-7645-5456-5
- Ireland For Dummies
  0-7645-5455-7

- Las Vegas For Dummies
  0-7645-5448-4
- London For Dummies
  0-7645-4277-X
- New York City For Dummies
  0-7645-6945-7
- Paris For Dummies
  0-7645-5494-8
- RV Vacations For Dummies
  0-7645-5443-3
- Walt Disney World & Orlando
  For Dummies
  0-7645-6943-0

GRAPHICS, DESIGN & WEB DEVELOPMENT

 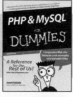

0-7645-4345-8   0-7645-5589-8

Also available:
- Adobe Acrobat 6 PDF
  For Dummies
  0-7645-3760-1
- Building a Web Site For Dummies
  0-7645-7144-3
- Dreamweaver MX 2004
  For Dummies
  0-7645-4342-3
- FrontPage 2003 For Dummies
  0-7645-3882-9
- HTML 4 For Dummies
  0-7645-1995-6
- Illustrator CS For Dummies
  0-7645-4084-X

- Macromedia Flash MX 2004
  For Dummies
  0-7645-4358-X
- Photoshop 7 All-in-One Desk
  Reference For Dummies
  0-7645-1667-1
- Photoshop CS Timesaving
  Techniques For Dummies
  0-7645-6782-9
- PHP 5 For Dummies
  0-7645-4166-8
- PowerPoint 2003 For Dummies
  0-7645-3908-6
- QuarkXPress 6 For Dummies
  0-7645-2593-X

NETWORKING, SECURITY, PROGRAMMING & DATABASES

0-7645-6852-3   0-7645-5784-X

Also available:
- A+ Certification For Dummies
  0-7645-4187-0
- Access 2003 All-in-One Desk
  Reference For Dummies
  0-7645-3988-4
- Beginning Programming
  For Dummies
  0-7645-4997-9
- C For Dummies
  0-7645-7068-4
- Firewalls For Dummies
  0-7645-4048-3
- Home Networking For Dummies
  0-7645-42796

- Network Security For Dummies
  0-7645-1679-5
- Networking For Dummies
  0-7645-1677-9
- TCP/IP For Dummies
  0-7645-1760-0
- VBA For Dummies
  0-7645-3989-2
- Wireless All In-One Desk Reference
  For Dummies
  0-7645-7496-5
- Wireless Home Networking
  For Dummies
  0-7645-3910-8